ETERNAL INDIVIDUALITY

Eternal Individuality

Towards a Karmic Biography of Novalis

Sergei O. Prokofieff

TEMPLE LODGE
London

Translated from the Russian by Simon Blaxland de Lange

First English edition 1992

Originally published in German under the title *Ewige Individualität, Zur karmischen Novalis-Biographie* by Philosophisch-Anthroposophischer Verlag am Goetheanum, Dornach, Switzerland in 1987

The publishers wish to thank Karla Kiniger and Arthur Osmond for editing the translated text

A catalogue record for this book is available from the British Library

ISBN 0 904693 39 2

Typeset by DP Photosetting, Aylesbury, Bucks
Printed and bound in Great Britain by
Cromwell Press, Melksham, Wiltshire

Contents

Appendices:

1. The Prophet Elijah in the desert
2. The Prophet Elijah's fiery ascension to heaven
3. John the Baptist
4. Raphael (self-portrait)
5. Novalis (Friedrich von Hardenburg)
6. John the Baptist, by Alexander Ivanov
7. Christ's Appearance before the People by Alexander Ivanov
8. Central part of the Deesis, from the Iconostasis by Theophanes
   the Greek
9. Sophia, the Wisdom of God
10. Intercession of the Virgin

(For full credits see final page of plate section)

Foreword

'. . . Through his revelations of wisdom there passed, like a red thread, the mystery of Novalis, Raphael, John.'

Marie Steiner

'Novalis must be experienced today as a living spirit-figure . . . In this way must also his eternal entelechy speak to us.'

Albert Steffen

'Thus there are two Michael streams: the one is associated with Michael himself, the Sun-Spirit, while the other is led by Elijah.'

Ita Wegman

The individuality who worked in his last earthly incarnation under the name of Novalis is, possibly to a greater extent than any other human individuality, the key to the mysteries of both the most distant past and the furthest future.

He also has a particular place in the spiritual–scientific research of Rudolf Steiner. If we cast our eye over all that the founder of the science of the spirit has said about him, the impression arises that the individuality of Novalis belongs, without any question, to the circle of those supersensible inspirers of Anthroposophy who have, from the start, invisibly accompanied its gradual incarnation on Earth in the twentieth century.

On this basis, the present work has a threefold purpose. Firstly, the intention is to answer the question as to the place which research into the karmic biography of Novalis holds in Rudolf Steiner's creative work and, above all, to discover where, amongst the manifoldness of his spiritual–scientific communications, we may find traces of the direct inspiration of this individuality which testify to his participation in the Anthroposophical Movement.

The answer to this question is connected, however, not only with a consideration of the *past* evolution of this individuality, in so far as this is known to us through modern occult research, but also with the necessity of finding a path leading to an understanding of his *future* mission amongst mankind, so closely connected as it is with the spiritual meaning of earthly evolution. The second purpose of the present work is, therefore, to indicate how this future mission of Novalis in Earth evolution gradually grows and receives its form from the rich karmic past in which it is rooted.

Finally, its third purpose, which in a certain sense also includes the first two, consists in the attempt to bring the individuality of Novalis still closer to the soul of every anthroposophist, through entering into the deeper foundations of his inner world, into the more hidden motivating forces of his soul and into the mystery of the occult powers which worked within him and, through him, guided mankind, those occult powers which in our time have, through Rudolf Steiner, called Anthroposophy into life; in other words: to bring the spirit-image of Novalis close to us so that he may become the intimate friend and spiritual companion of every anthroposophist in his most inward spiritual strivings, and a true helper in the fulfilment of the tasks of Anthroposophy in the modern world.

For, as will become fully apparent from what follows, the mission of Novalis amongst mankind is connected in a very direct way with the fundamental mission of Anthroposophy in our time, with its service to the central impulse of the whole of Earth evolution, the impulse of Michael-Christ.

As Rudolf Steiner has repeatedly testified, one of the most important tasks of Anthroposophy is that it should even now, within the womb of our fifth post-Atlantean epoch, prepare for the future sixth epoch, when that spiritual or Johannine Christianity—whose first messenger is the modern science of the spirit—will attain its fullest and highest flowering. This future spiritual epoch, which will begin roughly in the middle of the fourth millennium after the birth of Christ, will be particularly associated with the Slavic inhabitants of Eastern Europe. More will be said about this in the corresponding places of the present work which, it may be pointed out, was completed in the year before the thousandth jubilee of the Christianising of the most populous nation of Eastern Europe.

The baptism of Russia which took place in Kiev in the year 988 had significance not only for Europe, in so far as its Christianising was completed thereby, but for the whole of humanity. For by this means Eastern Europe gained access to the spiritual forces—the full development of which will enable the whole of mankind to rise in the sixth cultural epoch to a new, higher stage in its evolution.

If from the standpoint of this spiritual–historical perspective we now consider the personality and creative work of Novalis, we shall make the quite astonishing discovery that there is perhaps no other figure in our modern age who manifests so many of the most characteristic traits of the future sixth cultural epoch as does Novalis!

It was this 'discovery' which became for the author a key for understanding the personality and creative work of Novalis, and was one of the inducements towards writing the present book. For it became clear that in this personality of Novalis not only Middle and Western Europe but, above all, also *Eastern Europe* can contemplate their own respective futures as in a mirror.

Hence the individuality of Novalis can, as no other, serve as a bridge which spiritually unites Middle and Eastern Europe, prophetically anticipating, through his personality and creative work, the future transition of all mankind from the fifth to the sixth cultural epoch, a transition which, in its turn, represents the first stage on the path to the new aeon of world evolution, the aeon of Jupiter.

To facilitate *such* an understanding of Novalis as a spiritual *mediator* between the West and the East, and at the same time as *one who guides* humanity towards the spiritual culture of the future, is the intention of the present work.

Arlesheim, St John's Day 1987   Sergei O. Prokofieff

1

Origins

The theme of karmic research occupies a particularly important place in the full extent of Rudolf Steiner's spiritual–scientific communications. This theme was—as Rudolf Steiner himself states—directly connected with his principal life's task;[1] it is the alpha and the omega of his entire spiritual creative work. Already at the very beginning of his public activity as a teacher of Christian occultism, at the founding in the Autumn of 1902 of the German section of the Theosophical Society, the title which he chose for his introductory lectures was 'Practical Karma Exercises'.[2] And although at that time what he had in mind could not be realised, nevertheless this theme, like a seed resting in the depths of the Earth throughout the long winter period, was always present in the background of the manifold spiritual–scientific research in the years that followed, so that it might appear with full force at the Christmas Conference of 1923, and then find its highest manifestation and development in the karma lectures of 1924. Thus spiritual–scientific research in the field of karma not only forms a majestic spiritual bridge spanning the beginning and the end of the earthly evolution of Anthroposophy during the first quarter of the twentieth century, but at the same time represents the most important contribution of Anthroposophy to spiritual culture as a whole.

However, apart from the initial and final points in the development of the karmic research of Rudolf Steiner we may also observe how at certain periods, largely determined by the laws governing the coming into being of spiritual science, it is to be found again and again at the centre of anthroposophical considerations. In this sense the year 1909 occupies a quite special position. This is the year when Christ began to appear to human beings in an etheric form, the year when He began to become the Lord of Karma.[3]

In connection with these events, so decisive for the whole subsequent evolution of the Earth, Rudolf Steiner introduces an altogether new theme into the field of his spiritual–scientific investigations which is associated with the mysteries of 'spiritual economy' and in which the motif of karmic research and the karmic rulership of man and humanity appears with particular force.[4]

The first lecture on this theme was given on 28 December 1908, but this did to some extent still bear the character of an esoteric lesson—one was, for example, not permitted to take notes. It is, however, the lecture of 21 January 1909, given in Heidelberg almost exactly one year before the new appearance of Christ in the etheric realm was first proclaimed, which represents the real beginning of all the subsequent revelations regarding the mysteries of 'spiritual economy'. Between these two dates, at the Festival of Epiphany, which marks the incarnation of Christ through the Baptism by John in the Jordan, in the course of the lecture of 6 January 1909 in Munich, in a room adorned with reproductions of paintings by Raphael and on the occasion of an evening devoted to the work of *Novalis*, Rudolf Steiner for the first time revealed to his anthroposophical audience the karmic secret of this individuality when he pointed to the connection between Novalis, Raphael, John the Baptist and the prophet Elijah.[5]

This is a classic example of Rudolf Steiner's karmic research and, alongside two other examples from the Christmas cycle of the year 1910,[6] is the most significant anticipation of what he was to say on this theme in 1924.

In order truly to sense the full significance of this particular piece of karmic research for the evolution of Anthroposophy, and also to become aware of what a prominent place it occupies amongst the other elements of Rudolf Steiner's explorations in the field of karma, it is necessary to turn to the cosmic–earthly activity of this individuality amongst mankind as it found expression in the four incarnations referred to above, and most especially to his spiritual origins. We may find indications of these origins in the lecture cycle devoted to the Gospel of St Luke which was given by Rudolf Steiner in Basel in September 1909.

According to the spiritual–scientific information contained in this cycle, in the figure of Elijah–John the Baptist we have to do with the oldest individuality of mankind, who, during the ancient Lemurian age, gave to its whole evolution a direction which led it gradually 'from Heaven to Earth'. In a certain sense the individuality of the father of all humanity, Adam, stands before us here.[7] As an individuality who was connected from the beginning with earthly evolution and who stands at the inception of earthly humanity, he has, from the outset, been in very close connection with that high lodge of the rulership of humanity which Rudolf Steiner describes as the 'great Mother Lodge', led by Manu.[8] Thus in speaking of the incarnation of this individuality at the Turning-Point of Time as John the Baptist, Rudolf Steiner clearly indicates that his ego was sent to Zachariah and Elisabeth directly by Manu himself from the 'Mother Lodge'.[9]

This individuality also worked throughout the **Atlantean** evolution (which followed the Lemurian age) out of the forces which he received from the Sun-sphere, through his direct relationship with the central oracle of the Sun (this being a kind of earthly representative of the 'Mother Lodge'),[11] and with its highest Initiate. This relationship was subsequently expressed in the particular care which the Sun Oracle and its rulership gave to the direct descendants of the original 'principal pair' that had experienced the Moon-crisis[10] on the Earth. For the etheric bodies of these descendants and in particular the etheric body of **Adam**, the first man, whom Rudolf Steiner in his description of the Moon-crisis characterises as 'the strongest soul' in earthly evolution, were from the outset under the special protection of the leading Sun-Spirit, the Cosmic Christ.[12]

Rudolf Steiner refers in his 'Last Address' to another no less important connection of this individuality with the origins of the human race. This is his relationship to the sphere of the so-called 'Moon Teachers of Wisdom', to the sphere of the original Teachers of humanity who at the end of the Lemurian epoch left the Earth together with the Moon and formed in the spiritual domain of the latter a kind of 'cosmic colony' whence they have, since that time, guided and ordered the karmic relationships within earthly evolution.[13]

The spiritual–scientific facts to which we have referred also delineate the subsequent working of this individuality amongst mankind. Connected from the very beginning—through his spiritual origins and his proximity to the Moon Teachers of Wisdom—with the karma of mankind in its entirety, he acquired as a result of his direct relationship to the 'Mother Lodge' and its rulership, at a definite moment of his evolution, the impulse to unite with that people whose particular task it was to prepare the conditions on Earth for the incarnation in a human body of the Sun Logos, the Cosmic Christ. This was the people of the Old Testament who at the dawn of their existence had received this lofty mission from Manu himself.[14]

Once the individuality of Adam had, in Lemurian times, formed the 'gate' for the entry of the Luciferic-impulse into mankind, and had as a result gradually plunged into the world of matter, it was able to become a most effective participant in preparing for that event which was to give an altogether different direction to world-evolution. This event was Christ's incarnation on Earth at the Turning-Point of Time and the subsequent Mystery of Golgotha.

The decisive epoch and at the same time the most important turning-point in the history of the Hebrew people was when Moses, one of the most advanced pupils of the great Zarathustra, was active in their midst.[15]

6

Brought up at the court of the Egyptian Pharaoh and initiated by Egyptian priests, Moses was able to receive the high revelation of the Christ Being on Mount Sinai through the mediation of the Moon Elohim, Jahve, who served Him. As a result of this, Moses could become the direct witness before the Hebrew people of 'the God whose name cannot be uttered', 'I am the I am', the witness of the Christ Being in His approach to the Earth and of His working in the sphere of the earthly elements of fire, lightning and thunder.[15]

It was with this first great revelation of the Christ Being to the Hebrew people that the oldest individuality of mankind united himself in order, at the decisive moment, to save this revelation from becoming overwhelmed with total spiritual darkness, and the people of Israel from physical annihilation. He incarnated into this race at the time of Moses under the name of Phinehas and was able to rescue the great mission of Moses, which is so deeply connected with the mission of mankind on our planet. As a result of this deed, Phinehas was then able to rise to a still higher stage in his own development, to the stage described in the Bible as God giving to him 'the covenant of an everlasting priesthood'.[17]

This individuality subsequently, in the course of his continual incarnations amongst the Hebrew people, is given the task, in the person of the prophet Elijah, of not only developing and consolidating the revelation of the future impulse of the World Ego bequeathed to Moses, but also of raising it to a higher level. In this sense Rudolf Steiner calls Elijah the 'representative' of Moses, and he also refers on several occasions to the further development which Moses' proclamation regarding the coming of Christ to the Earth received as the result of the activity, in both physical and spiritual worlds, of the prophet Elijah.[18] However, this became possible for him only as a result of that quite particular initiation that he underwent: 'To this end it was essential that certain singular and very special forces be called up from the hidden depths of his soul—deep-seated powers as yet unknown to mankind, *even to the great teachers of that time*: something in the nature of a holy, mystical initiation of a new order, through which might come the revelation of such a God [of Jahve, the lunar reflection of Christ]—had to take place in the innermost being of Elijah.'[19]

All the 'miracles' subsequently wrought by Elijah are a consequence of this initiation, from the 'replenishing of the barrel of meal' and the 'raising of the widow's son'[20] to his relationship with the elemental process of nature. While Moses was able to experience the higher revelation of Jahve-Christ as a revelation of the World-Ego only through the *outer* elements of fire, lightning and thunder (for he was as yet unable to enter the 'Promised Land' and could only indicate the way to

7

it), Elijah, on the other hand, works wholly *within* this land, that is, he experiences the revelation of Christ–Jahve to a certain extent already in his own inner being.[21] This explains his altogether different relationship to the world of elemental nature, which is for him no longer the 'mediator' for a higher revelation, as it was for Moses, but rather something which he commands through the forces of the ego-revelation which he bears within his soul as a result of his 'mystical initiation of the highest order'.

Furthermore, we learn from spiritual science that in the figure of Elijah we have to do with an individuality who possesses such all-embracing spiritual forces—forces which are connected with the primal origins of mankind—that he can never *fully* incarnate on Earth. For in each of his incarnations his essential spiritual nature remains (one could say) hovering above the human body with which he can only unite in part. Rudolf Steiner makes this especially clear through the example of the relationship of the spiritual essence of Elijah to his physical bearer, Naboth.[22] And although Rudolf Steiner never calls Elijah a 'Bodhisattva', we nevertheless have every reason to speak of him as a 'Bodhisattva-like' being, especially if we consider the indications regarding his 'partial' incarnations and also his closeness to the Moon Teachers of Wisdom, whose emissaries on Earth are the Bodhisattvas.[23] Moreover, in the course of fulfilling his high mission amongst the ancient Hebrews, the individuality of Elijah gradually advanced so far in his own development that from a certain moment he became, in a way, their 'group soul': 'He may be regarded as the *Folk-Spirit* of the ancient Hebrew people', as Rudolf Steiner says.[24] This means that from a certain moment Elijah becomes the envoy of the leading Moon Elohim, Jehovah: 'Elijah must not be identified with this deity; he is that earthly reflection of him which is at the same time the folk-soul of the ancient Hebrew people. The spirit of Elijah is a kind of Jehovah differentiated, or in the words of the Old Testament, he is the *countenance of Jehovah*.'[25]

In the words in italics we have an indication of a further mystery associated with the activity of the individuality of Elijah. This mystery consists in that Elijah, as the bearer of the 'Folk-Soul', was at once the 'instrument' not merely of Jehovah but also of the true *spirit* of the ancient Hebrew people—at that time the *Archangel Michael*—who was then not the 'earthly' but the higher, supersensible 'countenance of Jahve'. The individuality of Adam–Elijah had been connected with both these Hierarchic Beings since ancient Lemurian times. For in Jehovah we have the creator of *earthly* man, that Being who had formerly played a decisive part in the process of endowing man with the substance of his ego[26]; and in Michael, the 'countenance of Jahve', his heavenly helper and mediator in this deed.[27] Furthermore, it is these two Hierarchic Beings who, belonging to the ranks of the Exusiai or Spirits of Form and the Archangels, have inspired the whole spiritual life of the ancient Hebrews from Abraham through Moses to Elijah and all the prophets who came after him.[28]

In the course of his initiation, Elijah[29] now spiritually unites with these two Hierarchic Beings who from the spiritual world led the ancient Hebrews to the fulfilment of their essential task—that of forming the sheaths for the incarnation of the Christ Being on Earth. He has become their *earthly* instrument and envoy. Thus from a certain moment in the history of the ancient Hebrew people there begins to work, in their midst, a new being whose body, soul and spirit are organised in such a way that the being of Elijah is able to enter into his body for the fulfilment of his mission only in part and, in so doing, forms in the spiritual world, from his 'soul nature', a vessel for the working of Michael, the Folk-Spirit, and, from his 'spirit nature', a vessel for the working of Jehovah, extending right into the events of nature: 'The man who lived as Elijah was an outstanding example of this. The words uttered by his mouth and the actions performed by his hands *proceeded not only from the part of his being actually present in his personality; they were manifestations of divine-spiritual Beings in the background.'*[30]

And so in Elijah we have:

spirit — Jehovah (Spirit of Form)
soul — Michael (Archangel)
body — Elijah (a Bodhisattva-like human being).[31]

2

At the Turning-Point of Time

The principal task which the individuality of Elijah had taken upon himself, that of carrying forward the impulse of Moses amongst the ancient Hebrews and preparing unceasingly for the coming of the Christ Being, the Bearer of the World-Ego, to the Earth, reached its highest point and at the same time its culmination at the Turning-Point of Time in his incarnation as John the Baptist. In this incarnation Elijah appears in the first instance as a kind of forerunner of Christ Jesus, in that he united the two principal mystery streams of antiquity, whose highest representatives before the events of Palestine were the individualities of Buddha and Zarathustra. For according to spiritual science both these individualities take a direct part not only in the evolution of Jesus of Nazareth,[32] but also of John the Baptist. The connection of the latter with the Zarathustra stream arises through his participation in the process of the further fulfilment and development of the impulse given by Moses, an impulse which ultimately can be traced back to the influence within the soul of Moses of the etheric body that he had received from the founder of the culture of ancient Persia.[33] Hence, the being of Elijah, who in a spiritual sense is a 'representative'[34] of Moses amongst the ancient Hebrews, also bears—when subsequently incarnated in John the Baptist—something of the forces of the mighty etheric body of Zarathustra. On the other hand, the Nirmanakaya of Buddha, abiding in the spiritual world, exerts through his astral body an indirect influence upon his ego. Rudolf Steiner refers to this as follows: 'The ego of this Being [the Nirmanakaya of Buddha] was now farther from the spiritual world and nearer to the Earth, much more closely connected with the Earth than the Beings who had formerly guided Elijah [that is, Jahve and Michael].' And immediately afterwards he continues: 'The *transition* leading to the amalgamation of the Buddha stream with the Zarathustra stream was now to be brought about.'[35] This transition, which John the Baptist fulfilled only prophetically, was a preparation for the eventual union of both streams in the cosmic-earthly Being of Christ Jesus. And so, if John the Baptist inherited a connection with the forces of the etheric body of Zarathustra, from his incarnation as Elijah, then in his incarnation at the Turning-Point of Time this was augmented by

10

inspirations flowing from the Nirmanakaya of Buddha. Hence 'the words spoken out of the mouth of John were uttered under the inspiration of the Buddha.'[36]

However, there were also higher Hierarchic Beings who continued to work through Elijah in his incarnation as John the Baptist—though now everything took place *one stage lower* than during his previous earthly existence. Instead of the Archangel Michael, there now worked in the soul of John the Baptist a quite particular Angel, of whom (notably) the beginning of St Mark's Gospel makes mention.[37] In order to understand his relationship to the sphere of Michael, it is necessary to turn once more to the supersensible influence which the Nirmanakaya of Buddha had on John the Baptist. For it was not only the inspirer of his preaching, but worked already at his birth as the awakener of his ego: 'Being nearer to the Earth, this force [the Nirmanakaya of Buddha] now worked as more than an inspiration; it had an actual formative effect upon the ego of John. Under the influence of the visit of her who is there [in the Gospel] called "Mary",* the ego of John the Baptist began to stir. The Nirmanakaya of Buddha was here working upon the ego of the former Elijah—now the ego of John the Baptist—awakening it and penetrating right into the physical substance.'[38]

Thus there is a twofold influence upon John the Baptist from the time of his birth. On the one hand, his ego 'is awakened' by the Nirmanakaya of Buddha, and on the other hand, because of being only partially incarnated in a physical body, it remains so selfless that a particular Angelic Being is able to work through it: 'John was still able to say: not I but the Angel within me has been sent down and uses me as a tool.'[39]

The ego of John is, therefore, from the time of his birth, under this twofold influence which proceeds from two Beings: an Angel and the Nirmanakaya of Buddha.[40] One could also say, the Nirmanakaya of Buddha 'awakens' the ego of John the Baptist in his earthly incarnation, in the sixth month of Elisabeth's pregnancy, when the child was still possessed of so high a degree of selflessness that the Being of the Hierarchy of the Angels was able to begin to work through him. This is the source of all the remarkable capacities and soul-qualities with which John the Baptist was endowed from his earliest childhood, and which subsequently led him to gain access to many of the mysteries of the Essene order and to be initiated in many of its secrets, even though he was not a member of it. For present purposes what is of particular importance is that in the individuality of John the Baptist there are working together

* This is a reference to the visit of Mary at Elisabeth's house, as described in the Gospel of St Luke (1:39–45).

11

the supersensible being of the Buddha and a certain Angelic Being, of which the former was, in a way, a preparation for the subsequent activity of the latter. This *combined* working of the two spiritual Beings, through John the Baptist, also testifies to the profound spiritual connection existing between them, a fact which can help us to unveil the mystery of the Angelic Beings whose earthly instrument John the Baptist was to become.

However, before turning to a consideration of this mystery it is necessary to address our attention to an event where the connection between the Nirmanakaya of Buddha and the Angelic Being who inspired John the Baptist are presented with particular clarity. This is the scene where the tidings of the birth of the Nathan Jesus child, as recorded by St Luke, is proclaimed to the shepherds in the field. In the second chapter of St Luke's gospel, verses 8–14, we read: 'And in that region there were shepherds in the field, keeping watch over their flock by night. And *an Angel of the Lord* appeared to them, and the glory of the Lord shone around them, and they were filled with fear. And the *Angel* said unto them, "Fear not; for behold, I bring you good tidings of great joy which will come to all people; for unto you is born this day in the city of David a Saviour, who is Christ the Lord . . ." And suddenly *there was with the Angel a multitude of the heavenly host*, praising God and saying: "Glory to God in the highest, and on Earth peace, goodwill towards men."'

In this scene there is first the appearance of an Angel, and then 'suddenly' he is joined by 'a multitude of the heavenly host', which according to the spiritual research of Rudolf Steiner is none other than a supersensible imagination of the 'Nirmanakaya of Buddha'.[41] First the Angel brings tidings of the birth of the Lord (*Kyrios* in the Greek text of the Gospel of St Luke), and then Buddha brings to the shepherds the new revelation from the spiritual worlds—his sublime message of peace. We also encounter this phrase about the approach of the Lord (*Kyrios*) at the beginning of St Mark's Gospel, where there is a reference to the Angel who proclaims through John the Baptist: 'Prepare the way of the Lord, make his paths straight.'[42] In each case we have one and the same proclamation issuing from one and the same Angelic Being. In each case the proclamation has to do with the birth or the coming of the 'Ego, the Ruler of the soul-forces': this is how Rudolf Steiner translates into today's language the word '*Kyrios*', Lord, that we find in both Gospels.[43] Of John he adds the following: 'Hence John the Baptist declared to his disciples: Through the Waterman Initiation, I can place at the disposal of my Angel only those powers which enable him to proclaim the coming of *Kyrios*, the Lord.'[44]

If we once more recall what we have already said from various aspects regarding the working of the Nirmanakaya of Buddha through John the Baptist, we may sense the full significance of the fact that, in the two scenes from the Gospels to which we have referred, *both* Beings—the Angel and the Buddha who is connected with him—manifest their activity in his spirit-body. It is this deeply intimate relationship between these two Beings, together with their combined activity at the Turning-Point of Time, which enables us to unveil the mystery surrounding the Angel who works through John the Baptist and who is also the Hierarchic Being who with respect to John the Baptist has taken upon himself the tasks which the Archangel Michael had formerly fulfilled with regard to Elijah—which is to say, *he is the spiritual successor and inheritor of Michael's mission in the sphere of the Angels.*

Rudolf Steiner speaks more fully about this Angelic Being who is so intimately associated on the one hand with the Nirmanakaya of Buddha and on the other with the Archangel Michael in connection with one of the most important spiritual events of our time—the ascent of the Archangel Michael to the rank of the ruling spirit of our present age. In describing this event in the lecture of 18 May 1913, Rudolf Steiner poses the following question in conclusion: 'If a promotion of Michael has taken place, if he has become the guiding Spirit of Western civilisation, who will come in his stead? The place must be filled. Everyone must say to himself: "Then some Angel must also have been promoted, and must enter the ranks of the Archangels. Who is it?" '[45] In the next lecture Rudolf Steiner himself answers this question, at the same time unfolding the mystery of this particular Angelic Being: 'When a man from being a Bodhisattva becomes a Buddha, then his Guardian Angel is, as it were, set free; it is such Angel Beings who, after the fulfilment of their mission, ascend into the realm of the Archangel Beings. Thus we are actually able to grasp how an Archangel ascends to the nature of an Archai and an Angel Being to an Archangel Being . . .'[46]

This ascent of the two Hierarchic Beings, who are thus related by the principle of spiritual succession, belongs to the time between 1841 and 1879. Here it should be borne in mind that the place which was 'made vacant' in the Hierarchy of the Archangels as a result of Michael's ascent to the rank of Time-Spirit was no ordinary place, but one which, since ancient times, has belonged to the *ruling Sun Archangel*.[47] Thus in order that he might take up his place, the Guardian Angel of the Gautama Buddha, once he had in the sixth century BC been freed from the task of guiding the human being that had been entrusted to him and had thereby been enabled to ascend to the rank of Archangel, had to make the sacrifice of consenting to work in the sphere of the Angels for almost a further two and a half thousand years, even though he was—in so far as his inner qualities were concerned—already an Archangel. It was this sacrificial deed which enabled him to participate in the manner described in the events of Palestine, though now no longer as the Guardian Angel of a Bodhisattva incarnated in a human body, but as the collaborator and guide of a Buddha working in a spirit-body. For as he continued to work in the spiritual world nearest to the Earth after the Buddha's enlightenment beneath the Bodhi tree, he was able to participate in the events of the Turning-Point of Time far more directly as an Angel than would have been possible had he been of the rank of an Archangel.[48] Here we have one further testimony of the fact that the Angelic Being working through John the Baptist was the direct successor of Michael in the sphere of the Angels and had for six centuries passed through a stage of development whose aim was that he would take Michael's place in the sphere of the Archangels at the beginning of the new epoch of his rulership amongst mankind.

Thus instead of the Archangel Michael working through Elijah, we have working through John the Baptist the particular Angelic Being who had formerly been the Guardian Angel of Gautama Buddha. However, everything has, as we have seen, now moved one Hierarchy lower.[49] If we then take into account this 'shift' in the ranks of the inspiring Hierarchies, we also need to ask: Who, with respect to John the Baptist, adopted that role which the Moon Elohim, Jahve, actively fulfilled with regard to Elijah?

It follows from what has been said that this must have been a Hierarchic Being who stood one stage lower than the Elohim Jahve, that is, one who belonged to the Hierarchy of the Archai or Spirits of Time. In other words, one is speaking of the ruling Time-Spirit of the fourth post-Atlantean cultural epoch, the epoch to which belongs the most important event of the whole of Earth evolution—the Mystery of Golgotha.

In the lecture of 12 June 1910 Rudolf Steiner characterises in some detail this Hierarchic Being who was originally the ruling Archangel of the people of ancient Greece.[50] Subsequently, through having fulfilled to perfection his mission of guiding the cultural life of ancient Greece, he was able to ascend to the rank of Archai and become the ruling spirit of his entire epoch. This also enabled him at the Turning-Point of Time, as the new Time-Spirit, to participate in a quite special way in the events of Palestine and in the spreading of Christianity. For according to Rudolf Steiner, in order that it might be spread amongst mankind, 'it was not merely necessary that this event [the Mystery of Golgotha] took place but that certain guiding and ruling Spirits from the Hierarchies worked towards this end.'[51]

14

Already before the beginning of the events of Palestine, the activity of this Archai, the Time-Spirit of the fourth post-Atlantean epoch, brought about in Southern Europe, Asia Minor and Northern Africa such a degree of unity between the Greek, Hebrew and Roman cultural impulses that from these it was gradually possible to form those sheaths within which Christianity could then begin to spread over the Earth. Rudolf Steiner speaks in this connection of the body, soul and spirit of early Christianity, these corresponding respectively to the Roman, Hebrew and Greek elements.[52] The fact that at that time Christianity, born as it was out of the Hebrew soul, could be united with the two other elements was a direct result of what the 'Greek' Time-Spirit had previously accomplished. So successful was he with his task of preparing humanity for the coming to Earth of the Christ Being that at the time of the events of Palestine he won the opportunity to rise still higher in his own development, to ascend from the rank of a Time-Spirit to that of a Spirit of Form. At this point, however, something quite special takes place which Rudolf Steiner describes in the following words: 'A most remarkable and interesting event now occurred. At a definite moment *which coincided approximately with the descent of Christ upon Earth* [that is, with the moment of the Baptism in the Jordan], the Greek Time-Spirit renounced for our present epoch the possibility of rising into the Hierarchy of the Spirits of Form and became the guiding Time-Spirit who then works on through the successive epochs. *He became the representative guiding Spirit of exoteric Christianity . . .*'[53] Thus if in the century immediately preceding the birth of Christianity the 'Greek Time-Spirit' prepared the three sheaths in which Christianity was to be born, through the merging and interpenetration of the Greek, Hebrew and Roman elements, so now after the events of Palestine, as a result of his sacrificial renunciation from ascending to the rank of the Spirits of Form, he was able to become the guide and inspirer of the true evolution of the Christ-impulse within these sheaths. In renouncing this ascent to the rank of the Spirits of Form, to the sphere of the Second Hierarchy, he remained more directly connected in this spiritual sphere of the Third Hierarchy with the whole earthly evolution of humanity. However, this is not the end of the process. For in characterising this Time-Spirit as he fulfils the new mission which he took upon himself at the moment of the Baptism in the Jordan, Rudolf Steiner twice refers to him as he who 'stands' or 'goes' *before* the Christ-impulse, that is, as His forerunner: 'He becomes the representative guiding Spirit of exoteric Christianity, so that the Archai Being—the guiding Spirit of the Greeks—*himself forms the vanguard of the Christ-impulse.*' And a little later in the same lecture Rudolf

Steiner speaks of him as 'that common Time-Spirit who was in the vanguard of the Christ-impulse.'[54]

Christ has a trinity of forerunners, each of them walking before Him at a different level of world existence. On Earth He is preceded by John the Baptist: 'There was a man *sent from God*, whose name was John. He came for testimony, to bear witness to the light, that all might believe through him. He was not the light, but he came to bear witness to the light.'[55] Then there is the Angelic Being who works through John. Of him it is said: 'Behold, *I send my Angel before thy face*, who shall prepare thy way.'[56] And finally, there is the 'Greek Time-Spirit', who 'is in the vanguard of the Christ-impulse'. Thus the words with which John characterises his principal mission, 'I am not the Christ, but I have been sent *before* Him'[57] can also—although in a more spiritual sense—justly be related to the two other Hierarchic Beings working through him. For the fulfilment of their mission at the Turning-Point of Time, each of these three Beings had to offer a certain sacrifice; only thereby was it possible for them truly to approach and serve the Christ-impulse. The sacrifice offered by John finds its highest expression in his words: 'He must increase, but I must decrease.'[58] The Angel who works through him renounced (as we have seen) his ascent to the rank of the Archangels, and the Time-Spirit who inspired John renounced at the moment of the Baptism in the Jordan his elevation to a Spirit of Form.

We shall now, on the basis of what has been said up to this point, turn once again to the personality of John the Baptist as recounted in the Gospels, and we shall be able to distinguish with full clarity two kinds of inspiration in his words and actions. On the one hand, an Angelic Being works within him. As we have seen, this is the same Angelic Being who appeared to the shepherds in the field before the revelation of the Nirmanakaya of Buddha. His task was to proclaim the birth of the Cosmic Ego of Christ in the man, Jesus: 'In John there lived an Angel whose mission was to herald in advance the Egohood that was to be present in the *most all-embracing* [that is to say, cosmic] sense in Jesus of Nazareth [from the moment of the Baptism in the Jordan].'[59] Thus as he feels in his soul the inspiration of this Angelic Being, John the Baptist says of him: 'I myself did not know Him; but *he who sent me to baptise with water* said to me, "He on whom you see the Spirit descend and remain, this is he who baptises with the Holy Spirit."'[60] These words refer to the union of the World-Ego of Christ with Jesus at the Baptism in the Jordan[61] as expressed in the imagination of the dove, and also to His descending Spirit-Self, through whose forces He was able to baptise by the Holy Spirit.[62]

John the Baptist receives an altogether different kind of inspiration from the Archai who, as the Christ Being entered into the sheaths of Jesus of Nazareth, changed from being the ruling Time-Spirit of the fourth post-Atlantean epoch to the 'guiding Spirit of exoteric Christianity'. For by renouncing his ascent to the rank of the Spirits of Form, this guiding Spirit was from the moment of the Baptism in the Jordan able to become the mediator between the world of man and the revelation from the sublime macrocosmic sphere of the Father. Not even the Angelic Being who worked through John was able to be such a mediator, for in the sphere which is directly associated with the earthly evolution of mankind, that of the Third Hierarchy, the Angels represent the impulse of the Holy Spirit, the Archangels the principle of the Son, and only the Archai the principle of the Father.[63] Thus at the Baptism in the Jordan, there sound, *through the mediation* of the ruling Archai of that time, these mighty, truly cosmic words: 'This is my beloved Son; today I have begotten thee.'[*][64]

As for John himself, the inspirations of the ruling Archai of his time laid upon him a task of the highest order. As the representative of earthly humanity in the fourth post-Atlantean cultural epoch it fell to him to recognise Christ out of the forces of his individual ego working within the intellectual or mind soul, to encounter Him and, long before the Apostle Peter, to utter the words which ushered in the new aeon in human evolution. These words germinate within the soul of John the Baptist as the direct Inspiration of the ruling Being of the Hierarchy of the Archai and stir him to the world-historical testimony: 'And I have seen and have borne witness that this is the son of God.'[65]

This sublime deed of acknowledgement of John, at the foundation of which there lies a profound understanding of the mystery of the descent of the Sun Being of the Christ into the sheaths of Jesus of Nazareth, leads us to the question: What is the source of these spiritual forces of higher knowledge which enabled John to be the first of all men to *recognise* the Christ on Earth and to declare Him to other human beings? If we are to answer this question we must turn to the lecture of 2 May 1910, where Rudolf Steiner refers to how at the very time when, at the Turning-Point of Time, the Christ-impulse was beginning to spread from the East there comes to meet it from the West a certain soul-quality which forms in man a kind of *organ of cognition* for perceiving the Christ Being on Earth. This new faculty is *conscience*. 'These are two things that belong together. As Christ appears in the East, so conscience awakens in the West that through it Christ may be received. In the simultaneous occurrence and *comprehension* of the Christ event . . . we may behold an infinite wisdom

---

[*] Or in another translation: 'You are my beloved Son, in whom I am well pleased.'

that holds sway in [human] evolution.'[66] On the other hand, the evolution of conscience, the new cognitive organ for the Christ Being, is connected very closely with *the evolution of the forces of the ego in the individual human being*. And while amongst the Egypto-Chaldean peoples the evolution of the ego was somewhat delayed and in Northern Europe, in contrast, ahead of its time, in the figure of John the Baptist there stands before us a powerfully and harmoniously developed ego that appears within the intellectual or mind soul and is hence most fully capable of recognising out of the forces of conscience—this new organ of cognition—the Christ Being who appeared on Earth historically, as the World-Ego, in the fourth cultural epoch of the intellectual or mind soul.[67] Thus the words that arise within John the Baptist through the inspiration of the ruling Archai of that time, 'This is My beloved Son, today have I begotten Him', sound in his soul, in his ego, as the voice of *world conscience*; they awaken in him a higher knowledge of the Christ Being. Hence we may say: John the Baptist appears before Christ at the Jordan as the representative of the conscience of all mankind, and he thereby becomes for all future ages the archetype of one who 'has recognised Christ out of the forces of conscience as an organ of cognition', the first 'witness of the Light . . . that has come into the world,'[68] testifying to all mankind: 'This was He of whom I said, "He who comes after me ranks before me, for He was before me."'[69]

3

The Representative of the Conscience of Humanity

'Conscience . . . takes the place of God on Earth, and is hence to that extent the highest and last.'

Novalis

We may now ask what it was that enabled John the Baptist to become the representative of the conscience of all mankind at the Turning-Point of Time although he was born and grew up amongst the Hebrew people, whose entire life was founded on the *law* and was therefore essentially foreign to the impulse of conscience. As we have already seen, the principal prerequisite of conscience is a strongly developed individual ego,[70] a condition that John had been able to fulfil—albeit in a quite special form—in his incarnation as Elijah. This comes to expression in the Old Testament. For what Moses experienced as the revelation of the 'I am' *from without*, in the thunder and lightning on Mount Sinai, and which then took the form of the Ten Commandments that govern the behaviour of the human ego from without,[71] becomes in Elijah for the first time to some extent, an *inner experience*. This comes imaginatively to expression in that Elijah begins to work on the Earth with natural forces such as thunder and lightning.[72] This inner experience of the 'I am' forms within him the foundations for the subsequent development of the impulse of conscience.

However, if we want to find a still deeper reason why John the Baptist was so especially suited to be the bearer of the impulse of conscience, we need to return to the very beginning of human evolution and recall that, as Adam, he participated directly in the Fall. According to the Old Testament, this event ends with Adam, having tasted of the Tree of Knowledge of good and evil, being forced to leave the higher regions of the spiritual world, at whose gates the higher powers, guiding earthly evolution, place the Cherub with the flaming sword to guard them.[73]

If we try to express in earthly words what the image of the Cherub with the flaming sword at the gates of Paradise is addressing—in imaginative language—to all mankind, we would have to say: 'Your state of soul has changed (because you have tasted of the fruit of the Tree of Knowledge). Henceforth the celestial realms have distanced themselves from you.' These words have since then lived in the innermost depths of every human soul, but they have lived with quite particular—one could even say 'primordial'—strength in the soul of Adam himself throughout all his subsequent incarnations until his appearance at the Turning-Point of Time as John the Baptist. From this we may see why it was that John the Baptist was especially predisposed to be the bearer of the impulse of conscience. This was a consequence of the effect that the imagination of the Cherub, together with his cosmic words, had upon his soul in the course of his many incarnations; it formed the mighty impulse in his soul which eventually led him to baptise in the Jordan, and also served as the foundation for the evolution of the 'organ for recognising the Christ'—conscience.

There is, however, a further element—in the activity of this individuality amongst the people of the Old Testament as Elijah and, earlier on, as Phinehas—which merges with this original impulse; it has to do with the relationship of Phinehas and Elijah to the impulse given by Moses. As we have seen, the former (Phinehas), because of his boundless devotion to the impulse of Jahve, rescues the mission of Moses amongst the people of the Old Testament, while the latter (Elijah) leads it to a higher level. Thus the individuality of Phinehas-Elijah, in living and working amongst the ancient Hebrews, constantly finds himself at the point of intersection of two impulses: the impulse of Moses proceeding from without; and from within, from the depths of his soul, the impulse of the Cherub and of his words at the gates of Paradise. From without the law, from within the moral memory of the imagination. This means that the soul of the individuality of Phinehas-Elijah experienced already on Earth in a physical body what an ordinary human being of those times (and this remained the case until the beginning of the twentieth century) experienced only *after death* before entering into Kama-Loka. Rudolf Steiner describes this experience in the following words: 'Before one's Kama-Loka one is confronted by two figures . . . One of these is Moses—there is no doubt in one's mind that it is Moses whom one is meeting—holding out the Tablets of the Law. In the Middle Ages they spoke of Moses "with his stern law". And in one's soul one is keenly aware of how far in one's inmost being one has transgressed against this law. The other figure is he that is called "the Cherub with the flaming sword" who pronounces judgment on these transgressions.'[74]

From these words we may see that Moses manifests to the soul after death the 'stern law', while the Cherub *judges* any deviations from it—which is to say that the Cherub in this scene appears as *the imagination of cosmic conscience*, imparting the judgment of the entire spiritual cosmos on man and his deeds.[75] Here is repeated on a small scale for every human being what formerly took place with regard to the whole of humanity at the dawn of earthly evolution—the event known as 'the expulsion from Paradise', the immediate witness of which was the individuality of Adam. The fact that this individuality in the course of his subsequent incarnations bore within himself this memory-image of the Cherub and his words eventually brought it about that when the ego of Adam, through his incarnations in the ancient Hebrew people, had attained the necessary strength, the mighty imagination of the Cherub, the representative of cosmic conscience, that worked in the depths of his soul was transformed in his ego into the impulse of *personal human conscience*; this was at the same time the initial stage of the incarnation of the awakening conscience of all humanity at that time. This transformation in the soul of Adam—in his incarnation at the Turning-Point of Time as John the Baptist—of cosmic conscience into the conscience of humanity, the organ for perceiving and recognising the approaching Christ, enabled him to experience anew the ancient cosmic words of the Cherub at the gates of Paradise and to proclaim them to all mankind. Instead of saying, 'Your state of soul has changed. The celestial realms have distanced themselves from you,' he was able to proclaim out of the forces of his personal conscience: 'Change your state of soul, the celestial realms have come near to you.'[76] This new proclamation means: The impulse of the World-Ego (the Kingdom of Heaven) has now approached mankind, and hence the soul-condition of human beings must now also change. The world epoch of the 'law' has ended. In the souls of men, the impulse of conscience must now awaken. These transformed words of the Cherub have since that time lived in every human soul, and continue to do so today; every human being knows them as the voice of his own conscience: 'Change your state of soul . . .' The very fact that every man can inwardly hear his voice and follow it is a testimony that *at this moment* 'the celestial realms' have really come near to him.

'For the law was given through Moses; grace and truth have come through Jesus Christ': these words from the prologue of the Gospel according to St John[77] are perhaps the most direct expression of the essential nature of the proclamation of John the Baptist. For as Adam he was once the first witness of the descent of the whole of mankind from the 'celestial realms' to the Earth, from above downwards on the path decreed by the law; and as the Baptist he was the first witness of the beginning of the ascent from the Earth back to the 'Kingdom of Heaven', from below upwards on the path of 'grace and truth'.

What Paul the Apostle later set forth in his Epistles, as the teaching of the old and the new Adam, appears here not as a teaching but as a historical reality, which finds its expression in the following words of John the Baptist that characterise his relationship to the Being of Christ: 'You yourselves bear witness, that I said, I am not the Christ, but I have been sent before Him. He who has the bride is the bridegroom; the friend of the bridegroom, who stands and hears Him, rejoices greatly at the bridegroom's voice; therefore this joy of mine is now full. He must increase, but I must decrease. He who comes from above is above all; he who is of the Earth belongs to the Earth, and of the Earth he speaks;[78] He who comes from heaven is above all. He bears witness to what He has seen and heard, yet no-one receives His testimony; he who receives His testimony [that is, principally John himself] sets his seal to this—that God is true. For He whom God has sent utters the words of God, for it is not by measure that God gives the spirit; the Father loves the Son, and has given all things into His hand. He who believes in the Son has eternal life; he who does not obey the Son shall not see life but the wrath of God rests upon him.'[79]

This can also shed a completely new light upon the whole character of John the Baptist's activity amongst the people of the Old Testament. For this task—as the one who prepares this people for the coming of the Christ Being to the Earth—was, firstly, to strengthen the forces of the individual ego within each human individual and, secondly, to awaken— on the foundation of this strengthened ego—the impulse of conscience which is capable of perceiving the World-Ego of Christ as He approaches the Earth. The first part of this task—the strengthening of the individual ego—was accomplished by John with the help of his preaching, which always preceded the actual process of baptism. Through his words he transmitted to his listeners part of his 'Elijah-forces', something of the spirit of Elijah, which enshrouded him like a mighty supersensible aura and which, as we have seen, was unable fully to enter into the earthly sheaths of John the Baptist (see p 8). Rudolf Steiner describes this process in the following words: 'The spirit of Elijah shows us in how manifold a way it must enter human hearts, so that many may gradually receive the Christ-impulse in the course of history. The significance of the Baptism by John was that Elijah was ready to prepare the way for Christ. This was what was encompassed in the deed of the Baptism by John in the Jordan: 'I will make a way for Him, I will prepare a path for Him within the hearts of men; I shall not merely hover above man, but will enter into their hearts, so that He (Christ) may enter also.'[80]

Somewhat earlier in the same lecture, Rudolf Steiner explains what is meant by the expression, 'the spirit of Elijah': 'When we consider this connection [Rudolf Steiner here refers to the process of the Baptism by John], there appears before us, for the first time in its true light, the spirit of Elijah that also worked within John the Baptist. Then we may conclude that in Elijah there stands before us the spirits of the Jewish people, the spirit of the Old Testament people. What kind of spirit was this? It was in a certain sense *the spirit of the ego* . . .'[81]

Such was the first part of the mission of John the Baptist. As for the second part—the awakening of the impulse of conscience in the egos of those who came to him to be baptised—this was accomplished by him in the process of baptism itself. This process of baptism consisted in that the person being baptised was fully immersed in water and remained under water until a partial separation of the etheric body from the physical body took place. As a result of this he was for a short time able to have perceptions of the spiritual world nearest to the Earth. And as his ego had been temporarily strengthened by the preaching of John the Baptist, he was at these moments—when a higher consciousness was awakened within him—able to have conscious supersensible experiences. What lit up within the soul of one who had passed through such an experience was none other than an inner revelation of the impulse of conscience, the awakening of the 'inner organ of *cognition*' that has the capacity to perceive the Christ as He approaches the Earth. 'Hence the baptism by John was a matter of cognition. "Change your whole outlook, do not simply look backwards . . . but turn your eyes to something new: the God who can reveal Himself within the human ego is approaching; the celestial realms have drawn nigh." The Baptist did not only preach this, but enabled men to recognise it by making it possible for them to partake in the baptism in the Jordan. Those who were baptised knew henceforth from their own clairvoyant perception, even though this may have lasted but for a few moments, that the words of the Baptist gave expression to a fact of world historical significance.'[82] Thus John accomplished the second part of his task through making the experience of the renewed words of the Cherub at the gates of Paradise accessible to all human souls, and unfolding to them the mystery of how the impulse of world conscience henceforth becomes the impulse of individual conscience, which makes possible a direct perception of 'the God who can reveal Himself within the human ego'.[83]

This twofold task which John had to fulfil amongst the ancient Hebrew people drew him inevitably into conflict with the Pharisees and Sadducees, with the scribes and the doctors of the law. We shall especially single out two moments in the story of this conflict as it is set forth in the Gospels. John says to the Pharisees and Sadducees who approach him: 'You brood of vipers! Who warned you to flee from the world conflagration to come? Bear fruit that befits repentance, and do not presume to say to yourselves, "We have Abraham as our father"; for

I tell you, the divine Father is able from these stones to raise up children to Abraham.'' '84

These words express clearly what it was that John had to do. 'Do not presume to say to yourselves, "We have Abraham as our father."' This means, 'Do not think that you can inwardly strengthen the impulse of the individual ego by turning to the group ego, which works through the generations in the sense of the formula, "I and Abraham are one".' And then: 'You brood of vipers!' (meaning, sons of the wisdom of the law) 'Who warned you to flee from the world conflagration?' (that is, from the ancient condemnatory imagination of the Cherub with the *flaming* sword). 'Bear fruit that befits repentance': this means, 'The celestial realms have come nigh', or: 'Learn to judge not according to the law but according to conscience'. And finally, the last admonition: 'Even now the axe is laid to the root of the trees; every tree therefore that does not bear good fruit is cut down and thrown into the *fire*.' '85 In these words we have an indication of the transition from the epoch of the law to the epoch of conscience and freedom. The tree of the law no longer has the power to bear good fruit, for the times have changed.

Thus John reveals to the Pharisees and Sadducees the essential character of his life's task, and accordingly erects an impassable barrier between himself and them. Like them, John, as a member of the ancient Hebrew race, lives and works in accordance with the law of Moses,86 but inwardly he judges his actions and the actions of others on the basis of his *conscience*, the transformed voice of the Cherub in his soul, which opens up the way to a true knowledge of Christ. Thus the people say of John: 'John performed no sign, but everything that John said about this man was true.' '87 This 'judgment according to conscience' estranges John from the fundamental attitudes and also the customs of the ancient Hebrews, and eventually leads him to the open conflict with Herod and to his martyrdom.88 The reason for this tragic outcome is that he stands amidst the people of the Old Testament as the first prophet and representative of the New Testament, and through his martyrdom he becomes the first forerunner of the cosmic-earthly destiny of the Christ.

The principal task of John the Baptist, the representative of the conscience of the whole of earthly humanity—meeting the Christ on Earth and *recognising Him*—also determined John's destiny after death, and had a decisive influence upon his activity in the spiritual world after his martyr's death, which in itself had been a direct consequence of his service to the Christ Being. For according to Rudolf Steiner, '. . . conscience is a prophetic premonition of how our deeds will be experienced after death.' '89 It was on the strength of this that a condition arose for John after his death where he was, in accordance with the forces working within his soul, able to pursue—albeit in an altogether different form—the principal direction of his earthly activity. Thus he creates around Christ Jesus, from out of the spiritual world, a spiritual atmosphere of such a kind as can best enable Him to accomplish His deeds: 'John the Baptist has gone [into the spiritual world], but what he is, as the spirit of Elijah, has remained; in this spirit, Christ Jesus can *best* work, and His words flow most easily; in the *atmosphere* that has remained, in the *atmosphere of Elijah*, His deeds may best leave their mark.'[90] This is, so to speak, the first stage of John's service to the Christ Being after his death. At the second stage the entelechy of John gradually becomes the group-soul of the Twelve Apostles.[91] Finally, at the third stage it unites with Lazarus during the latter's initiation by Christ Jesus at Bethany.[92]

These three steps or stages are a reflection of the three conditions of this individuality in the past which, through his connection with Christ, have been transformed into the seeds of future conditions. Thus the first stage is, in a sense, a repetition—albeit in a wholly metamorphosed way—of the existence of this individuality as Adam who in deepest antiquity accompanied, as in a spiritual atmosphere, the earlier stages of the earthly evolution of mankind. Now, however, this oldest human soul, transformed by the Christ-impulse, wields a new, youthful strength. In the Gospel of St John, for example, there is a reference to this soul's supersensible participation in the feeding of the five thousand, that is, in the prophetic experiencing of the fifth cultural epoch,[93] in the form of the 'lad' who brings to Christ Jesus the five loaves and two fish, corresponding to the forces of the five higher and the two lower members of man's being,[94] from whose union with the Christ-impulse the spiritual foundations for the fifth post-Atlantean epoch can be laid within human souls. For it is in this epoch that the individuality of John is to begin his new *Christian* mission amongst mankind (of which more will be said later), and his two incarnations in the fifteenth and eighteenth centuries—permeated as they were with the entire fullness of the rejuvenating forces of the Christ-impulse, as the true Bread of Life[95]— were a preparation for this.

At the second stage, again in a wholly metamorphosed form, this individuality repeats his existence as Elijah, the bearer of the impulses of the group-soul of the ancient Hebrews, though now as the group-soul of the Twelve Apostles. And finally, in the process of uniting with Lazarus–John, he repeats—again at a more spiritualised level—his existence as John the Baptist, the first man on Earth who 'recognised the

25

Christ' and, through this union, he becomes worthy of being supersensibly present at the Mystery of Golgotha itself.

These are the consequences for his life after death of the further evolution of the impulse of conscience which John the Baptist experienced while still on the Earth.

4

After the Turning-Point of Time

Before turning to a consideration of the incarnations of the individuality of John the Baptist in the Christian era, it is necessary that we focus our attention upon one particularly important aspect of his nature. As the reincarnation of Adam, who had in the Lemurian epoch formed the gateway for the entry of the forces of Lucifer into the evolution of humanity, this individuality had, as a result of this event, come to be separated from his sister individuality, who at the time of the 'Fall' had been held back in the higher worlds, where she became the guardian of the unfallen, primordial etheric forces of mankind, symbolised in the Bible by the image of the Tree of Life. This sister soul of Adam, the individuality who had preserved the original, paradisaical condition of humanity, was to incarnate *for the first time* amongst mankind as the Jesus of the Luke Gospel.[96] As this 'paradisaical soul' was therefore a kind of 'heavenly archetype' of humanity, it represented from the very beginning the highest goal and focus for all the spiritual strivings of the 'earthly Adam', in so far as these were directed towards the attainment of the forces of the Tree of Life, towards gaining access to the unfallen cosmic etheric forces from which he had been separated since ancient Lemurian times.

This also explains why, between these two souls, there had always been a connection—which was in evidence during Mary's visit to Elisabeth, when the ego of the 'earthly Adam' (John the Baptist) was stirred through the contact with the 'heavenly Adam'—with the spiritual forces of his heavenly sister soul (the Jesus of St Luke's Gospel).[97] Subsequently, both individualities grew up together, as has been depicted—in a spirit-filled way—in many of Raphael's paintings,* and later on they often met and had long discussions at the door of the house of the Essene order in Nazareth, an order with which they were both connected but of which they were not actually members.[98] Despite this, however, their affinity, for all its deep karmic foundations, remained no

---

* This longing of John the Baptist for the Jesus of St Luke's Gospel (the Nathan Soul) as for his higher archetype is depicted with a particular intensity of feeling in one of the last of Raphael's Madonnas, 'Madonna del Passeggio'.

more than outward, for only through the mediation of the Christ Being, or to be more precise, through uniting with the impulse proceeding from the Mystery of Golgotha, was the individuality of Adam–Elijah–John the Baptist able to enter upon the path leading to his gradually being united with the lost forces of the Tree of Life, with the primordial etheric forces that had been preserved by the Nathan Soul.

Only after he had—as a result of his spiritual union with Lazarus–John—been supersensibly present on the Hill of Golgotha was this individuality able in the spiritual world to enter upon this path of becoming once again like his archetype, the 'heavenly Adam', the Nathan Soul. This path was then to be reflected in his two subsequent incarnations, as the Italian artist Raphael and the German poet Novalis. That this could happen is, according to Rudolf Steiner, 'one of those facts that can make one so clearly aware of the extent to which the mighty impulse of the Mystery of Golgotha brings about immense changes in human souls.'[99]

Like Elijah and John the Baptist, Raphael does not incarnate fully in his physical body.[100] The greater part of his spiritual entelechy remains *outside* his physical sheath, with the result that the individuality of Raphael is in constant association with the beings of the spiritual world. Thus there is in his case a repetition—though at one stage lower—of what we have already observed in connection with Elijah and John the Baptist. For just as the former was associated with the Archangel Michael and the latter with the Angel who prepared the arrival on Earth of the 'Lord of Karma', so was this individuality in his incarnation as Raphael and also, as we have seen, in his incarnation as Novalis, especially connected with the *Nathan Soul*, to the ideal of which—as the bearer of the primordial, Christ-permeated etheric body—he has since his spiritual participation in the Mystery of Golgotha striven with all his forces. Hence this path of inner purification and transformation that he had undergone led him to become, as Raphael, ever more youthful and spiritualised in his soul-qualities, ever more like the heavenly being of the Nathan Soul.

Thus Raphael, as kind of leitmotif of his artistic creativity, depicts ever and again in his picture the Holy Family of the Luke Gospel (and only very rarely that of the Matthew Gospel). It is also well known that the most moving of these (the *Sistine Madonna* and certain others) were painted directly from spiritual visions in which the Mary of the Luke Gospel and the Nathan Soul appeared to him as the highest goal of his spiritual strivings.[101] With this, however, we touch upon a profound mystery in the life of Raphael, which is associated with that all-embracing law of spiritual existence that Rudolf Steiner characterised in his lectures as the 'principle of spiritual economy'. According to this law the etheric and astral bodies of the most advanced human individualities do not dissolve in the spiritual world after the physical death of their bearers, as is generally the case, but are preserved in the higher worlds and used for the good of mankind's further evolution. This happens in such a way that, through certain occult processes, spiritual impressions are taken from these preserved etheric and astral bodies which are then incorporated in the corresponding sheaths of other human beings seeking incarnation on the Earth. And amongst these most highly evolved etheric and astral bodies preserved in the higher worlds, the etheric and astral bodies in which Christ Himself once dwelt on the Earth, that is, the supersensible sheaths of the Nathan Soul, occupy a quite special place. Etheric and astral impressions taken from them and then reproduced were, throughout the Middle Ages and even until the Renaissance (fifteenth century) to be embodied in the corresponding sheaths of those living on the Earth who were karmically predisposed for this. Thus according to indications of Rudolf Steiner, in the period from the fourth/ fifth to the tenth/twelfth centuries AD impressions taken from the preserved etheric body of the Nathan Soul were incorporated in the etheric bodies of many people. For those who received such impressions at this time in their etheric bodies, there could be two sorts of consequences. Firstly, 'they were always able to experience something akin to a Pauline revelation *on a small scale*',[102] that is, something similar to Paul's enlightenment before Damascus. Secondly, they were able 'in a certain sense to receive spiritual revelations of the events of Palestine'. But the most important aspect of what they were thus able clairvoyantly to experience with regard to the events of Palestine was, apart from the scene of the Crucifixion, the image of the 'Madonna', the image of 'Mary with the Jesus Child'.[103] Such experiences were also the source of early Christian and medieval art, especially painting.

The *overwhelming majority* of such 'incarnations' of the impressions of the etheric body of the Nathan Soul took place principally in the centuries referred to. However, if we take into consideration the quite particular nature of the individuality that lived within Raphael and also the immediate effect that *his* art has upon us, it does not seem impossible that Raphael, who lived at the transition between the fifteenth and sixteenth centuries, was nevertheless able, as were many anonymous artists of the Middle Ages, to receive into his own etheric body an impression of the etheric body of the Nathan Soul.[104] The deeper reasons for this fact are to be sought principally in the yearning of this individuality, as the reincarnated Adam, for his heavenly archetype for the 'sister soul' with whom he was originally united.

29

In the figure of Raphael we have a direct continuation of the inspired art of the 'first Christian centuries', born as it was 'from the forces of the etheric body of the Nathan Soul, in whom there lived the pristine, virginal forces of a true knowledge of natural and spiritual things. Rudolf Steiner says: 'Thus everything we feel at Christmas time flows together in the picture of the Mother Mary and the child, that picture which hovered so often before painters in earlier times, especially in the first Christian centuries, and of which the last echoes have been preserved in Raphael's Sistine Madonna. The Sistine Madonna *was born out of the great instinctive knowledge of nature and the spirit which prevailed in ancient times*. For it is a picture of the imagination which must in fact come to a man who inwardly contemplates the weaving of the mysteries of Christmas in such a way that this becomes for him a living picture.'[105]

As regards the 'Pauline revelation on a small scale', there is in Raphael's biography at any rate one soul-experience which he himself compares in a poem with Paul's experience before Damascus. The poem was written by Raphael on one of the sketches for the fresco *The Glorification of the Sacrament*. Raphael does not actually describe the experience itself, for it had to remain a secret of his own soul life. Nevertheless, the fact that it is connected with one of his most important works of art is already of some significance:

> As Paul spoke not of what he once had seen,
> So now do I keep silence, for love's balm
> Has cast caressing veils around my heart,
> To shield my joys in blissful mystery's balm.[106]

This is also confirmed by Rudolf Steiner in the lecture of 5 October 1917, where he speaks of how the figure of Paul the Apostle and his spiritual Damascus experience was the central question of Raphael's inner life and the most important theme of his later creative work.[107]

However, not only are the spiritual sources of the works depicting the 'Madonna and child' revealed to us through knowing the mystery that an impression of the etheric body of the Nathan soul worked within the etheric body of Raphael, but the spiritual sources of his last and perhaps most important work, *The Transfiguration of Christ*, also became more accessible to our understanding. For the scene of the Transfiguration, as described in the three Synoptic Gospels, has a particular relationship to the spiritual individuality of Raphael, not only because in this scene the prophet Elijah (that is, the spiritual entelechy of John the Baptist) appears with Christ, but above all because the revelation of Christ Jesus, out of the Sun-sphere (Devachan) that the three disciples experience, was the result of His union with the *etheric body* of Jesus of Nazareth.[108] That is why a work devoted to this theme occupies a special place in Raphael's creative activity. This majestic picture was completed by the artist only in its upper part, which depicts the Transfiguration itself. And, like a symbol of his brief earthly life, there appears before us an image of Raphael lying on his death-bed in his studio with his last and never completed painting, *The Transfiguration*, at his feet, which in Raphael's interpretation is at the same time a supersensible representation of the *Mystery of the Resurrection*.

The spiritual influence of the etheric body of the Nathan Soul on Raphael is not, however, the only source of higher influences in his life. For it is not only the so-called 'lower stream' of Hierarchic inspirations, which, proceeding initially from the Archangel Michael, then passed through an Angelic Being, and finally found expression in the working of the forces of the etheric body of the Nathan Soul that are manifested in Raphael. His soul was also permeated by the Hierarchic inspirations of the 'upper stream'. This 'upper stream' appears, in the case of Elijah, in the form of the direct influences of the Moon Elohim, Jahve, and then in the case of John the Baptist in the revelations proceeding from the ruling Time-Spirit, the Archai who had sacrificially renounced his further ascent and had, from the moment of Christ's incarnation on the Earth, become the guiding Spirit of exoteric Christianity. This stream, too, now descends one stage lower and is manifested in the inspirations which Raphael receives, in particular, from a certain Being of the Hierarchy of the *Archangels*.[109]

The very name, 'Raphael', is an indication of the source of these inspirations. For immediately before the birth of the future artist, his mother, with whom he was to be connected in a particularly intimate way,[110] received from the spiritual worlds the indication that her child be consecrated to the Archangel Raphael and that he should bear this name. This spiritual connection of the artist Raphael with his Hierarchic patron was also expressed in that his birth and his death both fell on Good Friday, a time in the yearly cycle which stands quite especially under the influence of the Archangel Raphael.[111] Here too, in order to gain a better understanding of this relationship we need to recall once again that its foundation lay in the fact that the artist Raphael, as we have seen, bore in his etheric body an impression of the etheric body of the Nathan Soul, that is, the forces of the 'Tree of Life' that has been transformed by Christ,[112] the forces of eternal youth and *cosmic healing*, a soul substance through which the Archangel Raphael might best be aided in his work.

In the Bible this Archangel is mentioned only once, in a story which, moreover, is not included in the canonic Old Testament. This is the story

31

of the righteous sage Tobit, for the healing of whose blindness the Archangel Raphael is sent from the spiritual world. In this Old Testament narrative the Archangel Raphael appears not only as the healer of outer physical sight but also as the awakener of the inner spiritual vision through which the physically healed and spiritually enlightened Tobit and his son, Tobias, can recognise Raphael as his saviour.[113] In other words, the Archangel Raphael appears in this story not only as the healer of the physical, but also as the *mediator* between outer and inner vision and, in the case of Raphael the artist, makes it possible for him to express experiences of a purely soul-spiritual nature through line and colour in a beautiful, harmonious and yet also a remarkably exact way. Rudolf Steiner refers to this particular mystery of Raphael's art, a mystery which decisively distinguishes it from that of all the other artists of the Renaissance, in the following words: 'Every high point in the history of art depicts the spiritual in sense-perceptible form, or rather raises the sense-perceptible to the sphere of the spiritual. Raphael, the painter, is valued so highly because, *to a greater degree than any other painter*, he was able to depict in the realm of the senses something that rises up into the realm of spirit.'[114] This also explains the remarkable therapeutic powers of Raphael's art, as Rudolf Steiner has indicated on a number of occasions and in various connections; it is sufficient to recall the sequence of 15 paintings which Dr Felix Peipers put together, under his direction, as material for a 'therapeutic meditation'.[115]

This intimate relationship of the artist to the Archangel of healing, and through him to the sphere of Mercury as a whole, was expressed in the especially deep connection that he had with this spiritual sphere, even after his death. Rudolf Steiner refers to this as follows: 'Then we behold him wander through the Mercury sphere where, in association with the great cosmic healers, he transformed for his spirituality the power that had been his to create *what is so infinitely whole and healthy* in colour and line.'[116]

If we trace this remarkable transition from John the Baptist to Raphael, the question inevitably arises: How was it possible that the individuality of John, this last of the prophets of the Old Testament—who was still connected in all the fibres of his soul with the people of the Old Testament, and who through the many centuries of his history and his strictly monotheistic spiritual life was so distant from, and even hostile to, the 'pagan' world around him (and, above all, that of Greece and Rome)—was able in the person of Raphael to become so sensitive a venerator and connoisseur of the art and culture of antiquity in all their diverse manifestations? 'And so,' says Rudolf Steiner, 'we may observe the remarkable fact that through Raphael the world of Greece reappears in the Christian world. Thus we see in Raphael a Christianity emerging at a time which in a certain sense represents an anti-Christian environment around him.'[117]

The second part of this observation—that which refers to Raphael as one who in his whole personality and creativity brings the new tidings of Christianity—can be understood without any particular difficulty. For at the moment of the Baptism in the Jordan John's great Old Testament mission came to an end forever and his new mission, that of the New Testament, began. Through meeting Christ on the Earth and through *recognising* Him by means of the revelation of the ruling Archai of that time—'This is My beloved Son, today I have begotten Him'—there began for John a new epoch which placed an altogether new task before him. We shall have more to say later on about this new task. Meanwhile, what is of particular importance for us is the fact that, in a certain, more spiritual sense, his presence and participation in the Baptism of Jesus—that is, the direct experience of the incarnation of the ruling Sun-Spirit in the Man Jesus of Nazareth—was for John a kind of 'spiritual baptism', an inner, and final, transition from the Old to the New Testament. How far this 'spiritual baptism' was consciously experienced by John is borne out by his own words in the Gospel of St John (quoted on p. 22).

Herein also lies a more inward reason why Novalis, as though out of some deep, vague memory, in describing the scene of the Baptism, does not only describe it in the first person, from the point of view of John, but also from the standpoint of Jesus himself (see p. 78). For what in all its fullness united then with Jesus of Nazareth also overshone John, transforming the last Old Testament prophet into the *first Christian*, the first human being of the new aeon of evolution.

Now the question arises in connection with the first part of Rudolf Steiner's observation. How could 'the world of Greece reappear in the Christian world' through Raphael? Whence did he, who in his past incarnations did not have any relationship to the 'pagan' world, acquire this deep connection to and understanding of the culture of Greece, this love of his for the Roman world, to the extent that he became the first archaeologist of his time, who organised and led excavations and restorations of the architectural monuments of ancient Rome?[118] In order to answer this important question, it is necessary to recall a spiritual law which states that all that has been experienced by a man in one incarnation in a more spiritually outward way, for example in the form of an inspiration coming from above, in the next incarnation, after passing through a higher metamorphosis and fully uniting with the soul in the period between death and a new birth, appears as an inner soul-spiritual quality that belongs to the soul, to the ego of the person concerned.

Thus the Jahve revelation, formerly experienced by Elijah, became in his next incarnation as John an inner power of the soul, a spiritual impulse that filled his whole ego.[119] The inspirations experienced by John the Baptist during the Baptism in the Jordan that proceeded from the ruling Archai of that time—whose essential task in the century prior to the founding of Christianity was the preparation of the spiritual and cultural–historical sheaths of body, soul and spirit necessary for this event—led in consequence to the most intense working together with this Archai on the part of the soul of John after his death. As a result of this, the fundamental spiritual–historical mission of this Hierarchic Spirit of preparing and carrying forward exoteric Christianity was, in the new incarnations of John the Baptist as Raphael, able to become the inner impulse of his own ego. And as this mission, as we have seen, consisted in harmoniously uniting the cultural impulses of Rome, Judaism and Greece (which formed the sheaths for the arising of Christianity), Raphael was permeated by this task to the very depths of his soul. Out of the forces of his ego he endeavoured to bring Christianity (which was born for him out of Judaism at the Baptism in the Jordan) into a harmonious interrelationship with the worlds of Greece and Rome. This was the reason why in the course of his incarnation at the turn of the fifteenth and sixteenth centuries he was active only in the spirit of *exoteric*, and not esoteric, Christianity.

5

The Herald of Spiritual Christianity

'I say to everyone, He lives,
The Risen One is He;
For he is hovering in our midst,
There evermore to be.'

Novalis

'There is no religion that is not Christianity.'

Novalis

The life of Novalis was filled by even more significant spiritual experiences when, with the death of his bride Sophie von Kühn at Easter 1797, he gained access to inner spiritual faculties and above all to the capacity of seeing and reading in the astral light.

'An *initiation* experienced through the grace of higher powers'—thus does Rudolf Steiner characterise this fundamental experience of Novalis, which he later described in the third and fourth hymns of his cycle of poems, *Hymns to the Night*. If we study this poetic description of the soul-processes through which Novalis passed at that time, we may find therein an exact reflection of certain moments on the Path of Initiation that are familiar to us through the book, *Knowledge of the Higher Worlds: How is it Achieved?* Thus for Novalis, the approach to the threshold of the spiritual world is accompanied at first by a feeling of ever-growing solitude ('. . . as solitary as none have been before . . .') and then by a sense of the most oppressive fear ('driven by unspeakable anguish'). However, this fleeting experience is at once overcome through Novalis' spiritual strength, and as a result his spirit is freed from the fetters of his physical body: 'my liberated, new-born spirit took wings over the neighbouring area', and the inner Sun of the higher ego lights up within his soul.

Two experiences are particularly characteristic of a right entry into and a conscious life within the spiritual world: that at the moment of union with it a veil of oblivion is cast over all earthly things; and that the sources of higher memory, the first fruits of the working of the higher ego within the human soul, become manifest in its depths.[120] Rudolf Steiner describes both these experiences as the receiving of two 'draughts': oblivion with regard to the physical world, and memory with respect to the spiritual. In *The Divine Comedy*, Dante also describes this stage of inner development in the image of the two rivers of oblivion and memory, Lethe and Eunoe, in which the would-be initiate must bathe. 'Earthly glory flew away, and my sorrow with it': in these words Novalis characterises the *effect* of the first draught. He describes the process of receiving the second in greater detail: 'Far and wearisome was my pilgrimage to the holy grave and the cross was heavy. He whose mouth the crystal wave has moistened, which, *indiscernible to the ordinary senses*, issued from within the dark womb of the hill at whose foot the earthly flood bursts forth, he who has stood up upon this border-region of the world and has looked out over that new land, night's dwelling place, such a one does not return to the bustle of the world, to the land where light abides in eternal restlessness.'/The next step is that the soul orientates itself in this 'new land' which has opened up to it at the 'border-region of the world' and finds its place therein. Rudolf Steiner characterises this initiation process as 'building a hut'[121] in the spiritual world, this being associated with the experience of finding one's true home in this new world. 'Night's dwelling-place', that is, the spiritual sphere where every man dwells unconsciously as he sleeps, and where Novalis was, through his initiation, able to awaken in full consciousness, now gradually becomes his new home. 'In the heights he builds himself huts, shelters of peace . . .'[122] writes Novalis in the fourth Hymn.

What, however, was revealed to Novalis in the spiritual world as a result of his initiation? These experiences, as with the process of initiation itself, were reflected only partially and very incompletely in his *Hymns to the Night* and other poetic works, and remained within the holiest regions of his soul. Hence at this point we need to turn to what has been imparted by spiritual science, where we find an exact description of what Novalis came to perceive as a result of his glimpses into the higher worlds. For what was revealed to him in this spiritual contemplation was first and foremost the cosmic mystery of the Nathan Soul, which is associated with the supersensible origins of mankind, together with the mystery of death and resurrection, which is associated with the working of the Christ Being on the Earth.[123] Thus what is in our time the focal point of anthroposophical Christology was revealed to him through direct vision. For '. . . not only a great vista of past ages of the Earth and the cosmos but the Christ Being Himself appeared before his spiritual eye. He was able to say of himself with regard to the Christ Being that he was one who *with the eyes of spirit has actually seen* what is revealed when "the stone is lifted" and when the Being—who has furnished earthly existence with the proof that life in the spirit will forever overcome death—becomes visible.'[124] Novalis was here once more experiencing what his spiritual eyes had beheld when, after his incarnation as John the Baptist, he had united supersensibly with Lazarus and was therefore able to be spiritually present at the 'lifting of the stone':

> Uplifted is the stone—
> Mankind is now arisen—
> To Thee we all are wed
> And nevermore feel bonds.

'The initiation conferred upon him, as it were through grace, brought to life within him all that he had achieved in earlier incarnations . . . And because he looked back through the ages with his own awakened eyes of spirit, he was able to affirm that nothing in his life was comparable in importance with the experience of having discovered Christ as a living reality. *Such an experience is like a repetition of the event of Damascus*, when Paul, who had hitherto persecuted the followers of Christ Jesus and paid no heed to what they had to say, received in higher vision the direct proof that Christ lives, that He is present, and that the event of Golgotha is unique in the whole process of the evolution of humanity. Those whose eyes of spirit are open [in this case, Novalis] can themselves behold this event.' Thus the fundamental Christian truth was revealed to Novalis' inner experience: 'Christ was not only present in the body that was once His dwelling-place, He has remained united with the Earth; *through Him the power of the Sun has united with the Earth.*' Novalis speaks of the revelation that came to him as 'unique' and he maintains that only those who with their whole souls wish to participate in this event are men in the true sense.

The source of this revelation is, for Novalis, the *mystery of the heart*, which, when it is comprehended in a conscious way, leads to a direct experience of Christ, to an inner 'Damascus event'. Novalis himself refers to this profound Christian mystery in the following lines:

> O nurse, my Beloved,
> My yearning breast,
> That I in slumber,
> In love, may rest.
> Now feel I death's
> Youth-bringing flood,
> *To balm and ether,*
> *Is changed my blood—*
> By day are faith

And courage my food,
At night I die
In holy ardour's mood.

'To balm and ether is changed my blood'—Rudolf Steiner was later to
refer to this spiritual process of the ceaseless transformation—within the
human heart, of blood into etheric substance—as the mystery of 'the
etherisation of the blood', and he described it in detail in the lecture of
1 October 1911. The essence of this mystery is that since the Mystery of
Golgotha, parallel to the stream of etherised human blood flowing from
below upwards, from the heart to the head, there has in every man
flowed another stream, that of the etherised blood of Christ Himself:
'Since the Mystery of Golgotha it has always been possible for the etheric
blood of Christ to flow together with the streams from below upwards,
from heart to head' ... 'so that ... in man ... the [etherised] human
blood-stream unites with the blood-stream of Christ Jesus.'[125] And if,
through studying modern spiritual science or, in the case of Novalis,
through special karmic dispensation, human beings are able to bring this
etherised stream of divine blood to consciousness, they will gain access to
an experience of the Christ-Being, who works both within man and in
the whole aura of the Earth:

Through the countless happy hours
When I found life's fairest flowers,
Only one stayed true to me;
One when in my deepest grieving
I learnt in my heart's own weaving
*Who it was that died for me.**

After his initiation into this mystery, Novalis was also granted a full
awareness of the human heart as a new, higher organ of knowledge. This
mystical secret of the etheric heart, which Rudolf Steiner was later to call
'heart-logic' (as opposed to 'head-logic') and by means of which he was
able to accomplish all his spiritual research,[126] was revealed to Novalis as
though at one stroke of higher spiritual inspiration. 'The heart is the key
of the world and of life,' he writes during his last illness and, feeling the
Christ-impulse to be his only source of help in his physical sufferings, he
adds: 'Thus Christ is, from this standpoint, indeed the key to the world.'
A key to the world and to all its secrets—thus can the heart, and Christ
who works within it, be described. A meeting of this kind between

* In the hand-written version, the last line has the word 'me' instead of 'us'.

microcosm and macrocosm—between man and God—is alone capable of solving all the riddles of life and death. This is for Novalis the true 'transfiguration of the heart' which is the foundation of any real religiousness. 'All our inclinations would seem to be nothing other than applied religion. *The heart would appear to be the religious organ.* Perhaps the higher testimony of the productive heart is none other than *heaven* itself.'

But this was not all. In the same lecture Rudolf Steiner goes on to say that, apart from this microcosmic stream of etherised human blood flowing from below upwards, from the heart to the head, there is a second, macrocosmic stream within man that flows from the spiritual world in the direction from above downwards, through the region of the head towards the heart. Rudolf Steiner characterises the first stream as the bearer of man's *intellectual* faculties and the second as the stream that corresponds to his *moral* qualities.

These two streams work within man in completely different ways during day and night. By day the 'intellectual' stream is dominant, and because of this it becomes possible for man to maintain a fully waking consciousness with regard to all perceptions of the other world. While at night, during sleep, the second, 'moral' stream is dominant, carrying all the moral impulses which he is to make manifest in his waking life into him from the macrocosm.

In the future, which, however, has already begun, man must find in himself the forces whereby the one stream may be *fructified* by the other. As a result of this, says Rudolf Steiner, 'what will be accomplished in humanity . . . is that the two poles . . . the intellectual and the moral, will become more and more one, they will merge into a unity'.

This can come about if, on the one hand, with the help of right meditation, man is able to lead the forces of the day stream over into the night stream, that is, the forces of *waking consciousness* living in the 'intellectual stream' into the 'moral stream'. This means that such a man will be able to awaken in full consciousness in 'the world of night', in the 'moral ether-atmosphere'. He will then come to experience this conscious penetration into the world of night as a kind of real passage through death and resurrection in the 'moral fire' which rays forth in the spiritual world from the Christ Being. It was through such a 'night' experience, an experience of 'dying and becoming', that Novalis passed, and we find a reference to this in his words

> . . . at night I die
> In holy ardour's mood.

39

But just as, in human life, outbreathing is impossible without in-breathing and the conditions of night without those of the day, so does the leading of the forces of the microcosmic stream over into the macrocosmic stream necessarily presuppose the leading of the macrocosmic stream over into the microcosmic, that is, the penetration of day waking, or 'intellectual', consciousness by the *moral force* proceeding from the 'world of night', so that human beings 'will be permeated to an ever increasing degree, also during the day, by the direct working of the good from the spiritual worlds'. Novalis also speaks of this second process, which in the order of events is actually the *first*, as follows:

> By day are faith
> And courage my food . . .

This mutual fructification of the two streams, which is connected with the leading of consciousness over into the realm of night, into man's macrocosmic state of being, and of morality into the realm of day, his microcosmic state of being, brings Novalis to an experience of what he sees as the future condition of mankind: 'There will come a time when man will constantly be both asleep and awake.'

If we were to express this through the imagery of ancient Hebrew occultism, we could say that in the course of this experience there takes place first the mutual contact and then the complete interpenetration of the two trees, the Tree of Life (the nightstream) and the Tree of Knowledge (the day stream), the interweaving of which has—since the time of the Fall—been treasured in the spiritual world by the Archangel Michael as the highest ideal of earthly evolution.[127] For the Archangel Michael is that Spirit in our cosmos who makes particular efforts to lead man towards uniting in his soul the intellectual and the moral principles, his head and his heart,[128] and this is the most important prerequisite for the perception of the Etheric Christ.[129]

These observations shed a clear light on the part which the being of Novalis plays from the spiritual world in the principal supersensible event of our time, the new appearance of Christ in the etheric realm. For through his personal experience of Christ he has become the great forerunner of, and spiritual guide towards, that renewal of the Damascus experience which from our time, and increasingly during the next three thousand years, will gradually be made accessible to the widest circles of people. Rudolf Steiner says, in describing this new appearance of Christ, that 'all those who prepared the way for Him [for Christ as he appeared in a physical body] will become recognisable in a new form to those who will have experienced the new Christ-event. Those who once dwelt on

Earth as Moses, Abraham and the *prophets* will again become recognisable to human beings.'[130] We may add: in the first instance these words relate to the greatest of all the prophets, to the prophet Elijah (and also to his reincarnation as John the Baptist), who raised to a higher stage the ego-impulse which was the fundamental impulse of the religion of Jahve, whose foundation was laid in antiquity by Abraham and, in particular, by Moses.[131]

This is further confirmed by the following fact. In the lectures of 30 November and 2 December 1911,[132] Rudolf Steiner speaks in detail about the three calls or revelations which mankind has received during the last three millennia: the call from the sphere of the Father through Moses, from the sphere of the Son through John the Baptist,[133] and finally, in our time, from the sphere of the Spirit through modern spiritual science. If at this point we recall that in the figure of Phinehas we have to a certain extent the saviour of the work of Moses (and hence of the first revelation as a whole), in the figure of Elijah its chief promoter, and in the figure of John the Baptist the great herald of the second revelation,* it will not be difficult for us to surmise that this individuality participated *supersensibly* in the third revelation and above all in what can be seen as its focal point, the new proclamation of Christ in the etheric realm. Thus we should say: alongside the Bodhisattva who in three thousand years' time will become the Maitreya Buddha there also works the 'Bodhisattva-like' individuality of Novalis,[134] who is in our time the most important spiritual *preparer* of the new appearance of Christ in the etheric realm, and at the same time one of the supersensible inspirers of modern spiritual science, of Anthroposophy.

It is already possible to sense from those descriptions—where we find in Novalis echoes of his supersensible meeting with Christ—a remarkable degree of correspondence with the manner in which Rudolf Steiner characterises the appearance of the Etheric Christ which begins from our time onwards in connection with the gradual development amongst mankind of the forces of the new 'natural clairvoyance': 'Many a human being will have this experience when sitting silently in his room, heavy-hearted and oppressed, not knowing which way to turn. The door will open, and the Etheric Christ will appear and speak words of consolation to him. The Christ will become a living comforter to men.'[135] The following poetic words of Novalis bear a certain resemblance:

> Through the countless happy hours
> When I found life's fairest flowers,

* This is why Elijah appears together with Moses in the scene of the Transfiguration.

Only one stayed true to me;
One when in my deepest grieving
I learnt in my heart's own weaving
Who it was that died for me*

And elsewhere he says:

He died, but you can every day
Receive His love when sore oppressed,
You will find comfort, come what may,
By drawing Him gently to your breast.

He brings new blood, forever living,
Into the hard and dying bone;[136]
In answer to your heart's free-giving
He is eternally your own.

In the same lecture Rudolf Steiner describes how Christ will work amongst men in *the etheric body* with so intense a degree of spiritual reality that 'it [the etheric body of Christ] is able to work in the physical world as a human physical body works.' And then he continues: 'It will differ from a physical body in this respect only, that it can be in two, three, nay even in a hundred, a thousand places at the same time. This is possible only for an etheric, not for a physical form.' Novalis refers to the remarkable way in which the Christ-impulse will work amongst men in the future as follows: 'The perfected human being must be able to live in several places and in several human beings at once—he would have to be constantly present in a wide circle and at a great number of events.'

The spiritual mystery of Christ as the 'Lord of the Elements', wherein His spiritual countenance is everywhere manifest, is also known to Novalis. He writes:

He is the star, He is the Sun,
The spring whence endless life does run.
From plant and stone, from sea and light,
His childlike features shimmer bright.

And in one of his fragments Novalis refers to this mystery as follows: 'If God was able to become man, he can also become stone, plant, animal *and*

---

* In preparing this poem for publication Novalis replaced the 'me' in this line by 'us'. In the original manuscript the word is 'me'.

element, and perhaps there is in this way a perpetual redemptive power in nature.'

And so the more we immerse ourselves in the manifold references of Novalis to the Christ Being that are cast like diamonds throughout his creative work, the more strongly we feel: this individuality will surely be one of the first to appear in the twentieth century around the Etheric Christ, for in his last incarnation he had been prepared in so complete a way to encounter His etheric manifestation in the spiritual world nearest to the Earth.[137] Since then he has passed through the spiritual world in the retinue of the Etheric Christ, as one who leads many human souls after their death into His etheric sphere,[138] and at the same time prepares for his own future mission of coming to Earth in his new incarnation as the envoy and *herald of the Etheric Christ*.

All that we have considered can also be analysed in a chronological sense. On 6 January 1909,[139] at the *Festival of Epiphany*, Rudolf Steiner reveals to anthroposophists for the first time the mystery of the karmic connection between Elijah, John the Baptist, Raphael and Novalis. This occurs in the year which according to his spiritual-scientific investigations was also the year that marked the beginning of the etheric manifestation of Christ, of which he first spoke in Stockholm on 12 January 1910,[140] that is, five days after the Festival of Epiphany, the festival of the appearance of the Christ Being at the Turning-Point of Time in a physical body. The next lecture on this theme was that given on 23 January of the same year in Strassburg at the inauguration of the Novalis Branch, where the theme of Novalis and the theme of the Second Coming are united into an indissoluble whole. The lecture as a whole culminates in a threefold call *to the spirit*, firstly to the spirit of Novalis, then to 'the spirit of spiritual science itself', and finally to the spirit of the Masters of Wisdom and the Harmony of Feelings, to the spirit who in all three cases is *one and the same spirit* and who was to permeate, as an inner impulse, all the work that was to take place within the newly formed branch.[141] The next lecture associated with the theme of the new advent was given by Rudolf Steiner on 25 January 1910, when there appears as a completely new element a reference to how, in the 'spiritual retinue' of the Etheric Christ, all those who have prepared His physical incarnation on the Earth, namely 'Moses, Abraham and all the prophets', can be seen with the eye of spirit. And in all these three lectures[142] (and also in many later ones on this same theme) there resounds in a new, a renewed form, as the principal motif running through them, the original *call* of John the Baptist, the first herald of Christ Jesus on Earth—the call which two thousand years ago proclaimed the appearance of Christ in the flesh and in our time His

43

appearance in the etheric realm. For 'we are letting the call sound forth today, even as John the Baptist, as the forerunner of Christ, and Christ Himself once let it resound: A new age is at hand, in which human souls must take a step upwards into the kingdom of heaven!'[143] Or in another lecture: 'We can repeat today the words of St John's Gospel [spoken by John the Baptist]: "Change the disposition of your soul so that your own faculties open the spiritual world to you." For human beings with etheric clairvoyance will behold the Christ appearing before them in an etheric body.'[144]

Is not this call to the supersensible beholding of Christ, to a new experience of the Damascus event, the fulfilment of what Novalis had a century before experienced and imparted to all mankind? For if Rudolf Steiner on more than one occasion refers to the experience of Paul before Damascus as the prophetic anticipation of the spiritual events of our time, does this apply any the less to Novalis, who lived not in the fourth cultural epoch, still permeated as it was with traces of the spirituality of olden times, but in the modern epoch at the threshold of the nineteenth century, the most materialistic century in the entire evolution of humanity? 'Novalis speaks of the revelation that came to him as "unique", and he maintains that only those, who with their whole soul wish to participate in this event, are men in the true sense' (see p. 37). And does not Rudolf Steiner, in speaking of the new advent, place before us the task of 'participating with our whole soul in this event' in order that we may become 'true men'? For in this, as in so much else, Rudolf Steiner and Novalis are completely one: Rudolf Steiner, who speaks to us of 'the growing together of the experience of being in and with Christ and the experience of real and true humanity' and indicates that ' "Christ gives me my humanity" must be the fundamental feeling which wells up in the soul and pervades it'[145]; and Novalis, who also testifies to this out of his personal spiritual experience:

> Through Him am I a man become;
> My destiny transfigured shines through Him . . .[146]

Thus we can come to experience, with an ever greater sense of reality, how the inspirations of that individuality, whose mission amongst mankind Rudolf Steiner referred to on several occasions as 'the fourfold heraldship of the Christ-impulse', flow directly into the most important message of modern spiritual science[147]: Elijah: '. . . a mighty herald . . . a preparer of the Christ-impulse'; John the Baptist: 'the herald of Christ Himself'; Raphael: 'A herald who has brought tidings of the spiritual Christ who will again be comprehended by spiritual science.' Novalis:

the herald who ... is permeated by an anthroposophical Christian impulse', the proclaiming of which 'is like the dawning of a new Christ idea'; for Novalis bears within himself that which 'is for Christianity a proclamation for the future'.

6

Novalis' Sources of Inspiration

Before turning to a more detailed consideration of where in modern spiritual science or Anthroposophy one may find traces of the spiritual inspirations of the individuality of Novalis, it is necessary that we consider his life's path and the spiritual foundation of his biography from a particular viewpoint which has been given much weight in our present studies. This viewpoint, which has served as a key to the understanding of many secrets associated with his karmic biography, is the *Hierarchic* one, which has led us to a knowledge of the inspirational sources of the life and work of this individuality in his last and in his previous incarnations. As a point of departure we may take the aspiration, to which we have frequently referred, of the individuality of Adam for his 'heavenly archetype', for the Nathan Soul, an aspiration which, however, acquired the actual forms for its fulfilment only after this individuality had, as John the Baptist, participated in the events of the Turning-Point of Time. These 'actual forms' whereby the Adam individuality gradually approached his heavenly archetype appeared initially in a more outward fashion. The ancient karma that had connected John the Baptist with Jesus of Nazareth, with the Nathan Soul who now incarnated on Earth for the first time, was renewed through their childhood friendship, and thereafter through their many meetings and conversations with one another.[148] Here we have, so to speak, the first stage of their 'drawing near to each other' on the *physical plane*. The next and more spiritual stage of this process was, as we have seen, the permeation of the etheric body of Raphael by the imprint of the *etheric body* of the Nathan soul which had been preserved in the higher worlds. Finally, the third stage in this development was the further, and more inward, approach of this individuality, now in the person of the poet Novalis, to its ideal—the Nathan Soul who abides in the spiritual worlds. In the case of the latter, this new, spiritual stage was expressed in that, as he was preparing for his incarnation on the Earth at the end of the eighteenth century, he received into his astral body, or to be more precise into his intellectual or mind soul, an imprint of the *astral body* of the Nathan Soul which had been preserved in the higher worlds.[149] This astral body, being thus united with his soul before he was born, is then stirred

46

into activity as a result of the profound shock sustained by Novalis in the spring of 1797 in connection with the premature death of his bride, Sophie von Kühn. The consequence of this was that, in the Easter of that same year, there began the process to which we have already referred of the birth of the higher man within him: '. . . then from the blue expanses, from the heights of my ancient bliss, a tremor from a gleam of dawn— and at one stroke the bonds of birth, the fetters of light, were sundered. Away fled the splendour of Earth and my sorrow fled with it. My pain flowed together into a new and unfathomable world. O spirit joy of night, slumber of heaven, you came over me. The place where I was, lifted itself gently upwards; over this place hovered my free, new-born spirit.' In correspondence with this fundamental experience of Novalis and with the wholly new relationship to Christianity and its Founder that derives from it, we may cite Rudolf Steiner's characterisation of the inner experiences of those people to whom it was vouchsafed to become bearers of an imprint of the astral body of the Nathan Soul: 'in their astral bodies there lived a direct access to strength and devotion, an immediate sense of certainty with regard to the holy truths [of Christianity]. A deep fervour, an utter conviction [in the reality of Christianity] and, under certain circumstances, also the capacity to substantiate this conviction, resided within such human beings.'[150] 'Thus it was that these people were able *to impart the great Christian truths*. For their astral bodies, *whence their knowledge sprung*, had been interwoven with an imprint of the astral body of Jesus of Nazareth Himself.'[151] In other words, they have been able to work amongst mankind as *heralds* and '*bearers of Christianity*':

> Though all are faithless growing.
> Yet will I faithful be,
> That one on Earth is showing
> His thankfulness to Thee.

But does not Rudolf Steiner also speak about this, albeit in considerably more detail, in the words already quoted (p. 37) about the 'revelations' which Novalis received regarding the Christ Being and the Nathan Soul[152] and which he then incorporated in the form of sublime poetry in his creative work? It is indeed the case that these revelations, this new testimony of Christ by Novalis, are the direct result of the activity within his soul of the astral body of the Nathan Soul. This is the reason for the remarkable—one might almost say unearthly—purity of his soul and also for his capacity, frequently attested by Rudolf Steiner, of reading in the 'astral light', a capacity which is always associated with the higher development of the astral body.[153] A number of Novalis' sayings spring from this secret source: '. . . to trace higher influences in myself and to forge a path of my own into the world of my origins'—this he feels to be 'the most essential aspect of my existence'. Of the conscious experience of how the forces of a higher spiritual revelation work within his own soul he says: 'One [man] has more capacity for receiving revelations than another.' And there is a further saying of his which sounds with particular force in our age of purely materialistic attempts to 'make the cosmos our own': 'We dream of journeys through the universe: but is not the universe in us? The depths of our spirit we do not know. The path of mysteries leads within. Eternity, with its worlds of past and future, is in us or nowhere.'

Perhaps the most characteristic trait of this new revelation which comes wholly to permeate Novalis is the feeling for the complete renewal or rejuvenation of the world, man and humanity,[154] which is why, as though through a premonition, he himself chose the poetic pseudonym 'Novalis'—the 'new man', the 'man of the future'. This underlying soul mood of the poet comes most fully to expression in the following poem, where the influence of the forces of the astral body of the Nathan Soul, which enabled him to sense the presence of Christ in the Earth's aura, and at the same time in his own soul, is manifested with particular power. The poem concludes with the image of the 'world-renewing feast' which is to embrace the whole of man's being:[155]

> I say to everyone, He lives,
> The Risen One is He;
> For He is hovering in our midst,
> There evermore to be.
>
> I say to all, and everyone
> Repeats it to his friend,
> That Heaven's new Kingdom soon will come
> And nevermore have end.
>
> With senses new we now behold
> The world as Fatherland;
> We drink new life in joy untold
> That flows forth from his hand.
>
> And now the fear of death is driven
> Below the deepest sea;
> To everyone the power is given to view his destiny.

The darksome way that He has trod
Leads unto heaven on high,
And only to those who hear His word
Shall come the Father nigh.

No longer does one need to mourn
When someone's eyes are closed,
The grief of parting is reborn
As sweetness juxtaposed.

And now will every goodly deed
With fresher beauty glow,
And wondrously forth from this seed
Will heavenly blossoms grow.

He lives, and shares His company
Though all support has ceased!
And thus for us this day shall be
A world-renewing feast.'

This sheds light upon the nature of the relationship of Novalis to the 'world of night', for the forces of the Nathan Soul that had worked within his astral body from the very beginning have a deep affinity with the forces which in the ordinary course of life work upon man only *at night, during sleep.* Rudolf Steiner refers to this relationship in the following way: 'This [Nathan] Soul remained behind at that time [in the Lemurian age]; it could not enter the physical process of mankind's development [through incarnations]. It lived on, invisible to the physical world of man . . . and could only be perceived by those who rose to the heights of clairvoyance, who developed those forces that awaken in the state we otherwise know as sleep. *In that state man is near to the forces that live and work in purity in the sister-soul* . . . This soul only became visible, could only show itself, when human beings attained clairvoyant vision in their sleep . . . In most instances it was only recognisable in those special conditions of clairvoyance that expand man's spiritual vision into sleep consciousness.'[156] Thus we may say: it was the presence, in the soul of Novalis, of the imprint of the astral body of the Nathan Soul which enabled him to enter in full consciousness into the 'world of night' and to experience therein the 'Damascus event'.[157]

With this, however, not all has yet been said about the soul life of Novalis and the higher sources of the inspirations that worked within him. For we can also trace in him the working of that spiritual law which we have already considered in some detail (see pp 33–4). This law concerns the metamorphosis which the influences of the higher hierarchies that work in any one human incarnation in a more spiritually outward way undergo in the person's next incarnation, where they become inner forces of his individual ego. For instance, the impulses of the ruling Time Spirit of the fourth post-Atlantean epoch, which worked in a more spiritually outward way (that is, not through his ego but through his sheaths) within John the Baptist, appeared within Raphael as the spiritual forces of his own ego, forces which enabled him to bring about a harmonious synthesis of the Judaeo-Christian, Greek and Roman elements in his art. And by the same token, the Inspirations of the Archangel Raphael, the Archangel of healing, that worked in his life in a more spiritually outward way, appear in his next incarnation, as Novalis, as spiritual forces belonging to his individual ego which are manifested in the particularly intimate and direct connection that he had with the spiritual sphere of *Mercury* and the Beings related to it. For this reason, once he had entered the spiritual world as a result of the awakening of the forces of the astral body of the Nathan Soul within his soul, Novalis did not—because of the connection which he had by now developed with the Mercury Beings—find himself in the Luciferic sphere of illusory visions and mediumistic experiences (a danger which threatened many 'romantics' at that time) but, following the spiritual leadership of the Spirits of Mercury, attained to true spiritual percep-tions, to the realm of objective or '*true imaginations*.'[158] In other words, through the initial (for this incarnation) connection of his ego with the Mercury Spirits, Novalis was enabled from the outset rightly to orientate himself in the spiritual world, thus achieving what Rudolf Steiner describes as the 'awakening or transmuting of the inwardness of night into the day'.[159] It is this fundamental experience that underlies the other aspect of Novalis' so very intimate relationship to the world of night, which for him is a symbol of consciously entering the spiritual world, an endeavour which is expressed in a spiritually inspired way in his *Hymns to the Night*: 'Now wend I down to holy, ineffable, mysterious night,' he writes in the first hymn. And then: 'To us more heavenly than those radiant stars are the endless eyes that night *has opened in us*. But the domain of night is beyond time or space,' he adds in the second hymn.

Thus we may say: if, according to Rudolf Steiner, such a '. . . livingly perceptive comprehension of the Moon-sphere [that is, the "world of night" in Novalis' expression] is the starting-point of the one path of initiation', then only if man becomes inwardly aware of the 'influences of Mercury' can 'the world of visions [that is revealed to him] pass over into a world in which he can [objectively] perceive the spiritual'. For 'in

50

this Moon-sphere the world of imaginations is revealed to us as a reality during the day.'

According to Rudolf Steiner, this whole process is connected with the birth within man of the higher or 'second man', in whom there 'lives the power of the Moon-sphere'. In the case of Novalis, this 'second man' who awakens within him is, through his connection with the Mercury Beings, enabled *rightly* to enter the sphere of the Moon and to behold, in the glimmer of 'the night that has awakened in the day', the ascent of the spiritual Sun: 'We behold the Sun a second time, spiritually. It is as yet fleeting and undefined, but we know that we are perceiving it spiritually. We gaze into the inner being of the sun.'[160] What then emerges is an experience of the night Sun as a living being, as the radiant countenance of the Sun God. Novalis has recounted this sublime experience in the following poetic words:

> O single night of rapture,
> Eternal poem—
> The Sun for all of us
> Is God's own countenance.

Elsewhere he writes, weary from ceaseless spiritual watchfulness: '. . . and a refreshing, earthly sleep has closed his eyes *for another Sun*.'

But this is not yet all. The conscious entering of the Moon-sphere leads man not only to the experiences already described, but (and this is of particular importance) also to a perception of his own *higher ego*, or to use the anthroposophical term—his *Spirit-Self*. However, in the present aeon of evolution, that of the Earth, man does not as yet possess the Spirit-Self as his own property in the same way that he possesses his ego on Earth. In our time his Spirit-Self still rests in the bosom of the Hierarchy that stands immediately above him, the Angels, the realm of whose activity is, precisely, the sphere of the Moon (which is why in spiritual science the Angels are also called the 'Spirits of Twilight'). Hence a man who is by his karma especially predisposed for this can, through the mediation of the Angels, be overshone by the Spirit-Self as he consciously enters the sphere of the Moon.

Moreover, this 'being overshone by the Spirit-Self in the Moon-sphere is not something abstract, for it comes about in the form of a direct encounter with one's Guardian Angel, that is, with the 'guardian' of one's Spirit-Self. Thus the meeting with the Spirit-Self and the meeting with one's Angel are, at a certain level of inner development, really one and the same. Rudolf Steiner refers to this fact as follows: 'Today, instead of using the complicated expression, "We are in connection with the

Hierarchy of the Angeloi", we can simply say, "We are in connection with what is to come to us in the future as our Spirit-Self".[161] And then he continues: 'Our ego must meet that higher ego, that Spirit-Self which we still have to develop and which in a certain respect is of like nature to Beings of the Hierarchy of the Angeloi'; in other words, 'we must from time to time meet with a Being of the Hierarchy of the Angeloi.' In the lecture about the three meetings of the human soul with the cosmic principles of the Father, the Son and the Spirit from which these words are taken, Rudolf Steiner goes on to say that the meeting with the Angelic Being who is the bearer of our Spirit-Self takes place every time a man goes to sleep at night.

That such a meeting with one's Angel or higher ego in the spiritual world is possible was still known in late antiquity. Plutarch, for example, describes this as an experience of the daemon or genius that 'hovers above man's head'. 'This genius,' says Rudolf Steiner in explanation of this observation of Plutarch, 'is none other than the Spirit-Self in process of becoming, though born by a Being belonging to the Hierarchy of the Angeloi.' The classic example of such a Being is the 'Daemon' that inspires Socrates, as described by Plato in his Dialogues.

A meeting of this kind, which takes place 'at every midnight hour', generally happens unconsciously, although for Novalis, after his awakening in the Moon-sphere, it gradually becomes more and more conscious—not only in the sense that 'the feeling which we may have, in our waking state, of our connection with the spiritual world, is an after-effect of this meeting with the genius' but also as a direct, 'face-to-face' meeting with it. Novalis gradually works towards this meeting. And if (in the lecture that is being referred to) Rudolf Steiner speaks at some length of the need to feel 'the holiness of sleep', there surely stands behind this that spiritual experience which Novalis expresses as follows: 'The duration of sleep is eternal. *Holy sleep*—do not bless too seldom him who is consecrated to night in this earthly work of the day.' And then when Rudolf Steiner speaks of how 'sleep [or, as Novalis would say, 'night'] unites us with the spiritual world, sleep sends us over into the spiritual world', is it not these feelings and experiences, albeit expressed not in spiritual-scientific concepts but in the language of poetry, which we meet everywhere in the work of Novalis? For example, when he writes: 'Night has become the mighty womb of revelation', or:

> But true to the night
> My inmost heart remains,
> And to her daughter,
> All creating love.[162]

And if Rudolf Steiner says that, as a consequence of the nightly meeting with the 'genius', one gradually becomes pervaded with the feeling that the 'true world is that of the genius',[163] then that is surely the same mood as sounds forth in the words of Novalis: 'The outer world is the world of shadows, it casts its shadows into the realm of light.'[164] For him, this 'realm of light' is the divine 'world of night', 'the mighty womb of revelations', where the sources of the spiritual inspirations which nourish his life and creativity are to be found.

7

The Forerunner of the Sixth Cultural Epoch

'The true writer of fairy-tales is a seer of the future.'

Novalis

We shall now endeavour to find, amongst the poetic works and the numerous sayings of Novalis, traces of the spiritual development described above. His awakening in the Moon-sphere, his conscious relationship to the spiritual powers of the night, led him gradually to a meeting with his *higher ego* or Spirit-Self. Novalis speaks of this as follows: 'This ego of a higher kind is related to man as man is to nature or as the wise man is to the child. Man longs to become like it, just as he seeks to make the not-self like himself. Such a fact cannot be demonstrated. Everyone must experience it himself. It is a fact of a higher kind which only the higher man encounters.'[165]

Rudolf Steiner likewise speaks in a quite particular way of Novalis' experience of the Spirit-Self. In his book, *The Riddles of Philosophy*, he writes in the section about Novalis: 'It is the tendency of this age, as can be seen in its representative thinkers, to search for the higher spirit nature in which the self-conscious soul, which cannot have its roots in the world of sense reality, is rooted behind the outer sense-perceptible world. Novalis feels and experiences himself as having his being within the higher spirit nature. What he expresses, he feels through his innate genius as the revelations of this *very spirit nature (Geistnatur selbst)*.'[166] In these final words one needs only to exchange the places [in the German phrase] of the words 'natur' and the 'selbst' for the hidden meaning to become clear.

How can this inner process be described, by means of which one may approach this 'ego of a higher kind'? Here Novalis encounters one of the greatest problems of any spiritual research. How can what has been experienced in the spirit be communicated in earthly, human words? Where can one find those human words which would be capable of communicating the living breath of the spirit, of expressing the inexpressible, for in the spiritual world everything is completely different from how it is in the physical? Rudolf Steiner too had to struggle with this awesome problem for many years. Once, in his later years, he

54

was asked: 'When you were writing *The Philosophy of Freedom*, were you already consciously aware of the Hierarchies of which you speak in *Occult Science* and elsewhere?' To this question Rudolf Steiner replied: 'I was aware of them, but the language that I employed at that time did not allow the possibility of formulating anything about them. That came later.'[167] And in the last preface that he wrote to *Occult Science—an Outline*, in January 1925, he wrote: 'so then I had before me the results of conscious spiritual vision. They were things "seen", living in my consciousness, to begin with, without any names. To communicate them, some terminology was needed, and it was *only then*—so as to put into words what had been wordless to begin with—that I looked for suitable expressions in the traditional literature. These I used quite freely. In the way I apply them, scarcely one of them coincides exactly with its connotation in the source from which I took it.'

Novalis proceeds in a similar way to that of Rudolf Steiner. He too takes certain concepts from the spiritual life of his contemporaries or from more ancient sources, concepts which, in his usage of them, acquire an altogether new spiritual–scientific meaning. For instance, the word 'philosophising' means for Novalis not simply reflecting about abstract categories of being, but a highly concentrated 'thinking about thinking' leading to meditation which, in its intensity, embraces the whole man, to a confidence in 'the absolute independence and the boundless propensity of meditation'. It is in this sense that we should understand the process of 'philosophising', when Novalis refers to it as a path to the higher ego: '*Philosophising* is a superior form of the self conversing with itself in the manner described above, a true self-revelation: the arousing of the true ego through the idealistic ego. Philosophising is the foundation of all other forms of revelation. The resolve to philosophise is a summons to the true ego that it shall awaken to self-awareness and be a spirit.'

The process of 'romanticising'—which in the way that Novalis uses the word is a particular kind of soul activity that also represents a path into the spiritual world—is another aspect of the inner life. These two paths, which are essentially only two sides of one and the same whole, are similar to those two paths into the spiritual world of which Rudolf Steiner speaks in *Occult Science*: the one opening through the development of one's thinking in the sense of *The Philosophy of Freedom* (according to Novalis, the path of 'philosophising'); the other leading directly into the world of imaginations as described in the penultimate chapter of *Occult Science—an Outline* and in *Knowledge of the Higher Worlds: How is it Achieved?* According to Novalis this is the path of 'romanticising': 'The world must be *romanticised*. In such a way can one regain one's original sense of purpose. Romanticising is none other than a qualitative

55

potentising process. The lower self is in such an operation identified with a better self. It is as though we ourselves were such a qualitative exponential series. This operation is one that is still completely unknown . . .' In both cases the aim is a conscious experience of the Spirit-Self as a 'true' or 'better' ego (self).

If at this point we recall that in his book, *Knowledge of the Higher Worlds: How is it Achieved?*, Rudolf Steiner compares this awakening of the higher ego within man with the image of a mother bearing and giving birth to a child, we shall be able to view the following words of Novalis in a completely new light: 'The great mystery is open to all and remains eternally unfathomable. The new world is born of grief, and ash is dissolved in tears as a draught of eternal life. In everyone there dwells the heavenly mother, bearing each child in eternity. Do you not feel the sweetness of birth in the throbbing of your breast?' And now Rudolf Steiner, writing about the same process: 'This is not a figurative event but a veritable *birth* in the spiritual world, and if the higher self having now been born is to be capable of life, it must enter that world with all the necessary organs and aptitudes. Just as nature must see to it that a child is born into the world with well-formed ears and eyes, so must the laws of man's own development ensure that his higher self comes into existence with the necessary faculties. And these laws which govern the development of the higher organs of the spirit are none other than the laws of healthy reason and morality belonging to the physical world.* The spiritual man matures in the physical self as a child in the mother's womb.'[168]

And again Novalis: 'The fair mystery of the Virgin, which renders her so inexpressibly alluring, is the foretaste of motherhood, the presentiment of a future world that slumbers within her and shall develop out of her. She is the most appropriate image of the future.' Thus is the ideal archetype of the human soul, which gives birth to the higher ego, revealed to Novalis in the image of the Virgin Mother.[169] Indeed, if one compares these lines with the corresponding places in *Knowledge of the Higher Worlds* and *Occult Science*, one can only say with Rudolf Steiner: 'We would not [in Novalis] find a spirit who expresses himself in words and teachings of the kind that we can give in spiritual science, but nevertheless a spirit *who through his words gives expression to exactly the same substance.*'[170] This enables one to understand many of the more hidden thoughts and feelings of Novalis as contained in his *Spiritual Songs* and his

* Novalis in his poetic language calls such a union of the 'laws of reason and morality' in the sphere of the physical world 'moral grace'.

Songs of Mary, which are none other than poetic descriptions of certain initiation experiences.

If we would further characterise this process of the birth of the higher ego within man, and also those 'organs and aptitudes' which it needs to have, we could say, employing anthroposophical terminology: just as the ordinary ego recognises itself and the world by means of the instrument of logical thinking, so does the higher ego recognise the spiritual reality that surrounds it through the mediation of the supersensible organs of Imagination, Inspiration and Intuition. Surely it is not surprising that Novalis should write words such as these: 'the productive *imagination* . . . is the beginning of a true permeation of the self by the spirit, which never ends;'[171] or when he says: 'without *inspiration* there is no spirit-manifestation. Inspiration is manifestation and counter-manifestation (*Gegenerscheinung*), appropriation and communication all at the same time'*; or when in another place he writes of the '. . . arousing of the holy sense of *intuition*'. Thus we may have the feeling that, in Rudolf Steiner's words, the entire creative work of Novalis speaks to us '. . . in the most comprehensive way [of the] knowledge of these spiritual scientific truths.'[172]

However, Novalis' encounters in the spiritual world are not limited to these experiences of his higher self. For once he has arrived at such experiences he undertakes a further step, which enables him to have a direct knowledge of the Angelic Being who is connected with his higher self (the Spirit-Self), and who continually inspires him.

This new, supersensible experience appears for him initially only in the form of an inner exchange or 'conversation' with a higher spiritual Being: 'It seems to one as though one were involved in a conversation and an unknown spiritual Being were in a most wonderful way giving rise to the development of the most conclusive of thoughts. This Being must be of a higher nature, for there is something about him that does not belong to a being that is bound to the world of appearances. He must be of a homogeneous nature, for he [the spiritual Being] treats him [man] as one would a spiritual Being, and asks of him only the very rarest manifestation of selfhood.' However, this inner conversation subsequently acquires an even more definite character, so that the 'unknown spiritual Being' gradually receives a more concrete form and is revealed to his inner vision as an Angel or Genius.

The poet turns frequently, and in a variety of forms, to this higher source of his spiritual inspirations:

---

* The beginning of this fragment may be found on p 61, and more about the 'new world inspiration' on pp 59 and 63.

An *Angel* bendeth o'er you
And bears you to the strand
And, filled with joy, before you
You see the promised land.

And in another poem:

Oh! then God bends down to us,
With His love He draweth near;
When we long for life to leave us
Then His *Angel* does appear;
Brings the cup of life renewing,
Courage and comfort he imparts . . .

Or, naming his inspiring Angel his 'genius':

It cannot be intoxication—else
I'd not been born for this star—only by chance in this mad world
Too closely drawn
To its magnetic circle.

Was moral grace's perfected awareness
Mere intoxication? Belief in human kind
The plaything of an happy hour?
If this be drunkenness, what then is life?

What leads the wise man through the vale of life,
The beacon lighting up his higher being—
Must He but build in patience here below,
Then lay him down, and be forever dead.

No drunken frenzy art thou, *voice of genius*,
Thou image of our immortality,
Thou consciousness of that fair treasure
That only individuals recognise.

Bearing in mind the general mood of the *Hymns to the Night*, we may be
drawn to compare these poetic lines with the following mantric words of
Rudolf Steiner: 'I am going to sleep. Until I wake, my soul will be in the
spiritual world. There it will meet with the guiding power of my earthly
life, who abides in the spiritual world and hovers around my head; there

it will meet my *genius*. And if I am sufficiently awake, I will have had the meeting with my genius. *The wings of my genius have beaten upon my soul.*'[173]

The Genius, the inspirer of Novalis, is a Being belonging to the Hierarchy of the Angels. Novalis speaks of him again and again in his Fragments: 'Every effective action is accompanied by a higher Being.'— 'Contact with a higher Being.' And: 'The main thing is synthetically to forge a true method—forwards and backwards.* The method of the divine genius.'[174] It is from the inspirations of this Angel and from his inner guidance that the conviction awakens within Novalis: 'Christianity must again become alive and effective', a condition that only 'the new world-inspiration' can fulfil. Anticipating this in a real way in his soul, Novalis strives towards this high ideal, towards an all-embracing union—transcending every confession—of all the spiritual streams of mankind into a single whole, a single spiritual organism, which Goethe once called the 'great, immortal individual'. For according to the deep conviction of Novalis, there is in the world '. . . no religion that is not Christianity': 'Just as human beings are the sons of Gods, so, out of what human beings in the physical world experience by rising to the events of Golgotha, will the body be formed for those new Gods of the future, of whom Christ is the leader.'[175]

From this all-embracing idea, which was the high Inspiration of his Angel (and not from the unhelpful and often politically tinged ecumenical movements of our time), the following words were then able to arise: 'For me, it [the unifying impulse] is none other than the solemn call to a new communion, *the powerful wing-strokes of the Angelic herald as he flies past.*'[176] With these words, the 28-year-old Novalis, at the moment of the birth within him of the intellectual or mind soul, refers directly to his Hierarchic inspirer, that Being whom he was enabled consciously to meet in the spiritual world a year before his premature death: 'The mortal quavers in his foundations, but the immortal begins to shine more brightly and comes to learn who he is.'[177]

---

* Elsewhere Novalis characterises this spiritual process as follows: 'Only the backward-looking eye brings one forwards, for the forward-looking eye leads one backwards.' Here he speaks of what Rudolf Steiner was later to call 'complete clarity with regard to the conception of time', of which the latter writes in his short biography, *Correspondence and Documents 1901–1925, Rudolf Steiner—Marie Steiner-von Sivers* (RSP, AP 1988): 'It was the knowledge that this is a *backward*-moving evolution—the occult-astral—that intervenes in *forward*-moving evolution. This knowledge is the condition for spiritual vision.' Here, however, there is an essential difference between Novalis and Rudolf Steiner. What Rudolf Steiner attained as a result of his own spiritual development, that is, through his own forces, was granted to Novalis as a kind of higher inspiration.

'If we behold his countenance, as it has been handed down to us in pictorial form, we may be astonished how childlike, and yet how wise, these features are. *It is as though an Angel was gazing through them,*' said Albert Steffen about Novalis.[178]

This meeting with his Angel, and also what preceded it by way of the birth in his soul of the higher ego or Spirit-Self, the mediator for the working within man of the new Holy Spirit,[179] the Spirit of Whitsun, which proceeds from the sphere of the Cosmic Christ, made Novalis the first prophet and apostle of the future epoch of the Spirit, the *sixth cultural period*. This is referred to in the Book of Revelation through the image of the community of Philadelphia, the brotherly community of love, which embraces the whole of humanity. Hence some of the words spoken in the spirit to the author of the Apocalypse about the community of Philadelphia can also be applied to Novalis, as its true forerunner: 'I know your works. Behold, I have set before you an open door [this refers to the door into the spiritual world], which no one is able to shut. I know that you have but little power [in his short earthly life Novalis only managed to accomplish a little], and yet you have kept my word and have not denied my name . . . He who conquers, I will make him a pillar in the temple of my God [the two pillars in the spiritual temple of the Old Covenant were the individualities of Elijah and Moses. When the individuality of Elijah has fulfilled his future Christian mission, he will then become a new pillar in the spiritual temple of the New Covenant]. Never shall he go out of it. And I will write on him the name of my God, and the name of the city of my God, the New Jerusalem—which comes down from my God out of heaven and my own new name.'[180]

We shall subsequently speak further about the relationship of Novalis to the image of the New Jerusalem, and also about the most important motif of his entire creative work, that of the return to the spiritual kingdom of the Father through union with the divine Son. What is of importance for us now is to consider the presentiment of that all-embracing experience of the spirit which Novalis bore within his soul and which will become common to all mankind only in the sixth cultural epoch. Let us call to mind some of his observations where he indeed speaks of this future world epoch of the Holy Spirit:

'The *Holy Spirit* is more than the Bible. He shall be our teacher of Christianity, and not dead, earthly, ambiguous letters.'

'The world is a universal metaphor of the *spirit*, a symbolic picture of the same.'

'All that we experience is a sharing of information. And so the world is truly a sharing of information—a revelation of the *spirit*.'

'The world is macro-anthropos. There is a world-*spirit*, just as there is a world-soul. The soul shall become the *spirit* of the bodily world. The world is not yet ready—so little like the world-*spirit*—from one God shall spring an all-God. From one world—a universe . . . With the cultivation of the *spirit* goes the cultivation of the world-*spirit*—and hence religion.'

'For many there is a lack of *spirit* in the present—hence so much the more will they have *spirit* in the future.'

'What is man? A perfect metaphor of the *spirit*.'[181]

'The world of *spirits* is indeed already open to us, it is always discernible. If we suddenly became sufficiently flexible, we would see ourselves in its midst.'

'Man has been able at every moment to be a *supersensible being*. Otherwise he would not be a citizen of the world but an animal.'

'The resolve to philosophise [see p 55] is a summons to the true ego that it shall awaken to self-awareness and be a *spirit*.'

'In former times everything was a manifestation of *spirits*.'

'We are on a mission. We have been called to cultivate the Earth. If a spirit were to appear to us, we would at once gain mastery over our own *spirituality*—we would be inspired at once by ourselves and the spirit[182]—without inspiration there is no *spirit* manifestation.'

'Mankind is the collective organ of the *Gods*.'

Rudolf Steiner, in characterising the sixth cultural epoch, lays particular emphasis on three of its qualities:

1. All pain and suffering felt by another will be experienced as one's own and it will be impossible to experience happiness if the other is unhappy. In other words: a universal, all-human brotherhood, or true Philadelphia, founded upon the principle of love.
2. Absolute religious freedom, which will be founded on the fact that at that time the whole of earthly life will become an expression of the supersensible, an expression of the spirit, so that the very meeting of two people will be a religious act and sacrament.
3. A pneumatology or spiritual science akin to modern Anthroposophy.

We find all three of these qualities developed to a remarkable degree in Novalis. They are the three pillars on which his whole life is based and to which his entire creative work aspires. When he proclaims love as the highest principle of the universe or speaks of how the whole of life must become an unceasing service to God, or, finally, when he tells of the future epoch of the 'new world-inspiration', whereby the spiritual world will become open and accessible to all, in all these ways he appears not only as a prophet, but as a living representative of the 'new moral epoch', of the 'golden age' that is approaching![183]

At this point, however, one may ask: from what source in the soul of Novalis do the spiritual inspirations proceed which make him the forerunner of the sixth cultural epoch and which bring it about that its three most characteristic qualities, as referred to above, become the spirit-soul foundation of his entire creative work and inner orientation? The answer to this question is contained in Rudolf Steiner's lecture of 9 October 1918 entitled *The Work of the Angel in Man's Astral Body*. There Rudolf Steiner refers to the three particular characteristics of the sixth cultural period as those soul qualities which Beings of the Hierarchy of the Angels (the Guardian Angels) are striving, under the guidance of the Spirits of Form, to implant in the form of images (Imaginations) in human astral bodies as a soul-spiritual foundation of the spiritual epoch that is to come. Thus in the astral body of *every* human being in our time, in the fifth post-Atlantean epoch, '. . . one of the choir of the Angels is working for the future of mankind.'[184]

Such an Angel works in the soul of Novalis. But as he was the reincarnation of the first earthly man, we are in his case—as distinct from other men—concerned with the oldest and also one of the most powerful of the Guardian Angels that is associated with the evolution of earthly humanity. In the third chapter of his book, *The Spiritual Guidance of Man and Humanity*, Rudolf Steiner describes in some detail how the Angelic Beings who guided mankind during the third, Egypto-Chaldean epoch were already at that time able to come in contact with the cosmic Being of the Christ as He gradually approached the Earth. It was these Angelic Beings who, once they had received the Christ-impulse into themselves during the third cultural epoch, then became the chief inspirers of those men who were able as a result of this to become the most important earthly preparers of the events of Palestine.

One of these Angels was the Guardian Angel of the individuality who was later to appear, in recent times, under the name of Novalis. This Angel was at that time one of the first who received the Christ-impulse into himself, which he did with particular intensity, and was therefore able to lead the human soul that he was guiding to incarnations in which it contributed as Phinehas, Elijah and then as John the Baptist, in a highly significant way to preparing for the coming of the Christ Being to the Earth. Then, in the course of the fourth, Graeco-Latin cultural epoch, these Angelic Beings distanced themselves somewhat from the direct guidance of human beings and, so to speak, left them for a while to their own devices in order that, from the fifth post-Atlantean cultural epoch onwards (an epoch which in a spiritual sense is the repetition of the third on a new level), they might again receive this guidance, though now wholly in the spirit of the aims and intentions of the Christ Being. For this is how the result of the spiritual progress and evolution comes to expression in the realm of the Angelic Beings,[185] namely that '. . . in our fifth cultural period it is the Angels who bring the Christ down into our spiritual evolution.'[186]

It is to this important spiritual circumstance of our time that modern spiritual science or Anthroposophy owes its origin (in the year 1911, Rudolf Steiner still employed the term 'theosophy' when speaking of this): 'And if nowadays Theosophy is cultivated, this constitutes recognition of the fact that the superhuman Beings who formerly guided humanity are now continuing their task as leaders in such a way as to be themselves under the direct guidance of the Christ.' As in the figure of Novalis, we have to do with an individuality who is guided by an Angel whose spiritual evolution, in the sense referred to above, is particularly far advanced. If we take this into account, we must quite naturally proceed to the acknowledgement of the fact that in Novalis 'inspirations of greatest magnificence concerning matters of spiritual science are to be found everywhere, . . . that from him comes something that finds its way into mankind like a seed and will spring to life in the future . . . and we feel that a stream of living Theosophy goes out from him that is, however, *inspired throughout by the power of Christianity*.'[187] In these observations of Rudolf Steiner it is the final words, 'inspired throughout by the power of Christianity', which speak most pertinently of the manner in which the spiritual forces of these Angels, and above all those of his own Guardian Angel, were working in the soul of Novalis; and it is under the guidance of the latter that he truly comes to a spiritual–scientific understanding of the Christ as a cosmic Being who has, since the time of the Mystery of Golgotha, been working as the new Spirit of the Earth.[188] For 'in order to gain a true knowledge of the Christ, there is a real need for those inspiring forces which are now [in the fifth post-Atlantean epoch] being manifested by the superhuman Beings [Angels] who formerly guided the Egypto-Chaldean epoch and are now under the leadership of the Christ. There is a need for a *new inspiration* of this kind . . .'[189]

This 'new inspiration', which now issues from the Angel-sphere bordering upon the Earth, is what Novalis has in mind when he speaks of the 'new world Inspiration' which alone is capable of saving modern Christianity from total ruin. Moreover the prominent position which the Guardian Angel of Novalis occupies amongst the Angelic Beings enables him to call forth within Novalis an enlightenment of a special kind which represents a repetition of the event at Damascus. The influence of these Angelic Beings led to Novalis, like Paul, 'in this respect prophetically foreshadowing the future',[190] to experience already at the end of the eighteenth century what humanity as a whole was to experience only from the twentieth century onwards.

Already during his last incarnation Novalis was able to accomplish that which streams into the fifth post-Atlantean epoch as the most important demand which the spiritual world places upon contemporary humanity: 'Men must, purely through their consciousness soul, through their conscious thinking, come to *perceive* what the Angels are doing to prepare the future of humanity.'[191] This means that *every* man must 'succeed in *beholding* what the Angel is unfolding in his astral body.' It is such a vision that Novalis attains. This becomes possible for him as a result of the union in his soul of the forces of his Angel with the forces of the imprint of the astral body of the Nathan Soul residing within it. Through the mediation of this imprint, Novalis continually senses the activity of the Angel in his astral body, and this experience, in turn, fills his soul with the three fundamental moral ideals of the sixth cultural epoch. What for the majority of human beings still takes place in the depths of unconsciousness becomes for him an immediate spiritual reality: 'Spiritual science for the spirit, freedom of religious life for the soul, brotherhood for the bodily life—this resounds like cosmic music through the work wrought by the Angels in human astral bodies.'[192]

Throughout his short earthly life the soul of Novalis was constantly immersed in this 'cosmic music', all his spiritual endeavours were permeated by it and the inner sources of his 'magical idealism' lay therein.

However, this faculty of consciously perceiving the spiritual activity of the Angelic Being in his astral body has a further highly important consequence for Novalis. In the lecture of 9 November 1914, Rudolf Steiner, in referring to the particular character of the preparation for the sixth cultural epoch in Eastern Europe, speaks of how one of the results of an incarnation in a Slavic race (he chooses as an example that of Russia) is that one has a natural predisposition for an intimate connection with one's Angel after death. What comes about in a Russian through a certain natural inclination, which is determined by the place of his birth and expresses his essential task of eventually becoming the bearer of the impulse of the sixth epoch, appears in Novalis as a *consciously attained and inwardly experienced condition of soul*. In other words, what Rudolf Steiner describes as the capacity 'to identify in consciousness with . . . [one's] Angel', 'to grow together with one's Angel' in order then 'to behold the spiritual world with one's eye of spirit',[193] which a Russian has quite naturally after death, Novalis already possesses *to a certain extent* during his life in a physical body, just as humanity as a whole will come to possess it during earthly life in the sixth cultural spoch—if, of course, the stage of development designated by the higher powers is attained. What Novalis calls 'magical idealism' is none other than his capacity to behold 'with an Angel's eyes' not only the spiritual world but also the world of the senses: 'It [the creative work of Novalis] makes so deep an impression because whatever we have before us in immediate sense-perceptible reality, whatever the eye can see and recognise as beautiful, appears with a well-nigh heavenly splendour in the poetry of Novalis through the *magical idealism* that lives in his soul. Through the magical idealism of his poetry, he can make the most insignificant material thing live again in all its spiritual light and glory.'[194] Or, to express the same thought in Novalis' own words: this is 'the art of transforming everything into divine wisdom (*in Sophien*)—or the other way round.'

If we take into account all these facts testifying to Novalis' relationship to the Angelic Being who guides him, and also what we have described by way of his relationship to the Spirit-Self, we must say: *In the figure of Novalis we have to do with a true representative of the sixth cultural epoch.* What in the Slavic East is only gradually being prepared and, moreover, *not* as an *individual* but as a *national* trait—which comes to expression in a natural capacity to work ever more consciously with one's Angel, thus enabling a soul that incarnates in such a folk gradually to become prepared for receiving into itself the substance of the Spirit-Self—was at the end of the first quarter of the fifth post-Atlantean epoch manifested to the whole of humanity in the figure of Novalis, a man who stood at the summit of the cultural evolution of his time.

For this reason, the creative work of Novalis, and also his brief earthly biography, of which Rudolf Steiner says that 'it is itself a work of art',[195] will in the course of time come to have an ever greater significance for the understanding of the spiritual–historical evolution of mankind and, in particular, for understanding the essential nature of the sixth cultural epoch. For in his life and personality we have a wonderful (one could say) 'magical mirror'. In him every man can see the extent to which he stands close to or far away from the ideal to whose unceasing service the entire life and creative work of Novalis was dedicated, and which is set before the whole of humanity as *the next stage of spiritual attainment.*

It follows from such an understanding of the soul-spiritual qualities of Novalis' inner world that the steps in the evolution of his spirit which he had achieved in his previous earthly life were able to strengthen still further the capacities that such a soul would come to have after death. Rudolf Steiner tells us that since the last third of the nineteenth century the Archangel Michael has been waging a battle in the spiritual sphere closest to the Earth, in order that the etheric form of Christ may *rightly* be reflected in the substance of the world ether, and that in this battle he chooses as members of his host particularly those human souls who are now in the world between death and a new birth, and who having passed in their previous incarnation through the Russian or another Slavic race are hence capable after death of identifying especially strongly in their consciousness with their Angel. To this 'heavenly host' that is directly connected with the sphere of Michael, Novalis surely also belongs. As he possesses all the qualities that we have described, not out of a national, but rather out of a *universally human* disposition, he can participate in the *preparation* taking place in the sphere of Michael for the new appearance of Christ in the etheric realm with particular awareness and intensity— a spiritual task in which he takes a *leading role*. Novalis, who was able already at the end of the eighteenth century to pass through an experience akin to that of Paul before Damascus,[196] has, as a result of his conscious meeting with the Spirit-Self, become in the course of the nineteenth and twentieth centuries the leading individuality in Michael's host as he fights for the new advent of Christ in the supersensible world nearest to the Earth. 'This event of Christ's appearance . . . can only be brought about if the rulership of Michael is extended ever more and more. This process still continues in the spiritual world. One could say that a battle is being waged by Michael, on the plane that borders upon our world, for the coming of the Christ . . . so that in the spiritual world we can plainly perceive a conquering impulse on the part of Michael for the coming of Christ . . . Michael must fight the battle to which I have referred so that He does not appear in a false guise, in a subjective human imagination, so that He appears in a true image.'[197] And if Rudolf Steiner says that those souls who after death '. . . are fitted to identify themselves with their Angel' and are thereby '. . . quite particularly suited to call into being the forces which can present in purity the picture whereby the Christ is to appear', Novalis belongs to the first rank of those individualities who are able to contribute *especially powerful forces* towards the attainment of this goal. Moreover, it is he who is to be regarded as the great teacher and guide of the Slavic and especially the Russian souls in the spiritual world as they seek to accomplish their allotted task. Hence one can say with certainty: the individuality of Novalis will in the future come to have an immense significance for the spiritual evolution of the Slavic East. Novalis will be recognised there in a completely new way as a forerunner and prophet of that mission which—according to the will of the world rulership—Eastern Europe is intended to accomplish.

'If one receives Novalis into one's soul, one is fashioning an organ for the future,' Albert Steffen has said of him.[198] And indeed, the life and work of this poet-messenger serve as an organ whereby all men may arrive at a perception of the impulses of the sixth cultural epoch.

It follows from the words of Rudolf Steiner quoted above that a necessary prerequisite for the appearance of Christ in the etheric realm is that the 'rulership of Michael amongst men is extended ever more and more.' The process of the new advent will take place in the course of the next three thousand years, that is, until the beginning of the last third of the sixth cultural epoch.[199] However, its spiritual foundations must be laid during the modern period of Michael's rulership, which will last approximately a further three centuries. Consequently, Novalis is, in this respect too, one of the most important preparers of mankind for the sixth cultural epoch. He, who has been connected with the sphere of Michael since the arising of ego-humanity,[200] will be taking up his task in the course of the fifth post-Atlantean epoch or, to be more precise, during the next 200–250 years, which are under the sway of the Sun Time-Spirit.

If we take as a *temporal mid-point** of earthly evolution the middle of the Atlantean age, the modern fifth post-Atlantean cultural epoch becomes the reflection of the third epoch of the ancient Lemurian age, which is to say that it is a reflection of the last stages of the time *before* the Fall, corresponding to the paradisaical condition of mankind immediately prior to the Luciferic forces' intervention in human evolution.[201] This can be expressed chronologically with somewhat more precision: the *beginning* of this process of the 'Fall', which lasted a fairly long time, until the expulsion from Paradise, comes at the moment of the Lemurian age whose reflection in our fifth post-Atlantean epoch is the end of the dark age of the Kali-Yuga. Thus in the year 1900, from which time humanity is again living in an 'age of light', there gradually begins the spiritual reflection, in earthly evolution, of the ancient paradisaical condition of humanity *before* the Fall. In other words, from our time onwards, and increasingly as the future progresses, it will become possible for mankind—although in a completely different form and on a far higher level—to return to the primordial paradisaical condition through a conscious perception of, and a union with, the higher worlds of spirit. The ascent to this primordial paradisaical condition will pass through

---

* The spiritual mid-point of earthly evolution is the Mystery of Golgotha, which took place at the end of the first third of the fourth (Graeco-Latin) cultural epoch of the post-Atlantean period.

certain stages,* and will be connected quite especially with the coming of that new 'moral age' whose impulses will, by the middle of the sixth cultural epoch, gradually embrace the whole of humanity, and which will reach its culmination during the concluding seventh epoch.[202]

This 'age of morality', which will begin approximately three thousand years after our time (although preparation for it must be set in motion already today), coincides with that moment in human evolution when the new Bodhisattva, working amongst mankind, attains the stage of Buddha-hood and appears as 'a bringer of good through the Word, through the Logos,[203] as the Maitreya Buddha who bears new tidings of Christ and the Mystery of Golgotha. This new spiritual proclamation of the Maitreya Buddha will then spread amongst mankind not only as higher knowledge or as a new spiritual teaching, but it can work as 'a magical moral power' amongst men and will have the capacity '. . . of carrying to hearts and souls a full conviction of the eternal, deeply significant brotherhood of intellect and morality.'[204] For the Maitreya Buddha 'will have the task of enlightening human beings concerning the Mystery of Golgotha, a purpose for which he will endeavour to find the most meaningful and profound ideas and words . . ., so that through his words the nature of the Mystery of Golgotha will become *magically* imprinted in the human soul. *Hence in this respect also we are approaching what we may call the future moral age of man. In a certain sense we could refer to it as the coming golden age.*'

It is this moral or golden age that Novalis feels himself called to prepare,[205] and he already has a presentiment of it in his soul: 'eternal peace is already with us—God is amongst us—America is here or nowhere—the *golden age* is here—we are magicians [magi]—we are moral . . .' Or in another place he writes: 'To be the apotheosis of the future, of this truly better world, this is the essential injunction of Christianity.' And in another of his sayings: 'We are on a mission: we have been called to cultivate the Earth.' For Novalis this means that we must work towards the bringing into being of a new 'moral universe'. And when we are confronted by this perspective which so stirs the spirit, 'we must seek to become *magicians* so that we may become truly *moral*. The more moral, the more in harmony with God—the more divine, the more united with God.' This is a premonition of that future age when 'teaching will have a magical-moral power', when a new 'magical morality will stream into the hearts of men.'[206] We may call this future age, the path to which—and also the first anticipation of which—is

---

* More will be said later about the initial approach to this condition, which will come about already in our time.

represented by the 'magical idealism' of Novalis, the time of the blossoming of a true 'white magic'.[207] This will be an age when natural, intellectual and moral principles will cease to be separated from one another, just as they were not separated from one another in the paradisical childhood of mankind.

As an example of an actual premonition of such a connection between the natural and the moral, a section from a letter of Novalis to Friedrich Schlegel may be cited where he writes that he 'has come upon the idea of a moral astronomy' and has 'made the discovery of a religion of the visible universe' (Teplitz, 20 July 1798). What this means he speaks further about elsewhere in the following words: 'Day is consciousness of the wandering star, and while the Sun, like a god, ensouls the centre in eternal self-generated activity, one planet after another opens an eye after a longer or a shorter time, and in the cool of sleep is refreshed for new life and contemplation. Thus there is a religious aspect to this—*for is the life of the planets anything other than service of the Sun*? Here too you come towards us, ancient childlike religion of the Persians, and we find in you *the religion of the universe*.' Thus to experience the universe, in which the spirits of the planets continually pay cultic homage to the central Sun-Spirit, this is 'magical idealism', contemplating the world 'with the eyes of Angels', with the eyes of divine beings, where the moral-spiritual structure of the universe is revealed as an ordered progression of Hierarchic Beings: '. . . the moral law appears here as the only true, great law of progression in the universe.' Man is eventually to become the last member of this Hierarchic whole. That is his highest designation, as Novalis writes out of his feeling for the future: 'God wants Gods!' And in another fragment: 'Every man who now lives by God and through God shall himself become God.' Both these observations are essentially a metamorphosis of the words of Christ, 'I have said: you are Gods' (John 10:34), though Novalis' words are not merely borrowed from the New Testament but are derived from his own spiritual experience.

Finally, as a culmination of everything, there is the principle of total renewal ('Behold, I create all things new', Revelation 21:5): 'The child and his John . . .' ('Where children are, there is a golden age')—'. . . The Messiah of Nature. *New* Testament—and *new* Nature—as the New Jerusalem.' In these words of Novalis there is a direct premonition of the future Jupiter condition.[208] This distant future condition will shine its dawning rays into the sixth cultural epoch, which Rudolf Steiner calls 'the age of love', when 'what may be called Christian love will be manifested in an altogether different form', when 'this deepest of teachings, that of the mission of earthly love, in its connection with the Mystery of Golgotha', will become recognised for what it really is.[209] In this sixth epoch there will awaken in man 'a love for every kind of existence . . . whether of the physical plane or of higher planes'. The symbol of this love, for Novalis, is the image of the child. This is not only because of what is said in the Gospel about only children being able to enter into the Kingdom of Heaven (Matthew 18:3) but principally because in the sixth cultural epoch mankind will, to a certain extent, come consciously to master those forces which work within every child as cosmic forces during early childhood and which then, upon emerging into the full light of consciousness, appear as forces of love for all that exists: 'A child is love made visible. We ourselves are a visible seed of the love between Nature and spirit of art.' '*Love is the foundation for the possibility of magic. Love works in a magical way.*' One could also say that in these last-quoted words of Novalis his spiritual eye beholds the future Jupiter condition, the New Jerusalem, as though through the prism of the sixth cultural epoch, whose dawning light is, as we have seen, associated with the beginning of the development within man of the forces of 'magical morality'. Thus Novalis prophetically beholds in the spirit what Rudolf Steiner describes in the following words: 'We see the preparatory forms, which are to survive as the forms of the next Earth incarnation, as Jupiter, come forth *through the power of the white magicians: we see the New Jerusalem arising out of white magic.*'*[210]

Then all nature will become moral and love will ray forth from every natural process, as wisdom does now.†[211] This sublime state will not, however, come at once, but will have to be preceded by a period when all that exists can be spiritualised, or, to express this in spiritual–scientific language, a pralaya: 'There will come a time when Nature is no more— it will gradually become a world of spirit.' On Jupiter this transformation of the natural world will take place existentially, though the spiritual foundation for such a transformation must be laid during the sixth cultural epoch through the development of a new *spiritual consciousness*, in which the seeds for the entire future of the Earth are contained.[212] Novalis feels himself to be a representative of this spiritual consciousness. He calls it a 'complete' or 'higher' consciousness, and this consciousness is the source of the words: 'The system of morality must become the system of Nature.' We need only to compare these words with the following observation of Rudolf Steiner: 'that the moral world order of

* Compare with Novalis' words quoted on p 68: 'We must seek to become *magicians* so that we may become truly *moral* . . .'
† The motif of love as a magical power and at the same time as the spiritual foundation of the New Jerusalem is present with particular power and poetic immediacy in the lines quoted on p 97.

the present is the germinal force of a future natural order; this is the most real thought that there can be.' Novalis comprehends this 'most real thought', in that for him, as for Rudolf Steiner, 'the moral is not merely something that is thought out; something is moral . . . when, impregnated with reality, it is a seed for future outer reality.'213

Out of a direct inner experience of this sublime truth, Novalis goes on to write: 'The first chapter of physics belongs to the spirit world. Nature cannot be explained in a static way, but only as something that is proceeding onwards, *to morality*.'—'God has nothing to do with Nature—He is the goal of Nature, that with which it shall one day be in harmony. *Nature is to become moral* . . . It shall be explained through morality.' Nature can attain this stage only through man and his spiritual activity; only through him can it begin 'to harmonise with God', with that God of whom Novalis writes: 'Theosophy. God is love. Love is the highest reality—the ground of everything.' But in order that this might be fulfilled man must become 'the messiah of nature', and for this purpose he must consciously master those spiritual forces which worked unconsciously within him in the period of early childhood. For only with their help will he be able to transform himself and liberate the natural world (Letters to the Romans 8:19–22): 'Mankind is the higher meaning of our planet, the nerve that connects this limb with the higher world, the eye which it raises to the heavens', in the hope of its spiritualisation in the Jupiter aeon.

'*The New Jerusalem*' will find a certain preliminary fulfilment already in the sixth cultural epoch. In the *Phila*-delphian epoch it shall become an *inner reality* within man, representing 'the presence of God's love in our innermost self.' For the truth which Rudolf Steiner formulates in the following words appears to Novalis to be quite unshakable: 'The highest power and morality are needed to receive the Christ-impulse into ourselves so that it becomes power and life in us.'214

If this is able to become a reality within man, then—according to Novalis—'Christendom will again be alive and effective', and from the human heart—'man's holy organ'—its impulses will be able to permeate the whole of human social life. Then 'the New Jerusalem will be the capital of the world', a symbol of the spiritual brotherhood of all 'souls that thirst for the supersensible.' Novalis wishes to serve this vision of the social future of the sixth cultural epoch with the whole of his being, yes, 'true unto death'. And it is to *such* a service and faithfulness to these higher spiritual ideals that he would lead those who are now capable of understanding the spiritual reality that lies behind them. In our time, anthroposophists are called to understand it, and to take the first steps towards its realisation, for modern spiritual science is none other than the conscious preparation of mankind for the sixth cultural epoch, that of the Spirit-Self.[215] Hence we may say: this call of Novalis is directed in the first instance to the anthroposophists of the twentieth and twenty-first centuries (for many of whom he was a companion and guide in the spiritual world). This is a call to be his constant companions in proclaiming 'the divine Gospel', whose mysteries are now revealed to us in Anthroposophy, 'with word and deed', so that the new spiritual epoch, 'the holy time of everlasting peace', might dawn upon the Earth: 'When, oh when? This is not something that one can ask. One must just be patient, it will come, it must come, this holy time of eternal peace, when the New Jerusalem will be the capital of the world; and until then one must be cheerful and courageous before the perils of the time. Companions of my faith, proclaim the divine Gospel with word and deed, and remain faithful to the true, eternal faith even to death.'

8

The Karmic Biography of Novalis according to His Own Testimony

'Here is the future in the past.'

Novalis

'Life had liberated from his soul the wisdom of previous incarnations that slumbered within it.'

Rudolf Steiner, 26 October 1908

In the previous chapter we considered the inner path of Novalis' spiritual development; we should like in this chapter to try to discover—in his own words—references to his past earthly lives as they have been described in the present work.

For Novalis himself his previous incarnations were not a reality of which he was fully conscious; in the epoch of the Kali-Yuga it was extremely difficult to come to a direct clairvoyant perception of one's past lives.[216] Nevertheless, the idea of reincarnation in its new Christian form appeared before him with full clarity as a fruit of his spiritual experience. He writes of this as follows: 'As earthly man we strive towards spiritual development—towards the spirit as a whole. As extraterrestial, spiritual beings, towards earthly development—towards the body as a whole ... With us the thousand-year kingdom lasts perpetually. The best of us, those who have attained to the spirit-world during their lifetime, only appear to die ... whoever does not attain perfection here attains it, perhaps, in yonder realm, or else must begin a repeated earthly life-cycle.—In yonder realm ought there not also be a death whose result is earthly birth?'

Or: 'The synthesis of soul and body is called a person—the person is related to the spirit in the same way as the body is to the soul. It, too, falls apart and then arises again in an ennobled form.' And in another place: 'When a spirit dies, it becomes a man. When a man dies, he becomes a spirit.'—'Free death of the Spirit, free death of man.' Behind these concentrated words stands Novalis' deep insight into the mystery of birth and death, into the mystery of Mary–Sophia and Christ Jesus, regarding

73

which he wrote poetry of so high a degree of inspiration. Even the motto which he chose for his life, 'Christ and Sophia', can ultimately be understood only on the basis of an insight into the mystery of death and the mystery of birth, and also into what unites them: the law of repeated earthly lives.*

Novalis describes this all-embracing cosmic law in a particularly incisive—one might even say personal—way in one of his later poems, 'The Song of the Dead', where he concludes what he says about the union of the human soul after death with the stream of the world ether by means of the following lines:

> We have mysteriously
> Flowed forth ever on this tide
> Into life's expanse of ocean,
> Deeply into God.
> Forth from His heart's outward streaming
> We return to our own circle,
> And the spirit of highest striving
> Dives into our inmost vortex.

Here there comes before us in purely poetic form an image of the human soul's ascent after death to the highest regions of the spiritual world ('the heart of God'), and its return from thence into the cycle of Earth-existence, though now with a new task apportioned to it by 'the spirit of highest striving'.

This law of reincarnation, which worked with particular force in the soul of Novalis, embodies that magical power which is able to transfer, into the present, events of the most distant past, and awaken memories of the most diverse spiritual and historical happenings. Although it was not as yet possible for Novalis to gain an insight into his previous incarnations, nevertheless these incarnations with all their mighty and, at times, also truly cosmic experiences stood imperceptibly beside him from beyond the threshold of his earthly consciousness. In this sense the short life of Novalis was indeed a continual conscious–unconscious *remembering* of his rich cosmic–earthly past. Rudolf Steiner refers to this feature of his life in the following words: 'This young man, who left the physical plane at the age of twenty-nine and who gave more to the German spirit than hundreds and thousands of others, *lived a life that was really the memory of a previous one*. Through a quite definite event the spiritual experiences of

---

* More will be said about this 'motto' in Chapter 12.

74

earlier incarnations were called forth, appeared before his soul, and flowed out from this soul in tender, rhythmically surging poems . . .'[217]

The memory of his previous incarnation as Raphael is perhaps most clearly displayed in the words which he wrote as an immediate impression upon seeing the *Sistine Madonna* in Dresden: 'Love is the ultimate purpose of world history—the sole centre (Unum) of the universe.' (We shall see later on why it is that, in the course of acknowledging the cosmic working of the principle of *love*, there arises within Novalis a memory of his life as Raphael.) And in full concord with these words, though expressed in a more intimate way, the following may also be cited: 'Was Raphael a painter of souls? What does that mean?' For does not this cry of astonishment which once burst forth from Novalis testify to his deep recollection of the degree of *love* for every man and for the whole of existence that is necessary for entering into the soul of another being, for depicting its highest aspirations in works of art?

This mystery-filled being of Raphael, and in particular his mighty cosmic experiences after his early death, form the spiritual background against which the outward life of Novalis took its course. Countless are the channels and paths whereby the memories of what—as a result of his past life—he experienced in the spiritual worlds between the sixteenth and eighteenth centuries poured into his soul, for it was in these centuries that the supersensible School of Michael was active in the high Sun-sphere.[218] And so, having been spiritually awakened through the shock which he sustained as a result of Sophie von Kühn's death, he wishes once more to lead 'the life of Raphael' in the spiritual worlds, he again seeks access to those sublime truths which he experienced between his two incarnations: 'He wants to pass over already now into the supersensible, *he wants to lead again the life of Raphael*, not really touching the Earth, but living out in poetry his magical idealism, without wishing to be touched by earthly life.'[219]

If we turn from the life of Raphael to that of John the Baptist, we find between these two earthly lives, when this individuality was abiding in the spiritual world, experiences of a very particular kind which arose as a result of his spiritual connection with Lazarus–John.

The memories of these experiences were to form the spiritual foundations of Raphael's life: 'The earthly personality of Raphael was completely yielded up and was only present through what Lazarus–John gave to this soul to be poured out in colour and line for all mankind.'[220] In Novalis too, the memory of his connection at the Turning-Point of Time with John the Evangelist and of having shared spiritually in an experience of the central event of earthly evolution rays forth like a flash of lightning:

Uplifted is the stone—
Mankind is now arisen—
To Thee we all are wed
And nevermore feel bonds.

In these four lines from the fifth Hymn to the Night one can sense an echo of his memories of having been supersensibly present at the Mystery of the Resurrection. This motif appears with even greater clarity somewhat earlier in the prose part of the same Hymn, where all the most important moments of the events of Palestine, which the entelechy of John the Baptist views from on high and in which it participates spiritually, are described as though in retrospect from the spiritual world. Indeed, if we contemplate the meaning of these lines, we may have the feeling that Novalis derives his images, in an absolutely direct way, not from outward Gospel sources but from the astral light itself. This becomes particularly discernible when the order of the events which he is speaking of suddenly becomes reversed and, after his description of the Resurrection, Novalis enters by means of his spiritual sight into the inner experiences of the Apostles, into their memories of their wanderings and conversations with Christ Jesus *before* the Mystery of Golgotha. From these few lines there arises an impression similar to that which comes upon us when reading what Rudolf Steiner communicates from the Fifth Gospel in the lecture of 2 October 1913, where he describes in some detail the inner experiences of the Apostles after Pentecost, when they beheld their life together with Christ Jesus on Earth in spiritual retrospect. Something of this vision shines through the words of Novalis. This is his memory of that time when, after his incarnation as John the Baptist, he overshone the company of the Apostles as their new group-soul. And if we take into consideration that, in the company of the Twelve Apostles, all the principal spiritual streams are represented, we may understand why it was precisely the archetype of the assembly, the original council, that stood before Raphael's inner vision as one of the most central ideas in his entire work. This lofty idea was to find its most complete embodiment in two of his frescos, *The School of Athens* and *The Glorification of the Sacrament*. Novalis, too, refers to the memory that lives in his soul of the spiritual connection with the company of the Apostles, of 'His disciples', in the following words:

76

Where I hold Him ever
Is my fatherland;
And those gifts will fail me never
He bequeaths me with His hand:
Brothers long forsaken
See I now in His disciples waken.

With this Novalis' conscious–unconscious memory of his supersensible participation in the awakening of Lazarus is also connected. The verses that follow make this plain:

When my world around was shattered,
Canker-gnawed, my flowers were scattered,
Heart and blood moved listlessly.
All my hopes of life lay dying,
Every wish was buried lying,
Only pain was left to me.

As I thus in silence languished,
Craved to leave, with sorrow anguished,
Yet through foolish fear did bide,
I from gravestone, suddenly,
From above was wrested free,
And my soul was opened wide.

This mysterious connection of Novalis with John the Evangelist was not altogether hidden from his contemporaries and friends. Some of them even observed in Novalis' outer countenance a certain resemblance to the 'beloved disciple' of Christ Jesus. For example, Ludwig Tieck wrote about Novalis as follows: 'The outline and expression of his face approximated closely that of John the Evangelist, as we see it portrayed in the wonderful big picture by Albrecht Dürer preserved in Nürnberg and Munich.'[221] But this affinity is manifested not only in an outward resemblance. Novalis' whole attitude of soul, his relationship to the cosmic sphere of Christ, is a clear expression of this basic element of Johannine Christianity: 'Theosophy. God is love. Love is the highest reality—the ground of everything.' Again, these words of Novalis are not a mere repetition of the corresponding utterance of John the Evangelist (1 John 4:8 and 16), but the result of an inner experience of the very essence of Johannine Christianity. They testify to his spiritual kinship with those who, out of their personal experience, have recognised the central Mystery of the Christ and the Sophia and 'journey with You [Christ] and the heavenly Virgin in the realm of love.'

Novalis' conscious–unconscious recollection of the events of the Turning-Point of Time extends to still greater depths, to the life of John the Baptist and his martyrdom. Such a memory shines through the following lines: 'Martyrs are spiritual heroes. Every man has his years of martyrdom. Christ was the great martyr of our race. Through Him martyrdom has become infinitely meaningful and holy. 'Oh! that I had a taste for martyrdom.' Do not the sentiments of the first martyr of the new Christian era sound forth in these words?

Of all that Novalis has written, however, it is the following lines which manifest his connection, in its full spiritual reality, with the being and the essential mission of John the Baptist (the reason for the description being in the first person has already been discussed on p 33):

> When [there follows a description of senses'
> glow and inner longing],
> Then the heavens open up before me
> And God's Spirit descends upon me.
> The Baptism
> The vision. [All kinds of religious
> transformations] . . .
> God's revelation in human form.

This is the record of Novalis' direct memory of the Baptism in the Jordan, of the mystery of God becoming man. In the life of John the Baptist this central event is preceded by his preaching. Novalis refers to this in these words: 'The true spirit of God moralises. The moralist is *John*.' For John this is a time of inner trial and preparation for this chief task, that of the change from being the last prophet of Jehovah to becoming the first witness of the Christ, as He incarnated on Earth in the sheaths of Jesus:

> For your example and your teachings
> Showed us a religion
> Simple and worthy of Jehovah,
> Exalted, holy, God's own son.

The above observations can also shed light on the enigmatic figure of the singer of Hellas, spoken of in the fifth 'Hymn to the Night'. An understanding of this figure is made possible through the knowledge that the forces of the mighty Archai who was the guiding Spirit of exoteric

Christianity worked through John the Baptist, then like an echo through Raphael, and also through Novalis. According to the fifth Hymn, the mysterious singer wanders from Greece to Palestine in order there to receive the light-filled tidings of the birth of the Conqueror of Death. From Palestine the youth makes for Hindustan, where 'a thousand hearts inclined to him, and the joyful message burgeoned thousandfold.'[222]

In this figure of the youthful singer we may discern the destiny of exoteric Christianity—whose inspirer had in the past been the ruling Archangel of Greece—as read by Novalis in the astral light. At the Turning-Point of Time he overshines John the Baptist, awakening him to a universal-historical 'recognition' of Christ on Earth (see p 16). At the end there is a reference to the future working of this Archai, who brought about the spreading of exoteric Christianity over the entire Earth, even to its most distant regions (Hindustan). All three stages of this line of development, Greece—Palestine—Hindustan, are reflected in the soul of Novalis. Thus to some extent the mysterious singer is Novalis himself, he who works out of the inspirations of the Spirit-ruler of exoteric Christianity.

A similar 'recollection' appears in Novalis' letter to Friedrich Schlegel of 20 January 1799, where the motifs of Christianity and Greece are, like two wings of a high Hierarchic Being, united in a single whole which encompasses the entire 'universe', in space and in time:[223] 'To be the apotheosis of the future, of this truly better world, is the essential injunction of Christianity. With it there ends the religion of antiquity, the spirituality of the ancient world, the restoration of olden times as the second great wing. Both maintain the universe, as the body of the Angel, in an eternal state of suspension, in an eternal *enjoyment* of space and time.'

The spiritual memory of Novalis extends still further into the past: the frequent meetings of the two families, of the two women—the Luke Mary and Elisabeth. Here Novalis' recollections become especially distinct. As mere poetic metaphors they seem almost impertinent, but they appear in a completely different light if one is aware of the actual— or historical—reality that stands behind them. In his *Spiritual Songs* Novalis writes about his relationship to the Luke Mary and her child:

> Countless times you stood by me.
> I watched you with a childlike glee,
> Your babe with both his arms entwined me
> To show that he again would find me;
> Your smile was filled with tenderness:
> You kissed me too—oh sweetest time of heavenly bliss!

In order that we may inwardly approach this remarkable scene, we must place ourselves with full intensity in the world of Raphael's Madonnas and take note of certain basic motifs that recur again and again. Thus in the picture that bears the name 'Canigiani' one of the many meetings of the two families is depicted with Mary, Joseph and Jesus on the one side and Elisabeth and John the Baptist on the other. The gestures of both children are strongly reminiscent of the words 'your little child gave me his hands' (a similar motif also occurs in the picture entitled *Madonna del Passaggio*). Moreover, of the sixteen pictures where the two boys, Jesus and John, are depicted with Mary, ten portray Mary looking not at Jesus but at John the Baptist; and in the case of seven of these she also embraces the latter with one arm (though in the *Madonna with the Diadem*, Mary, while embracing John, is looking with him at the sleeping Jesus).

Thus we see that, for Raphael, Mary's relationship to John and John's to Mary and Jesus was a central motif in the artistic representations (in fifteen of the sixteen pictures on this theme John is looking at Jesus, and in one only is he also pointing at him). While Novalis, who has the capacity of reading in the astral light, penetrates even more deeply than Raphael into his own past and condenses it in concrete images as may be found in poems such as 'Through the countless happy hours', 'Who, O Mother, you have seen' and 'In countless pictures I behold you'.

Finally, this theme of Novalis' memories of his existence as John the Baptist culminates in the following lines:

> Whom I saw let no one question,
> Nor at His hand caught my attention,
> This I now shall ever see;
> This of all life's hours retaining—
> Like my wounds—from now remaining
> Ever open joyfully.

In connection with these lines, Rudolf Steiner once said to Ludwig Kleeberg that, in them, Novalis' spiritual contemplation of the Nathan Jesus boy, the future bearer of the Christ on Earth, holding himself—the boy John—by the hand, found its reflection.[24]

Novalis' remarkable capacity of anticipating the future, and his whole appearance as a *prophet* of the new 'golden epoch', speak to us with absolute clarity of the extent to which the mighty spiritual forces of the prophet of all prophets, Elijah, worked in the depths of his soul. Friedrich Schlegel, in a letter to his brother written in 1792, describes as follows his first meeting with Novalis, who at that time was still a student in Leipzig (Novalis had just reached the age of 20, and was such at the very beginning of the period associated with the development of his ego-forces): 'A man who was still very young—with a slender, noble frame, a very refined face and black eyes, with a wonderful expression whenever he speaks with *fire* about something beautiful—indescribably much fire … with impetuous *fire* he expressed, on one of the first evenings, his opinion that there is absolutely nothing evil in the world and that everything is again approaching the golden age.' This is the impression which Novalis made upon the man who was to be his closest friend, Friedrich Schlegel. And this characterisation of Novalis' 'fiery spirit' is to a remarkable degree in harmony with an observation of his own in a letter to Schiller, where he swears to him an oath of allegiance and writes of his readiness to defend him against the assaults of his enemies with 'the *fiery* zeal of an Elijah.'[225]

'About our ego — as the *flame* of the body in the soul', writes Novalis in one of his fragments. This leitmotif of the 'inner flame of fire' which serves as the revelation of the individual human ego has already been considered at some length in connection with the description of the life and spiritual mission of the prophet Elijah.[226] In the case of Novalis, however, this inner fire is something altogether different from the fiery nature of the Biblical prophet. For now—after the Mystery of Golgotha—this 'fire of Elijah', this inner fire of the individual ego, acquires a completely different significance: it becomes, so to speak, a 'new organ of knowledge' which exalts its possessor to his archetype, his source, to the 'spiritual fire of the Resurrection', in whose light the apocalyptic Christ appears. Rudolf Steiner refers in the following words to this highly important characteristic, which only Christians of the future will have—amongst whom Novalis may without doubt be reckoned: 'They [the Christians of the future] will understand not only the Christ who has passed through death, but also the triumphant *Christ of the Apocalypse, resurrected in the spiritual fire*, whose coming has already been predicted. The Easter Festival can always be for us a symbol of the Risen One, a link reaching over from Christ on the Cross to the Christ triumphant, risen and glorified, who raises all men with Himself to the right hand of the Father.'[227]

Such an experience of the 'apocalyptic Christ', who has been resurrected 'in spiritual fire' and leads the whole of humanity to the macrocosmic sphere of the Father, was also attained by Novalis; in the following lines from the sixth 'Hymn to the Night' he brings this knowledge to expression:

Come down to the bride of sweetness,
Jesus the Beloved:
Take comfort, dusk brings evening's greyness
To the lovers, the afflicted.
A dream breaks all our bonds asunder,
Leads to our Father's realm of wonder.

And the same theme rings out still more clearly in the *Spiritual Songs*:

A Saviour, a Redeemer came,
A son of Man, in love and might
And did an ever-quickening flame
Within our souls as fire ignite.
We only now saw heaven open
As our ancient fatherland,
Now were faith and hope awoken
We felt ourselves at God's right hand.

The motif of the 'ever-quickening flame', which appears in the above lines, is repeated again and again in Novalis' other writings. For example, in the fifth Hymn to the Night the description of the flame 'as the highest thing in the world' is given wholly in the spirit of the old Zoroastrian religion: 'All races have, in a childlike way, revered the tender, thousandfold flame as the highest thing in the world.' Subsequently, and especially in the *Spiritual Songs*, the motif of fire is increasingly brought into connection with the figure of the Risen Christ:

Go to that tree of wonder,
Give space to silent longing;
From it goes forth a fire
Th'oppressive dream consuming.

And in another context:

In cooling streams now send Him here,
In flames of fire let Him appear,
In air and oil, in tone and dew
Let Him imbue our Earth all through.

In these last quoted words we can feel that it is the experience of Christ, revealed in the 'spiritual fire', which leads Novalis to a knowledge of His higher cosmic Being. Christ stands before him as the new Spirit of the

Earth, permeating its whole organism. But this is not all. For with his knowledge of the present role of Christ in the evolution of the Earth is also revealed to Novalis the mystery of His higher Sun-nature: as the central Sun-Spirit 'He died cosmically from the Sun to the Earth'[228] in order then to arise in 'the spiritual flame', in its aura. And this new knowledge which Novalis bears within his soul is the spiritual fruit of the fact that in olden times Elijah was not only, like Moses, able to proclaim the Jahve-impulse to the people of the Old Testament, but could already behold, through Jahve's gate of the Moon, the Sun-sphere of the Christ. Thus 'Elijah proclaimed the Christ-filled Jahve', as Rudolf Steiner says.[229] In the following lines by Novalis, we can find an echo of these experiences:

> Lo, there comes to Earth below
> Blessed Child of all the skies,
> Winds of life again do blow,
> Round the Earth ring melodies,
> *From the long extinguished sparks and ashes*
> *Now ever radiant fire newly flames and flashes.*

However, Novalis speaks with particular certitude about this fundamental mystery of cosmic Christianity, of how since the Mystery of Golgotha Christ has *not* abided on the Sun but has been active in the spiritual surroundings of the Earth, by means of the imaginative, poetic pictures of his fairy-tales: 'The Sun stood in the sky, fiery-red with anger, its mighty flame sucked after its robbed light, and as forcefully did it seem to draw it to itself, so did it become ever more pale and blotchy.[230] Its flame became whiter and more powerful the paler the Sun became. It sucked the light ever more strongly into itself and soon the glory round the day-star was consumed and it remained there as a mere faintly gleaming disc . . . At last, nothing of the Sun remained other than a black, burnt out residue which fell down into the sea. The flame had become inexpressibly brilliant . . . It rose slowly into the heights and moved towards the North.' This cosmic event, according to Novalis, signifies a new aeon of evolution: 'It [the flame] has come. Night is past and the ice is melting.' And elsewhere in the fairy-tale: 'Warmth approaches, eternity begins.'

The special relationship of Elijah to the sphere of Michael also finds its reflection anew in a metamorphosed form in Novalis' fairy-tale. Having over a period of centuries contemplated from the spiritual world the gradual descent to the Earth of the Michaelic cosmic Intelligence (from the Turning-Point of Time until the nineteenth century), he refers to this process in the following imaginative picture: 'The old hero had hitherto also assiduously pursued his invisible calling, when all at once the King called-out, full of joy: "All will be well. Iron, cast your sword into the world, so that they may learn where peace reigns." The hero tore his sword from its sheath, placed it with the tip towards the sky, then took hold of it and threw it out of the open window over the town and the icy sea. Like a comet it flew through the air and seemed to disintegrate with a bright sound on the foothills of the mountains, then to fall down in *sparks* of purity.' But what formerly sank down, like myriads of shining sparks into the heads of human beings on Earth, must unite, in our time, in the modern age of Michael—through the awakening of a new spiritual consciousness in the souls of men—with the spiritual flame of the Resurrection, as Novalis prophetically indicated:

> . . . From the long-extinguished sparks and ashes
> Now ever-radiant fire newly flames and flashes.

In one of his Fragments, Novalis describes this 'spiritual flame of the Resurrection' no longer in the poetic images of a fairy-tale but in the form of a concrete spiritual experience which underlies the fundamental task of man in the earthly world. For through contemplation of this flame, the entire life of man becomes an unceasing service of the divine: 'Ordinary life is a priestly act of service, almost of a vestal nature. We have here to do with nothing other than the receiving of a holy and mysterious flame . . . It depends on us, how we tend and await it. Should the manner in which we tend it be, perhaps, the yardstick for our faithfulness, love and solicitude towards the highest things, for the character of our being?' These words contain an essential clue to the central mystery of Novalis' inner life, which we can understand only once we have taken the following words of Rudolf Steiner into consideration: 'For it is indeed true that as the Christ was revealed in advance to Moses and to those who were known to him [that is, in the first instance Phinehas] in the sense-perceptible fire of the thorn-bush and of the lightning of Sinai, so will He appear to us in a *spiritualised fire of the future*. "He is with us always, until the end of the world", and He will appear *in the spiritual fire* to those who have allowed their eyes to be enlightened through the event of Golgotha. Man will behold Him *in the spiritual fire*. Formerly, they beheld Him in a different form; then will they behold His true form *in a spiritual fire*.'[231] This is the 'greatest event of [Novalis'] life', his 'one great act of insight into the Christ Being',[232] an act of which we have already spoken (see p. 36) and which we must now characterise from one further point of view. For what Novalis

84

experienced in this case was none other than a supersensible baptism with spirit and with fire.

If John baptised those who came to him with water, and if his baptising was the last reflection of the ancient Mysteries of Atlantis, the last echo of the Mysteries of the great Sun-Oracle,[233] which enabled its adherents to behold the Christ working on the Sun and then approaching the Earth, we should regard the inner experiences of Novalis as the manifestation of a new baptism, of that baptism which was wrought for the first time by Christ Jesus Himself upon Lazarus in Bethany and which called him forth from a death-like sleep.[234] At that time, before the Mystery of Golgotha, Christ had to accomplish this baptism through His direct spiritual–*physical* presence. After the Mystery of Golgotha, however, baptism by spirit and by fire can be achieved in a purely soul-spiritual-way. This is what the Apostle Paul experienced. Something of this kind also happened with Novalis.

Baptism by the spirit: of this we have already spoken in connection with the description of Novalis' meeting with the Spirit of the ego (the Spirit-Self) and with the Angelic Being associated with it, the representative of the Holy Spirit in the supersensible sphere nearest to the Earth. To what has already been said about this it should be added that, in our time, Christ works through the entire Hierarchy of the Angels in the Earth's surroundings, through the mediation of His *Spirit-Self*.[235] Thus a conscious meeting with one's own Angel is at the same time a way of approaching the forces of the cosmic Spirit-Self of Christ, or (which is the same thing) the supersensible baptism that proceeds from His new Holy Spirit (John 20:22).

Baptism by fire—Novalis' insight into the mystery of the divine fire of the Resurrection, in whose light and warmth is revealed the victorious Christ celebrating His triumph over death: 'In the fire which Paul beheld on the road to Damascus we should see the miraculous, spiritualised fire . . . In this fire all that was great and noble in the past will be born in the future.'[236] When we read these words it is impossible not to recall that Rudolf Steiner also characterises Novalis' supersensible experience of the Christ Being as a repetition of the Pauline Damascus event (see p 37). Thus it is that spiritual experiences which would seem at first sight to be wholly unconnected and even far removed from one another are now united in a single whole and concentrated in a single focal point in Novalis' heart, solely filled, as it was, with the wish to strive towards higher knowledge.

In light of the above, it is of particular significance that in Novalis' life the 'event of Damascus' is, in a remarkable way, connected with the memories of his life as Elijah, which worked karmically within his soul. For, already in the ninth century before Christ, Elijah had been so able to exert his influence from the spiritual world upon the individualities of the later Old Testament prophets that he awakened in them higher spiritual forces and a clear awareness of their mission. Rudolf Steiner compares this *first* example of such a supersensible influence with Paul's experience before Damascus. The incident in question here is Elijah's calling and consecration of his successor and pupil, Elisha, to his role as a prophet.

This act of receiving Elisha into the prophetic stream founded by Elijah takes place in two stages, the first of which also occurs geographically in the region of Damascus. Firstly, Elijah–Naboth shortly before his death calls his pupil to a new service, 'casting his mantle upon him', that is, as we have seen, overshining him with his spiritual power;[237] and then—after his death—he crowns this summons from the spiritual world with a true initiation, as a result of which the entirety of Elijah's spiritual power (his 'mantle') is transferred to Elisha.[238] The most significant aspect of this process of calling and consecration is that, when describing it, Rudolf Steiner is able to compare Elijah's part in it with the risen Christ's own supersensible influence upon the Apostle Paul and also upon other Apostles and disciples: 'It was in Damascus that Elisha was to be sought, and it was there that he was to receive this spiritual enlightenment. This enlightenment was to come to Elisha in the same way as we know it to have come to Paul the Apostle at a later time. And after Elijah had chosen his successor, the vengeance of Jezebel fell upon him.' And so this first calling of Elisha occurs *before* the death of Elijah, before the 'vengeance of Jezebel', and then it continues after Elijah's death, when it becomes a true initiation: 'And in the same way that the individualities of those who have passed through the portal of death may work with a particular force from the spiritual world, so did Naboth–Elijah, after his death, extend a powerful influence upon Elisha, as did Christ Jesus Himself—after His death, after the Resurrection—upon His disciples. Elijah–Naboth's influence upon Elisha was great indeed.'[239]

The comparison inherent in these words may be understood as follows. As we have already discussed at some length, there was a part of the spiritual being of Elijah which was, from the outset, not fully incarnated in his physical body. Later on, with the fulfilment of his mission, this part of his being that was not incarnated became ever more powerful until finally, like a mighty aura, it was able to encompass the whole Hebrew people and came to serve as a kind of mediator between this people and the principal force guiding them, the Moon Elohim, Jahve.[240] But—according to Rudolf Steiner's indications—as the reflection in the sphere of the Moon of the Sun-impulse of Christ was manifested in Jahve, so was the calling of Elisha at Damascus also the effect on him of this reflected Christ-impulse which proceeded from Jahve. This reflected impulse then reaches Elisha *through the part* of Elijah's spiritual being which was not incarnated in Naboth's physical body, and only later, after Elijah's death, through his spiritual being *as a whole*. In other words: in the initiation of Elisha,[241] the lunar *reflection* of the Christ-impulse (Jahve) works upon him from the spiritual world, through the mediation of the spiritual aspect of a particular human being—in this case the prophet Elijah. The latter, as the reincarnation of Adam, the first man, is in his turn the *earthly reflection* of the heavenly being of the Nathan Soul.

Thus *before* the Mystery of Golgotha we have, in connection with the 'event of Damascus', as experienced by the prophet Elisha and subsequently by other prophets (for example, Ezekiel and Daniel), a twofold reflection: the reflected activity of the Christ-impulse in the sphere of Jahve and the reflected activity of the Nathan Soul through the mediation of its 'brother-being', the reincarnated Adam (Elijah). While in the experience of Paul the Apostle, and also of other disciples of Christ Jesus after His Resurrection from the dead (1 Corinthians 15:3–8), we are no longer dealing with the reflected but the *direct* influence of the Christ and the Nathan Soul upon them. Rudolf Steiner describes this—as exemplified by Paul—as follows: 'When Paul has his vision before Damascus, He who appears to him then is the Christ. The mantle of light, in which Christ is clothed, is Krishna [the Nathan Soul] . . . because Christ has taken Krishna as His own soul-sheath, through which He then works on further . . .'[242]

This spiritual light which surrounds the etheric manifestation of Christ is none other than the *astral light* radiating from the translucent astral body of the Nathan Soul (as a result of the Mystery of Golgotha), from its 'soul-sheath', of which Novalis bears an imprint within his soul (see p 46): 'And the stars, which send down the light of the day as though in secret during the night, appear to him as no more than feeble rays of light, while meantime the truth of the spiritual was rising up in his consciousness, a consciousness which for him, as seer, is illuminated *with a dazzling bright astral light* whenever he is able to transport himself in spirit into the night.'[243] In this 'dazzling bright astral light' there was revealed to Novalis, as it was to Paul, who on the road to Damascus was 'suddenly illumined by a light from heaven' (Acts 9:3), 'in the night of *the soul* the riddle of death, *the riddle of the Christ*.'[244]

A still more ancient memory, which, however, works as a real spiritual force in the depths of Novalis' inner soul-life, is his connection with the life of Phinehas, the great, younger contemporary of Moses who, nevertheless, has for outer history remained somewhat obscure. We have (p 17) already spoken at some length of how Phinehas, as a reward for saving the people of Israel from physical annihilation and also for his steadfast faithfulness with regard to spiritual union with higher powers, received from Jahve the 'covenant of an everlasting priesthood'. It is this impulse, which continued to work through all the subsequent incarnations of this individuality, that eventually appears in Novalis as the endeavour to turn the whole of earthly life into a ceaseless inner service to God, where a man who is able to sacrifice the lower aspect of his being to the higher powers can become a priest in the invisible Temple of the Holy Spirit, in the only temple of the future 'golden age'. The following two observations testify to this: 'Our whole life is a service to God'; and: 'Ordinary life is a priestly act of service, almost of a vestal nature.'

However, with the words which God addresses to Phinehas: 'Wherefore I give him my covenant of peace. And he shall have it, and his seed after him, even the covenant of an everlasting priesthood,'[245] something further is connected. For this 'covenant of peace and of an everlasting priesthood' is also an indication to us of the direct connection of Phinehas with the stream of Manu–Melchizedek, with the stream that has its sources in the Mother-Lodge of the rulership of humanity. Melchizedek is 'the King of Salem, that is, the *King of Peace*', says Paul.[246] According to Psalm 110, he is 'a priest for ever' and in this sense Phinehas belongs wholly to his stream.

Novalis speaks about this affinity to the stream of Manu–Melchizedek. For example, at the end of his essay *Christenheit oder Europa* (Christendom or Europe) he writes about its aims: 'Just have patience, it will, it must come, *this holy time of eternal peace*, when the New Jerusalem will be the capital of the world.'

In the Book of Genesis (ch. 14) we may read about the meeting between Abraham and Melchizedek: 'And Melchizedek, King of Salem, brought forth *bread and wine*: and he was the priest of the most high God.' The symbols of bread and wine are an indication of the essential nature of that spiritual stream which issues from deep antiquity and finds its continuation and culmination in the scene of the Last Supper: bread as an indication of the path of the earthly Adam, and wine as an indication of the celestial path of his 'sister-soul'. Both paths have their origin in the Mother-Lodge and both must come together through the earthly activity of the Christ Being.[247] But what in the time of Melchizedek, and until the Last Supper, had still to be represented by means of outer symbols can, since the Mystery of Golgotha, and especially since the new appearance of Christ in the etheric realm which begins in our time, be experienced in a purely spiritual way through the direct connection with Christ which arises in the act of offering an inner sacrifice of love, thus bringing about a mystic act of consecration (communion) in the holy of holies of the human soul. Novalis refers to this inner achievement as follows:

> They beheld the—
> Infinite fullness of *love*,
> And extolled the nourishing substance
> Of body and blood.

For just as a communion, having its foundation in the physical symbols of bread and wine, is associated with the historical Mystery of Golgotha, so after the spiritual Mystery of Golgotha, which is taking place in our time in the higher worlds, and its most important consequence, the new appearance of Christ in the etheric realm,[248] the possibility of a purely spiritual, *etheric communion* opens up, to an ever increasing degree, before the whole of mankind.

Novalis passes through such a purely spiritual communion already at the end of the eighteenth century, as though prophetically anticipating the future. Through this means, the mystery of what corresponds to his inner experience in the macrocosm is revealed to him: 'A wonderful vista of the future opens out before Novalis. He sees the Earth transformed; he sees the present Earth, in which the residue of ancient times is still contained, transformed into the body of Christ; he sees the waters of the Earth permeated with Christ's blood, and he sees the solid rocks as Christ's flesh.'[249] We find an echo of this knowledge in some lines by Novalis which we have already quoted:

> In air and oil, in tone and dew
> Let Him imbue our Earth all through.

This remarkable historical–mystical process can be traced as follows: Melchizedek gives Abraham bread and wine. Christ transforms them during the Last Supper into His flesh and blood, which since His Resurrection have become spirit. Since the Mystery of Golgotha this spiritual flesh and blood can be administered to every man in an inner act of spiritual knowledge, and such a communion leads to a receiving of Christ as the new Spirit of the Earth. From without inwards and from within again outwards—such is the path of the ruling Christ-force in the gradual transformation of the Earth: 'Novalis is also aware of the mighty truth that, since the event of Golgotha, the Being we call the Christ has been the planetary Spirit of the Earth, the Earth-Spirit by whom the Earth's body will gradually be transformed.' This is the knowledge that stands before Novalis when he says: 'Faith in the boundless capacity of all earthly things to be the bread and wine of eternal life.' In other words: when human life as a whole is exalted to a sacrificial consecratory act of love, everything that is earthly will become the 'bread and wine of eternal life', the body and blood of the new Spirit of the Earth, and man will have attained the dignity of an 'everlasting priesthood' which will never end. In the figure of Novalis we may see the extent to which the aspiration towards this sublime ideal permeated the whole of this brief earthly life, which in its karmic foundations was a metamorphosis, and also a continuation and development of that high mission which was entrusted by God to Phinehas.

In conclusion we must touch upon the oldest and most all-embracing memory that worked unconsciously within the soul of Novalis as his deepest inspiration: 'The first man is the first beholder of the spirit. Everything appears to him as spirit. What are children if they are not first men? The fresh look of a child is more exuberant than the notions of the most confirmed visionary.'

This reference to the first man, Adam, as a being who was still connected with the etheric cosmos surrounding the Earth, and who possessed the forces of a primordial 'cosmic youth', those forces which in our time are active only in the small child until approximately the age of 3,[250] reveals to us (does it not) the most essential feature of Novalis' mood of soul. For this is the origin of his ceaseless aspiration towards this source of universal life and cosmic youth, and of his knowledge that 'Christ is the new Adam' who is able, though now in a different form, one that is appropriate for the present condition of human consciousness, again to endow mankind with those cosmic forces of which it has become almost wholly bereft. This is the fundamental knowledge which, associated with the very foundations of Novalis' being, unites in a single whole, like a majestic arch embracing the whole of human evolution, the beginning and end, the alpha and omega of mankind's earthly history: 'The Bible begins with Paradise, *the symbol of youth*, and ends with the eternal kingdom, the Holy City.' 'Paradise' and the 'Holy City'—both of these are for Novalis 'symbols of youth' and total renewal: 'And He who sat upon the throne said, Behold, I make all things new.'[251] The whole history of man on Earth is embraced, as though in a single movement, in the above words of Novalis: its beginning—the paradisaical condition of mankind in the ancient Lemurian epoch. Man has not yet tasted of the Tree of Knowledge of good and evil, his whole being rests within the cosmic bosom of the Hierarchies, he continues to live in the world in such a way as he was created by the Gods on Old Moon and borne by them to the Earth; for the epoch of Lemuria is a repetition of Old Moon in the context of the Earth incarnation.[252] And its end—the coming of the Jupiter condition as the new spiritual aeon of evolution, when humanity will ascend to the level of the Angels and all human beings will again become cosmic Beings. The beginning and the end, alpha and omega, Moon and Jupiter; and the central impulse of the Earth, 'Christ is the new Adam', which unites them. The history of humanity, as Novalis understands it, is the history of man's relationship to the principle of 'cosmic youth', to the impulse of the Cosmic Christ.

In the scene where Christ Jesus is taken into custody in the Garden of Gethsemane, by night in the light of the moon[253] and the torches, something occurs which is mentioned only in the Gospel of St Mark. There we read: 'And a *young man* followed Him, with nothing but a linen cloth about his body; and the soldiers seized him. But he left the linen cloth and ran away naked.'[254] Rudolf Steiner elucidates these words as follows: 'Who is this young man? Who was it who escaped? Who is it that appears beside Christ Jesus almost without clothing and then slips away naked? It is the *cosmic youth-impulse*, it is the Christ who slips away, He who has now but a loose connection with the Son of Man . . . The new impulse has none of those things which olden times could wrap around mankind. [This is a reference to the irregular *Moon*-forces that entwine themselves round man like a snake.] It is the entirely naked, new cosmic impulse of earthly evolution. It remains with Jesus of Nazareth, and we find it again.'[255] In these words from the Gospel, and Rudolf Steiner's commentary on them, we may see a reference to the primordial forces of 'cosmic youth' brought by Christ to the Earth, forces which man possessed only in the so-called 'paradisaical' condition which was his until the Fall and over which the human beings who were ruled by demonic Moon Beings proved to be powerless in the Garden of Gethsemane. Thus in this scene the retarded forces of Old *Moon* are conquered by Christ for all mankind. Only after this can the Mystery of Golgotha—the central event of *Earth*-evolution—be fulfilled. Then on the third day the *youth* again appears. Later on in the Gospel of St Mark we read: 'And when they [the women] entered the tomb, they saw a young man sitting on the right side, dressed in a white robe; and they were terrified.'[256] 'This is the same youth,' says Rudolf Steiner, that is, 'the cosmic youth-impulse'. He stands spiritually before the women in such a way as every man will appear in the new aeon of *Jupiter*.[257]

From the standpoint of Christian–Rosicrucian wisdom this process can be expressed as follows: the original paradisaical condition of humanity was still connected with the forces of Old Moon, with a direct experience of participating in the higher divine cosmos: 'Ex Deo Nascimur.' After the loss of this primal state and the separation of mankind from the sources of the 'forces of eternal youth', as a result of the Fall, a new influx of these forces into earthly evolution took place through the most important of all earthly events, the Mystery of Golgotha: 'In Christo morimur.' And finally, as a result of the free union of each individual human being with the Christ-impulse, which is to say, through the gradual alliance with the forces of 'cosmic youth' which the new Holy Spirit that proceeds from Him makes possible, he can again, though on a new level, attain the original stage and enter the Jupiter aeon as a cosmic being acting out of love and freedom: 'Per Spiritum Sanctum reviviscimus.'[258]

All that we have adduced here, from the sources of modern spiritual science, and of the Rosicrucian wisdom which it has renewed, lived, in the form of artistically poetic premonitions, in the soul of Novalis. Thus his unfinished work, *The Novices of Saïs*, the content of which can be traced back to the mystery-wisdom of the third cultural epoch—this being the reflection in the post-Atlantean age of the period of Old Moon[259]—was intended by the author to have ended with the theme of the 'New Testament', with a description of the central event of the Earth and the subsequent birth of a 'new Nature—a New Jerusalem'. In these last words Novalis gives a prophetic glimpse of the future Jupiter condition, which he experiences in the forms of the sixth cultural epoch, the first anticipation—within the confines of 'Earth'—of the cosmic aeon of the future.

This motif appears in the most diverse forms and aspects in Novalis' creative work. We shall cite here three more of his spiritually poetic observations from the *Hymns of the Night*. For example, in the fifth Hymn he writes: 'Night became the mighty womb of revelations; thither the Gods retraced their steps, fell into slumber, in order then to emerge in wonderful new forms over the changed world.' 'Night', as Novalis understands it, is the all-embracing sphere of cosmic spirituality; the 'changed world' is that 'new world' which will, from our time onwards, be gradually revealed to human beings through their newly awakened supersensible faculties as heralded by modern spiritual science, and which Novalis *already* inwardly experiences:

> Now dawns the new world's radiant light
> And darkens sunshine's rays so bright.

Here Novalis' poetic vision startles us with its remarkable occult precision. His description, as quoted above, of the disappearance and new manifestations of the old Gods—which in Nordic mythology is known as 'Ragnarok' or the Twilight of the Gods—corresponds exactly in its spiritual essence with what has been given through anthroposophical research: 'If one particular part of humanity experiences the new age on that very soil where Nordic mythology flourished [and Novalis belongs to such a part of humanity], it must be understood by these people that the old clairvoyance ['the first man is the first spirit-visionary,' says Novalis] must assume a *different aspect*, once man has undergone development on the physical plane [Novalis: 'emerge in wonderful new forms']. That, through which the old clairvoyance was proclaimed, has become silent for a while; for a certain time . . . the world of Odin, Thor, Baldur, Hodur, Frey and Freya was hidden from his sight. But it will light up again before him, after such a time when other forces have meanwhile been working upon man's being. And when the human soul beholds the *new world* [Novalis: 'the changed world'] with the new clairvoyance which is initiated through etheric vision . . . Odin and Thor will again become visible to man, though now in accordance with the new development through which his soul has passed.'[260] These words are also directly associated with the whole character of the spiritual rulership of humanity in the modern fifth and the subsequent post-Atlantean epochs. Thus according to Rudolf Steiner, the Angelic Beings who led mankind during the third, Egypto-Chaldean-Babylonian epoch, having withdrawn from this leadership in the Graeco-Latin epoch, in our time begin again to guide mankind, though now under the rulership of the Christ Being Himself. Something similar will occur in the sixth cultural epoch, when the Archangels who guided human beings during the ancient Persian epoch will join the Angels in their rulership of humanity. To them will eventually be added the Archai, who ruled over human beings in the ancient Indian epoch.[261] So that 'men will come ever more and more to feel how everything which is of a pre-Christian nature can be enabled to reappear on a higher level, at an elevated degree of lustre and style.'[262]

This motif appears with even greater clarity in the fourth 'Hymn to the Night', which ends with the words:

> Truly I was before you were
> With others of my race
> The mother* has sent me
> To inhabit your world

* This refers to 'Mother-Night', an image of the spiritual world from which man comes. The words in brackets have been added from the prose edition of the Hymn.

And to hallow it   (5)
With love
To give
A human meaning
To your creations.
Not yet have they ripened,   (10)
These divine thoughts.
As yet the traces
Of our present (revelation)
Are few.
Some day your clock shall indicate
The end of time,
When you will
Become like us,
And, full of yearning (and ardour),   (20)
Will be extinguished and die.
I feel within me
Activity's end,
Heavenly freedom,
Blessed return.
Wild with grief   (25)
I perceive your remoteness
From our homeland,
Your resistance
To the old
Wondrous heaven.   (30)
In vain is your rage,
Your frenzy.
The cross stands there
Invincible,
A victory-banner   (35)
Of our race.

The first section of this part of the Hymn is a kind of metamorphosis of
the words from the Gospel, 'Before Abraham was, I am,'[263] that is, an
allusion to the original paradisaical condition of humanity. Then in lines
15–16 there is a reference to the final state of mankind, to the 'Holy City',
the 'New Jerusalem', when 'time shall be no more'.[264] And then in lines
21–24 there is a description of the highest fruit of the union of the
beginning and the end of human evolution, when the historical process
will have culminated in a 'blessed return' to its origins, albeit on a new
level, in accordance with the individual freedom that has been striven for

on the Earth, a quality which, in the new aeon of evolution, will become 'heavenly freedom', that is, a freedom which opens up the possibility of higher cosmic creativity. Finally, the last four lines (33–36) speak of that power with whose help this union of beginning and end, of alpha and omega, can be achieved by those men who, not in a physical but in a *spiritual* sense, represent a new race amongst *mankind* (36), a new race of human beings who are permeated by the impulses of a spiritual, cosmic Christianity, a Christianity which is under the direct rulership of the Archangel Michael.[265] Later in his life, Rudolf Steiner speaks in a similar sense about the 'race of Michaelites', those men who have in full freedom received the modern impulse of Michael–Christ, with which the individuality of Novalis is so intimately connected, receiving it into their soul and spirit, into their human nature as a whole, in so intense a way that in their subsequent incarnations it can work as a transforming force even to the extent of the physical body itself.[266]

And one further example. In the sixth, and last, 'Hymn to the Night' Novalis *on four occasions* uses the word *Vorzeit* ('former times'). The first occasion is when he is characterising the soul condition of one who can still recall mankind's original state:

> Oh! lonely stands and all downcast
> He who loves the time that's past.

The next three verses (4, 5, 6 in the Hymn) all begin with this word and characterise, in turn, three great stages in human evolution. The first verse describes the primeval condition of humanity as it was before the great Atlantean catastrophe. The next verse speaks of the post-Atlantean period that ensued, of the 'ancient tribes', amongst which the people of the Old Testament and their history may be reckoned. The last of these three verses has as its theme the events of the Turning-Point of Time. And then the motif of the last spiritual homeland appears once more—together with the motif of the yearning for 'return':

> Unto our homeland we must go
> That we this holy time may know.

The hymn concludes with a sublime description of sinking again into the Father's bosom ('And sink us in the Father's womb') through a union of the human soul with the combined forces of the Christ-impulse and the Sophia-impulse, the representatives of the World-Spirit and the World-soul in our cosmos.[267]

95

All this also has a direct relationship with the cultic act of laying the Foundation Stone of the First Goetheanum on 20 September 1913. In the address which he gave at that time, Rudolf Steiner speaks of humanity's 'call' or 'cry of longing' for the spirit, of the new spiritual revelation, and of the answer to this cry through the coming of modern spiritual science or Anthroposophy to the Earth. This 'cry of yearning for the spirit'[268] and the answer to it in the form of Anthroposophy is a direct continuation, and at the same time a spiritual reflection, of those events which are familiar to us as the preparatory stages of the Mystery of Golgotha in the supersensible worlds. In connection with them Rudolf Steiner also speaks of 'humanity's cry to the spiritual world for help' and of the answer, which is manifested in the three cosmic sacrificial deeds of the Nathan Soul.[269] So we have the call for help of the descendants of the *earthly Adam* from below and, from above, the answer from his 'sister-soul' in the higher worlds.

Perhaps what is most remarkable about the address which Rudolf Steiner gave at the laying of the Foundation Stone of the First Goetheanum is that he commences his communications from the Fifth Gospel, that imperishable Gospel which is preserved in the Akashic Chronicle. The first of what he gives from this source is the reading of the macrocosmic Our Father, which expresses the whole tragedy of the situation of earthly humanity since the Fall. However, this first reading of the 'primeval macrocosmic prayer'[270] is preceded by an indication of particular importance. Rudolf Steiner here refers to the connection of the four canonic Gospels with the *Earth* and of the Fifth Gospel with the *Moon and Jupiter*, with the alpha and omega of earthly evolution.

As we have seen, this is also the principal motif of Novalis' life: uniting the beginning and the end of the Earth aeon through the Christ-impulse. If, then, we become aware that the inner mood of the macrocosmic Our Father must for many thousands of years have been the fundamental soul mood of the individuality of the first man, Adam, it does not seem extraordinary when in the work of Novalis we find, veiled in the form of poetry many of those facts which Rudolf Steiner, in his address of 20 September 1913, draws from the sources of the new anthroposophical revelation. Thus we find already in Novalis a premonition of, and to a certain extent even a conscious quest for access to, this higher supersensible Gospel. 'In the Gospels,' he writes, 'lie the basic characteristics of future, higher Gospels.' Or: 'The new Gospel, of which Lessing has foretold, will appear in the manner of a Bible: but not as an individual book in the ordinary sense.' And in another Fragment he makes the observation: 'Devotional books—sermons—prayers—new Gospels.' Or as a question: 'Is it not possible to conceive of the existence of several

Gospels? Must one be absolutely historical? Or is history no more than a vehicle? Perhaps also a *Gospel of the Future*?' And finally, at the end of the essay, *Christendom or Europe*, we find words which truly sound like his testament to the Christian peoples of Europe: '. . . proclaim with word and deed the divine Gospel . . .'

These remarks of Novalis are like one great question directed to the spiritual world, a question to which only modern spiritual science can give an answer; it is 'that answer which can be given where spiritual science can be present, with its Gospel of the knowledge of the spirit', with the 'macrocosmic . . . Gospel of knowledge: the Fifth Gospel.'[271] Novalis, as he penetrates with his poetic intuition of genius into the sphere of the 'future, higher Gospels', wholly encompasses in his soul this tragic 'lunar' mood which fills us when we acquaint ourselves with what is revealed 'as the first of what is given from the Fifth Gospel'. As we hearken to his poetic revelations, we may at the same time call to mind the words and the entire mood of the 'ancient, undying prayer': 'The old world was drawing to an end. The pleasure-garden of the youthful race was fading; the human beings, growing up children no longer, were striving upwards in a space unconfined and desolate. The Gods had disappeared with their retinue. Nature was left lonely and lifeless. With an iron chain it bound barren number and strict measure. Life's measureless bloom fell apart in dark words as though in the dust of air.' And elsewhere, even more clearly defined, he says:

> That holy world was long ago:
> I wander sadly to and fro,
> With grief as my companion staying.
> Have I so sinfully been straying?

But Novalis lives in the epoch since the Mystery of Golgotha. Hence this 'Moon' mood arises in him only as a memory, at such time when an awareness of the principal event of Earth blazes forth within his soul:

> The Cross stands there
> Invincible,
> A victory-banner
> Of our race.

It is this conviction which reveals to Novalis the path onwards from Earth to the future Jupiter condition, to the New Jerusalem. For he knows for sure: on the Hill of Golgotha the foundation was laid for the future aeon of love:

How he was moved by love alone,
All to us has given away,
To be God's City's cornerstone
Himself into the Earth did lay?

In this universe of the future whose first foreshadowing will be the 'golden age' which will begin approximately in the second half of the sixth cultural epoch man will no longer be separated from his true homeland, from the spiritual world. Then will the words of Christ be fulfilled: 'Unless you inwardly turn and become like children, you will never enter the Kingdom of Heaven.' And then: 'The more a man in humility brings to life the child within himself, the greater is he in the Kingdom of Heaven. And whoever receives one such child* in my name receives me.' These words from the Gospel can only be understood on the foundation of other words of Christ Jesus: 'Among those born of women there has arisen no one greater than John the Baptist; yet he who is least [the child] in the Kingdom of Heaven is greater than he'[272] 'Unless you inwardly turn . . .'—The premonition of the necessity of this process arises in the soul of Novalis first as a prediction, a prophecy as 'the singing of the song of the return', and then as an immediate inner reality:

I feel within me
Activity's end,
Heavenly freedom,
Blessed return.

Since early Christian times, Angels have always been depicted with the heads of children. For in a child there still lives something of what is manifested in all its fullness in the being of an Angel. Thus every child is an unconscious bearer of a portion of Angel existence, or Jupiter existence. Rudolf Steiner speaks of this as follows: 'The spiritual world speaks through the child . . . It is not the child that is speaking, but the Angel is speaking out of the child . . . his ego is not merely the fourth member . . . but at the same time the lowest member of an Angel . . . for we can speak of these members of an Angel in connection with this period [from birth until the middle of the fourth year], and of the child's ego as the lowest member of the Angel.'[273]

We find an allusion to this particular mystery of human evolution in the following words of Christ Jesus: 'See that you do not despise these

* In the authorised version, this is expressed in the words: 'not withstanding he that is least in Heaven is greater than he.'

tender embryonic forces within man [that which is to serve as a foundation for Jupiter]. For I tell you that the Angels who guide the being of a child [this means the child in every man] always behold the face of my Father who is in Heaven.'[274]

This *conscious* aspiration towards childhood as a Path of Initiation, leading to a purely spiritual existence, appears in classic form in the conversation of Christ Jesus with Nicodemus. 'Unless one is born from above, one cannot see the Kingdom of God,' Christ says to him. To this Nicodemus replies: 'How can a man be born when he is old? Can he enter a second time into his mother's womb and be born?' These words represent the answer of a humanity that has become wholly entangled in the consequences of the Fall. But Christ counters Nicodemus' question: 'Unless one is born of Water *and the Spirit*, one cannot enter the Kingdom of God.* That which is born of the flesh is flesh, and that which is born of the Spirit is Spirit.'[275] And again, baptism by *water*, just as birth which is of the flesh, is of the Moon; while baptism through the spirit of the ego (the Spirit-Self) is a spiritual birth, the anticipation of the future aeon of Jupiter. In a small child the one and the other are *unconsciously* united. In the first three years of childhood we have, on the one hand, a powerful manifestation of the forces of heredity, which are associated with the influence of the Moon, and on the other hand the forces of the Angel (of the Spirit-Self), who still bears in his bosom the child's future earthly ego.

The conversation of Christ with Nicodemus (cited above) has a fundamental significance for an understanding of the entire theme that we are considering. For what was before the Mystery of Golgotha not yet understood by Nicodemus becomes for Novalis the central yearning of his soul:

> May only children see your face†
> And trust th'assurance of your grace?
> May bonds of later years now sever
> And let me be your child for ever;
> For childlike love and trust sublime
> Still live within me from that golden time?

---

* These words correspond spiritually to the assertion that only a man who has brought to life the child in himself can enter the Kingdom of Heaven.
† Compare this verse with the words: 'For I tell you that in heaven their [children's] Angels always behold the face of my Father who is in Heaven' (Matthew 18:10).

And in another poem:

> For all His thousand gracious gifts
> His humble child I will remain.
> We know that He is in our midst
> When two are gathered in His name.*

In these lines Novalis refers in poetic form to that same ideal of modern initiation of which Rudolf Steiner writes as follows: 'What then becomes manifest as man's highest ideal . . .? Surely this: Drawing ever nearer to what we may call a conscious relationship to the forces which work within man unknown to him during early childhood.' This is at the same time the goal of the whole of earthly evolution: 'The significance of evolution through successive earthly lives is gradually to make the whole individual human being, including the conscious part, into an expression of the *forces* which rule over him under the influence of the spiritual world—though he does not know it—during the first years of his life'[276] (that is, principally the forces of the Angel who is guiding the person in question, of the representative of the principle of the Spirit-Self). Like Rudolf Steiner, Novalis also knows that from these forces, or to be more exact, from the cosmic sphere to which they belong, there flow all human ideals, all impulses of true artistic creativity, all natural faculties of healing[277] and, finally, those 'best forces whereby knowledge of the spiritual world, true clairvoyance, is attained'. But this is not all. If a man is able to transform these best forces of his soul into a faculty of 'true clairvoyance', the highest possibilities are opened to him: 'For genuine clairvoyant self-knowledge leads *the man of the present day* to see that powers are to be discovered *in* the human soul which emanate from the Christ./These powers are at work during the first three years of childhood without the human being himself doing anything about it. In later life they *can* be brought into effect, if the Christ be sought within the soul by inner meditation.'[278] Novalis was such a man. In his striving to 'find the Christ' he discovered through 'inner meditation' that Christ can be found, in the depths of the human soul, only by means of those forces which remain within man as forces untouched by the Fall, as the forces of primordial childhood: 'It is essential to pay heed to what has remained childlike in man, for it is by way of this childlike nature that warmth can be imparted to the other faculties through the Christ-principle. The

---

* These verses should also be compared with Novalis' words regarding the 'second higher childhood' which is a kind of 'rediscovered Paradise' (in the second part of *Heinrich von Ofterdingen*).

100

childlike nature must be developed in order that the other faculties may follow suit. Everyone has the childlike nature within him and this, when wakened to life, will also be responsive to union with the Christ principle.'[279] There is a further observation by Rudolf Steiner which sounds as though, from out of the spiritual world, the entelechy of Novalis was speaking through him: 'To affirm the necessity that the age of childhood casts its Sun-filled eye over his entire life, this is indeed the Christianising of a man.'[280] In their aphoristic manner, these words are like a hitherto unknown, by chance lost and newly rediscovered fragment by Novalis in which is expressed that which he would *in our time* wish to impart through Rudolf Steiner to men on Earth.

All that has been said hitherto can be illumined from yet another side. In the lecture of 11 September 1910 Rudolf Steiner says that, although the fourth post-Atlantean epoch witnessed principally the development within man of the intellectual- or mind-soul, there were nevertheless, on Earth at that time, individual human beings who were able, to a certain extent, to develop the first elements of the *consciousness-soul*, which has the capacity of being open to higher regions and receiving the *inspirations* of the Spirit-Self (of the Angel). In the esoteric tradition of the ancient Hebrews such men were called 'Sons of Man', and at the Turning-Point of Time a clear example of such a person was John the Baptist,[281] whom an Angelic Being guided, and through whom such a Being worked.

The counterpart to a 'Son of Man' was a Being such as was called by the same esoteric tradition of the ancient Hebrews a 'Son of God'. This Being possessed the entire fullness of the forces of the Spirit-Self, Life-Spirit and Spirit-Man and was, through them, continually in a fully conscious relationship with all the higher Hierarchies: 'Esoterically speaking, one calls the first man the divine man—because he stands in a relationship to the higher Hierarchies—or the Son of God; the other one calls the Son of Man.'[282] 'Thus one may make a distinction between the "Son of Man", who grows upwards from below, and the Son of God, the "Son of the living God", who grows downwards from above.'[283] In the lecture of 25 February 1911 Rudolf Steiner describes in some detail how in the course of the first three and a half years in the earthly life of every human being the forces of the higher Hierarchies, the forces of the 'Son of God', are continually active, and how they are later gradually transformed into the activity of the forces of the consciousness-soul, that is, of the 'Son of Man'. In the same lecture Rudolf Steiner refers to the goal of earthly evolution as the awakening of the 'Son of God' within the 'Son of Man' or (which is the same thing) the conscious development, at a later age, of the spiritual forces of early childhood.

The individuality of Novalis has been connected in a most intimate way with this goal of earthly evolution, with the endeavour to awaken the 'Son of God' within the 'Son of Man', ever since the time of his incarnation on Earth as John the Baptist. For at the Turning-Point of Time, John, who through being inspired by an Angelic Being was already at the stage of the 'Son of Man', was at the Baptism in the Jordan the first in the entire history of the Earth to behold, and at the same time to participate in, the historical descent of the Son of God (Christ) into the Son of Man, into Jesus of Nazareth. This is why Rudolf Steiner says in this connection: 'It belongs to such things that we are able to place ourselves in a right relationship to what streams forth through the Baptism of John, to the healthy, fructifying forces of childhood.'[284]

This fundamental experience is preserved within the entelechy of John even after his death, and reappears then in metamorphosed form in the work of Raphael, especially in his 'Madonnas', of which Rudolf Steiner says: 'Anyone who gazes at Raphael's Madonnas can see that from the eyes of his children there shines forth the divine, the hidden, the superhuman, *which in the early stages after birth is still connected with the child.* This is something one can observe in all Raphael's pictures of children . . .'[285]

However, this impulse, which has its origins in a first-hand experience of the Baptism in the Jordan, reaches a still higher manifestation in the incarnation of Novalis. For if a man of our time is able, even if only to a certain extent, at an age of full consciousness to awaken within himself the forces of early childhood, or (which amounts to the same thing) to make baptism by the spirit and by fire an inner reality, the consequence of this for him will be a *personal experience of the Damascus event*, a fulfilment of the words 'Not I, but Christ in me'. This is the experience of which we were able to say that it was the central event in the spiritual life of Novalis (see p. 37): 'And if we try to develop in ourselves a human nature that is akin to the soul of childhood, but which is fully permeated with the reality and content of the spiritual world, we shall have a conception of that Ego-hood, that Christ-hood, of which St Paul is speaking when he sets before men the challenge of the words: "Not I, but Christ in me"—meaning the childlike soul that is permeated with full and complete ego-hood. In this way the human being is able to permeate his Son of Man with his Son of God and will be in a position *to fulfil his earthly ideal: to overcome his external nature and once again to find the connection with the spiritual world.*'[286]

The final, italicised, words of this quotation make it clear that Novalis' Damascus experience is also the beginning of his fulfilment of that mission which was originally associated with his destiny as the reincarnated first man, Adam. This mission, as we have seen, is at the same time the ideal and goal of all earthly evolution: again to find a conscious relationship to the spiritual worlds, to the primordial 'paradisaical' state which was wholly lost to mankind through the 'Fall':

> Thus is the holy battle fought,
> The wrath of Hell is turned to naught,
> And flowering everywhere around
> Our former Paradise is found.
>
> The Earth is stirring, green, alive,
> And filled with spirit all men strive
> Their Savour lovingly to meet
> And with o'er-flowing heart to greet.
>
> The winter wanes, a New-Year morn
> The crib's High-altar doth adorn.
> It is the first year of the world
> Which this Child has Himself unfurled.

It follows with absolute clarity, from all the facts that we have considered so far, that Novalis was, as no one else in recent times, a true forerunner of modern spiritual science. Thus we find scattered throughout his creative work seeds of many ideas and insights which we subsequently encounter only in Anthroposophy: 'And so we see that in this Novalis there lives, in a distinctively individual form, everything which has now been given to us through spiritual science.'[287] This is so because Novalis was, in the course of his brief earthly life, able to bring to life within himself the spiritual forces of *early childhood*, to awaken the 'Son of God' within the 'Son of Man'. This is also why the theme of the development and experiences of the spiritual forces of childhood occupies what would seem to be so prominent a place in his works.[288] Moreover, these spiritual forces worked within him in so intense and so real a way that, on the basis both of his appearance as a man and of his work as a whole, we could hardly imagine him other than as a youth, an 'eternal youth' who, nevertheless, bears within himself the wisdom of a thousand years. The oldest soul of humanity manifests to all men, in the figure of Novalis, the path towards complete spiritual renewal, towards the sources of primordial cosmic youth.

'His outer appearance was at first reminiscent of those pious Christians who are portrayed in a modest fashion . . . To him this secret place [the spiritual world] was transparently his original home; from here he beheld the sense-world and its relationships . . . Novalis seemed both to speak and write out of a profound sense of the spiritual past, out of a primal depth which could only dimly be expressed in the everyday world of the present . . . The poetic, religious thoughts of Novalis . . . sounded like wonderful oracles full of promise, and they [human beings] found in his utterances a strength, almost as the pious Christians in the Bible. Indeed, Novalis was, in the deepest sense, a Christian and religious,' Henrik Steffens was later to write after meeting him in 1799 in Freiburg.[289] And Novalis, out of a semi-conscious feeling for his deeper nature, himself writes:

> Now burns with mighty power that hidden fire—
> My ancient being—deep in this earthly structure . . .[290]

And so we see how the *Damascus motif*, the experiencing of the mystery words, 'Not I, but Christ in me', runs through all the stages of Novalis' karmic biography. Already in his incarnation as Elijah (even though still only in an indirect and preparatory way), this fundamental motif makes its appearance in his destiny (see p. 85). In his incarnation as John the Baptist it appears again with greater clarity through the fact that a certain Angelic Being was working through John.[291] After the Turning-Point of Time this motif appears, no longer in a 'reflected' but in a *direct* form, in Raphael, who in the draft for one of his poems himself mentions a Damascus event in his life.[292] This fundamental experience later enables him, in the *Sistine Madonna*, to portray the holy child in such a way that, in him, there not only arises before us the figure of the Luke Jesus (that is, the Nathan Soul), as in Raphael's other pictures, but the Christ-impulse shines forth through the childlike features of his face.[293] Hence Rudolf Steiner says of the *Sistine Madonna*: 'Something [of what works within man in the early years of childhood] can be observed in all Raphael's portraits of children, with one exception only. There is *one* such portrait of which this could not be said, and that is the Jesus-child of the *Sistine Madonna*. Anyone who looks this child in the eye knows that more shines forth from the eye of this child than could be present in a human being. Raphael has made this distinction, that in this one child of the *Sistine Madonna* there lives *something which experiences, as though in anticipation, a quality of pure spirit, of the Christ Himself.'*[294]

Finally, in the figure of Novalis himself, the entire process of development that has been described, which at each stage is connected with a new aspect of an experience of the Damascus event, reaches its culmination and becomes a kind of foundation stone for the whole of his *future task*, of which more will be said in the next chapter. Thus, if we consider this theme from a new aspect, we may see that all the individual threads come together in one single whole wherever we may turn in the creative work of Novalis. And however diverse the various elements of his output may seem at first, nevertheless they will, through deeper examination, be seen to lead to a single centre and to share one central source: a direct, supersensible meeting with the Christ.

'To recognise the forces working in human nature during childhood is to recognise the Christ in man.'[295] This remarkable observation of Rudolf Steiner we find in the *first chapter* of his little book, *The Spiritual Guidance of Man and Humanity*, which may indeed serve as a commentary on Novalis' life. For in this first chapter all the underlying motifs of his soul-spiritual development are united in a single whole: his relationship to the higher ego (the Spirit-Self), and his meeting with the 'Genius', the Angelic Being who guides him; his inner experience of Christ; and the description of that region of the human soul where He can alone be found—the realm of the primordial divine forces of childhood that were not touched by the influence of Lucifer (which is to say) in that part of every man where the Being of the Nathan Soul continues to be present. 'It is the best part of mankind which in these three years [in the first three years of life] we have around us.'[296] The best part of *mankind . . .*' is the Nathan Soul:

> For childlike love and trust sublime
> Still live within me from that golden time.

All these themes are already familiar to us from the preceding chapters; they all testify to the real presence and activity in the world of what could be called 'the spiritual guidance of man and humanity', that 'spiritual guidance' with which the individuality of Novalis was so deeply connected in his last, and in all his previous incarnations.

9

The Future Mission of Novalis amongst Mankind

*'What forms the human being if it is not his own biography? And nothing
so forms a noble human being as does the history of the world. Some people
would rather live in the past and the future than in the present.'*

Novalis

*'We stand in a relationship with every region of the universe—and similarly
with both future and past.'*

Novalis

The study of the various incarnations of the individuality of Novalis, as
has been made in the foregoing chapters of this book, on the basis of what
has been given through modern spiritual science, sets an important
question before us. If, on the one hand, in the incarnations of this
individuality as Phinehas, Elijah and finally as John the Baptist there
comes before us what could be described as the spiritual fruit of his entire
'pre-Christian' development—which reaches its culmination at the
Turning-Point of Time—then on the other hand, beginning with the
latter incarnation and still more so in the two subsequent incarnations in
the fifteenth and eighteenth centuries, we may gain an ever clearer
impression of a kind of *preparation* of this individuality for completely new
tasks amongst mankind. What might these new tasks be?

If we turn directly to the earthly lives of Raphael and Novalis for all
the remarkable things which these personalities accomplished for the
general cultural development of their epochs in the artistic realms of
painting and poetry, nevertheless both these incarnations *in an esoteric
sense* had far less influence on the further spiritual progress of humanity
than, say, the personalities of the prophet Elijah or John the Baptist had
in the past. The reason for this lies, amongst other things, in that the
earthly activity and creativity of both Raphael and Novalis belonged
wholly to the *exoteric* culture of mankind. If we take into account the full
significance of the spiritual individuality standing behind these personalities, we may rightly regard both these incarnations as the means
whereby this individuality is preparing for a definite spiritual mission in

the future. The principal aim of the present chapter is to attempt to unveil the mystery of this future spiritual mission of the individuality of Novalis.

However, in order that we may gain a clearer comprehension of this spiritual task, it is necessary first to turn once more to the pre-Christian incarnations of Novalis, focusing on one particular aspect which we have not hitherto considered.

As we know through spiritual science, the chief task of the ancient Hebrew people was to prepare, by dint of the stream of heredity, the physical sheath for the incarnation on Earth of the cosmic Being of the Christ. The hereditary forces work mainly in man's physical and etheric bodies and come more outwardly to expression in the particular characteristics of the build of his physical body and in the whole configuration of the etheric forces of his blood. The esoteric significance of Old Testament history from Abraham, the forefather of the ancient Hebrews, until Jesus of Nazareth, lay in the preparation of these two bodies and also, more indirectly, of certain qualities of the astral body. In the Old Testament the principal reference to this important occult fact is the appearance in the grove of Mamre (Genesis 18) of the three men (Angels), who reveal to him the mysteries of the physical, etheric and astral bodies immediately after Melchizedek has initiated him into the Mystery of Jahve or the 'divine I am',[297] when he has, as a result, received the name Abraham instead of his former name of Abram (Genesis 17).[298] For this reason, in artistic portrayals of Abraham's meeting with the three divine messengers, as, for example, the 'Trinity' of the Russian icon-painter Rublyov, the Angelic figures are positioned in such a way that behind one of them rises a mountain—an indication of the mysteries of the physical body; behind the second a tree—an indication of the mysteries of the etheric body; and behind the third a temple-building—an indication of the mysteries of the astral body.[299]

Into this stream of development the individuality that we are considering now appears as a younger contemporary and distant relative of Moses–Phinehas. This occurs at that particularly dramatic moment of Old Testament history when, as a result of unlawful mingling with other races, the ancient Hebrew people were threatened by the danger of losing the spiritual predispositions, in the stream of heredity, of that *physical body* in which Christ was to incarnate. This would have made it impossible for the Hebrew people to fulfil their principal task within human evolution, and the consequence of this, at that time, would have been gradual, physical death.

This critical situation is described in the Old Testament in the twenty-fifth chapter of the fourth Book of Moses (Numbers), where it speaks of the wrath of Jahve–Elohim towards the ancient Hebrew people (25:3) and of his wrathful wish to 'consume in jealousy' all the 'children of Israel' (11). Only the intervention of Phinehas, who manifested thereby a very high example of utter devotion to the will of Jahve, that is, a readiness to serve only the goals of the highest rulership of mankind, rescued the Hebrew people from total *physical* annihilation at that time. 'And the Lord spoke unto Moses saying: Phinehas, the son of Eleazar, the son of Aaron the priest, has turned my wrath away from the children of Israel, while he was zealous for my sake among them *that I consumed not the children of Israel in my jealousy*' (Numbers 25:10–11).

What is at issue in this scene is primarily the damaging and destroying of the spiritual forces of the *physical body*, attested by the reference to the twenty-four thousand 'children of Israel' who died in those days from the plague: 'And those that died in the plague were twenty and four thousand' (verse 9). A twofold law underlies this number, one that is associated with the inner structure of the physical body, each of whose twelve parts can be overwhelmed by the forces of evil and death in two directions—in the terminology of spiritual science we would now say: in an Ahrimanic or a Luciferic direction. This danger of the destruction of the spiritual forces of the physical body could at that time be warded off from the ancient Hebrew people only through the removal of these two times twelve sources of 'damage' from their midst, with the aid of certain magical, occult acts. This was accomplished by Phinehas under the direct guidance of Jahve-Elohim. Thus Phinehas was able to rescue all those spiritual forces in the hereditary stream of the ancient Hebrew people, from which the physical body for the incarnation on Earth of Christ Jesus was eventually to be formed.[300]

The next incarnation of the individuality of Phinehas amongst the people of the Old Testament occurred in no less dramatic a period of their history. Now the principal danger threatened not so much the physical body as the *etheric body* into which Christ was later to incarnate as He descended to the Earth.

The chapter which is devoted to this difficult spiritual task of the prophet Elijah—of keeping the etheric forces of the Ancient Hebrews in a pure state and preventing them coming into the possession of Ahab and his demonic inspirer, Jezebel, who wanted to use them in the battle against the future new aeon of evolution—begins with the words: 'And it came to pass after these things that Naboth the *Jezreelite* had a vineyard, which was in Jezreel . . .' The word 'Jezreelite' comes from the same root as the word 'Israelite', and in this connection it is used in the same sense as in the story in the Gospels about Nathanael, of whom Christ Jesus says that he is a 'true Israelite'. In other words, in the present instance, as with that of Nathanael, the word 'Israelite' refers principally to the degree of Naboth's initiation into the old mysteries. This particular one is the fifth stage, where the Initiate bears the name of that people to which he belongs, and it signifies that he is now becoming a kind of guardian-spirit of the entire race.[301] Naboth-Elijah is, in this incarnation, such a guardian-spirit of the Hebrew people, or to be more exact, of the most inspired and purest etheric forces of this people (the 'vineyard').[302] Thus when Ahab demands that he hand the vineyard over voluntarily or sell it to him, he answers: 'The Lord forbid it me, that I should give you *the inheritance of my fathers!*' (1 Kings 21:3)[303] that is, the stream of the etheric forces which flows through the generations of the ancient Hebrew people, beginning with father Abraham.

As in the story of Phinehas, so in that of Naboth–Elijah, we find certain numerical relationships which refer to secrets now no longer of the physical but of the etheric body and which come to expression, not through the law of twelve but through the law of seven, not in a spatial but in a temporal organism. The physical body is the bearer of the forces of death. Thus in the story of Phinehas two times twelve thousand *dead* people are spoken of. The etheric body, however, is the bearer of life. Thus the story that is associated with it speaks not of 'dead' but of 'remaining' Israelites, of which the Bible says there are *seven* thousand. In this sense Jahve–Elohim says to Elijah: 'Yet I have left amongst the Israelites seven thousand men: all the knees that have not bowed before Baal and all the lips that have not kissed him' (1 Kings 19:18).

So, we have the following order of events. The eighteenth chapter of the first Book of Kings tells of Elijah's great spiritual victory over the priests of the Luciferic cult of Baal, the consequence of which is that it becomes possible for the etheric forces of the ancient Hebrews to be preserved in a state of purity and inviolability. A further reference is made to this in the nineteenth chapter in the picture of the seven thousand Israelites who did not bow down before Baal. And, finally, in the twenty-first chapter this battle for the higher etheric forces of the ancient Hebrews enters its last, concluding stage, for now Ahab and the demonic Jezebel seek directly to gain possession of the 'vineyard', the etheric body of the people, itself. This final stage of the battle is, however, concluded by the total victory of Elijah–Naboth, although the battle costs him his physical life.

Thus for a second time this individuality rescues the mission of the ancient Hebrews within human evolution, now enabling not only their physical but also their etheric forces ultimately to become the foundation for those physical *and etheric bodies* into which the Christ-Being was to descend at the Turning-Point of Time.

The forces of the next member of man's being, his astral body, do not really underlie the laws of earthly inheritance. Therefore the individuality of Elijah is able to participate in their preparation only from the spiritual world. The scene of Elijah's ascension into heaven 'in a whirlwind' (2 Kings 2:1 and 11) refers to this participation in a more imaginative form. 'In a whirlwind' means in this instance: in the spiritual forces of that astral body in which the Christ-Being was subsequently to incarnate amongst the ancient Hebrew people. This cosmic astral body had, like a mighty cloud-aura, enshrouded the people of the Old Testament from the very beginning[304] and Elijah, as the representative of his group ego (see p. 8), was connected in a particularly direct way with it, both in his life in the physical body and after his death in the spiritual world. This mighty astral aura, in whose surroundings Elisha, Elijah's pupil and successor, beholds him in imaginative form in the scene of the spiritual ascension of his teacher, and which is portrayed in so visually impressive a manner in many Russian icons (see Plate 2), then during the time between the earthly lives of Elijah and John the Baptist gradually permeated to an ever greater extent the etheric–physical stream of hereditary flowing 'down' through the generations of man, so that by the time of the Turning-Point of Time we can already speak of its actual incarnation amongst the Hebrew people.[305] Thus the principal task of Elijah when he came again to Earth as John the Baptist was to awaken within the individual members of the ancient Hebrew people the spiritual forces of this mighty astral aura that slumbered in the depths of their souls. This was the goal which John the Baptist strove to attain by means of his preaching, seeking thereby to awaken within their souls the astral forces of wisdom, so that the true meaning of the writings of the prophets who proclaimed the coming of the Messiah might be revealed before their eyes. For it was out of the forces of this cosmic astral body— which overshone them from the spiritual world—that the Old Testament prophets were able to foresee and foretell His future incarnation.

This preaching and the enlivening of the cosmic forces of human astral bodies which it called forth was, in a certain way, the high-point and at the same time the culmination of the pre-Christian mission of John the Baptist. On the other hand, what was described in the third chapter as his awakening amongst the ancient Hebrews of the impulse of conscience— the new organ of cognition for the Christ, the Bearer of the impulse of the World-Ego, as He came to the Earth—belonged already to the beginning of the new, 'future' mission of John the Baptist.

An allusion to this future mission is contained in the prologue of St John's Gospel, where the individuality of John the Baptist is brought into a direct connection with the mystery of the incarnation of the Logos. However, this connection can only really be understood on the basis of all that has already been said about the individuality of Phinehas–Elijah–John amongst the ancient Hebrew people. For if, on the one hand, Rudolf Steiner considers the stages of the 'incarnation' of the Logos contained in the prologue of the Gospel of St John from the aspect of cosmic history, as corresponding to the evolutionary stages of Old Saturn, Old Sun and Old Moon,[306] in their microcosmic or 'earthly' aspect these stages correspond to the gradual formation of the three sheaths for the incarnation on Earth of Christ Jesus. Thus in the gradual formation—through many series of generations—of the future physical body of Christ Jesus, we have the first 'microcosmic' deed of the Logos on the Earth, in the gradual formation of the etheric body His second deed, and, finally, in the incarnation of the astral body[307] His third deed. And in all these three deeds the individuality of Phinehas–Elijah–John works directly as the earthly preparer of the incarnation of the Logos, incarnating on each occasion amongst the Hebrew people at the very moment when the preparatory deeds of the Logos amongst men were threatened with the greatest danger.[308]

All that has been said hitherto reaches its highest culmination in the scene of the Baptism in the Jordan, during which John was able, out of the forces of conscience—the new organ of cognition which he was the first human being to use in this way—to recognise the Christ as He incarnated on the Earth, and to proclaim Him to mankind as the Representative of the World-Ego.[309] This deed relates to the beginning of his new mission amongst mankind, and is at the same time the *principal spiritual impulse of the incarnation through which he was then passing*. Hence Rudolf Steiner says of him: 'We see how this individuality [John the Baptist] is to be an instrument for preparing an *understanding* of the Christ-impulse.'[310] And in another lecture, in characterising the mission of conscience at the Turning-Point of Time, he says: 'In the simultaneous occurrence of the fact of the Christ-event and the *understanding* for the Christ-event (through the impulse of conscience) ... we see the authority of an infinite wisdom that is inherent in evolution.'[311] John also awakens this impulse of conscience in many of those who were to become the closest followers of Christ Jesus (for example, Andrew and John, son of Zebedee). Thus after his death John the Baptist continues to be connected with the whole circle of his pupils. For this connection after death is the karmic consequence of the fact that the impulse of conscience had been awoken within them, in the manner described.[312]

If we turn from this central incarnation of John the Baptist at the Turning-Point of Time to his next incarnation, as Raphael, we shall be able to understand this enigmatic figure only if we realise that the impulse which filled him with the same power, as the impulse of conscience had filled John the Baptist, was that of *love* and *compassion* (sympathy) for all that lives in the world. This impulse was later transformed from the spiritual world, through the inspirations of his father, Giovanni Santi (who died young), into a yearning for higher *beauty* which filled him on the Earth, and which he then embodied in his works of art.[313] Their principal theme was reflected in his numerous portrayals of the Luke Mary and the Nathan Soul, to whose pure unfallen etheric forces (which in their primordial purity are still related to the principle of the Life-Spirit) his soul was ever inclined. The creative work of Raphael was filled with the constant yearning again to resurrect in his works the primordial etheric forces of the Tree of Life, and throughout his short life his whole soul was devoted to an inner contemplation of the Luke Mary and the Nathan Soul, whose imagination again and again appeared before his inner eye.[314]

Raphael yearned for the complete purifying and spiritualising of the intellectual- or mind-soul, which arises out of the forces of man's etheric body and is evolving towards its higher archetype, the Life-Spirit.[315] This is the reason for his being inwardly attracted to the world of antiquity, the fourth post-Atlantean period, when the intellectual- or mind-soul was actually developed. From a spiritual point of view, Raphael, with his high ideal of beauty, was, more than any of his contemporaries, inwardly a true representative of the Renaissance. This also comes to expression in that Raphael in his earthly life was, in fact, unable to pass beyond the bounds of the intellectual- or mind-soul. He dies in his thirty-seventh year, less than two years after the completion of the fifth seven-year period of his life.[316]

Even a cursory examination of the portrayals of the Madonna and Child in Raphael's paintings can enable one to feel what a power of love must have filled his soul, and how pure his heart must have been to be able to create *such* pictures. After the powerful and deeply tragic shocks of his early childhood (the occult foundations of which have already been indicated in the present book)[317] the whole of the rest of his life, until his premature death, was of an exceptionally harmonious and cloudless character. Wilhelm Kelber, in his book on Raphael, refers to this as follows: 'Raphael's life from his eleventh year onwards is probably the happiest human life that we know. No event from the subsequent years of his life is known which signifies a misfortune, a failure, a disappointment or an adverse destiny. The waves of time have taken him joyfully on their backs and borne him from one goal to the next. If we knew nothing of the family events in his childhood, we would have to have thought something of the kind in order to explain such a favourable manner of life on Earth.'[318]

In order that we may understand this remarkable phenomenon, so unusual for that stormy and eventful age, it is necessary to recall a remark that Rudolf Steiner once made: only the life of a man who has a super-abundance of forces of love in his soul can, under certain conditions, acquire such an exceptionally light-filled and harmonious character; for the forces of love, if they are rooted in a heart of absolute purity, also have the capacity to draw towards themselves, from the surroundings, only forces of love. Indeed, there was hardly anyone amongst the artists, poets, or worthies of either Church or State who was so loved by those around him as was Raphael. But all the same, this all-prevailing love was in a deeper sense no more than an outward reflection, a kind of echo, of that great love which he himself bore within his soul and so generously bestowed on his surroundings.

Raphael's younger contemporary and the biographer of many of the eminent artists of that time, Vasari, described his basic soul-quality in the following words: 'Amongst his particular gifts there is one that I find of such significance that I am quietly amazed how heaven could have given him the power, an artist amongst artists, to bring forth an effect so contrary to what one would naturally expect, namely, that artists, whenever they worked together with Raphael, were at once of the same mind and so harmonious that every trace of ill-humour fled before his face and every mean and vulgar thought fell from their souls; a mood of concord that had otherwise never reigned. The fact of the matter was that they were under the spell of his friendliness and capabilities, and, moreover, under the sway of the genius of his good nature. This was so filled with noble amiability, so overflowing with a benevolent *love*, that one saw even the animals bore him reverence and men were reduced to silence. The story runs that whenever a painter with whom he was familiar, or whom he hardly even knew, came to him about a drawing that he needed, Raphael left his work in order to be of help to him. And there were always countless numbers at work with him whom he supported and instructed with a *love* as though he were approaching not artists but his own sons.' Vasari also emphasises when describing Raphael's life, in contrast to his biographies of other eminent artists, that with him 'it was a matter of keeping on the same level as both artist *and man*.'[319] We may sense something of these qualities of Raphael in his famous self-portrait, painted around 1506, despite the fact that it has been severely damaged through repeated restorations in the eighteenth and nineteenth centuries (see Plate 4).

All that has been said hitherto about sympathy and love as the

113

fundamental soul-impulses of Raphael also has a direct relationship with a profound mystery of his spiritual life to which Rudolf Steiner referred in his 'Last Address' in terms of the consequences, as manifested in the depths of Raphael's inner life, of his supersensible participation at the Turning-Point of Time in the initiation and subsequent earthly destiny of Lazarus–John, the future author of the Apocalypse and the fourth Gospel: 'This earthly personality of Raphael was completely yielded up and was only present through what Lazarus–John gave to this soul to be poured out in colour and line for all mankind.'[320]

What was Lazarus–John, the 'disciple whom the Lord loved' (John 13:23), able to give to the entelechy of Raphael? Only that for which the Lord Himself particularly loved him, namely, that capacity of his which Rudolf Steiner described at some length in the concluding chapter of *Occult Science*: his sublime capacity of transforming wisdom into love in his true, Christ-filled ego. For herein consisted the fundamental mystery of the initiation of Lazarus, where through contact with the Christ-sphere all the ancient wisdom of mankind which he had gathered in his former incarnations gradually succumbed to death, in order again to resurrect from his ego, through the mediation of the Christ-impulse, as the highest faculty of love. From this time forth the motif of spiritual love becomes the fundamental motif of the rest of John the Evangelist's life. 'God is love' (1 John: 4-8)—these words represent for him the highest spiritual experience, from which derive his last earthly words spoken by him to his followers and pupils before his death as a kind of final testament to all mankind: 'Little children, let us love one another.'[321]

Thus under the influence of this supersensible relationship, Raphael—according to what Rudolf Steiner says in the 'Last Address'—was able to become the one 'who on Earth had unfolded *so great a love* for art, whose soul had *been aflame with love* for colour and for line.'

Both the chief characteristics of the soul-disposition of John the Baptist and Raphael, which we designated as the impulse of conscience in the case of the one and an unusual capacity of love and a sympathy for all living things in the case of the other, also find, echo-like, their reflection in the work of Novalis. Thus in the second part of his unfinished novel, *Heinrich von Ofterdingen*, we find some remarkable words regarding the significance of conscience in human life, an inspired poetic hymn which reveals the high purpose assigned to this divine power within man. 'Awakening voices of higher Nature' within man is what Novalis calls it through the mouth of Sylvester, one of the heroes of the novel: 'Make the nature of conscience intelligible to me' Heinrich asks him. 'If I were able to do that,' answers Sylvester, 'I would be God, for in so far as one comprehends conscience, it arises.' Then Heinrich himself tries to define what the voice of conscience within man actually is: 'Conscience itself,' he says, 'this power that engenders meaning and worlds, this germ of all personality, appears to me as the spirit of the world-poem . . .' To this Sylvester replies: 'Conscience is manifest in every serious ending, in every fully formed truth. Every inclination, every capacity formed into a picture of the world through thinking becomes a manifestation, a transformation of conscience. All training leads to what one can only call freedom, by which is meant not a mere concept, but the creative ground of all existence. Freedom is mastery . . . And it is precisely this all-embracing freedom, mastery or dominion that is the essential nature, the impulse of conscience. In it is revealed the holy uniqueness, the untramelled creativity of the personality, and every action of the master is at the same time a part of the process of getting to know the high, simple, uncomplicated world—the Word of God.' And then, in answer to further questions of Heinrich, Sylvester continues: 'Indeed conscience is the innate mediator within every man. It takes the place of God on Earth and is, accordingly, for so many the highest and the last. But how removed has been the kind of learning that has prevailed hitherto—which has been called a doctrine of virtue or morality—from the pure form of this sublime, fully comprehensive, personal thought. *Conscience is a man's most personal nature in its most radiant form, the heavenly human archetype.*'

In these final, italicised words appears what could be called the most intimate soul motif of John the Baptist's entire life. We should seek its origin in the scene where Mary visits his mother Elisabeth, as described in the first chapter of the Gospel of St Luke, when as Mary, who is carrying the Nathan Jesus, the sister-soul of Adam, 'the heavenly human archetype', approached her, 'the babe leaped in her womb' (v. 41). In this scene we have to do with the beginning of John the Baptist's 'ego' development; and this development is called forth while he is still within his mother's womb *through the impulse of conscience*, which is at this moment awakened within him for the first time by 'the heavenly human archetype' (the Nathan Jesus-child), who represents his (John's) 'most personal nature in its most radiant form.'[322] This first awakening within the young John of the impulse of conscience, as a new organ of knowledge, is manifested with such power that this impulse is also transmitted to his mother, which is how she is able to acknowledge and proclaim this profound mystery to her visiting relative: 'And Elisabeth was filled with the Holy Spirit and she exclaimed with a loud voice: "Blessed are you among women, and blessed is the fruit of your womb!

And why is this granted to me, that the mother of my Lord should come to me . . .?' (vv. 41–43).[323]

Let us return to the conversation of Heinrich and Sylvester from the second part of Novalis' novel. After further elucidations on the part of the latter, Heinrich again returns to the theme of conscience in the following words: 'Everything which makes experience and earthly effectiveness intelligible belongs to the sphere of conscience which connects this world with higher worlds.'

In these words of Heinrich, Novalis' understanding of the true place of conscience in human evolution as a higher organ of knowledge, as a connecting thread or as the true 'religio' between the heavenly and the earthly worlds, finds its expression. Thus in the next speech of Heinrich the theme of conscience passes over directly into that of religion, and the theme of religion into the theme of love, into an inner sense of 'the divine presence of the most personal Being, or . . . of *His love* in our deepest selves.' Here the memories of his life as John the Baptist, which worked latently within Novalis, change into memories of his life as Raphael. It was not for nothing that Novalis wrote his profoundest observations about the cosmic significance of the principle of love (see p. 75), when he had just seen Raphael's *Sistine Madonna* in Dresden for the first time. In the same way, one of the most perceptive poems from his poetic cycle *Spiritual Songs* testifies to his inner connection with the life of Raphael. For the supersensible image of Mary and her holy child, which he bears within his soul, is at the same time a reawakening of those spiritual experiences which had once led Raphael to the creation of his Madonnas and, in particular, to the most perfect of them, the 'Sistine':

> In countless pictures I behold you,
> Mary, lovingly portrayed,
> But none of all these can depict you
> As my own soul sees you arrayed . . .

And in the next poem:

> Oft, when I dreamed, I saw you there,
> With heart so inward, and so fair.
> The child-God from your arm is bending,
> His playmate's grief in pity tending;
> But you uplift your gaze on high
> Withdrawing to the glory of the sky.

116

These lines are reminiscent of that brief story which Raphael once related to the famous sculptor Bramante in answer to his question as to how he, Raphael, had been able to achieve such an inimitable perfection in his portrayals of the Madonna and Child. There he speaks of a nocturnal dream experience,[324] in the course of which, in answer to his repeated inner requests and prayers, the as yet unfinished picture hanging on the wall of his studio suddenly turned into a sublime vision of Mary with the holy Child in her arms.[325] Thus like mighty spiritual waves, the conscious–unconscious memories which Novalis cherishes of his two previous lives, with their powerful impulses of conscience and love, rise up from the depths of his soul.

However, everything in the world is in continuous development. Thus in Novalis' life, too, something new is now added to these two impulses. For just as conscience was a fundamental aspect of the soul disposition of John the Baptist, and love and sympathy for everything that lives a fundamental soul quality of Raphael, so if we now turn directly to Novalis himself we can also find in him one particularly characteristic trait which is at the same time a sort of key for understanding his whole personality and its disposition of soul. This trait or particular characteristic, which belonged to Novalis from the very beginning and formed his whole soul-life from within, can be defined as: 'reverence and wonder before the facts of the world'.[326]

If, in a wholly unprejudiced way, we contemplate the only authentic portrait of Novalis, that of Franz Gareis (as it was before its recent restoration), and also the sculpture of Friedrich von Schaper, we may become convinced in a fully objective way of the validity of the above statement.[327] In this fundamental characteristic of Novalis' disposition is also rooted that particular impression of enlightened and wise childlikeness which he almost invariably made upon those who were around him. This was, however, no ordinary 'childlikeness' but the revelation of the higher forces of *reverence and wonder* that worked within his soul, the presence of which gave to his face this unrepeatably individual expression of, at once, 'childlikeness' and the deepest, primordial wisdom—qualities which were indissolubly united in an all-embracing feeling of wonder at all the miracles and secrets of the world. It was this feeling of wonder which streamed from his face like rays of an invisible sun.

Albert Steffen once referred to this fundamental soul-quality of Novalis in the following words: 'Novalis feels wonder before he thinks, and hence his thoughts about everything which he sees on the Earth are associated with the origin of the same.'[328] Perhaps the most convincing confirmation of this characteristic of Novalis is the whole world of his

117

Fragments which, like the diamond sparks of a rushing mountain stream, express in the most diverse hues above all wonder and reverence for the mysteries of world-existence that surround us everywhere. Is not his prose fragment, *The Novices at Saïs*, an inspired poetic hymn, at whose foundation lies a feeling of infinite wonder and reverence for the innumerable mysteries of the kingdoms of nature, and his unfinished novel, *Heinrich von Ofterdingen*, a testimony of wonder and reverence for the mysteries of human life and poetic creativity? Finally, are not his poem-cycles, *Hymns to the Night* and *Spiritual Songs*, in the whole of their inner mood, the purest expression of wonder and reverence for the profound secrets of the spiritual world, secrets which find their sublime focus in the Mysteries of Christianity? Truly, the creative output of Novalis is, in its whole inner orientation, none other than an expression of that 'fundamental mood' which Rudolf Steiner characterises as the foundation and point of departure of any true spiritual path and which he calls 'the *path of veneration*, of devotion to truth and knowledge'.[329] It was this mood—which in our time represents the gate to the spiritual temple of the modern Mysteries, and is for this reason the *first* to be spoken of in the book, *Knowledge of the Higher Worlds*—which formed the foundation of the soul-life of Novalis. Thus in the soul-disposition of Novalis we find, in a certain sense, a contrast to what we encounter in John the Baptist. For if the fundamental inner impulse of the latter—that of conscience—relates to the life after death (see p. 24), the fundamental soul quality of Novalis relates, in contrast, particularly *to the life before birth*.[330] In his 'Last Address', Rudolf Steiner characterises this existence of Novalis before birth as the supersensible life of 'Raphael' in the planetary spheres, and at the end of his description he says: 'He [Novalis] wants to pass over into the supersensible, *to lead again the life of Raphael* [in the spiritual world] and not really touch the Earth . . .'[331] The content of these words can be deepened still further through observations of Rudolf Steiner about the forces which Novalis, in his creative work, drew directly from his spiritual past. For example, in the lecture of 22 December 1908 he says: 'In the case of Novalis we cannot really speak of an [ordinary] single life, for his was like a memory of an earlier life.'[332]

However, the soul qualities of wonder and reverence are not only the consequences of the spiritual life of the human soul before birth and in previous incarnations but are also active forces in the present. For according to Rudolf Steiner, it is these qualities which in our time lead man in his inner development beyond the confines of the earthly world into the realm of the supersensible or, in Novalis' words, into the all-embracing spiritual sphere of the *night*. But on this path there is a further, *third* quality which needs to be added, one that in our fifth post-Atlantean epoch occupies what could be described as a central position on the horizon of the soul-life of mankind. This soul quality or faculty is that of *faith*: 'Indeed,' says Rudolf Steiner in this connection, 'it is always this wonder and this astonishment which guide us to the supersensible [to the "realm of night" in Novalis' words], and it is at the same time also that quality which one usually calls faith. Faith, wonder and astonishment are the three soul forces which lead us out beyond the ordinary world.'[333]

In our time of stormy scientific and technological development and strongly growing intellectualism, *faith*, it would seem, plays an ever diminishing role in human life, and yet it is the forces of faith, according to modern spiritual science, which are the principal source of the spiritual forces that nourish the fifth post-Atlantean epoch, just as the forces of love will nourish the sixth, and the forces of hope the seventh cultural epoch. 'Thus at present it is essentially the power of faith, in the astral body, which shines into the soul and gives our age the characteristic ... that the power of faith is the most significant force of our time,' as Rudolf Steiner says.[334] In this occult sense, faith is not in the least at variance with true knowledge. 'I believe what I know for certain.—*Knowledge is but the foundation of faith*. We should know in order that we may ever more be able to rise to the forces which represent the forces of faith in the human soul.' This is what Novalis has in mind when he says: 'Science is only one half, faith is the other.' And in another fragment: 'Faith is a mixture of will and knowledge.' Rudolf Steiner then continues in the same lecture: 'In our soul we must have what enables us to look towards a supersensible world, what can direct all our thoughts and ideas towards such a world. If we do not possess forces such as are expressed in the word "faith", something within us is laid waste, we become parched and dried up like the leaves of Autumn.'[335] Faith, according to the way it is defined by spiritual science, is that fundamental power of the human astral body which alone is capable of directing all our thoughts and ideas towards the supersensible world. And Novalis understands it in the same sense: 'The *wondrous power of faith*—all faith is wonderful and wonder-working. God is in the moment when I have faith in Him ... Faith represents the influences and sensations of another world *perceived in this one*—it is the perception of a transmundane act. True faith relates only to the things of another world. To have faith is to have awareness of waking and working and sensing in another world.'/And in another fragment he puts it still more clearly: 'Man has the possibility of being a supersensible being in every moment. Without this he would not be a world-citizen—he would be an animal. To be sure, presence of mind in this condition, the finding of oneself, is very difficult, in that such a condition is so ceaselessly, so necessarily, bound up with changes in the rest of our situation. But the more we are able to be conscious of this condition, the more living, powerful and satisfying is the conviction that arises out of it—faith in true revelations of the spirit.'

In other words: only a man who experiences himself as a spiritual, supersensible being can have 'faith in true revelations of the spirit.'

In these last words of Novalis we have a prophetic anticipation of that profound metamorphosis which will in future, beginning from our present twentieth century, gradually have to take place with regard to the power of faith within the human soul. This higher metamorphosis of the power of faith in earthly evolution is directly connected with the new appearance of Christ in the etheric body. Rudolf Steiner refers to this as follows: 'We have also pointed out that the capacities of human beings will be enhanced and that, from our epoch onwards, a sufficiently large number of people will grow up able to behold the Christ, so that what has hitherto had a justified place in the world as faith will be succeeded by what may be called the vision of Christ.'[336] Novalis, too, knows of this future transition of the power of faith into the forces of higher supersensible vision. He knows of this not through a dim mystical feeling but directly from his own personal experience of Christ, from his Damascus event. He experiences the Christ Being, in a supersensible vision that is born of a flaming faith, as the highest revelation of 'Heaven on Earth'. It is to an experience of such 'visionary faith' that he summons all other human beings:

> For all His thousand gracious gifts
> His humble child I will remain.
> We know that He is in our midst
> When two are gathered in His name.
> O go ye forth throughout the land,
> And bring the erring ones inside,
> Stretch out to everyone your hand,
> That they with cheer may with us bide.
> *Heaven's reign on Earth has now begun,*
> *In faith we may behold its light;*
> For those who in our faith are one
> The heavens are open to their sight.[337]

Thus we may see that in the future, which is already here, the old form of faith, based as it is on a more or less vague feeling, yields its place to a higher vision which will, however, be none other than a further and higher metamorphosis of that same power of faith, in man's astral body. For if Rudolf Steiner calls the power of faith the fundamental spiritual power of the astral body and, through this, of the *whole* fifth post-Atlantean epoch, of which the first third has not yet passed, it really cannot be said that the power of faith is going to disappear from human evolution—on the contrary, it will continue to work within man, with an ever-growing strength, and will undergo a process of ever higher metamorphosis.

Rudolf Steiner speaks as follows about the significance of the power of faith for man's astral body and also for the present cultural epoch: 'This is what we may call that human sheath in which the power of faith is active, and we may name it the faith-soul or—as I prefer—the faith body. It is the same as that to which we have hitherto given the more abstract name of astral body. *The most important power of the astral body is the power of faith*, so the terms of 'astral body' and 'faith body' are equally justified.' And in the following lecture: 'The sheath to which yesterday we gave the name of faith body is mirrored or reflected in human souls [astral bodies] in our present *fifth* epoch.'[338]

We can, however, understand this metamorphosis, through which the power of faith is now passing within the human astral body, only if we consider one further process taking place today in man's astral body. This second process is connected with the extraordinary development in the modern world of the forces of the intellect. Thus with regard to the astral body of a human being of our time, we must say: its foundation is the power of faith that works within it, while into the sphere of this power intellectual forces of the greatest strength have been introduced as a result of the cultural development of mankind over the course of the last few centuries. There are two ways out of this situation. One possibility is that the intellectual forces, through becoming wholly materialistic in character, will lead to the destruction of the power of faith, in man's astral body, as a result of which the astral body will gradually become 'parched and dried up as the leaves in Autumn', and human life on Earth will be increasingly filled with insuperable 'fear, worry and anxiety' and also with what Rudolf Steiner defines by the word 'nervousness', which leads to the gradual sickness of the whole soul body.[339] The other outcome, in contrast, is that the power of faith within the human soul is *strengthened* to such a degree that in its yearning for the supersensible it is also able—so to speak—to embrace the intellectual principle, that is, the power of thinking, which similarly flows through the astral body. However, this will be possible only when the power of faith in the astral body is permeated by a real *moral will* which is directed towards a new knowledge of the supersensible worlds in accordance with the present stage of evolution. Rudolf Steiner speaks as follows about the need for this process: 'Progress will only be made in this respect when men not only develop a heightened intellect for themselves, but also lift it up into the astral world.' This is possible today only with the help of the metamorphosed forces of faith. For *only a faith which is permeated by a will that strives towards higher knowledge is capable of transforming the modern intellect into a new capacity of conscious clairvoyance.* '. . . In the course of the next three thousand years the etherically visible Christ can and will approach ever more clearly the man who has advanced to intellectual clairvoyance in this way.'[340]

Novalis, too, refers in the following words to such a transformation of the intellectual forces—with the help of forces of faith which have been permeated by sacrificial will—into a higher faculty of spiritual vision which leads to a direct experience of the Christ: 'In the will is the ground of creation. Faith is the effect of the will upon the intellect . . .' And so in this process faith is manifested no longer as the bearer of vague feelings that have nothing to do with knowledge, but as a *mediator*, with whose help a creative, moral will—which could also be regarded as a 'selfless prayer'—permeates the intellectuality of the human head in meditation and bears it (and with it also human *self-knowledge*) into the spiritual world, thus making man one who, with the help of a spiritualised intelligence, is able consciously to behold such a world. This power of faith is what Rudolf Steiner, in a somewhat different connection, first described as 'a special power of wisdom' and then as 'a special power of spirit-wisdom.'[341]

With this we have the only true picture of the faith of the future, the metamorphosed faith which is capable of becoming a new spiritual organ for the conscious perception of supersensible facts and, above all, for the moral will which comes to birth in the spiritual world and which is made conscious with the help of the spiritualised intelligence—and is then experienced by man as *free* will: 'Faith is the perceiving of the *realised will.*'

The above two quotations from Novalis bear witness to his remarkable insight into the future nature of faith as the 'visionary faith' of the new age of light. In these observations Novalis truly touches upon the deepest motivating forces of the fifth post-Atlantean epoch and also upon the fundamental mystery of the human astral body as the source and bearer of the power of faith within man.

If in this connection we recall that in the astral body of Novalis there worked the forces of the imprint of the astral body of Jesus of Nazareth (the Nathan Soul), it becomes ever clearer to us why, in his brief earthly life, Novalis became not only the first prophet of the 'visionary faith' of the future but also its first representative:

Heaven's reign on Earth has now begun,
In faith we may behold its light . . .

And merely by knowing *what* the word 'faith' means in the mouth of
Novalis, it is possible really to understand the words which appear in his
letter to the district official, Just, written during his last illness in
November 1800 and sounding like his spiritual testament: 'Religion is the
great Orient in us, which seldom becomes dull. Without it I would be
unhappy. Thus does everything unite in One great, peaceful thought, in
One *still, eternal faith.*'

This mystery of the future metamorphosis of the power of faith within
man was, however, not the only mystery of the future which was
revealed to Novalis' spiritual eyes alongside what has already been
described regarding his insight into the past evolution of the Earth and of
humanity.

There were many other mysteries of the future in its connection with
the further evolution of the Christ-impulse which were revealed to his
inner eye—and in particular one which is especially connected with his
own future mission amongst mankind. Such a clear awareness of this
future mission of Novalis can also help us to come closer to an
understanding of this remarkable individuality. If at this point we recall
that we were able to characterise the fundamental soul qualities of John
the Baptist simply with the word *conscience*, the fundamental soul
qualities of Raphael with the words *love* and *sympathy* for everything
living, and that in the case of Novalis we were able to discern as the
fundamental characteristic of his soul disposition *faith, reverence* and
wonder before the mysteries of world-being that were revealed to his
inner eye, it follows from this sequence of soul conditions that we have
a clear picture of that high task, that essential mission, which it will
eventually be Novalis' lot to accomplish amongst mankind in the course
of his further service of the Christ Being and for which his three
incarnations at and after the Turning-Point of Time were a preparation.
For according to what has been given through modern spiritual science,
these three groups of soul qualities—conscience; love and sympathy;
wonder, reverence and faith—will in the future which, however, is
already our present, be those soul-spiritual substances out of which the
cosmic Being of the Christ will gradually fashion for Himself His sheaths
amongst mankind: the physical body out of all the deeds of the human
conscience (John the Baptist anticipates this stage through the fact that by
means of his Baptism he opens the gate for the direct union of God with
man's *physical body*);[342] the etheric body out of all manifestations of love

123

and compassion; and the astral body out of all feelings of faith, wonder and reverence before the mysteries of existence.

As to how this task of first preparing and then leading mankind towards this lofty goal appeared in full actuality, at a certain moment of his life before Novalis' inner eye, the following words of Rudolf Steiner, in which he describes the inner revelations of the poet-visionary, bear witness: 'Novalis is also aware of the mighty truth that, since the event of Golgotha, the Being we call Christ has been the planetary Spirit of the Earth, the Earth-Spirit by whom the Earth's body will gradually be transformed. He sees the body of the Earth gradually becoming the body of Christ. And in a miraculous deed of co-operation, all that is of Earth and all that is of Christ become one before his eyes: he sees the Earth in future time as a *great organism* in which man is embedded and whose soul is Christ.'[343] A little later he says, even more clearly: 'And whereas human beings of ancient times looked back to the primeval Gods, yearning to be united with them in death, Novalis recognises the God *who in time to come will have as His body all that is best in us and which we can offer* [as deeds of conscience, love, wonder and faith] *to the body of Christ.* He recognises Christ as that Being *to whom humanity offers itself in order that He may have a body.*'[343] It is this deep insight which Rudolf Steiner calls 'the greatest event of his life', 'the uniquely great insight into the Christ Being'. Thus does the ancient past unite for Novalis with the distant future of humanity and the Earth into one indissoluble whole.

As the individuality who bears within himself the first man, Adam, his personal cosmic-earthly destiny encompasses the deepest sources of earthly humanity, when it was still in the paradisaical state of childhood and inseparably connected with the world of the higher Gods: 'Thus Novalis was able to behold those times when the Gods lived amongst men, when everything ran its course in a spiritual way, when the spirits and souls [of human beings] had not yet descended into earthly bodies.'[344] Moreover, Novalis was, in his inner eye, able to behold his own connection with the Turning-Point of Time, when he was the first amongst men to recognise Christ on the Earth,[345] and as a result of this entered upon a spiritual path which is wholly united with the sublime perspectives of the future evolution of the Earth and humanity—in so far as this is connected with the further working of Christ amongst mankind—and which is also a revelation of the future mission of Novalis himself: 'But this Christ-impulse at first finds nothing with which it can clothe itself. Therefore it must obtain a sheath through the further evolution of the Earth, and when the Earth has come to its end, the fully evolved Christ shall be the final man—as Adam was the first man—around whom humanity will have gathered in all its multiplicity.'[346]

Novalis refers to this great future of humanity in the following words: 'All these are no more than indications, disjointed and unrefined, but they reveal to the historical eye a universal individuality, a new history, a new humanity, the sweetest embrace of a young, astonished Church and a loving God, and the ardent receiving of a new Messiah amongst its thousand members all at the same time.' As he did not as yet have at his disposal the benefit of spiritual-scientific concepts for giving expression to this sublime truth, Novalis calls this future condition of 'Godmanhood' either 'a universal individuality' or 'a new humanity', or else he uses the picture of a mystical Church of the future. What he really wanted to say could hardly be better expressed than did Rudolf Steiner in the following words, which he spoke wholly in the spirit of the above description of Novalis' inner experiences: 'We see humanity in perspective before us, like a great organic formation. As human beings come to understand how to make their actions part of this great organism, and through their own deeds weave their impulses around it like sheaths, they shall then in the course of earthly evolution lay the foundations for a great community which can be permeated and made Christian through and through by the Christ-impulse.' In these words we have a comprehensive description of the entire future mission of Novalis amongst mankind, the preparations for which were made in those three incarnations when he presented humanity with successive archetypes of that path whereby it will be able in future to fashion sheaths for the Christ Being: manifesting, in his incarnation as John the Baptist, the mystery of the fashioning of the physical sheath[347]; in his incarnation as Raphael, the mystery of the fashioning of the etheric sheath; and in his incarnation as Novalis, the mystery of the astral sheath, thus laying the spiritual foundation for his future earthly task. But this is not all. As he himself passed through these three stages, the physical, etheric and astral, he at the same time prepared himself for attaining in this process of development a still higher stage, that of the ego, in order then—from his next incarnation onwards wholly permeated by the Christ-impulse even in his ego—to appear as a Master before mankind and to lead it to the fulfilment of the goal referred to above: that of working out of the forces of conscience, love, wonder and 'visionary faith' upon the creation of 'a great community which can be permeated and made Christian through and through by the Christ-impulse.'

In this future mission of Novalis, to the fulfilment of which all his subsequent incarnations will be dedicated, we also have a certain counter-pole to what in deep antiquity, in the Lemurian age, entered into human evolution *through* the individuality of Adam. As in that distant time it was Adam who was the 'instrument' in the hands of the world-rulership with whose help humanity, in its paradisaical innocence, was to enter upon the path towards earthly being, so in future this individuality will have the task of occupying the leading position in the process of mankind's gradual return to its original cosmic state, in the process of its new ascent to those spiritual spheres whence it formerly descended in order to find freedom and individual ego-consciousness on Earth. This will be the highest expression of that all-embracing cosmic law according to which every human individuality who has accomplished some kind of significant deed within the context of the spiritual evolution of humanity must, in course of time, repeat this deed, though now as a certain polarity with regard to the first deed, so that through the second deed the consequences of the first deed can be turned, for the good of the further evolution of the Earth, into their opposite.[348]

This polarity in the cosmic-earthly activity of the individuality of Adam is formed, on the one hand, by the process of the gradual descent of humanity from the spiritual sphere into the earthly as a result of the so-called 'Fall' and, on the other, by its future, but then fully conscious, re-ascent into the sphere of spirit as a result of the gradual forming in its midst of the 'great immortal Individual.'[349] For what this individuality, in the three incarnations referred to above manifests to us as the impulses of conscience, compassion, wonder and 'visionary faith' is none other than the beginning of the fulfilment of the *essential meaning of the whole of earthly evolution*, the beginning of balancing out the world-karma of mankind, a task to which it will be the principal mission of Novalis to make a contribution. '*The purpose of Earth-evolution* is that there may be implanted into the evolutionary process, as a whole, powers which could otherwise never have come into existence—astonishment, wonder, compassion and conscience'[350]—in order that by the end of evolution on Earth a condition will have been reached which can be regarded in the highest sense as a counter-pole of the original paradisaical condition of mankind. This higher condition can be brought about only if human beings gradually transform the Earth in accordance with its new planetary Spirit—the Christ—through the fashioning of His sheaths: 'When the Earth has attained its goal, it will, like man, be a fully developed being which befits the Christ-impulse . . . when the goal of Earth-evolution is attained, He [Christ] will be enveloped in the threefold vesture woven from the powers that have lived in men and which, when the limitations of man's lower ego have been transcended, will become the sheaths of Christ.'

Thus at the conclusion of earthly evolution there will be a renewal of that primordial condition of a direct connection with the divine-spiritual world which is described in the first two chapters of the Book of Genesis. In the penultimate chapter of the Apocalypse, John the Evangelist refers to this future condition of the Earth in the following words: 'And I heard a great voice from the throne saying: "Behold, the dwelling of God is with men. He will dwell with them, and they shall be His people, and God Himself will be with them; He will wipe away every tear from their eyes, and death shall be no more, neither shall there be mourning nor crying nor pain any more, for the former things have passed away" (21:3–4).' These words form, in the wonderful compositional structure of the Bible, a counter-poise to the words which Jahve–Elohim speaks to Adam when he is driven out of Paradise.[351] Hence the writer of the Apocalypse continues: 'And He said to me, "It is completed! *I am the Alpha and the Omega, the beginning and the end*" (21:6), that is, the beginning and end of ego-development, which began when Adam (and through him the whole of mankind) was endowed with the principle of the ego (Genesis 2:7), and will culminate in the highest point of the evolution of this ego, with its readiness fully to unite with the next principle, the Spirit-Self, so that wholly united they will make the transition to a new cosmic aeon. But—as has been described—this will come about only when the sheaths have been fashioned amongst mankind with which Christ can be clothed in order that humanity may be led to the Jupiter stage of existence: 'What is physical in our Earth falls away at the end of the Earth period and human souls in their totality pass over into the Jupiter condition, the next planetary condition of the Earth. From the evolutionary stage that it will have reached by then, it passes over to the next stage of Earth evolution, that of Jupiter existence. Just as the ego of an individual human being is the centre of his further evolution, so for the whole of future humanity it will be the Christ Ego in the astral and etheric bodies of men who will go on to ensoul Jupiter existence, in the next stage of planetary evolution.'[352]

This can also be characterised from a more inward point of view. The four group-souls of primordial humanity, which in the terminology of occultism are called 'Bull', 'Lion', 'Eagle', and 'Man' and which passed through their evolution on Old Moon, also came over into the Earth aeon. On the Earth they continued to influence the evolution of humanity from the Sun-sphere until approximately the end of the first third of the Atlantean age.[353] Here forces of the 'Bull' Spirits worked more on the evolution of the human physical body; the 'Lion' Spirits on the etheric body; the 'Eagle' Spirits on the astral body; and the 'Man' Spirits on the evolution of the new-born ego. Subsequently, beginning from the middle of the Atlantean epoch, these four kinds of Spiritual Beings gradually withdrew from the direct guidance of mankind, a necessary prerequisite for the gradual development of man's inner freedom, which is associated with a complete independence from the Spiritual Beings who had formerly served as man's guides. However, in world evolution nothing disappears without trace. And so it is the case that what had been given to mankind at the very beginning of earthly evolution, without man's own participation, must, by the end of Earth evolution, in full freedom and out of the higher spiritual consciousness that will have been acquired, again be attained by human beings as a foundation for the transition to the future Jupiter condition.

In this sense the conscious participation of human beings in the begetting of the 'great immortal Individual' is none other than the re-creation—though now out of man's own inner forces—of that spiritual structure of humanity in which the Sun forces of the 'Bull' Spirits which worked within it at the beginning of earthly evolution will again begin to be active—then, however, imbued with the transforming power of the Christ-impulse—in the physical sheath of the 'immortal Individual'; the forces of the 'Lion' Spirits in the etheric; and the forces of the 'Eagle' Spirits in the astral. As regards the fourth category of Spirits, which at the beginning of earthly evolution worked from the Sun as 'human archetypes', as 'Spirit-men',[354] their activity also appears in a new form—imbued with the Christ-impulse's transforming power—as the 'higher Ego' of all mankind,[355] in order then to unite with the three sheaths fashioned by human beings, and thereby to form the complete embodiment of the 'great immortal Individual'[356] brought by Christ from the Sun to the Earth.*

Thus the whole of earthly evolution will eventually become fused together in one single entity, in so far as its beginning karmically determines its end. And with the fulfilment of the great mission of the Earth, of becoming a complete expression of its new Planetary Spirit, that most ancient individuality of mankind, who, beginning from his incarnation at the Turning-Point of Time and on through his incarnations in the sixteenth and eighteenth centuries, has already been preparing for participation in this mission, is especially deeply connected.

---

* All that has been said above represents at the same time the beginning of the new union of the Earth with the Sun.

10

Novalis and the Birth of the New Mysteries in the Twentieth Century

'The time has come—now no longer shall the mystery be hidden.'

Novalis

All that has been said hitherto about the individuality of Novalis leads us directly to the important question regarding his participation in the founding of the New Mysteries of Michael on Earth in the twentieth century. These Michaelic Mysteries were spiritually anticipated by the *three stages* of the supersensible preparation of Anthroposophy in the higher worlds.[357] Thus according to Rudolf Steiner, in the first third of the fifteenth century a significant spiritual event took place in the spiritual worlds which was enacted in the sphere of the First and Second Hierarchies, as a result of which the cosmic Intelligence was transferred in the human organism from the region of the heart to the nerve-sense organisation, that is, to the region of the head.[358]

This important cosmic event was at that time observed from the sphere of the Sun by Michael and the human souls connected with him, amongst whom was the individuality of the future Raphael. The experience of sharing in these cosmic events led him to the decision to incarnate on Earth in the last third of the fifteenth century (in the year 1483). His intention was to contribute all his forces towards enabling the inner change in man's being, that had been brought about by the Hierarchic Beings, to find its *right* expression in the evolution of earthly humanity—in other words, towards preventing the forces of opposition from making use of this supersensible event and the new cosmic-earthly situation for a complete separation of the activities of the head- and the heart-forces within man. In accordance with the stage that human evolution had reached at that time and the historical conditions that existed on the Earth, the individuality of Raphael chose the fine arts as the most suitable means of attaining this goal.

Thus already at the end of the fifteenth century Raphael was able to bring to the Earth tidings of this cosmic event and the possibility associated with it of a completely new balance between head and heart, a balance which he manifested to humanity as an actual personality throughout his own earthly life and especially through his art. So in the life of Raphael as well as in his art, we have a source of healing and harmonising forces which can also help modern man to establish a right relationship between the intellect which has since then worked within his head and the spiritual forces of his heart.

Today it is very difficult to have even an inkling of the extent to which the fulfilment of this challenging task demanded of Raphael an exertion of all his spiritual and physical forces, especially if one takes into account the number and quality of the works of art which he created in so short an earthly life. However, the semi-conscious memories of what he had experienced in the spiritual world became, in course of time, so powerful in Raphael that only the forces with which his soul had been endowed, as a result of the supersensible connection at the Turning-Point of Time with Lazarus–John, were able to maintain his entelechy in the physical body until 1520.[359] Moreover, these supersensible memories concerned not only the first stage of the cosmic forming of Anthroposophy, but were also connected with his participation in the founding of the second stage, which Rudolf Steiner describes as the supersensible School of Michael in the Sun-sphere. This School arose at the end of the fourteenth century,[360] and once it had received a new cosmic impulse in the first third of the fifteenth century, as a result of its participants having shared in an experience of the event in the region of the higher Hierarchies referred to above, it continued to extend its influence 'through into the eighteenth century'.[361]

Only after the completion of the *entire* period of its supersensible activity does the individuality of Raphael again make the resolve to incarnate on Earth, in order now as Novalis (born in 1772) to bring to mankind tidings of the founding of the new cosmic Christianity that had taken place in the spiritual world under the direct guidance of Michael, a Christianity to which the future evolution of humanity must solely belong if mankind is truly to fulfil its mission on the Earth.

Rudolf Steiner speaks as follows about this message of Novalis, which is reflected in the most diverse ways in his creative work: 'If we examine his writings, we find that he *depicts the future of Christianity from out of its occult truths.*'[362] But with Novalis, as with Raphael, the connection with the earthly world is like a delicate and fragile thread. Thus in 1797, directly after the death of his first bride Sophie von Kühn, he makes the resolve to follow her in death, to return to the spiritual world: 'He wants to pass over at once into the supersensible, to lead again the life of Raphael, without really touching the Earth . . .'[363] For in the inner regions of his soul, he, like Raphael, aspires solely to the spiritual world, though now particularly to the nearest spiritual sphere, where at this time, at the end of the eighteenth and the beginning of the nineteenth century, the supersensible imaginative cult takes place in which Novalis feels himself in a semi-conscious way called to participate.[364]

In the year 1801, as a consequence of the inner resolve which he had made, Novalis crossed the threshold of death, in order, in the immediate spiritual surroundings of the Earth, directly to participate in the supersensible cult, the third and final stage of the heavenly preparation of Anthroposophy. Thus the individuality whom we are considering in a twofold way—as Raphael and as Novalis—was 'sent down by the Michael stream as a messenger to men on Earth' in order to bring to mankind tidings initially of the first and then of the second stage of the supersensible preparation of Anthroposophy in the bosom of the cosmic stream of Michael, thereby in these two incarnations 'preparing through art and through poetry the true Michael mood of soul.'[365]

And although, in accordance with the course of cosmic rulership, Novalis did not, after this, descend to the Earth at the end of the nineteenth century in order during the first quarter of the twentieth century to participate directly in the gradual incarnation of Anthroposophy in the earthly world and in its culmination—the founding of the new Michael Mysteries at Christmas 1923—nevertheless, it was he who was given the task in the spiritual world to be a guide and helper to many of the human souls who were seeking incarnation at the end of the nineteenth and in the twentieth century in order that they might participate *on Earth* in the stream of the New Mysteries. Furthermore, his invisible influence, help and participation can be traced in almost all the principal stages of the incarnation of Anthroposophy, especially from the autumn of 1908 onwards, the year before the Etheric Christ began to work amongst mankind (1909).

More will be said in the next chapter about this supersensible participation of Novalis in the earthly evolution of Anthroposophy. At this point we need to consider especially the direction in which the *earthly* activity of Novalis, from his next incarnation onwards, will unfold. We may attempt to characterise his future earthly mission in the stream of the New Mysteries in the following way.

It has already been shown above (pp. 27 and 46) that the principal inner impulse of all the incarnations of the Novalis individuality has been, from the Turning-Point of Time onwards, his constant yearning for his spiritual archetype, the Nathan Soul—a yearning which led him in his incarnation in the eighteenth century to the Damascus experience, to a prophetic foreshadowing of the etheric appearance of Christ to mankind, which was to begin from the twentieth century onwards.[366] This immutable yearning for the Nathan Soul is also what lies behind the quite particular configuration of his karma, which comes to expression in that, according to the law of spiritual economy, he receives in his incarnation as Raphael an imprint of the etheric body of the Nathan Soul[367] and in his last incarnation as Novalis an imprint of its astral body, whereby he becomes prepared in his next incarnation to embark upon the path leading to a yet higher stage—to receiving into himself one of the imprints of the Ego of Christ Himself which are preserved in the spiritual worlds by the Nathan Soul, and then appearing openly before mankind with his new mission.[368]

In the lecture of 31 May 1909, Rudolf Steiner speaks about the possibility of receiving such an imprint or copy of the Ego of Christ, as preserved within the ego of the Jesus of Nazareth (the Nathan Soul) and then 'multiplied', in the spiritual world. He says: 'For the future development of humanity, the copies of the ego of Jesus of Nazareth are waiting for us in the spiritual world. People who can strive *to the heights of spiritual wisdom and love* are candidates for these copies of the ego of Jesus of Nazareth; they become the Christ-bearers, true Christophori.[369] It is their task on this Earth to be the preparers of His second coming.'[370]

The Novalis individuality has from the very outset been particularly associated with this task of becoming 'on this Earth the preparer for His second coming'. And the reference contained in these words to the necessity of ascending 'to the heights of spiritual wisdom and love' clearly has to do with the preparation for the gradual transition from the fifth to the sixth cultural epoch, to which Rudolf Steiner alludes with absolute clarity in another lecture which he had given two weeks earlier: 'The anthroposophist becomes a living receiver of what is given through the revelation of Jahve–Christ to Moses[371] and to Paul. This is evident from what is said in the fifth letter of the Apocalypse, as the people of the fifth cultural epoch are those who are actually receiving into themselves what will be taken for granted in the cultural period of the community of Philadelphia. The wisdom of the fifth cultural period will blossom as a flower of love in the sixth. Mankind today is called to receive something new and divine into itself and thereby to make the ascent into the spiritual world.'[372] We see from this point of view also in how wonderfully harmonious a way all Novalis' most important spiritual strivings, and also his future mission as the representative of the sixth cultural epoch (see chapter 7), come together in the principal stream of mankind's spiritual evolution, and especially in the impulse of the New Mysteries that takes its course within it.

These New Mysteries are in their turn the continuation and further development of that stream of 'true modern esotericism' which in a spiritual–historical sense goes back to the middle of the thirteenth century,[373] and at whose source we find the leading Master of Christian esotericism, Christian Rosenkreutz, who was worthy of being the *first man* to receive into his ego on Earth an imprint of the Ego of Jesus of Nazareth.[374] In the twentieth century we have in Rudolf Steiner the founder of the modern Christian-Rosicrucian Mysteries amongst mankind and the chief furtherer of the work of Christian Rosenkreutz in our time,[375] through whose earthly activity the possibility of becoming a bearer of the imprint of Jesus of Nazareth's Ego will, from now onwards and ever more in the future, become increasingly accessible not only to high Initiates, but to all those who wish out of their own free will to acquire a new spiritual relationship to Christianity; this is possible today through the receiving of modern spiritual science, of Anthroposophy.

Rudolf Steiner refers in the following words to this world mission of the new Christian Rosicrucian Mysteries, to this fundamental task of 'spiritual–scientific world-movements': 'Part of the mission of spiritual movements in the world is to help human beings to become so mature in soul that in ever-increasing numbers they will be able to receive into themselves an imprint of the Ego of Christ Jesus . . . And here you can realise on what deep foundations spiritual science rests. It is not a theory, not a sum of concepts given merely for the enlightenment of men; it is also a reality and imparts realities to the soul. A man with spiritual understanding and inner experience of Christianity will help to bring it about that, either in the present or in a later incarnation, an imprint of the Ego of the Individuality, who was Christ Jesus, will be woven into his own ego.'[376] From this it follows that this spiritual stream of 'modern esotericism' founded by Christian Rosenkreutz in the thirteenth century, will, in the twentieth century, become accessible to all men of good will, thanks to the spiritual-scientific endeavours of Rudolf Steiner. In the future it will also be taken further by the individuality of Novalis, intimately and deeply connected in the spiritual world as he is with both these Masters. For in aspiring towards the Nathan Soul, as his archetype, Novalis at the same time aspires towards the exalted ideal of the New Mysteries: that of becoming a true 'Christ-receiver' on the Earth, which is to say, being permeated by Him to the very core of his being, to his ego, and hence becoming an active proclaimer of the New Mysteries of the ego amongst mankind.[377]

Thus two karmically determined impulses of Novalis' inner development unite in his mission for the future. His 'microcosmic' aspiration towards receiving into his ego an imprint of the Ego of Jesus of Nazareth (the Nathan Soul) and his 'macrocosmic' aspiration of contributing towards the fulfilment of the most important mission of the Earth: the fashioning of the three sheaths within mankind in which, as a macrocosmic counterpart to the Baptism in the Jordan, the Christ Being will eventually incarnate. This whole process of development will, however, take place against a background of the gradual withdrawal from the Novalis individuality of the higher Hierarchies—a phenomenon which we have been able to trace through his various incarnations, where the Hierarchies from the Spirits of Form to the Angels have successively exerted their influence upon him. For this individuality will work on into the future not out of the inspirations of the Hierarchies, but solely out of the individual impulse of his own ego.[378]

What is distinctive here is the total absence of any relationship on the part of Novalis to the historical Rosicrucian stream. In contrast to Goethe[379], for example, Novalis in his incarnation in the eighteenth century was never directly connected with any of the outward occult associations or esoteric societies—the bearers of traditional occultism. His connection with the Rosicrucian stream, from the outset, rested upon a far deeper foundation. As the source of this connection went back to the events of the Turning-Point of Time, and in particular to sharing supersensibly in the experience of the Mystery of Golgotha through his spiritual bond with John–Lazarus, it was maintained in a quite special way through all the subsequent incarnations of this individuality. In order truly to understand this connection in its full significance it is again necessary to recall that, on the one hand, we have in Novalis the chief preparer and harbinger of the sixth cultural epoch and the future forms of spiritualised Christianity, and, on the other, that, according to Rudolf Steiner's frequent assertions, *Rosicrucian or Johannine Christianity*[380] will in future times be the spiritual foundation of the next cultural epoch,[381] when the final revelation and fulfilment amongst mankind of the Rosicrucian Mysteries, the Mysteries of Christian Rosenkreutz himself, the Mysteries of Johannine Christianity, will take place.

Only upon the foundation of the future revelation of these Mysteries—for which modern Anthroposophy is a preparation—will the true esoteric synthesis of a spiritualised religion, art and science be made possible—a synthesis whose fulfilment will be the most important mystery-deed of Christian Rosenkreutz.[382] The Novalis individuality will, in his future incarnations, play a significant part in the fulfilment of this task.

For his 'future collaboration' with Christian Rosenkreutz in the earthly world the Novalis individuality has been gradually preparing himself during his three incarnations since the Turning-Point of Time. In his incarnation as John the Baptist he develops primarily a *religious* impulse. Hence Rudolf Steiner, in referring to John the Baptist in the lecture of 30 January 1913, speaks of his 'exclusively moral–religious attitude', of how 'his soul was wholly given up to moral–religious impressions.'[383] To these profound religious experiences, which, it is true, were also in a modified form manifest in his next incarnation as Raphael, were now added no less remarkable experiences in the field of art. And, finally, with Novalis the impulse towards *spiritualised science* is joined to his deep religious sense[384] and his boundless devotion to art.

Here we shall cite just two of his observations on this theme. One of these relates to a future spiritualised science of astronomy: 'Metaphysics and astronomy are one science. The Sun is to astronomy what God is to metaphysics. Freedom and immortality will come to be the foundations of *spiritual physics* in the same way that the Sun, light and warmth are the foundations of earthly physics.'

The second observation is an anticipation of the spiritual medicine of the future: 'Every illness is a musical problem—healing a *musical solution*. The shorter and more complete the solution, so much the greater is the musical talent of the doctor.' In other words: every illness is a dissonance which has arisen between the rhythms of the human organism and the rhythms of the cosmos;[385] and every act of healing is really its overcoming, the transformation of this dissonance into a consonance, that which brings all the functions of the human organism into a correspondence and a harmonious interrelationship with the great world or macrocosm. For Novalis, 'the world is the *macro-anthropos*'.

Thus in his last incarnation Novalis comes—not out of some sort of outward inheritance or historical Rosicrucian tradition, but purely out of the karmic guidance of his destiny—to an understanding of the essential tasks of the future evolution of mankind and of the new spiritual synthesis of religion, art and science that is necessary for its fulfilment in the spirit of the true Rosicrucian-impulse: 'The man of culture lives wholly for the future. His life is a struggle; his support and his purpose, *science* and *art*. The more one learns to live no longer in moments but in years and so forth, the more noble one becomes. Hasty agitation and petty spiritual endeavours vanish in the wake of great, peaceful, simple and all-encompassing activity, and a wonderful patience finds its place. *Religion* and morality, these foundations of our existence, become ever more triumphant.'

Or in another Fragment: 'All historical knowledge strives to become mathematical. The mathematical power is the ordering power. All mathematical *knowledge* strives, in turn, to become philosophical—animated or rationalised—then *poetic*—at length moral—and finally *religious*.'[386]

Thus, although he had no direct association with the Rosicrucian stream *on Earth*, Novalis is nevertheless deeply connected with it, and its great founder, in the periods when he is in the spiritual world *between* earthly incarnations. During his life in the supersensible worlds the individuality of Novalis fulfils on each occasion a quite special task, working in the higher worlds as the chief *mediator* and connecting link between the most diverse esoteric streams, which are now to come together on the ground of Anthroposophy.[387] And so, as he is an individuality who is connected in the spiritual world with the stream of the Maitreya-Bodhisattva, which is associated with the figure of Jeshu ben Pandira (see p. 41 and note 23), and at the same time with the Rosicrucian stream, at whose source stands Christian Rosenkreutz, Novalis is able to contribute a considerable degree of intensity towards furthering their spiritual union, in the twentieth century, in modern spiritual science. For it is as a result of their spiritual union that the foundation will be laid for the revelation of the new spiritual sources of Christianity that are associated with the modern Mysteries of the Etheric Christ, with which, as we have seen, the individuality of Novalis is so intimately connected: 'Life [today] is such that the religious longings of men incline towards the Christ, but the true sources of Christianity must be rediscovered. And it is to this end that *we see* the stream of spiritual life proceeding from Jeshu ben Pandira flowing together with that stream which is connected at the beginning of the thirteenth century with Christian Rosenkreutz . . . In this way the two streams work together, the stream of the Maitreya Buddha and the Western stream connected with Christian Rosenkreutz.'[388] The very fact that, in our time, these two streams can work together in the evolving and becoming of the Anthroposophical Movement on Earth is an important result of the mediatory influence of the entelechy of Novalis from the spiritual worlds.

In conclusion, there is one further highly important realm of the mediatory activity of the Novalis entelechy that should be mentioned. This is his direct spiritual mediation in the final and complete union of the *supersensible stream of Michael and the Rosicrucian stream.* In the Middle Ages, and also at the beginning of the modern age, these two streams evolved strictly parallel with one another: the Michael stream in the spiritual worlds and the Rosicrucian stream, the principal stream of Christian esotericism, on Earth. The connection between the two streams, in the periods referred to, was such that certain personalities—'the true Rosicrucians'—fashioned their lives of soul, which they aspired to dedicate to the service of Michael, in such a way that at certain moments of inner meditative concentration they became completely inaccessible to any outer, 'earthly' influences. Because of this, Michael was able to work through the souls of such people, without being in any danger of coming in contact with earthly events. At that time, from the fourteenth until the nineteenth century, this state of affairs was for the Rosicrucians a necessary pre-condition for 'their work with Michael'.[389] Only when they had prepared their souls by strict meditative work and true moral purification, and had also, at certain moments of life, renounced all connection with the earthly world, were the true Rosicrucians able to help Michael in preparing his future mission amongst mankind, a mission which he was to begin to fulfil in the last third of the nineteenth century: 'True Rosicrucianism lies absolutely in the line of activity of the mission of Michael. It helped Michael to prepare on Earth the spirit-work which he wished to prepare for a later age . . . In this way the true Rusicrucian striving formed *for Michael* the path here on the Earth towards *his* coming earthly mission.'

Until the Christmas Conference of 1923 (or until 1914, for as long as the esoteric school of which he was the leader continued to exist), Rudolf Steiner, too, adhered to this strict rule of the medieval Rosicrucians, demanding as it did the complete separation of spiritual work from any outward earthly activity, though with the significant difference that the medieval Rosicrucians were able to experience what was highest in their spiritual life, the meeting with Michael in the spiritual world, only in a lowered, dream-state of consciousness, whereas, since the beginning of the modern age of Michael, it has been possible to experience this meeting in a fully conscious way.[390] Only at the Christmas Foundation Meeting, where he united the Anthroposophical Movement and the Anthroposophical Society into a single whole through taking upon himself the chairmanship—that is, the direct leadership of not only its spiritual but also its earthly affairs[391]—did Rudolf Steiner unite the two streams referred to above: the heavenly stream of Michael and the earthly stream of esoteric Christianity (Rosicrucianism). What had previously been united only in the purely ideal way that has been characterised above was now, in the changed historical circumstances that had arisen through the free deed of one human spirit, united in a new, higher and wholly real unity on the Earth itself.

During the Christmas Foundation Meeting this was brought about in a concretely spiritual way through the fact that the spiritual substance of the Foundation Stone Meditation,[392] which was received directly from the cosmic sphere of Michael, was united, in a cultic act accomplished in the spiritual world nearest to the Earth, with the very essence of the Rosicrucian stream, through the supersensible presence and participation, in this sacred rite, of Christian Rosenkreutz and his closest pupils.[393]

The mantric expression of this new spiritual union was manifested in the insertion of the three Rosicrucian dicta into the spiritual substance of the Foundation Stone Meditation, as the quintessence of the whole of 'modern esotericism'.

This supersensible event took place at the Christmas Foundation Meeting initially *beyond* the threshold of the ordinary consciousness of the members of the Anthroposophical Society who were present. Shortly after it had ended, however, this event was brought with full force and clarity into their day-consciousness. This occurred in the following way.

In the lecture which was given on the anniversary of the burning of the First Goetheanum on the evening of 31 December 1923, the motif of Rosicrucian esotericism again appears[394] with a remarkable intensity, and is then developed further in the lecture cycle which represents a direct continuation of the theme of the evening lectures of the Christmas Foundation Meeting: 'Mystery Centres of the Middle Ages. Rosicrucianism and the Modern Principle of Initiation.' In this cycle, the theme of Rosicrucian esotericism is united more and more with the theme of the cosmic stream of Michael and with a description of the altogether new spiritual circumstances which arose in the evolution of humanity as a result of the beginning of his rulership in the last third of the nineteenth century. Both themes reach their highest culmination and most complete amalgamation in the final lecture of this cycle, which was given on 13 January 1924.

This day, 13 January 1924, has altogether a special significance for the further evolution of the Anthroposophical Society. For on this day the whole esoteric significance of the Christmas Foundation Meeting was alluded to from two important sides. On the one hand, there was the indication in the evening lecture (to which we have referred) to the 'mystical fact' of the union at this conference of the two principal spiritual streams of Christian humanity, the earthly and the heavenly; and, on the other, there was the first publication of the complete text of the Foundation Stone Meditation, as a mantric testimony of this union, in the first edition of the members' supplement to the weekly journal, 'Das Goetheanum'.

In accordance with the occult–cosmic laws connected with the mysteries of the numbers seven and twelve, it was nineteen days after the laying of the Foundation Stone of the General Anthroposophical Society on 25 December 1923 and—associated with it—the first sounding of the words of the Foundation Stone Meditation[395] that these words entered into the cultural life of mankind as a living testimony of the founding at the Christmas Conference of the new Rosicrucian–Michaelic Mysteries, which were for the first time in the whole of human history to unite the exoteric and the esoteric, to unite 'the complete openness [of the Society] with the deepest, most earnest and most inward esotericism.'[396]

From all that has been said in this chapter it is not difficult to feel that the individuality of Novalis is especially strongly connected in the spiritual worlds with the principal task of the new Rosicrucian–Michaelic Mysteries, which are the present-day continuation of the stream of 'modern esotericism' founded by Christian Rosenkreutz in the thirteenth century, and which, after the Christmas Foundation Meeting, stand under the direct guidance of the spirit of Michael.[397] Thus in his incarnation as Elijah, who was so deeply connected with the cosmic sphere of this ruling Sun-Archangel, the individuality of Novalis was, already at that time, able to serve as Michael's chief human instrument for the preparation on Earth of the incarnation of the Sun-Logos. And subsequently, his connection with the sphere of Michael enabled this individuality to become his spiritual envoy in the Christian era, the supersensible helper and guide of a great number of true Rosicrucians in their most inward endeavours to meet the spirit of Michael in the higher worlds, in order then, at the end of the first quarter of the twentieth century, to become, at the Christmas Foundation Meeting, one of the most important supersensible participants in the laying of the Foundation Stone of the New Mysteries, which arose out of the merging of these two occult streams, and were to serve as the foundation for the introduction of the esoteric principle into all realms of human life and practice. For what was the last earthly life of Novalis other than a constant endeavour, with the help of his 'magical idealism', to permeate the whole of earthly existence—even to its most insignificant details—with the spiritual principle, that is, true esotericism? This he accomplished upon the foundation of his clairvoyant insight into the mysteries of the supersensible sphere of Michael-Christ. 'Through the magical idealism of his poetry, he can make the most insignificant material object live again in all its spiritual light and glory.'[398]

Novalis' close friend and first publisher of his works, Ludwig Tieck, also refers to this essential quality of his soul disposition in the following way: 'To him [Novalis] it was the most natural thing in the world to regard the most ordinary and most familiar of objects as a wonder, and the strange and supernatural [the spiritual world] as something ordinary, with the result that everyday life surrounded him like a wonderful fairy story; and that realm which most people would dismiss as remote and inaccessible, or altogether call in question, was to him like a beloved home.'[399] Thus like no one else, Novalis in his last incarnation was a prophet and forerunner of the new Rosicrucian–Michaelic Mysteries. For according to Rudolf Steiner, this was '. . . one being, who came forth from Elijah–John, appearing before mankind in two different forms [as Raphael and as Novalis], *preparing* through art and through poetry *the true Michael mood of soul, sent down by the Michael stream as a messenger to men on Earth.*'[400] And then, turning to all the anthroposophists of the General Anthroposophical Society that had been founded at the Christmas Foundation Meeting, he adds, still more clearly: 'And so we see in Novalis a radiant and splendid forerunner of that Michael stream which is now to lead you all . . . while you are living, and when you have passed through the gate of death.'[401]

As he is one of the most important servants of Michael in the spiritual world, who also participated supersensibly in the Christmas Foundation Meeting and in the ensuing development of the New Mysteries amongst mankind, the individuality of Novalis will in his future incarnations, as a result of his inner connection with the sphere of Michael–Christ and his particular spiritual–karmic predisposition, be a leading individuality in the fulfilment *on the Earth itself* of that task which is the most important fruit of the merging, at the Christmas Conference, of the Rosicrucian principle of initiation[402] with the central spiritual impulses of our time, impulses which since the last third of the nineteenth century have been under the rulership of the new Time-Spirit, Michael. At the end of the lecture of 13 January 1924, Rudolf Steiner speaks about this central task flowing from the very heart of the Christmas Conference: 'The world must, in our time, find the way to receive once more the principle of initiation as such among the principles of civilisation. Only thereby will it come about that man, here on Earth, will gather in his soul something with which he can go before Michael, so as to meet Michael's approving look, the look that says: "That is right, that is cosmically right." Then is the will made firm, and man is incorporated in the spiritual progress of the universe. Then does man become a fellow worker in what is to be instilled into the evolution of humanity and the Earth through Michael, beginning now in this present Michael epoch.' If after reading these words we again look back over all that was undertaken and written by Novalis during his last earthly life, we shall have to say: In the way in which this was possible in his time, Novalis tried, with all the forces of his soul, to prepare the ground for what, in the sense of the above words, could be described as 'the acceptance of the principle of initiation as a principle of civilisation'. He tried to do this, not out of any kind of theoretical knowledge or historical tradition, but above all, because participation in the resolving of this fundamental task of our time is directly connected with the fulfilment of his future mission amongst mankind.

11

Novalis as One of the Supersensible Inspirers of the Modern Science of the Spirit

'Would that men could only know,
Our comrades of the future,
That in every joy of theirs
We actively are with them . . .'

Novalis ('The Song of the Dead')

In the Statutes of the General Anthroposophical Society that were resolved upon at the Christmas Conference of 1923, Rudolf Steiner added the following footnote to No. 2: 'The Anthroposophical Society represents the continuation of the Anthroposophical Society founded in 1912, but it would seek to establish, for the goals that were then defined, an independent point of departure in accordance with *the true spirit of the present time.*'[403] This footnote tells us two things: firstly, that in both foundations of the Anthroposophical Society, in 1912 and 1923, the same goals were set before it; and secondly, that now, in 1923, a new 'independent' point of departure must be established for their attainment, one that is 'in accordance with the true spirit of the present time', that is, in an occult sense, with the ruling Time-Spirit, Michael.

If, therefore, the founding anew of the Anthroposophical Society at the Christmas Conference was accomplished directly out of the Spirit of Michael,[404] it would be the case that at its first founding, in 1912, the Spirit of Michael was represented not directly but through the mediation of an individuality whose association with him in the spiritual worlds had been especially close. This state of affairs corresponds in a spiritual–historical sense fully to the more exoteric founding of the Society in 1912 and the more esoteric founding in 1923.[405]

As we know, its first founding took place in Cologne during the Holy Nights on 28 December 1912, after the final separation from the Theosophical Society.[406] In connection with this, so as to indicate to the newly founded Society its principal spiritual direction from the very start and also to bring the spiritual tasks lying before it to the consciousness of its members with full clarity, Rudolf Steiner chose as the theme for the

141

lecture-cycle which he gave simultaneously with this deed of founding that of 'The Bhagavad Gita and the Epistles of Paul'. He began the first lecture of the cycle with the words 'We are today, in a certain sense, at the starting point of the foundation of the Anthroposophical Society . . .' and at the end of the cycle, returning once more in the final lecture to this initial theme, Rudolf Steiner, having again referred to the Anthroposophical Society, suddenly speaks *twice* about the Anthroposophical Movement: 'For this reason it was this course of lectures which was given at the starting point of the Anthroposophical Movement. . .'[407]

What was the fundamental impulse of this lecture-cycle? The intention was to indicate the relationship of the wisdom of the East—the most mature fruit of the *past* evolution of humanity—to the rising wisdom of Christianity, a wisdom which bears within itself the seeds of mankind's *future* evolution.

It was, however, the concluding lecture, given on 1 January 1913 and signifying at one and the same time the beginning of the new year and the beginning of the activity of the newly founded Anthroposophical Society, which formed the culmination of the entire cycle. In this lecture Rudolf Steiner once again places, with a quite particular depth and exactitude, before the inner vision of his listeners the process of the division on ancient Lemuria, immediately before the Fall, of the soul-structure of the first man into two parts, one of which—the earthly Adam—was then directed by the 'world-rulership' down into earthly evolution, while the other part, in a certain sense his 'sister'—or 'brother'—soul was held back from this descent in the higher worlds: 'Then one must further suppose that beside the human soul nature which incarnated in the body of Adam there was a human entity, a human essence, which remained behind and did not incarnate at that time, which did not enter a physical body but remained in a soul condition. One needs only to visualise that before a physical human being had come into existence within human evolution there was one soul, *which then divided in two*. The one part, the one descendant of the common soul, took on a physical body in *Adam* and thus entering into incarnation, was overcome by Lucifer, and so on. As for the other soul, the sister-soul as one could call it, the wise rulers of the world saw beforehand that it would not be good if it, too, were embodied. It was kept back in the Soul-world; it did not, therefore, take part in the incarnations of humanity but was kept back.[408]

This 'sister-soul of Adam' which remained behind in the spiritual worlds has thenceforth been the heavenly guardian of the 'primal forces of wisdom' and the 'primal forces of love' which in its incarnation on

Earth at the Turning-Point of Time it then embodies in the sheaths of the Luke Jesus.

Later in the same lecture, Rudolf Steiner speaks at some length about the part played in the events of Palestine by the two masters, Zarathustra and Buddha, in order, upon the foundation of a repetition of facts already familiar to anthroposophists, to lead them to a completely new result of his spiritual investigations—to the revelation of the mystery of the remarkable figure of Krishna, the knowledge of which serves as a path to an occult understanding of Paul's experience before Damascus.

Thus at the end of this powerful lecture cycle, the mystery of the connection of Krishna with the Nathan Soul—who had remained in the spiritual world—was unveiled to anthroposophists for the first time, and there was also a first indication of his direct participation in the Damascus event. This profound mystery of the 'shining light' surrounding the form of the Risen One when He appeared to Saul on the road to Damascus[409] is an indication to us not only of the principal source of inspiration of the Apostle Paul's spiritual creativity, including his insight into the mystery of the relationships between the earthly and the heavenly Adam, but also becomes for us an important key for understanding the etheric appearance of Christ in our time: 'For human beings will not always remain the same; they will become more mature and find Christ, *as Paul found Him in the spiritual world through the event of Damascus, in this respect prophetically foreshadowing the future*'—a future which in our time has now become the present, when it gradually becomes possible for an ever greater number of people to attain to a 'beholding of Christ as Paul beheld Him.'[410]

Although in the lecture cycle, *The Bhagavad Gita and the Epistles of Paul*, we do not find any direct reference to the new revelation of Christ in the etheric realm, nevertheless this cycle occupies a key position in enabling us to understand this chief spiritual event of our time.

We find again in this cycle, focused in the single point of the cosmic–earthly activity of the Nathan Soul, all the principal motifs which we have already encountered in the previous chapters in the course of considering the various aspects of the karmic biography of Novalis. Thus if we work meditatively with this cycle—which in a certain sense has within it the quintessence of anthroposophical Christology and at the same time represents a kind of spiritual legacy and blessing for the newly founded Anthroposophical Society—we may clearly sense the supersensible participation in this event of the eternally youthful 'herald of Christianity', invisibly standing by and helping Rudolf Steiner from the higher worlds in his spiritual-scientific research. If we take into consideration the whole spiritual mood of the cycle, we should not be surprised if, at its very beginning, on the day following the introductory lecture (which was also the day following the founding of the independent Anthroposophical Society), in the meeting-room of the Cologne branch on the morning of 29 December 1912, a gathering was arranged by Rudolf Steiner on the life and work of Novalis—that spirit who was henceforth to become in the spiritual worlds the invisible guardian, the protective spirit, of the newly founded Anthroposophical Society.

The address which Rudolf Steiner gave at this morning gathering has unfortunately come down to us in a somewhat abbreviated version; nevertheless, even through a cursory comparison with other lectures on the same theme, one may be struck by the particularly intimate and heart-felt tone, and also by the remarkable directness, with which Rudolf Steiner addresses the entelechy of Novalis in the spiritual world.

Even the first words of this address are astonishing in their singularity: 'If in this way we hear the heart's ringing of *our beloved Novalis*, through which he told in so intimate a way of the mission of Christ, we sense something of a vindication of our spiritual stream . . .'[411] These words about the 'vindication' of the anthroposophical 'spiritual stream' through Novalis' earthly life, spoken as they were at the moment of the founding of the Anthroposophical Society, are indeed full of profound spiritual significance. The intimacy and directness with which Novalis is addressed, almost as though he were actually present in the room, arouses the feeling: the Christian Initiate of modern times is speaking these and the following words out of the life which he has shared in common with the entelechy of Novalis in the spiritual world. Similarly, the following words of Rudolf Steiner sound forth like an earthly echo of the spiritual conversation of the two spirits which took place at this moment in the super-earthly sphere: 'It is a wonderful thing to immerse oneself in the heart and soul of such a man as Novalis.' Then, even more clearly, he says: 'If we let ourselves be influenced by the way in which he allowed the spirit worlds to stream into his youthful heart in this incarnation and his perception of how *these spirit worlds were irradiated by the Christ-impulse*, then *we* feel this to be a summons to our own souls, our own hearts, *to strive with him* towards that which shone incessantly before him as a sublime light, a light to which this brief life of his was wholly devoted.'[412]

Turning then to the members of the newly founded Anthroposophical Society, he speaks the following words as a higher spiritual legacy: 'We feel how he [Novalis] was, in this incarnation, one of the prophets of recent times for *what we would seek in the spirit worlds*, and also how *we* can best be inspired in this quest through that inspiration which lived in the heart, in the soul of Novalis, and which was his through his being inwardly permeated by the Christ-impulse. And we may precisely in the present moment of our endeavours—in that, on the one hand *we are founding the Anthroposophical Society* which encompasses all the human riddles of the present moment, and on the other hand we would call to mind in connection with the Christ-impulse the light which streams forth so radiantly out of the Orient [this refers to the content of the lecture cycle]—*unite ourselves with what lived as an expression of the Christ-impulse in the soul of Novalis . . . We turn* longingly and probingly to the reincarnated soul of Elijah, of John the Baptist and of Raphael in Novalis *and feel with his soul* how the longing for a new spiritual life for mankind permeates and irradiates the whole of its spiritual vibrance . . . *then we take courage and feel that something of that power comes to us which can enable us to approach this new spiritual life of mankind in our own lives . . . Thus does he [Novalis] stand before us, and we should revere him in such a way that* he can, amongst much else, be one of the *mediators* who show us the way in which we may add to the spiritual revelations to which we aspire in the stream of our spiritual world-outlook: the right heart, the right love, the right enthusiasm, the right devotion . . .' Then at the very end of the lecture: 'He it is [Novalis] who can shine before us like a kind of *guiding star*, in such a way that *when we follow him in our experience* we at the same time have the good will *to raise ourselves to him through our work in knowledge with all the effort that we can muster*, and on the other hand to cultivate the living will to permeate with knowledge every human heart that seeks the spiritual in truth.'

There is hardly anywhere in the lecturing activity of Rudolf Steiner, apart from his 'Last Address', where we can find such penetrating and moving words about Novalis, such a powerful and at the same time such an intimate and heartfelt call to this spirit to become, from the spiritual worlds, the protector and helper of the young Anthroposophical Society, to be its mediator with respect to the cosmic power that we know as the power of Michael, with which the individuality of Novalis has been connected from the very beginning of the earthly existence of mankind. This means, however, that what at the Christmas Foundation Meeting of 1923 was fulfilled directly out of the forces of the cosmic sphere of Michael was accomplished at the end of December 1912 through the mediation of his 'radiant forerunner'.[413]

Thus if we consider as a whole the evolution of the 'Novalis theme' in Rudolf Steiner's lecturing activity, we may observe its first independent formulation in the autumn of 1908, on the threshold of the year that signified the beginning of the working of the Etheric Christ amongst mankind,[414] then its significant extension, whereby the individuality of Novalis was associated for the first time with the figures of Elijah, John the Baptist and Raphael. This happens in the lecture of 6 January 1909, almost exactly a year before the first public proclamation of the event of the New Advent, which took place in the lecture of 12 January 1910 in Stockholm, and before the two remarkable lectures about Novalis which framed it on both sides, that of 26 December 1909 in Berlin and of 23 January 1910 in Strasbourg at the dedication ceremony of the branch called by his name.

We shall now dwell in somewhat more detail upon the last two of these lectures, for they both have a quite particular significance for our theme. After a short introduction, Rudolf Steiner begins the first of these by saying that we should receive 'anthroposophical truths' into our hearts and souls 'as the message of Christ Himself'. And then he speaks of how at the time of Christmas it is important to recall those who, in their lives, have endeavoured to rise 'to those realms of spirituality where the Christ Himself is to be found.'[415] As an actual example of such a man, Rudolf Steiner in his lecture cites Novalis, whom he calles in this connection a 'truly Christian German poet . . . a truly theosophical poet', and to whom he then refers as a spiritual guide into these higher 'realms of spirituality'.

Then Rudolf Steiner describes in some detail an experience Novalis' father had after his son's death. When his congregation sang one of his son's 'Spiritual Songs' (that his son had written it, the father learnt only later) 'he was borne upwards into the spiritual heights, and became aware of their compelling power, the compelling power of the spiritual heights', a power which enabled him for a short while to shake off 'all the preconceptions of the material world' and to experience in his soul for the first time 'a breath of eternity'.

In reading this description and trying to penetrate into the spiritual reality that lies behind it, it is impossible to conceive of it in any way other than as an indication that in this moment old Hardenberg was enveloped by the mighty aura of his son which overshone him from the supersensible world nearest to the Earth and which called forth in him for the first time in his life a true spiritual experience. Thus it was that, a few months after his death, Novalis, through one of his songs, became for his father a guide into the higher 'realms of spirituality where the Christ Himself is to be found'.

Rudolf Steiner concludes this account with a call to the anthroposophists who were present at the lecture: 'Let us rise above the materialistic prejudices of the present day! Let us feel the compelling power of the spiritual life, and let strength and warmth flow from it into our hearts!' In the context of the lecture this means: Let us feel at this moment, as we hear the *Spiritual Songs* of Novalis (after these introductory words nine of his 'Spiritual Songs' were read by Marie Steiner), what his father once felt when the supersensible aura of his dead son overshone him from the spiritual worlds ... In other words: Let us open our souls to the inspirations of Novalis, let us allow him, who is at this moment invisibly present amongst us, to lead us consciously to the sphere of Christ, to those 'realms of spirituality where the Christ Himself is to be found.' This is the occult reality that stands behind the part of this lecture from which these quotations come. For, as Rudolf Steiner says somewhat later in the same lecture, only 'if we *allow the same deep feeling* for the Christ-event *to work in our souls as lived within Novalis* will we feel called upon ever and again to ask ourselves: How can we come increasingly to sense the truth of that mighty impulse which entered into mankind when Christ was born in Palestine?'

It is readily apparent from this lecture, if taken as an entirety, that an answer to this question can be given in our time only by Anthroposophy, and especially by the spiritual–scientific studies of the four Gospels. Here we approach an extremely important point, a mystery of considerable significance in Rudolf Steiner's spiritual work to which he himself alludes with full clarity at the end of the lecture.

Thus after the direct salutation to Novalis, the account of the spiritual experience of his father, the call to anthroposophists and the reading of the nine 'Spiritual Songs' by Marie Steiner, there follows an allusion to the particular significance of the spiritual–scientific studies of the Gospels in connection with an understanding of the most important event of the Earth, the Christ-event, and after this Novalis is spoken of again (in the last of the quoted passages).

If one enters inwardly into this remarkable compositional form of the lecture, one cannot understand it in any other way but the following: that the supersensible presence of Novalis, which had been called forth by the spiritual salutation of Rudolf Steiner and further strengthened by the reading of his poems, enabled Rudolf Steiner to reveal to the anthroposophists present at the lecture the mystery of the spiritual reality standing behind his many years of spiritual–scientific studies of the Gospels. Although Rudolf Steiner refers to this mystery only at the very end of the lecture, nevertheless the motif of 'Gospel studies' that is associated with it is introduced by him for the first time immediately after the reading of Novalis' *Spiritual Songs* and ends with the summons to awaken a deep feeling for the Christ-event—such a kind as lived within the soul of the poet-seer.

If one goes on to read at the end of the lecture about this mystery, which reveals the source of the impulses that led Rudolf Steiner to his Gospel studies, and in a certain sense to the growth of the 'anthroposophical movement in Central Europe', it is impossible to be unaware of the

supersensible presence of the individuality of Novalis beside Rudolf
Steiner throughout the entire lecture. Thus at the end of the lecture
Rudolf Steiner first speaks of how the spiritual life of the Anthroposophical Movement 'can be traced back ultimately to the sources which we
seek in those individualities whom we call the "Masters of Wisdom and
of Harmony of Feelings". Through them we shall, if we search rightly,
find the impulses which will enable us to work as we ought to work from
epoch to epoch, from age to age.' And only after these introductory
words does Rudolf Steiner turn to his real message: 'A great impulse has
recently come *to us* from the spiritual world. And today, on this solemn
Christmas evening, let us refer in our circle to this momentous impulse,
a sign, so to speak, which has flowed towards *us* in the course of recent
years from the spiritual world *as a measure taken by the astral plane*. It is
through this impulse that our Anthroposophical Movement here in
Central Europe has developed . . . The spiritual world has directed *us* to
become acquainted once more with the literal meaning of the Gospels, to
understand what is contained in their actual words . . . This we are told
by those who have given *us* this impulse from the spiritual world. Such
is the Christianity that is to come . . .'

These deeply significant words, which are so clearly indicative of
Rudolf Steiner's essential task as the modern teacher of Christian
esotericism, placed before him directly from the spiritual world, of
preparing and paving the way for a true, spiritual understanding of the
Gospels and laying the foundation for 'the Christianity that is to come',
appear in a lecture whose central theme is the personality and creative
work of Novalis!

Such an indication of Novalis' significance as a forerunner of the
anthroposophical understanding of the Christ-event (and hence also of
the spiritual–scientific understanding of the Gospels),[416] together with an
indication, in the same lecture, of the spiritual impulse which proceeded
from the 'Masters of Wisdom and of Harmony of Feelings' (and
especially from two of them, Christian Rosenkreutz and the Master
Jesus[417]), has in itself a deep spiritual reality—this consists in the *combined
working* of the individuality of Novalis with the high College of the
'Masters of Wisdom and of Harmony of Feelings', in the spiritual world
nearest to the Earth, and in particular with the two that have been
named.

This should not be understood to mean that the individuality of
Novalis belongs already *in full measure* to this high College; it would be
more correct to say that he is at present on the spiritual path which must
eventually, after his initiation has been completed, lead to a final entry
into this College. Nevertheless, even though he does not as yet fully

148

belong to it, the individuality of Novalis has, after his last incarnation, advanced so far in his inner development that, from the twentieth century onwards (after the end of the dark age of the Kali-Yuga), he will be able to become one of the principal collaborators and closest assistants of the College of the 'Masters of Wisdom and of Harmony of Feelings' in spiritually leading and guiding that spiritual stream whose *earthly representative* amongst men was Rudolf Steiner.

Perhaps the clearest testimony of the working together in the spiritual worlds of the 'Masters of Wisdom and of Harmony of Feelings' and the individuality of Novalis is given by the words which Rudolf Steiner spoke at the end of the second lecture about Novalis mentioned above (that of 23 January 1910), where reference is made to the need for anthroposophists to permeate themselves in their spiritual–scientific work with the *threefold Spirit* that works within the Anthroposophical Movement: the spirit of Novalis, the spirit of spiritual science, and the spirit of the Masters of Wisdom and of Harmony of Feelings: 'Let your endeavours here be permeated *as much* by the spirit of Novalis *as* by the spirit of spiritual science *itself* . . . May such a spirit unite you, that spirit who is, *at the same time*, the spirit of the Masters of Wisdom . . .'[418]

From all that has been said hitherto it becomes clear that, in the context of the lecture of 26 December, the spiritual collaboration of the entelechy of Novalis with the 'Masters of Wisdom and of Harmony of Feelings' is expressed above all in his direct *participation* in that 'measure taken by the astral plane' which was spoken of at the end of the lecture. Moreover, it was precisely this *participation* that Rudolf Steiner wished to emphasise through the fact of his reference to this 'measure' in a lecture devoted to Novalis.

Now here the question arises: what exactly was this 'measure, this action, of the astral plane' which enabled Rudolf Steiner to set about the spiritual–scientific studies of the Gospels, that is, to begin laying the foundations for a truly spiritual understanding of the Christ event?[419]

It is at the present time not as yet possible to speak openly about this 'measure' *in a direct way*. For according to the strict laws of the spiritual world, a hundred years must have passed before this happens. Nevertheless, it is possible to say something about its *essential purpose*. However, in order to be able to say something about this essential purpose it is necessary to dwell upon that period of time which divides the two lectures about Novalis that have been referred to, that time between 26 December 1909 and 23 January 1910.

In the first of these lectures, after speaking of the 'measure of the astral plane' Rudolf Steiner says: 'And all that we have attempted in our study of the Gospels of St John, St Luke and St Matthew, and which we shall still attempt in our consideration of the Gospel of St Mark, has arisen from this impulse and from how it has developed and taken shape.'[420] And what does Rudolf Steiner do after giving the lecture where he speaks these words? He undertakes a journey of two weeks to Sweden, where at the Stockholm Branch of the then Theosophical Society he gives a cycle of eleven lectures as a spiritual–scientific study of all four Gospels: 'The Gospel of St John and the Three Other Gospels.' This cycle was not recorded stenographically. Only some very brief notes taken by Marie Steiner have been preserved from these lectures, though even from these it is fully apparent that this cycle formed a kind of culmination and further deepening of all the Gospel studies that had gone before.[421]

It is, however, not only because of its content that this cycle occupies so special a place in Rudolf Steiner's lecturing activity, but above all because it was during this cycle, between the seventh and eighth lectures in the morning lecture of 12 January 1910, that the most important spiritual mystery of the twentieth century, the new appearance of Christ in the etheric body, was revealed for the first time before a small circle of listeners. From this morning lecture only a very brief, bare report by Marie Steiner has been preserved which, however, contains an indication by Rudolf Steiner that the 'spiritual' [that is, the spiritual–scientific] studies of the Gospels have the aim of preparing mankind for the new appearance of Christ.

In a compositional sense it is also of interest that the lecture of 11 January, which precedes the first proclamation of the event of the Etheric Christ, ends with this theme, and that the lecture of 13 January, which was given the day after, begins with it. And so this theme of the great significance for contemporary humanity of the new spiritual understanding of the Gospels is not only directly connected with the proclamation of the Etheric Christ but, in addition, the manner of its expression (in so far as one can judge from the very brief notes) represents virtually a word-for-word repetition of the corresponding portion of the lecture of 26 December 1909, which serves as an introduction to the unfolding of the mystery of the 'measure of the astral plane'. For this 'measure' which was accomplished by the 'Masters of Wisdom and of Harmony of Feelings' in the spiritual world nearest to the Earth—with the active participation of the individuality of Novalis—had as its chief purpose none other than that of *preparing the spiritual world nearest to the Earth for the new appearance of Christ in the etheric realm* and also, through Rudolf Steiner, their emissary on the Earth, of preparing earthly humanity for a conscious perception of this event.[422]

This 'measure of the astral plane', which consisted of several steps or stages and stretched over a number of years in the spiritual world nearest to the Earth,[423] was for Rudolf Steiner not only 'a sign' that he should embark upon the spiritual–scientific study of the Gospels, but in a certain sense represented one of the principal impulses for the evolution on Earth of the Anthroposophical Movement as such. 'It is through this impulse that our Anthroposophical Movement here in Central Europe has developed',[424] says Rudolf Steiner about the impulse proceeding from the 'astral measure', the principal result of whose positive outcome would be that Christ would be able to appear in the etheric realm from 1909 onwards[425] and also that it would, at the end of this year, be possible for the first time to speak of this 'measure' to anthroposophists, and then, sixteen days later, on 12 January 1910, to reveal to them the mystery of the Etheric Christ. It was first mentioned in Stockholm.[426] Eleven days later, in Strasbourg, Rudolf Steiner speaks about this event again *in a lecture devoted to Novalis*: 'Spiritual science has the weighty task of preparing human individuals for the great moment . . . [for] the return of the Christ . . .' And a little later he speaks about this preparation not only as a task of modern spiritual science as a whole, but as his own individual task: '*We have* the weighty task of preparing human individuals through spiritual science for the great moment.'[427]

'The return of Christ will signify an elevation of human beings to the sphere where Christ has His abode.' 'And if the spiritual eyes [of human beings] are opened, they will see Him as did Paul on the way to Damascus.'—These two observations of Rudolf Steiner, which also come in the lecture of 23 January devoted to the poet-seer, can be related in a particular way to Novalis, who already at the end of the eighteenth century had prophetically experienced the renewal of the Damascus event and was therefore able to ascend 'to those realms where Christ is to be found.' This whole lecture, *the first lecture given in Central Europe* which tells of the new Christ-event, ends (immediately before addressing the threefold spirit who inspires all anthroposophical work) with a reference to the original call of John the Baptist at the Turning-Point of Time that sought to awaken the forces of conscience and lead men to self-knowledge, a call which from our time onwards is renewed in the world through modern spiritual science: 'Change your ways . . . for the human ego is nigh unto the Kingdom of Heaven.'

Do we not find everywhere in the work of Novalis a soul mood that corresponds to these words? For example in his words 'Man has the capacity of being at every moment a supersensible being', or in another fragment where he speaks of the 'beginning of a true permeation of the self by the spirit, which never ends.' And if this is so, it should not appear to us in any way inconceivable that this individuality of Novalis should in our time be directly participating from the spiritual worlds in the spreading of the renewed call of John the Baptist amongst mankind, preparing—from the supersensible sphere nearest to the Earth—the etheric appearance of Christ in the same way that John had in former times prepared His physical appearance on the Earth.

This motif of the 'renewed call of John' runs in its diverse variations like a red thread through all the lectures of Rudolf Steiner devoted to the mystery of the New Advent, and especially in the period from January until the middle of May 1910.[428] For example, in the lecture of 10 May 1910 in Hanover, Rudolf Steiner says: 'As the Christ has to have a forerunner, so spiritual science had to appear in order to prepare for this clairvoyant age [in which Christ will be beheld].'[429] From these words it is particularly clear that in our time modern spiritual science, in its chief task of proclaiming and preparing humanity for Christ's New Advent, is in a spiritual sense a direct continuation of what John the Baptist accomplished at the Turning-Point of Time as the first proclaimer or herald of the historical manifestation of the Christ-impulse.

This task of being a herald of the Christ-impulse was in its highest spiritual form taken further by the individuality of John the Baptist in his subsequent incarnations, as Raphael and, especially, as Novalis. And he continues to be associated with this task in the spiritual worlds, while modern spiritual science has now been called to continue it *on the Earth* and to testify, through its renewed Johannine call, to the supersensible participation in the preparation of the New Advent of the threefold herald of the Christ-impulse.[430]

Following the development of the theme of Novalis in Rudolf Steiner's lecturing activity, those lectures of the next two years will be singled out in which the invisible inspiration of Novalis is expressed with a particular power. Apart from the ensuing three great Gospel cycles,[431] there were the lectures whose content was incorporated in the book published in the summer of 1911, *The Spiritual Guidance of Man and Humanity* (spoken of at some length in chapter 8);[432] or, for example, a lecture such as 'The Concepts of Original Sin and Grace' given in May 1911,[433] and in 1912 particularly the lectures associated with the description of the future fashioning of the new sheaths for the Christ amongst mankind out of the impulses of conscience, love, wonder and faith; and, finally, all the many lectures of this year devoted to the karmic biography of Novalis.[434]

The lecture of 16 May 1912 in Munich[435] is specially important in this respect. In this lecture, Rudolf Steiner first speaks about Buddhism and its founder, Gautama Buddha, who, as we have seen, spoke directly through John the Baptist at the Turning-Point of Time (see p. 11); then he goes on to speak about 'the fourfold heraldship' in the service of Christ by the individuality of Elijah–John–Raphael–Novalis, characterising the latter as a personality who is 'permeated by an anthroposophical Christianity'; after this he takes up the theme of studying the cycle of the year (one which was very close to Novalis),[436] and ends with a reference to the 'Anthroposophical Calendar of the Soul', which represents one of the paths that can lead modern man to an experience of the Etheric Christ. At the very end of the lecture he speaks of the project of constructing a 'Johannes-Bau' ('St John's Building) in Munich; the relationship of the Novalis individuality to this project will be spoken of later in this chapter.

This gradual waxing of the 'Novalis theme' culminates, of course, in the lecture of 29 December 1912, with the study of which we began this chapter. In memory of this lecture, Marie Steiner wrote in the foreword to its first edition: 'The art of the poet-seer, Novalis, introduced one of the evenings at which Rudolf Steiner gave guidelines to the Anthroposophical Society.'[437]

Thus from the very beginning, the future development of the independent Anthroposophical Society which was founded in December 1912 was placed under the 'sign of Novalis', and the deed of its founding was accomplished from out of that *spirit* who had found his poetic expression in the 'Spiritual Songs'.[438]

There is one further theme of considerable importance in the spiritual-scientific research of Rudolf Steiner which is directly connected with the individuality of Novalis—that of the Festivals. After all, is not one of the four Festivals of the year dedicated to John the Baptist (St John's)? Was there not a profound connection of this individuality with the sphere of Michael, especially through his incarnation as Elijah? And then there was his proximity at the Turning-Point of Time to the events of Christmas as a result of the Archangel Gabriel's twofold proclamation,[439] the visit of Mary to Elisabeth and then the childhood that Jesus and John spent together, as so many works of art bear witness; and of course the central part played by this individuality in the Mystery of the Appearance of God (Epiphany); finally, his supersensible participation in the Mystery of Golgotha through his connection with the first Christian Initiate, Lazarus–John (Easter). And if we turn to Novalis, is not the whole of his creative work a foreshadowing of the future Christianity of the Holy Spirit, a revelation of the Whitsun Mystery, of the future Mystery of the divine Sophia? 'Christ and Sophia'—were not these two words the principal motto of his life after the initiation which he received in 1797 at the grave of Sophie von Kühn? 'Novalis has become a witness for this

Christianity of the Holy Spirit'—with these words did Rudolf Meyer conclude his book about Novalis.[440]

Nevertheless, of all these Festivals, the individuality of Novalis is connected most of all with the Festival of Epiphany, when the most significant deed undertaken by him in human evolution is celebrated, and also with the Twelve Holy Nights, the time when humanity is prepared for the Mystery of the Appearance of God through the ascent from the earthly birth of Jesus to the cosmic birth of Christ. For it was after all at the Turning-Point of Time that John's testimony sounded forth, calling men to follow *not only* Jesus but also Christ.[441] And was he not after this testimony the first of all mankind to bear witness to the presence of the God Christ in the man Jesus of Nazareth, an event which signifies the highest point of the path from Jesus to Christ (John 1:34)? Thus this individuality is connected in the cycle of the year especially with the time of the Twelve Holy Nights, with the mysteries of spiritual birth, whose counter-pole, St John's tide, has to do with the *physical* birth of John the Baptist.

For this reason it is not fortuitous but of profound spiritual significance that Rudolf Steiner, year after year, constantly mentions either Novalis or one of his former incarnations in the period of the Twelve Holy Nights, in the time between Christmas and Epiphany, or in the days immediately before.

The two Christmas lectures of 1906 and 1907[442] form a kind of introduction to all that follows, for in both of them (even though only briefly) John the Baptist is mentioned in connection with the cosmic significance of his words about Christ as preserved for us in the fourth Gospel: 'He must increase, but I must decrease' (3:30). However, the Novalis theme really begins (as we have seen) shortly before the Christmas of 1908, in the lecture given on 22 December.[443] Then at the beginning of 1909, on 6 January, at the Festival of Epiphany—that is, on the day dedicated to the memory of the Baptism by John in the Jordan— the mystery of the three previous incarnations of Novalis was revealed for the first time, while at the end of that same year, on 26 December, that highly significant lecture—also connected with the theme of Novalis—was given which has already been spoken of in this chapter (see p. 146). Thus the year which had so fundamental a significance for the further evolution of mankind, the year when Christ first appeared in the etheric body, was framed on both sides by lectures devoted to the theme of Novalis.[444]

Then follows the year 1910. In the Christmas period of this year the entelechy of Novalis is mentioned twice: once on 30 December, at the inauguration of the anthroposophical branch in Esslingen, in the course of a lecture on *Raphael* given for this event, and on the other occasion on 1 January 1911 during the sixth, and last, lecture of the Christmas cycle, where the three previous incarnations of Novalis are mentioned.[445]

In the two Christmas lectures of the year 1911 the individuality of Novalis is not mentioned (apart from several references to the event of the Baptism by John in the Jordan), though nevertheless they are connected in a quite particular way with the central task of John the Baptist amongst mankind, with the spiritual gesture with which he reveals to humanity the path from Jesus to Christ. In both lectures this motif comes to expression in Rudolf Steiner's indication of the need for a new understanding of the mystery of the supersensible birth of Christ within the earthly man Jesus at the Baptism in the Jordan on 6 January, in contrast to the latter's own *earthly* birth on 25 December.[446]

If we turn to the Christmas period of the next year, 1912, in the course of which the 'Novalis theme' was in its many different aspects and variations considered by Rudolf Steiner with particular frequency, we again approach the lecture which he gave on 29 December during the founding of the independent Anthroposophical Society. Finally, this theme appears once again in the last 'pre-war' Christmas period, in the New Year's Eve lecture of 1913, where in the course of considering a whole series of Old Testament prophets Rudolf Steiner especially singles out Elijah as the leading Initiate of the ancient Hebrew people, in whom there lived 'echoes' of the three cosmic deeds of Christ through the Nathan Soul, the so-called 'pre-earthly deeds for the Mystery of Golgotha'.[447] For through the fact that their 'echo' lived with such strength in the soul of Elijah, he was able to receive not merely the revelations of Jahve (as did Moses), but also the Sun revelations of the Cosmic Christ that worked *through* the Moon Elohim. Moreover, in this same lecture Rudolf Steiner again characterises Elijah-Naboth, and then also John the Baptist, in such a way that the 'Bodhisattva-like' character of the individuality who was incarnated in them becomes clearly evident.

Thus we see how from year to year the individuality of Novalis participates ever more perceptibly from the higher worlds in the gradual development of the Anthroposophical Movement[448] in the earthly world, as though overshining it with his light from the spiritual heights. And so it is not for nothing that at the end of the lecture of 29 December 1912 Rudolf Steiner refers to his entelechy in the spiritual world as the 'guiding star' that 'lights the way' for the newly founded Anthroposophical Society, the star which it should 'feel its way towards', endeavouring to 'raise itself up to him [Novalis] in knowledge', that is, endeavouring above all to attain a relationship to and knowledge of the spiritual sphere of Christ such as Novalis himself had. The lecture then ends with the following words: 'And so may our path be illumined by what Novalis has said so beautifully and which can be a kind of *motto for what we have formed as a resolve at the starting point of the anthroposophical spiritual stream.*'[449]

These 'Christmas inspirations' of Novalis that we have described continue from the autumn of 1908 until the last Christmas before the war. Then they almost completely disappear for the whole period of the war, and become discernible again only from approximately autumn 1920.[450] Thus in the lecture given on Michaelmas Day, 29 September, Rudolf Steiner again speaks about Novalis, on this occasion giving particular weight to his relationship to mathematics, which has a purely *inspirative* character. And then, examining this phenomenon through spiritual-scientific means, Rudolf Steiner arrives at the conclusion that '. . . with such youthful spirits as Novalis, it is none other than a feeling that what you behold as mathematical harmony, what you weave through the phenomena of the universe, is actually the same loom that wove you during the first years of growth as a child here on Earth. This is to feel concretely man's connection with the cosmos.'[451] Novalis had such an experience of a direct connection with the cosmos through his awareness of the spiritual forces working within man in the first years of childhood, forces of which we have already spoken at some length in chapters 7 and 8. 'We stand in a relationship with all parts of the universe . . .' as he says in one of his fragments. In this sense his special relationship to mathematics[452] was one of many testimonies of his conscious relationship to the spiritual forces of early childhood.

The same motif appears again at Christmas 1920 in the third lecture of the cycle, 'The Quest for the New Isis, the Divine Sophia'[453]—a theme which, indeed, accompanied the entire earthly life of Novalis as one of its principal leitmotifs. In this Christmas lecture Novalis is spoken of as a 'select spirit' who in his relationship to mathematics was, at the end of the eighteenth century, still able to revive the ancient wisdom of the Eastern Magi, a wisdom which at the Turning-Point of Time had led them to bow before the reborn Zarathustra.

If we turn to the year 1921, we should pay special attention to the lecture on 'The Psychology of the Arts', which is devoted to a spiritual–scientific comparison of the soul-organisms of Novalis and Goethe.[454] In this lecture, Rudolf Steiner characterises with absolute clarity Novalis' physical organism as being permeated to such an extent by his mighty soul-spiritual principle that it became for him, so to speak, one single sense-organ. And this is a yet further testimony to the fact that in Novalis the condition of earliest childhood, when the entire organism of the child is still one undifferentiated organ of perception (that is to say, principally an organ of wonder and delight before the mysteries of the

156

world around him), was to a certain extent able to manifest itself anew in the full consciousness of adulthood, albeit at a higher level.

Then at Christmas 1921 Rudolf Steiner again speaks on the same theme as in the Christmas period of 1911, on the need for humanity to find, with the help of anthroposophically orientated spiritual science, the path to a real understanding of the mystery of the Baptism in the Jordan, to find the path to an understanding not only of the earthly birth of Jesus but above all of the supersensible birth of Christ.[455]

In the Christmas period of 1922 the influence of the inspirations that we have been considering comes to expression in a more indirect way. However, it can be felt in the mighty evocation of the Michael theme, in the allusion to the Spirit of Michael as the true guide for our time towards a spiritual understanding of the season of Christmas and, in particular, in the indication that Christ has taken upon Himself tasks which had formerly in earthly evolution been fulfilled by the 'Year-God'.[456] In this transition from the 'Year-God' to Christ, that is, in the transition from a more natural to a purely spiritual experience of the cycle of the year, one may sense what could be described as a higher 'hierarchic' fulfilment of the words of John the Baptist: 'He must increase, but I must decrease. He who comes from above is above all.'[457] (The participation of the entelechy of Novalis in the events of Christmas 1923 has already been spoken of in chapter 10.)[458]

If we gather together what we have said about the 'Christmas inspirations' of Novalis, which were especially active in the development on Earth of the Anthroposophical Movement in the period from 1908 until 1913 and then in the Christmas days of 1923, one highly important question stands before us with renewed strength to which we have hitherto been able to give only a partial answer, namely: why are all the principal stages of the development of the 'Novalis theme' in Rudolf Steiner's lecturing activity so clearly associated in the first instance with the season of Christmas? From the standpoint that concerns us now, the answer to this question is contained in the lecture about Novalis of 26 December 1909. There we find the following words: 'And if in the fifth epoch we celebrate a true Christmas Festival, we shall then be able to celebrate a true Easter Festival in the sixth epoch . . . In this way the Festivals of Christmas and Easter are linked together in the fifth and sixth epochs of our post-Atlantean period.'[459] In the light of all that was said in the chapter, 'The Forerunner of the Sixth Cultural Epoch', these words may serve as a key to understanding all the Christmas inspirations of Novalis as he prepares in the spiritual worlds for his future earthly mission of becoming, in time, on Earth, one of the most important guides of humanity from the fifth to the sixth cultural epoch, or, to be more precise, from *Christmas to Easter*, from the central Festival of the fifth to the central Festival of the sixth cultural epoch.

There is a further sphere of activity of the entelechy of Novalis which needs to be considered in this chapter. Rudolf Steiner concludes the Munich lecture of 16 May 1912 (referred to on p. 152), a lecture which is particularly devoted to a study of the 'fourfold heraldship' of Novalis throughout the sequence of his incarnations, with the following words relating to the impossibility—caused by a series of outer difficulties—of realising the original project of constructing a 'Johannes-Bau' in Munich: 'Thus have I tried to set before you today a particular aspect of our anthroposophically orientated conception, and in so doing we have fashioned a kind of substitute for what ought to have taken place on this occasion but could not, owing to the fact that official permission has not yet been granted: namely, the laying of the foundation stone for our Johannes-Bau. However, we would hope that in the not so distant future we shall succeed in putting this right. For in so doing we may also lay the foundation stone for a re-enlivening of the Anthroposophical Movement, as is our intention within the Western world.'[460]

For our present purpose what is of particular significance in these words is that Rudolf Steiner chooses *the theme of Novalis* as '*a kind of substitute*' for the laying of the foundation stone . . . of the Johannes-Bau' which could not come about at that time, a task which, in his words, should also have served as 'the foundation stone for a re-enlivening of the Anthroposophical Movement . . .'[461] This spiritual relationship to which attention is being drawn here between the entelechy of Novalis in the higher worlds and the need to create on Earth an *outwardly visible* centre for modern Christian–Rosicrucian esotericism is, in the August of the same year, artistically embodied in the first scene of the third Mystery Play, 'The Guardian of the Threshold'. Here is shown the entrance-hall belonging to a '*Rosicrucian* brotherhood', on whose walls hang portraits illustrating the principal stages of the karmic biography of Novalis: Elijah, John the Baptist, Raphael and Novalis.

The scene itself represents a turning-point in the history of the brotherhood. Inspired by a true reading and interpretation of the signs of the times, its leaders decide to open the doors of their temple to all those who wish out of their free will to work with them for the good of the further spiritual progress of mankind. Thus the motif of the spirit-temple which unites all men and is accessible to all men of goodwill is united in this sense with the 'fourfold heraldship' of the individuality of Novalis, whose task is to lay the foundation for the bridge which unites the esoteric and the exoteric history of humanity, or, in the context of the

Mystery Play itself, its first scene, the action of which is played out in the 'forecourt' of the Rosicrucian temple, and its last scene, which takes place within it.

And if in the forecourt of the temple the individuality of Novalis is referred to in a more exoteric way, through the presence on the walls of his portraits, in the temple itself his presence is manifested in a purely esoteric way, through the *complete harmony of the principal ideals of the temple with the central task of Novalis*:

> It is the loving purpose of Earth's soul:
> Not I, but Christ is living in my being.

Thus speaks Maria in the temple at the end of her monologue. And this formulation of the 'Damascus event', the principal formulation of all true Christian mysteries, is particularly close to the individuality of Novalis, for it alone opens up the path to the higher synthesis of wisdom and love, the spiritual foundation of the sixth cultural epoch.[462]

Benedictus, the spiritual head of the temple, refers to this higher synthesis of wisdom and love, which can be attained only through the *immediate presence of the Christ Himself*, in the following words, turning to Maria from his high altar:

> And in the sanctuary of wisdom
> The Christ will shine, and warm it
> With the sense of spirit love.

These words of Benedictus, just as the above-quoted words of Maria about the purpose of earthly evolution, occupy a central place both in this closing scene and in the play as a whole. As regards the first scene, the focal position there is without doubt occupied by the speech of the Grand Master of the Rosicrucian brotherhood, Hilarius Gottgetreu, as he turns to the twelve representatives of the streams associated with the principal world-views of contemporary humanity, a speech in which the motif of the 'spiritual rulership of man and humanity' appears with a particular power. In this principal motif of Hilarius' speech, *four* stages can be clearly distinguished.

At the first stage, we hear of 'those powers who guide the *purposes* of Earth's becoming' and who were able 'to reveal themselves in light' only 'at the beginning of time'; at the second, of the 'wise leaders', the 'exalted Spirit Beings', who 'were sent . . . from higher realms of being' so as to lead mankind onwards through the mediation of the ancient Mysteries. These Beings of the second kind, although of a lower standing than the first, were nevertheless—in comparison with human beings—of a higher, supersensible nature. They were in time able to choose, out of the ranks of humanity, individuals of a specially advanced spirituality and to initiate them 'into mystic *aims* and *wisdom's* teaching', that is, into the world 'purposes' established by the Beings of the first kind, and into the 'wisdom' which the Beings of the second kind need to fulfil these purposes. These chosen people were the first 'human Initiates'. They formed the third stage of this evolutionary sequence and are called in Hilarius' speech the 'pupils of the Gods'; and they eventually also chose pupils for themselves 'to be successors in the guardianship of the spirit-heritage.' The latter, in turn, formed in time the concluding, fourth stage.

After the epoch which was governed by the direct inspirations of the superhuman Beings of the first category had come to an end, evolution as a whole was guided by Beings of the second, also superhuman category, who, in ancient times, formed on Earth the first, indeed the original, Mystery School of wisdom. From this original School, there subsequently came forth all the 'human Initiates' who later founded schools for the Mysteries over the entire Earth:

> For to this time all Mystery Schools
> Which bear this name with justification are rightly descended
> From the first, which stems from cosmic Spirits.

Only when these superhuman Beings of the second category had trained sufficient followers and successors in the form of 'human Initiates' were they able to withdraw from the direct guidance of humanity and to move on to other tasks:

> When the first Master's pupils later
> Could cultivate this treasure worthily
> The exalted teachers turned once more
> Back to their own worlds of *life*.

If one compares this speech of Hilarius Gottgetreu with other utterances of Rudolf Steiner, it is not difficult to see that when he speaks of the first category of Beings, those 'who guide the purposes of Earth's becoming', he has in mind primarily the Beings of the Third Hierarchy, Archai, Archangeloi and Angeloi, who carry out the will and intentions of the higher Hierarchies regarding the Earth and humanity.[463] Man encounters these Beings of the Third Hierarchy, and especially the last of them, the Angels, on each occasion after death, in the Moon-sphere,[464] in the sphere of the world ether surrounding our Earth [the 'worlds of life' referred to in the quotation at the end of the previous paragraph]. However, in the Moon sphere he encounters not only them but also the so-called 'ancient Teachers of *Wisdom*' who in the earliest times of Earth evolution were the Teachers of a then as yet still youthful humanity. Subsequently, having endowed the earthly mysteries and their human Initiates with their wisdom, they withdrew to the sphere of the Moon (shortly after it had separated from the Earth), where they formed a cosmic colony which thenceforth became the focus of the ancient primordial wisdom.465 They had by then handed the earthly rulership of humanity on to their 'successors'—highly evolved human beings who in the East were known as 'Bodhisattvas': 'Although they [the latter] have always made their appearance embodied as men, yet they are the successors of those Beings who have taken up their abode on the Moon. *Hence the life of the Bodhisattvas is actually passed in community with the Beings who live in this cosmic lunar fastness.* There lie the springs of their strength, the sources of their thoughts.'466

In the course of many thousands of years, the various Bodhisattvas worked as emissaries and mediators between the Moon Teachers of Wisdom and the many generations of pupils of the different Mysteries.

Thus in the speech of Hilarius Gottgetreu we can distinguish four categories of beings, the first two of which are met with only after death, in the Moon-sphere:

1. The Beings of the Third Hierarchy, who rule the evolution of the Earth and humanity through purposes which they receive from the higher Hierarchies. In the spiritual world nearest to the Earth (the Moon-sphere), the fulfilment of these purposes is undertaken by the Angels.
2. The ancient Teachers of Wisdom, who formerly worked amongst men in etheric bodies, and then withdrew to the Moon (the Moon-sphere).467
3. Their emissaries, the Bodhisattvas, and also the other Teachers of humanity who had attained their stage of development (i.e., the 'Bodhisattva-like' beings).
4. The pupils of the Mysteries and spiritually striving human individualities.

What we have said here with regard to the speech of Hilarius Gottgetreu should now be compared with that part of Rudolf Steiner's 'Last Address' where he describes the entry of the Raphael individuality into the Moon-sphere after his death. In the Moon-sphere this individuality first comes in contact with the Moon Teachers and their wisdom, and then with those spiritual Beings who in former times furnished earthly existence with its *purpose*, that is the Angels, the representatives *in the Moon-sphere* not only of the Third Hierarchy but of the entire hierarchic cosmos as a whole: 'We become aware of how Raphael enters the Moon-sphere, and we see how he comes here into the company of the Spirits who live in the Moon-sphere and who are the spiritual individualities of the great original Teachers of mankind, with whose *wisdom* Raphael, as Elijah, had been deeply inspired; we see how he joins together with these Moon Beings and with all the souls with whom he has lived in earlier stages of Earth evolution.' Then from the Moon Teachers of Wisdom the Raphael individuality gradually moves on to still higher, purely Hierarchic Beings who are, however, also connected with the sphere of the Moon: 'We see how he spiritually unites himself there [in the Moon-sphere] with *the Earth's spiritual origins*, with that world of being which first made it possible for man to be, and for the earthly to be impregnated with the divine. We behold Raphael as it were completely "at home", united with those with whom he had most loved to be, in the Elijah existence, inasmuch it was they who, at the beginning of Earth existence, set the *goal* for the life of this Earth.'[468]

In these words of Rudolf Steiner from the 'Last Address' and in the fact of their profound inner relationship with the speech of Grand Master Hilarius from the first scene of the Third Mystery Play, we have not only a further confirmation that in the case of the Elijah–John–Raphael–Novalis individuality we have to do with a 'Bodhisattva-like' being, but above all a most significant sign of the spiritual participation of this individuality in the earthly evolution of Anthroposophy in the first quarter of the twentieth century. For in this scene, not only the portraits on the walls of the entrance-hall of the Rosicrucian brotherhood, but most especially the speech of Hilarius Gottgetreu, bring to outward expression the various stages of the karmic biography of Novalis, both in his earthly incarnations and, in particular, in the periods of his life in the spiritual world between death and a new birth.

If we return again to the connection that we have already observed between the project of the Johannes-Bau in Munich and the 'Novalis theme', we can move a step further in this direction if we take the following into consideration. In September 1912, that is, directly after the first performance of the Third Mystery Play, Rudolf Steiner gives a lecture cycle in Basel which is devoted to a spiritual–scientific study of the Gospel of St Mark and through which the theme of Elijah–John the Baptist–Raphael–Novalis passes like a red thread at a depth not hitherto attained. At the end of that same month Rudolf Steiner visits Dornach for the first time and, after a conversation there with Dr Emil Grosheintz, takes the decision to build the Johannes-Bau in Switzerland.

From the time of the laying of its Foundation Stone on 20 September 1913, that is, *roughly one year* after the lecture in which Rudolf Steiner revealed the mystery of the activity of the entelechy of John the Baptist after his martyrdom as the group-soul of the Twelve Apostles, that is, as the group-soul of the *first* Christian 'community',[469] there begins a whole series of communications out of the Fifth Gospel, where, too, John the Baptist has an essential place.[470]

The connection that is thus revealed between the history of the Johannes-Bau and the spiritual individuality of Novalis can be made still more concrete if we recall that one of the last artistic, creative deeds of Raphael was the completion of the dome of the Cathedral of St Peter's in Rome, a work begun by Bramante. Thus the idea of the dome, which, so to speak, comes into movement in the double-domed building,[471] was—alongside the theme of the 'Transfiguration' in his painting—one of the central artistic ideas with which Raphael was concerned especially in the last years of his earthly life, and with which he crossed into the spiritual world.

The intimate connection which Raphael had with the construction of the great dome of St Peter's Cathedral is borne out, for example, by the following section of his letter to his uncle, Simone Ciarla, written seven years before his death: 'I simply cannot any longer live anywhere other than in Rome because of the love that I bear St Peter's which has been entrusted to me in Bramante's place. But what place on Earth could be worthier than Rome, and what enterprise worthier than the Cathedral of St Peter's? For it is the first temple of the world and the greatest building that has ever been seen.'[472]

A further example of the inner relationship between the Johannes-Bau and the creative work of Raphael is Rudolf Steiner's reference, in the lecture of 5 May 1909 in Berlin—on the occasion of the dedication of the new premises of the Berlin Branch—to Raphael's two frescos, *The School of Athens* and the *Disputa*. Reproductions of the two frescos were, at the time, hanging on the walls of the room where the lecture was being given. Rudolf Steiner calls these two works of art 'two of the most significant pictures in the world . . . through which the way that the anthroposophist can make his ideals become the inner content of his soul stands so clearly before us.' He then speaks of how the first of these frescos depicts the *pre-Christian* evolution of mankind, while the second portrays the epoch of the late Middle Ages: 'Both these pictures can only be understood together, and only in a particular sequence. They speak of what has happened from *pre-Christian* times until deep into the Middle Ages; and they speak of it in an artistic way . . . For a *pre-Christian* world-view is expressed through the first picture; what has come to pass through Christ comes to expression in the forms of the second picture . . . They are, so to speak, the expression of how human evolution *from antiquity* until far into the Christian Middle Ages was conceived by a great human spirit.'[473]

After describing both pictures in more detail, Rudolf Steiner moves on to the principal theme of his lecture, namely, that it will in future be necessary to add to these two a *third* picture which, in his words, will eventually be born from the human soul 'which in its life's blood' will have 'that spiritual world-conception which comes towards us today in its first form as Anthroposophy.'[474] Rudolf Steiner then speaks as follows about this 'third picture': 'What is to come into being through the Spirit—who is sent through the Christ and who will [eventually] loose himself from his sheaths—will come to expression in the picture which may stand as a *great ideal* before the soul of every [anthroposophist]. As yet it cannot be painted, for the models for it are not yet available. But in our souls these two pictures [of Raphael] should be completed so that they stand as a trinity of pictures.'

These words, together with the above indication regarding the connection of the first picture with the age of antiquity and the second with the epoch of the late Middle Ages, may enable us to come to the following conclusion: in the first picture are represented men who are immersed in the study of the most ancient primordial wisdom of humanity, in the form in which it was still preserved in Greek culture. This picture portrays the working of the last reflection of the wisdom of the Father-God impulse amongst mankind. The second picture portrays the working of the *Son* impulse and the third, a picture which at that time (1909) no one had yet brought into existence on the Earth, will be an artistic representation of the essential nature of the new revelation of the *Spirit*.

In the same lecture, Rudolf Steiner further defines the 'great ideal' which this third picture will portray as an 'all-embracing ideal of freedom and love', that is, the ideal which future humanity will serve in the cosmos as the Tenth Hierarchy. Such a characterisation of this ideal in association with the indication of the connection of the 'third picture' with the new epoch of the Spirit, to which Anthroposophy now forms the gateway, tells us with full clarity *where* in our time we should seek the realisation of this mysterious work of art. For what was as yet impossible to create in 1909 was by the end of the next seven-year period able to become a reality in the portrayal of the 'Representative of Man'—

maintaining the balance between the opposing forces of Lucifer and Ahriman—which was painted in the Eastern part of the small cupola of the First Goetheanum, and also in the sculptural manifestation of the same motif in the Group.

In this artistic representation of the ideal human being, which sets before our eyes the whole of humanity in its future cosmic condition as the Tenth Hierarchy, working creatively in the world out of the forces of freedom and love, we have the *third* picture, begotten as it is out of the modern revelation of the Spirit.

Everything that Rudolf Steiner said in the Berlin Branch at the dedication of the first anthroposophically designed premises about the historical foundations of the three pictures is to a remarkable degree in harmony with what he expressed in his address at the laying of the foundation Stone of the First Goetheanum on 20 September 1913 in Dornach. For if, as we have seen, the first picture shows the epoch of the highest flowering of antiquity in, shall we say, the age of Plato,[475] and the second picture shows the flowering of Scholasticism, when for the first time it became necessary to *substantiate and defend* the principal truths of Christianity and, indeed, Christian culture in general, on the one hand from outward physical forces and, on the other, from the spiritual onslaught of the representatives of Mohammedan culture, we also find both these historical motifs in Rudolf Steiner's address at the laying of the Foundation Stone. Here, too, we find, alongside the theme of the Turning-Point of Time and the Mystery of Golgotha, references to the 'mystery wisdom of ancient Greece', to the philosophy of the 'great Plato' and then to 'that great *spiritual* conflict . . . inspired by the fire of love . . . which was waged by our forefathers when in yonder regions they were repelling the Ahrimanic onslaught of the Moors', a conflict which in our time anthroposophists 'are to carry forward'. While the address itself begins with a characterisation of the fundamental, conscious–subconscious yearning of modern mankind *for the spirit*, man's longing, his hope and his call for the new spirit-revelation.[476]

Antiquity, the Mystery of Golgotha, whose light continues to shine amongst mankind until the epoch of the later Middle Ages, and the modern revelation of the spirit—these are the three principal stages in the historical evolution of humanity which appear before us both in the 'three pictures' and in the address at the laying of the Foundation Stone of the First Goetheanum, a building whose focal point was to have been the sculptural group erected in the East together with the painting in the small cupola corresponding to it, these latter being artistic representations which spring directly from the sources of the new spiritual revelation, the modern Christ revelation through the *Spirit* of our time—Michael.[477]

Thus not only in an architectural, but also in a pictorial respect, we have before us in the First Goetheanum a work of art which in a certain sense represents the culmination and fulfilment of all Raphael's spiritual expectations, the manifestation of the artistic ideal of the 'third picture' which, for his part, he tried to approach in his last work, the *Transfiguration* on Mount Tabor.

In the upper part of this picture there is portrayed the cosmic revelation by Christ of His higher *Sun* nature, and in the lower part may be seen His disciples failing to drive out the demonic forces from the youth who is possessed by them, due to the fact that the Christ-impulse does not as yet work with the strength with which it will work amongst mankind *after* the Mystery of Golgotha, when it will bring the opposing forces of Lucifer and Ahriman into a state of equilibrium. In this sense we may say: this last work of Raphael depicts at the same time the world-historical question about the new revelation, the 'third picture', the answer to which—in a form appropriate for modern times—was given in the First Goetheanum as a total work of art, and especially in the painting and sculpture of its eastern part.

Novalis, too, aspired towards this higher ideal of artistic creativity which draws its impulses directly from the sources of the new spirit revelation. For his most hidden purpose was to lift the veil of mystery from the holy temple image of Isis, the Divine Sophia, a veil which conceals the picture of the whole future evolution of humanity. This signifies—in a spiritual–scientific sense—gaining access to the all-embracing cosmic sphere of the Holy Spirit, which has within itself the eternally alive seeds of all true art, science and religion.[478]

'I am the all, I am the past, the present and the future; no mortal has yet lifted my veil'—thus runs an ancient inscription over the sacred image of Isis in the temples of Egypt.[479] To this Novalis answers, 'and if no mortal, as the inscription says, can lift the veil, we must strive to become immortal,' which is to say that in our time man can himself lift the veil from the holy image in the temple through the forces of his higher ego. But what is then revealed?

'One man succeeded—he lifted the veil of the goddess at Saïs—but what did he see? He saw—wonder of wonders—*himself.*' 'Himself' in the eternal form of his higher, immortal ego, as the ideal of the whole of human evolution, an ideal which is encompassed in the two magic words, 'freedom and love'.[480] Is not this experience of Novalis, together with his own words which bear witness to it, a living metamorphosis of what Rudolf Steiner was later to describe in the lecture of 6 January 1918, at

Epiphany, where he speaks of how 'behind' the sculptural Group portraying the Representative of Man between Lucifer and Ahriman is hidden the new Isis, the Divine Sophia, above whom in our time stand the words: 'I am man, I am the past, the present and the future. Every mortal should lift my veil.'[481]

Thus the times do change. At the end of the eighteenth century, Novalis still had to become 'immortal' in order to lift the sacred veil of Isis; he had to approach the mysteries of existence through the direct revelation of his higher ego. In our time, after the end of the dark age of the Kali-Yuga and in the period of the new rulership amongst mankind of the Archangel Michael, *every* man can recognise something of the mysteries of higher existence with his ordinary faculties of understanding, mysteries to which the spiritual being of man himself—as is now revealed to us in the modern science of the spirit or Anthroposophy—is both the key and the solution. Moreover, while in Novalis' time there was a need for exceptional inner illumination—for which he was predisposed by his quite special karma—leading to a supersensible Damascus experience, in the new world epoch which is beginning in our time, this Damascus light will, like light on Tabor which has been transformed by the Mystery of Golgotha,[482] begin quite naturally to shine forth in the souls of an ever greater number of people. This is the beginning of the epoch of the new natural clairvoyance heralded by modern spiritual science, when it will become possible for human beings to behold the Christ Being in the spiritual surroundings of the Earth and to acquire a genuine knowledge of Him, not through outward documents or Church traditions, but through direct inner experience.

Novalis calls this future epoch the 'golden age': 'a new golden age with dark unbounded eyes, a prophetic age wondrous in deed and in healing, comforting and enkindling eternal life . . . a great age of reconciliation . . .' And what Novalis thus prophetically beholds is none other than the return of that ancient, legendary land of *Shamballa* which is so universally known in the East.

In ancient times, with the onset of the dark epoch of Kali-Yuga, this wondrous land—and, with it, the capacity of beholding the ancient Gods—withdrew into the distances of the world ether. The spiritual light of the primordial wisdom, which had hitherto worked amongst mankind as the revelation of higher spiritual Beings, as the 'holy dwelling-place of the Gods', became gradually extinguished. In the fifth Hymn to the Night, Novalis describes this gradual onset of Kali-Yuga, and the subsequent disappearance of the 'wondrous land' which is the true spiritual home of all human beings, in remarkably precise words fully corresponding to the occult-spiritual reality: 'The Gods had

167

disappeared with their retinue. Nature was left lifeless and lonely. With an iron chain it bound barren number and strict measure. Life's measureless bloom fell apart in dark words as though into dust and air . . . A hostile North wind blew chill over the frozen fields, *and the frozen homeland of wonders vanished into the ether* . . . No longer was the light the dwelling-place of the Gods and a heavenly testimony: they cast upon themselves the veil of night.'

From our time onwards the legendary land returns, it returns with the possibility of entering the 'etheric sphere' in a wholly new way, it again becomes visible as the 'spiritual atmosphere' of the Earth transformed by the Christ-impulse.[483]

Novalis' clairvoyant gaze prophetically beholds the approach of this mysterious land, for which the peoples of the East have yearned for millennia, as the dawning of the coming 'golden age' of which he often wrote:

> Far to Eastward dawn is gleaming,
> Grey old ages growing young . . .

And indeed, if, as Rudolf Steiner says, Initiates and Bodhisattvas 'at certain times' draw their forces from this same land,[484] does not then the 'Bodhisattva-like' individuality of Novalis, 'whose life has the aspect of a blessed memory of an earlier life of a great Initiate',[485] also to some extent belong to it?

But his life is filled not only with conscious–unconscious memories of the past, but also with direct spiritual experiences of his *present incarnation*. For in passing through the Damascus experience, through what Rudolf Steiner describes as an 'Initiation conferred upon him by grace',[486] he knows with his whole being, with the certitude of true prophetic vision, that it will be the Christ Himself, in the spiritual world nearest to the Earth, who will lead men into this enchanted land.

This prophetic premonition of a 'golden age', of the future mystic land of Shambala, blossoms like a 'blue flower' in the soul of Novalis and is then poured forth into his entire creative work, filling it with the special 'aroma' of the future. Through the event of Damascus, says Rudolf Steiner, 'man will ascend to a cognition of the spiritual world and will see the physical world permeated by a new land, by a new realm.'[487] Thus already at the end of the eighteenth century Novalis prophetically beholds the entire physical world permeated by a 'new land'. And he calls this new vision of the world 'magical idealism'.

Through the enchanted crystal of his 'magical idealism', the organ of perception of mankind's future condition, he then contemplates man's future evolution. Together with this exalted perspective, he also recognises his own world task of leading human beings to a conscious experience of the future revelation of the spirit. For Novalis knows that what he experienced in this incarnation as a higher, though still as yet an exceptional, revelation will in future also be accessible to other men; he knows: 'Later, other human beings, too, will enter the land of Shambala; they will see its radiant light, as Paul saw above him the light that streamed from Christ. This light will stream towards them also, the portals of this *realm of light* will open to them; and through these portals they will enter the holy land of Shambala.'[488]

Only the unshakable conviction that other people will also eventually find the path to this future enables him to say that 'only those who with their whole soul are willing to participate in this event are human beings in the true sense.'[489] So he invites all men to participate in this event:

> Oh! go out onto every highway,
> And bring the erring ones inside,
> Stretch out your hands to each in greeting,
> Inviting them with us to bide.
> Here on Earth with us is Heaven,
> In faith do we behold its light;
> Who of one faith with us become,
> The heavens are open to their sight.

But human evolution moves onwards. What for the nineteenth century, for the last century of the dark age of the Kali-Yuga, was represented by the 'magical idealism' of Novalis is fulfilled for our *age of light*—which has by now lasted almost a whole century—by Rudolf Steiner's Anthroposophy. 'The spreading of the anthroposophical world-conception has taken place in our time so that man can be prepared on the physical plane to perceive the Christ-event either on the physical plane or on higher planes . . . The purpose of all anthroposophical development will be to render men more and more capable of participating in what is to come.'[490]

The individuality of Novalis is, as he prepares in the spiritual worlds for his future mission, connected with his whole being with this new revelation of Christ in the etheric sphere which has begun in our time. For having in his incarnation as John the Baptist embodied the impulse of conscience, in his incarnation as Raphael the impulse of compassion and love for all that exists, an impulse that flowed forth into the realm of the beautiful, and, finally, in his last incarnation wonder, reverence and a deep faith, in brief, everything which 'forms the path leading to

169

supersensible knowledge',[491] Novalis was able to become from the higher worlds a supersensible helper and collaborator of him who in the twentieth century was the first to give the true—that is, issuing directly from conscious, spiritual contemplation—image of the Countenance of Christ: 'There must be sublime power in this countenance' so that as it stands before one through the work of a painter or sculptor the highest expression of *conscience* may be discerned in the particular way that the chin and mouth are formed; the mouth must convey the impression that it is not there for the purpose of taking food, but to give utterance to such moral strength and power of conscience as has been cultivated by men through the ages . . . In contrast, He will be given eyes whence the full power of *compassion* can flow, a power that eyes alone can express—not in order to receive impressions, but to enter wholly into the joys and sufferings of others. And a brow . . . which is conspicuously prominent above the eyes and curves gently backwards over the head, expressing *wonder* at the mysteries of the world.'[492]

Only in the two lectures of 8 and 14 May 1912[493] does Rudolf Steiner give this striking description of the outward physical appearance of Christ Jesus. And in both cases this description is united with the theme of Elijah–John–Raphael–Novalis. In the lecture of 8 May all four incarnations of this individuality are considered; while in the lecture of 14 May, immediately before the description of how Christ Jesus looked, there is a reference to Raphael. And in the lecture that follows that of 16 May, all the four incarnations again enter into consideration.'[494]

The correspondence to which attention is being drawn here is no mere 'fortuitous' interlacing of two themes but, on the contrary, has its esoteric foundation in the fact that in his incarnation at the Turning-Point of Time it was this individuality who, in the person of John the Baptist, was, at the Baptism in the Jordan, the first to experience the transformation of the man Jesus into the God-man Jesus *Christ*. For at that moment John was the first and the only human witness who was worthy to behold the total transformation of the countenance of the man who appeared before him after the Baptism in the waters of the Jordan. This was a man who had now become wholly different and transformed, and from whose brow there radiated wonder at all the mysteries of the cosmos, from whose eyes there shone an infinite compassion for all that exists and whose lips, it seemed, had from eternity served not the purpose of receiving earthly nourishment but only that of giving utterance to the revelations of the world conscience.

This sublime image of Christ Jesus as He had indeed once wandered the Earth was later to be imprinted upon the central figure of the sculptural Group and upon the central motif of the painting of the small cupola of the First Goetheanum, and also in the sketches for this painting.

If we thoroughly immerse ourselves in these works of art by Rudolf Steiner, we can in our time really approach an experience of the Christ Being in the spiritual world. However, there is another way of reaching this goal, and that is through awakening within us the impulses of conscience, compassion and wonder as they have worked since the Mystery of Golgotha in the spiritual–historical evolution of mankind. Rudolf Steiner describes this second path as follows: 'If you would portray the Christ, you must not attempt to consider something that is actually there in the world, but you must let your whole idea be quickened and pervaded by all that flows from a contemplation of the spiritual evolution of the world that is inspired by the three mighty impulses of wonder, compassion and conscience.'[495]

With this reference to the inner path to the Christ, a path which also had a particular place in the karmic biography of Novalis, we would now bring this chapter to a close.

12

'Christ and Sophia'
The Mysteries of the Sixth Cultural Epoch

'Novalis experienced the Christ mystery, the Mary mystery, in relation to the cosmic mystery.'

Rudolf Steiner, 22 December 1908

The study of Novalis' karmic biography presented in this book would remain incomplete if, in conclusion, we were not to touch upon the mystery of the second half of the dictum which the poet-seer chose, as a kind of motto, for his brief earthly life: 'Christ and *Sophia*'.

Much has already been said in the pages of this book about Novalis' experience of the Christ-sphere and about the new spiritual tasks which appeared before him as a result of this experience, tasks to which his last incarnation was devoted and which his future incarnations will also serve. It remains now to consider the question of Novalis' relationship to the cosmic sphere of the Sophia, a relationship which found its reflection in so many of his prose writings and, most especially, his poetic works.

The study of this question is, however, in the present epoch of human evolution, connected with exceedingly great difficulties, for a true understanding of and insight into the Sophia mystery is even more foreign to our materialistic age than the Christ mystery.

One of the reasons for this is that it is in accordance with the central rulership of earthly evolution that the Christ mystery *to a certain extent* be made manifest to humanity already during the fifth post-Atlantean cultural epoch, the foundation for which was laid in the twentieth century by anthroposophically orientated spiritual science, while as regards the Sophia mystery its full revelation to mankind will take place not in the fifth but only *in the sixth* or Slavic cultural epoch of post-Atlantean evolution.[496]

This mystery of the spiritual life, to which particularly the inhabitants of Eastern Europe will be called, was already in ancient times thoroughly familiar to those who were entrusted with the care of the spiritual flowering and evolution of the Slavic peoples.[497] Thus from the outset the spiritual life of Eastern Europe, as a foreshadowing of this future task of the Slavic peoples, has already had a vague inclination towards the Sophia principle, though without a clear understanding of its esoteric nature. It was not by chance that, shortly after the Cathedral of St Sophia in Constantinople was built, which became the central architectural work of the Christian East, churches dedicated to the 'Divine Wisdom' were erected in Russia, first at Kiev and then in Novgorod.

Thus Novalis' motto, 'Christ and Sophia', is at the same time the ultimate goal and high ideal of the sixth cultural epoch. Everything which was set forth in the chapter, 'The Forerunner of the Sixth Cultural Epoch', receives its most exact and most concentrated expression in these two words which Novalis wrote in his diary on 29 June 1789.

However, the initiation into the future mysteries of the cosmic Sophia which Novalis experienced was, in a remarkable way, prepared and called forth by certain definite facts of his own earthly biography, amongst which his meeting with Sophie von Kühn on 17 November 1794 played without doubt a decisive role. This young girl, who at the time of her meeting with Novalis was almost still a child, scarcely 12½ years old, made, as we shall see, what was in its way a unique impression upon him and in one single moment, as if by magic, transformed his whole life. Under the influence of this meeting and of the deep inner changes which it aroused within Novalis, the dreamy and romantic mood of the youth was suddenly stirred into new life, so that he became clearly and distinctly aware of the full significance of his true mission in his present incarnation.

But what was the deeper, spiritual meaning of what occurred as a result of this initially so enigmatic prompting of destiny? How was Novalis able, through no more than one earthly meeting, to find the path to the sphere of the highest and purest cosmic spirituality? Or, in other words, how could the 12-year-old Sophie von Kühn represent a kind of human gate which led his inner eye towards the all-embracing sphere of the cosmic Sophia? Despite the quite considerable number of external documents, memories and written testimonies that have come down to us, the veil of mystery which is spread over this meeting remains nevertheless impenetrable, and the historical facts that have emerged have hitherto placed before the unprejudiced researcher more questions than they have given answers.

In order to introduce what follows, we shall try to approach this mystery initially in a more 'methodological' way. As a point of departure we may take Goethe's study of the archetypal mineral, the archetypal plant and the archetypal animal. In his quest for the ideal-supersensible archetypes of the visible world, Goethe embarked in his natural scientific studies upon a path of ascent which led him through the various kingdoms of nature—mineral, plant and animal—to the human realm, at the threshold of which he stopped. This destiny of Goethe is then also experienced by his Faust. At the moment when he has attained his life's highest goal, he speaks the words: 'To stand on freedom's soil with people free', words of which Rudolf Steiner once said that they should be augmented to read: '[to stand] on freedom's soil with Christ in one's heart, leading one in earthly life to the Spirit',[498] if the world-historical task of this most remarkable poem of the fifth cultural epoch is to be *fully* accomplished. However, Goethe was unable to rise from the experience of the archetypal mineral, plant and animal to an equally concrete and living experience of the *archetypal man*, Anthropos, that is, of man's higher cosmic-earthly archetype as it appeared to all men through the historical intervention of the Christ Being into earthly evolution. And so, as was the case with his Faust, his inner evolutionary path came to an end when he had reached no more than the threshold of the 'promised land', the threshold of the future sixth cultural epoch. Having expressed, in the words of Faust quoted above, one of the highest ideals of the consciousness soul and, hence, of the entire fifth post-Atlantean epoch, Goethe remained there, unable to cross the threshold beyond which the rising Sun of the Spirit, the Sun of Manas, begins gradually to send its light into the consciousness soul.[499]

But where Goethe, in his inability to step beyond the fifth post-Atlantean epoch, came to a halt is the point where Novalis begins his spiritual path. And just as Goethe was able to rise spiritually from a single plant to its archetype, the 'archetypal plant', which is reflected in the myriads of individual earthly plants and is nevertheless none of them, so was it possible for Novalis—in this way taking Goethe's work further— to accomplish, in essence, something similar, although on a higher plane: he was able to rise from the particular earthly individual, Sophie von Kühn, to her higher archetype, the cosmic Sophia.

In his older years, Goethe also aspired to this same ideal with his entire being. But as he remained only at the threshold of the consciousness *soul*, and in many of his works even within the intellectual or mind *soul*,[500] Goethe was, in his poetic feeling for the future, able to comprehend this higher ascent to the archetype only in a *soul* sense and not spiritually. Thus at the very end of *Faust*, which is surrounded by distinctively Catholic symbolism (corresponding to the previous epoch of the intellectual or mind soul), the entelechy of Gretchen becomes Faust's guide into the world of the higher archetypes where, however, there appears to Goethe's inner eye not a purely *spiritual* union with the sphere of the cosmic Sophia, but merely a *soul* perception of the 'Mater gloriosa'.[501]

This is why *Faust*, and in a deeper sense also the whole of Goethe's earthly life, ends with this conscious–unconscious *longing* for a real perception of the *spirit* which lies beyond the threshold at which Goethe stopped at the end of his earthly path. It is this longing or 'pull' which comes to expression in the two famous lines with which he concluded the second part of *Faust*:

> The Eternal Feminine
> Draws us onwards.

As we have seen, this aspiration towards the 'Eternal Feminine', which—if viewed historically—represents an aspiration towards the ideals of the sixth cultural epoch, filled Novalis' being with considerable strength. What Goethe experienced purely poetically as the figure of Gretchen in the spiritual worlds, leading Faust's soul into the world of archetypes, was actually lived out by Novalis in his life[502] through his finding of the path from the earthly form of Sophie von Kühn to the cosmic archetype, the world-soul, the Divine Sophia.

'Christ and Sophia'—the experience of the spiritual reality behind these two words, which are the key to the central mysteries of the sixth cultural epoch, is what makes Novalis its principal representative who is, in Rudolf Steiner's words, able 'to experience the Christ mystery and the Mary mystery *in relation to the cosmic mystery*'.[503]

One of the aspects of this 'cosmic mystery' is of particular importance for what is to follow, and in order to understand this better it is necessary to dwell at some further length upon the path whereby Novalis was able to make the ascent from the image to the archetype, from the physically incarnated human individual, Sophie von Kühn, to a purely spiritual experience of the Divine Sophia.

We shall first turn to the figure of Sophie von Kühn herself and try to form an impression of her on the basis of the various testimonies that have come down to us, from herself, from Novalis and from other people who knew her well.

When viewed from an outward aspect, there was a striking contradiction between how she appeared to be and how she actually was. This girl, who at the time of her meeting with Novalis was really still only a child, was in her whole being at that stage of childhood when curiosity towards everything that is going on in the world and a high degree of receptivity are the most characteristic traits of the human soul; whereas in everything that pertains to outer development a certain retardation was clearly evident. For example, she was still at 13–14 years of age continuing to make the most naïve spelling mistakes, such as would

175

normally be associated with children of a much younger age. 'She was a girl of twelve and a half who had grown up in the country . . . untouched [by outer civilisation], accustomed to a simple, country life, barely educated, and who had the spelling of a seven year old.' She was 'indeed . . . still completely engrossed in her child-nature and was surrounded by the habits and customs with which she was lovingly encircled by those who were her intimate friends'—in such a way does Ritter-Schaumberg characterise Sophie von Kühn in his book, *Novalis and his First Bride*.[504] Novalis, too, refers to this remarkable childlike quality of hers. In a short description of her particular characteristics which he bequeathed under the title of *Clarissa*, we read:

'Her obedience to and fear of her father.'
'Inclination towards childish games.'
'She does not seem as yet to have reached the point where she can reflect for herself.'
'Her child-like dependence upon her mother.'
'Talent of imitation.'
'Her acute attentiveness.'

Moreover, because of this childhood innocence, her general lack of culture and her involvement solely in the narrow circle of the interests of her immediate environment, Sophie von Kühn was altogether incapable of sharing Novalis' intellectual and spiritual interests. When he was wholly engrossed in studying the philosophy of Fichte, there could hardly be anything in him that was more foreign to her than these preoccupations. Still more remarkably, she did not share Novalis' devotion to poetry, which had from the outset played so central a role in his life. 'She does not value poetry in any way,' observes Novalis in *Clarissa*.[505]

Nevertheless, despite the fact that even his spiritual interests were alien to Sophie von Kühn, something drew him towards her with an irresistible power. 'A quarter of an hour has wrought a transformation within me,' writes Novalis subsequently in one of his letters to Erasmus, recalling his first meeting with Sophie von Kühn.[506]

And in *Clarissa* he observes: 'She wants to be nothing. *She is something.*' But what was this 'something'? Why did a simple, provincial girl exercise not only on Novalis, but also upon her whole surroundings, an influence that was well-nigh magical? Novalis experienced this particularly strongly, though all the same it remained from the outset a mystery even to him, and Sophie von Kühn herself was an unsolved enigma.

Shortly after his first acquaintance with her, Novalis writes the following words in a poem dedicated to her and her sister:

176

'When both of them you see, there stands the riddle beside the solution . . .'

This motif of his view of Sophie von Kühn as a complete mystery appears once more some months before her death in an unpreserved letter to her sister Frederika von Mandelsloh, from the answer to which it is clear that Novalis, even two years after his betrothal to Sophie von Kühn, was still trying in vain to solve what was to him the tormenting riddle of her being. Frederika's reply runs as follows: 'However gladly I would like to comply with your wish to portray little Sophie's character (even though I would feel myself to be unequal to this task), how can I describe something which—as is the case with Sophie—*lies several stages above me* and which I am not in a position to judge in a right and fitting way?'

It follows from these words that even for those close to her, Sophie von Kühn remained a riddle until the very end of her life. And only the mysterious 'raying forth' of her being compelled her elder sister to say that she was 'several stages above' her. This spiritual radiance emanating from Sophie von Kühn was also felt by others: Schlegel, that lover of irony; Goethe, who had so deep a knowledge of the womanly soul; Novalis' brother Karl;[507] and even Ludwig Tieck, who knew Sophie von Kühn only through Novalis' stories—all these felt the power of the mysterious aura that surrounded her and which was later transmuted into what Tieck described as a kind of divine halo[508] . . . But there is, furthermore, the point that Sophie von Kühn was wholly unaware of the almost magical influence which, quite independently of her will and consciousness, she had on her surroundings. To this testify both her utterly naïve letters to Novalis and his own words which we have already quoted: '*She wants to be nothing* . . .'

Nor did Sophie von Kühn share in any way in Novalis' more personal feelings. In *Clarissa* he observes:

'She refuses to be on intimate terms.'
'She does not want to be troubled by my love.'
'Her dread of marriage.'
'My love often afflicts her.'
'She is thoroughly cold.'

But in moments of greater self-awareness Novalis himself also clearly realised that his feelings for Sophie von Kühn did not really have anything in common with an ordinary amorous passion; in their more inward nature they were altogether devoid of sensuality. 'Only homage, only inexpressible pleasure, only a wondrous affection—not a trace of wild, possessive passion,' writes Novalis in a letter to Karoline Just. And in a letter to Woltmann he expresses his relationship to Sophie von Kühn in the following manner: 'It is certainly not passion—I feel it so incontrovertibly and coolly, so clearly with my whole soul, that she was one of the noblest and most perfect people who have ever been on Earth or will be in the future.' And again, in his diary: 'Sophie is for me an object of religion, not love.'

This basic quality of Novalis' relationship to Sophie von Kühn was also emphasised by Rudolf Steiner. Thus in the lecture of 23 January 1910 he says: 'Indeed, what we know of his relationship to Sophie von Kühn should not be thought of as something that has to do with sensuality.'[509] And in another lecture: 'During his stay in Grüningen he got to know a thirteen year old girl. And mysteries of the soul were enacted that one would never, without defaming the soul's tenderness, call a love-relationship!' It was a relationship '. . . which can be understood only by recognising it in all its spirituality.'

If one traces the history of Novalis' relationship with Sophie von Kühn, the clear impression arises that their acquaintance and subsequent relationship had not been karmically determined through the past meetings of two individual egos. For in a spiritual, intellectual and, in a certain sense, even in an emotional respect there was too much that separated them. The encounter with Julie Charpentier which took place later in Novalis' life had an altogether different character. It was a meeting between two fully formed individualities, two sovereign egos.[510]

Sophie von Kühn's significance for Novalis was completely different. She was for him like a gate to a higher world, an inducement to direct his inner eye to yonder spheres. In the brief history of their relationship, Sophie von Kühn appears to us as wholly *transparent*, as one who enabled Novalis for the first time to behold the spiritual world *through her* (although wholly without her awareness).

From a spiritual–scientific point of view the earthly personality of Sophie von Kühn can be characterised as follows. In the first place, she was from her birth physically a very weak and sickly child, this being the reason why she was to some extent retarded in her purely physical development. A further expression of this circumstance was that her ego was incarnated in her body to far less a degree than would normally be the case with a 12-year-old child. Rudolf Steiner refers to this as follows: 'In point of fact, we have in Sophie von Kühn—as this girl was called—a being who was on the verge of death.'[511] Thus in many respects she was, until her meeting with Novalis, still at a stage of development corresponding not to the second, but to the first seven-year period in the soul–bodily development of the child. Hence the process of the gradual freeing of the individual etheric body from the maternal etheric sheath which had surrounded it from the beginning, a process which under normal circumstances has reached its fulfilment by the age of 7, had in the case of Sophie von Kühn not been fully completed by the time that she had reached her twelfth year.

As regards her astral body, it was because of the general weakness of her physical body and of the fact that her ego was not rightly incarnated, to a very large extent left to itself, it was given over to all such outward influences as might work upon it from Sophie von Kühn's environment in Grüningen. This was the source of certain of the characterisations given by Novalis in *Clarissa*, which would appear virtually impossible with respect to a 12-year-old girl but which, however, have their origin not in her but in the influence which her immediate surroundings had upon her astral body.[512]

It follows from all that has been said that it was not in her physical appearance (judging by the portraits of her that have been preserved, Sophie von Kühn could hardly be called a beauty, although there was a certain childish charm), nor in the particular qualities of her astral body and still less in her ego[513] that we should seek the source of those mysterious emanations which so many people in her environment, and above all Novalis himself, experienced. And if he himself, in the poem 'Anfang' ('Beginning') calls Sophie von Kühn 'a moral grace' (that is, a 'moral beauty') and Ritter-Schaumberg (in the book about Sophie von Kühn already referred to) cites as 'one of the principal qualities' of her inner disposition a 'probing conscience', 'a great inner conscientiousness'[514] we must say: the riddle of this 12-year-old girl, whose outer and inner image we have endeavoured to depict in some way in this chapter, is—together with the unusual impression that she made on her surroundings—to be traced to the quite special *etheric* body which she had brought with her to the Earth from its pre-earthly state of being.[515]

In this way we may approach a solution to the riddle of this 'contradiction' in the character and outward conduct of Sophie von Kühn, connected as it was with the circumstances of her incarnation at that time and consisting in the profound difference between the principal qualities of her etheric and astral bodies.

However, before turning directly to the mystery of *this* etheric body of Sophie von Kühn, it is necessary to consider in more general terms certain features of the working of the etheric body in the female organism. In a number of his lectures, and especially in that of 26 May 1910, Rudolf Steiner refers to how, with respect to the image of the ideal man, the male organism enters too deeply into physical matter, while the female is in a certain sense 'not fully incarnated'. In the lecture referred to he puts it thus: 'In the male organism the inner man has penetrated more thoroughly into matter and has embraced it more closely than has woman. Woman holds back more of the spiritual in a disembodied state; she does not penetrate so deeply into matter but keeps her bodily nature more flexible. It is characteristic of woman's nature that she retains a greater degree of free spirituality, and for that reason does not penetrate so far into matter and, in particular, keeps her brain more flexible.'[516]

For this reason the modern fifth post-Atlantean epoch, whose task it is to enter more deeply into matter than any other in the history of earthly evolution, has a strongly masculine character. Everything that is connected with the development of science and technology, with the gradual penetration of materialism into all regions of human activity and practice and also into art and religion, is associated with the essentially 'masculine' character of our age. In contrast, the future sixth epoch of post-Atlantean evolution, the first anticipation of the Jupiter condition, will have a strongly 'feminine' character, inasmuch as this epoch is to witness the development of far more spiritual qualities and capacities which can be attained only through incomplete incarnation in the physical body such as quite naturally already takes place in the female organism.[517]

Because of woman's state of 'not being fully incarnated' in her soul-spiritual nature, her etheric body has even today a number of specific qualities which quite fundamentally distinguish it from the etheric body of a man. In order that we may better understand this difference, we must turn to the process of the forming of the etheric body immediately before earthly incarnation in the Moon-sphere surrounding the Earth. In the lecture of 21 April 1924 Rudolf Steiner describes this process in such a way that the soul, as it abides in the Moon-sphere under the guidance of the Moon Teachers of Wisdom, contemplates the spiritual spheres of the planets in order through such contemplation to acquire the forces for the right forming of its future etheric body. 'As the Earth forces are able to live in the physical body through its formation, so in the etheric body do there live the forces which stream down on all sides from the encircling cosmos to the Earth,' says Rudolf Steiner elsewhere in this connection.[518]

Just as the whole spiritual cosmos surrounding our Earth is reflected in the Moon-sphere, so is this process repeated—though now in a more microcosmic way—in the human etheric body, which thereby bears within itself a reflection of the forces of the entire planetary system. 'In the etheric body there is perpetual mobility, mirroring the constellations of the stars as they change during a human earthly life,' writes Rudolf Steiner.[519] Only such an etheric body, one which is wholly transparent for the planetary forces of our cosmos, can become a right bearer of the higher members of the human being, his astral body and ego, connected as they are not with the world of the moving stars but directly with the Sun itself, as a gate to the world of the fixed stars.[520] Hence this condition of the human soul before birth—when the human astral body and ego are gradually forming their future etheric body in the Moon-sphere—can best be depicted with the help of an image of a Moon sickle that bears within itself the disc of the Sun:

And when, finally, the forming of the new human etheric body has been completed, immediately before the astral body and ego have united with it (which in the majority of cases leads to the gradual extinguishing of the spirit-consciousness that is natural to the soul in the spiritual world between death and a new birth) something of the greatest importance takes place. For immediately before that moment when spirit-consciousness is fully extinguished, the human being is given a clairvoyant insight into the principal events of his future earthly life. 'Just as at the onset of death a kind of memory-tableau [of the past life] has stood before the human ego, so now there appears a preview of the life that is to come . . . And what a man thus sees becomes the source of active forces which he must carry with him into his new life.'[521] But this is not yet all. For at that moment when the spirit-consciousness lights up for the last time, the human soul is not only shown a perspective of its next earthly life but, like a radiant *blessing* on the part of the entire spiritual cosmos which the soul is now leaving behind in order that it may incarnate on the Earth, once again experiences in a mighty cosmic imagination—which is, so to speak, an *imaginative memory*—its whole spiritual path from 'the cosmic midnight hour'[522] to the union with its newly formed etheric body in the Moon-sphere. As though in a single majestic panorama there again appears before it the memory of when its ego was abiding in the highest cosmic sphere of the fixed stars, to which is then added the memory of its life in the Sun-sphere and, finally, its present existence in the Moon-sphere. (In other words, it recalls its sojourn in higher and lower Devachan and in the astral world.) This entire path, through which it has passed, is then transformed before its inner eye into the all-embracing, radiant image of the Being who personifies the sum of the *wisdom* of our cosmos, whose head is overshone by forces from the sphere of the fixed stars, in whose heart there bloom the spiritual forces of the Sun-sphere and in the movement of whose limbs there work the forces of the planets and of the Moon.

This is the sublime imagination of the Divine Sophia, who is experienced by every man—albeit at various levels of consciousness—immediately before incarnation on the Earth as the source of the forces that are necessary for the fulfilment of the tasks that have been placed before him in the present earthly life. She it is who appears in the twelfth chapter of the Apocalypse of John the Evangelist as the woman clothed with the Sun, with a crown of 12 stars on her head and the sickle of the Moon beneath her feet.[523]

In our fifth post-Atlantean epoch such an experience of the cosmic Sophia is accessible to man only before his birth on the Earth. In the sixth cultural epoch, however, the experience of this cosmic imagination will become attainable to an ever greater number of people also while in the physical body, and this will then serve as the foundation for a wider dissemination amongst mankind of the mysteries of the Divine Sophia. (In our time such a clairvoyant experience can be attained only on the path of modern spirit-pupilship.)

As the human soul experiences this imagination immediately *before* its union with the already formed etheric body, it is possible for it to absorb a direct impression of this imagination, as a result of which the etheric body can become to a very high degree the mediator for the spiritual forces of the planets and to some extent also of the fixed stars. Now, such an 'elevation' of the receptivity of the human etheric body to the spiritual influence of the heavenly bodies surrounding the Earth will depend above all upon to what extent this imagination is *consciously* apprehended by the soul before its birth on the Earth. If the imagination is experienced with a sufficient degree of consciousness, the faculty that the etheric body has from the outset of being transparent with respect to the spiritual forces of the spirit-cosmos surrounding our Earth will to a certain extent be maintained during the initial period after one's incarnation on Earth.

Here, however, an essential difference can be observed between the way that the two sexes develop in this respect. The etheric body of a boy, has, as a rule, already lost this faculty by the seventh year of life (at the moment of the birth of the independent etheric body), while the etheric body of a girl (because of her general 'incomplete incarnation' in the physical body) keeps it for much longer, under normal circumstances until the thirteenth or fourteenth year, that is, until the onset of sexual maturity. Novalis refers to this facet of human evolution in the following fragment: 'The eternal virgin is none other than an *eternal female child*. This is what corresponds to the virgin where we men are concerned. A girl who is no longer a true *child* is no longer a virgin.'

Thus we may say: approximately until the age of 14 the etheric body in the female organism retains the faculty of being transparent with respect to the spiritual forces of the Moon, that is, to all the spiritual forces of our solar system that are reflected in its sphere.[524] This means, however, that every female organism can until the age indicated also be characterised in a spiritual respect by means of the afore-mentioned symbol of the Moon bearing within itself the forces of the Sun and the other planets. This state of affairs changes altogether with the awakening of the individual astral body at the time of sexual maturity.[525] For the astral body, through its activity being directed from the beginning almost exclusively towards perception of the outer world of the senses, draws the Moon forces that are active in the etheric body together into a single point and leads them over into the physical body, this then being expressed in the 'lunar rhythm' that now manifests itself within it. Until this moment, that is, until the awakening of the forces of the individual astral body, the etheric body in the female organisation still continues to be, to the highest degree, open to the influences of the entire planetary cosmos. With the penetration of the 'Moon rhythm' into the physical body, however, this primal condition generally completely ceases to exist.

If we now return to the 'riddle' of Sophie von Kühn, we may say that because of the general sickliness of her physical body, the retarded development (that is, the insufficient individualisation) of her astral body and the incompleteness of the incarnation process of her ego, her *etheric body*, in contrast, was able, to an unusually high degree to maintain a connection with the cosmic sphere of the Moon, and, through it, with the whole world of the planets surrounding our Earth. It was this quality of Sophie von Kühn's etheric body that Novalis—through his enhanced receptivity to everything spiritual—experienced with such particular power already from his first acquaintance with her, although the true reasons for his being so strongly drawn towards the 12-year-old girl remained for him, especially in the early period of their acquaintance, to a remarkable degree unconscious and her whole being—as we have seen—an insoluble riddle.

However, it became clear to him comparatively soon after his first acquaintance with Sophie von Kühn that his feelings for her could not really be associated in any way with the word 'passion' or even with the word 'love' in the ordinary sense.[526] Thus long before her death his relationship to her had begun increasingly to acquire not an earthly but a mystical–metaphysical character. For example, less than a year after his first meeting with Sophie von Kühn Novalis wrote the following in the poem, 'Anfang' ('Beginning') (1795):

> One day mankind will be what Sophie is
> To me—the perfection of moral grace—
> No longer will her *higher consciousness*
> Mistaken be for wine's haze of illusion.

One may have the impression that in this first meeting Novalis' inner eye gradually penetrated at this time 'through' the soul-etheric nature of Sophie von Kühn into the spiritual sphere surrounding the Earth and, through her special etheric body, united with the cosmic reality of the woman clothed with the Sun and the Moon beneath the feet.

Only through what has been said does it become clear why in the lecture, 'The Psychology of Art', which is concerned with a spiritual–scientific comparison between the spirit-soul organisations of Novalis and Goethe, Rudolf Steiner says very clearly that the beginning of the acquaintance between Novalis and Sophie von Kühn came at a time *before* she had reached sexual maturity: 'And this personality of Novalis enters more and more deeply into life and begins a love-relationship that spiritually is utterly real with a twelve year old girl, Sophie von Kühn. His love for this girl *who has not as yet reached sexual maturity* is clothed in the most wonderful poetry, in poetry of such a kind that one would never be tempted to associate this relationship with anything to do with the senses . . . This girl dies two days after completing her fourteenth year, that is, at a time when the reality of physical life affects most people so strongly that they descend into the sexual aspect of the physical body. *Before this event can take place in the case of Sophie von Kühn*, she is borne aloft into the spiritual worlds.' And a little further on he returns to this same thought, though expressing it in a rather more veiled form: 'And so if one tries to understand all that sprang from this wonderfully formed soul [of Novalis], which was able to love without coming into contact with outer reality, which was accordingly able to live with what was actually taken away from it *before a certain stage of outer reality had been reached*, if one takes into account all that flowed forth from this soul of Novalis, one acquires the purest impression of the nature of poetry.'[527]

Despite all that has been said about the etheric body of Sophie von Kühn, the riddle of her being has not been fully solved. For the spiritual 'transparency' of her etheric body and the heightened receptivity of Novalis' soul are not complete explanations of the mysterious fact that it was through this meeting and subsequent relationship with Sophie von Kühn that he gradually gained access to the all-embracing cosmic sphere of the Divine Sophia. Therefore in order that we may penetrate beyond the veil of mystery of the earthly being of this 12-year-old girl, we need to turn to that law of spiritual life which Rudolf Steiner, notably in the lectures which he gave in 1909, describes as the law of 'spiritual economy'. Thus in the lecture of 15 February 1909 he explains it by means of the Eastern teaching of the 'Avatars', that is, Beings of a higher order who have no need to incarnate in an earthly body for their own development and yet, from time to time, make the sacrificial resolve to incarnate amongst mankind solely in order to give a new impulse for a further step in human evolution. 'Such a Being,' says Rudolf Steiner, 'can, however, in order to intervene in the course of human evolution, enter, in what could be described as a vicarious way, into just such a body as human beings have.'[528] Now, the most important aspect of such an incarnation of an Avatar in a human being is that the sheaths of the latter can be preserved in the spiritual world and also that the spiritual imprints or copies that have thus been fashioned can be multiplied and transmitted to suitable human individuals before their birth on Earth in order that they may fulfil particular tasks in the spiritual evolution of mankind. In the lecture referred to above, Rudolf Steiner goes on to say that the greatest of all the Avatars who have ever incarnated on the Earth was the Christ Being, who at the Baptism in the Jordan united with the physical body of the man, Jesus of Nazareth. Subsequently, after the Mystery of Golgotha had been fulfilled on the Earth, the sheaths of Jesus of Nazareth were preserved in the spiritual world, multiplied there according to the law of 'spiritual economy' and later incorporated in the corresponding sheaths of the human beings who had been chosen for this purpose, as we were able to see occurring in a quite special way in the cases of Raphael and Novalis.

If, however, we consider, at a somewhat deeper level, all the events connected with the Turning-Point of Time, with the Baptism in the Jordan and its preparation, when through the wisdom of the world rulership the two families who were to serve as the gates for the coming of the Nathan Soul and Zarathustra to the Earth settled close by one another in Nazareth,[529] we can actually discern in all these events not one but *two* cases of an Avatar Being entering into Earth existence. Of the first case (from the point of time it was the second) we have already spoken; the second is the vicarious incarnation of a quite particular Avatar Being from the higher worlds in the Mary of the Luke Gospel.

In his book, *The Childhood and the Youth of Jesus*, Emil Bock refers to this mystery in the following words, which at the same time characterise the nature of the Luke Mary: 'In her being and countenance there is a reflection, in the most serene purity and perfection, of a divine archetype which hovers over mankind in the spiritual world. Just as in the child that she is to bear, who reflects and embodies the archetype of the child, is the embodiment of all that is childlike—a focal point of everything that pertains to childhood on the Earth—so is the Luke Mary an earthly image of the archetype of virginal womanhood, the embodiment of the "eternal feminine", the woman of women . . . Here was a human soul which, in all its outward insignificance, was wholly imbued and permeated by the world soul, and, through it, by the pure light-essence of the cosmos, which in the ancient world was called Isis-Sophia and in Christian times the "Holy Spirit".'[530] Thus in the figure of the Luke Mary we have a human being who was worthy of becoming the bearer of one of the highest Avatar Beings after the Sun-Spirit of the Christ Himself, of that exalted Being who, in the ancient world, was called the Divine Isis and in the early Christian communities and in places where *esoteric* Christianity was nurtured, the Divine Sophia.[531]

This incarnation of an Avatar who ranks as the second in significance in our cosmos, an event which, unique in its way, took place outwardly almost wholly unobserved within the history of human evolution, did, however, acquire an immense significance for the further evolution of the Earth through the law of spiritual economy, which was at work also in this case. For in the same way that the sheaths of Jesus of Nazareth which had been permeated by the Christ Being were preserved and then multiplied in the spiritual world, so did something similar take place with the sheaths of the Luke Mary—which had been permeated by the cosmic Being of the Sophia—after she had passed over into the spiritual world in the twelfth year of the Christian era (she was then about 25 years old).[532] The only difference is that whereas the imprints of the supersensible sheaths of Jesus have already been an active force during the remainder of the fourth and in the fifth post-Atlantean epochs, the imprints of the etheric and astral bodies of the Luke Mary will be active amongst mankind only from the sixth cultural epoch onwards.

In this sense the teachings of the twelfth-century Italian mystic Joachim of Fiore are realised. He taught that after the age of the Father God, which includes the whole pre-Christian evolution of humanity, and the age of the Son God—whose beginning can be traced back to the deeds of Christ Jesus at the Turning-Point of Time—that followed it, there will eventually ensue the age of the Holy Spirit, the age which will see the dawning of the wisdom of the Divine Sophia amongst mankind. From a spiritual–scientific point of view, the beginning of this new age of the Spirit coincides with the shifting of the point of the Spring Equinox into the constellation of the Waterman, from which region the water of the new cosmic wisdom will flow forth into human life on Earth. From a historical standpoint, this time will correspond with the beginning of the sixth cultural epoch.

Despite the fact that the incorporation of the imprints of the supersensible sheaths of the Luke Mary into the etheric and astral bodies of human individuals on the Earth will as a rule take place in the sixth cultural epoch, nevertheless under particular circumstances, as a very rare exception, this can also occur in our time. The *exceptional nature* of such an 'incorporation' in our time is principally due to the especially deep immersion of the *whole* of mankind in the sphere of matter, as a result of which even the female organism, for all its general state of not quite complete incarnation, is in the majority of cases not sufficiently plastic to become the bearer of these imprints. If, nonetheless, such an event does take place today, in very rare cases, the female organism concerned will be able to hold on to this imprint in its etheric body only *until* the onset of sexual maturity, the reason being that the modern etheric body does not as yet have those inner qualities which it will have in the sixth cultural epoch, and which will enable it to retain such a divine imprint beyond this particular threshold of life.* Then it may happen that, at the moment when the individual astral body is awakened, the imprint of the divine etheric body begins to leave the human etheric body and withdraws all its life-forces back into the spiritual world with such strength that death can occur shortly after the coming of sexual maturity.[533] This is what happened in the case of Sophie von Kühn in the fifteenth year of her life, after she had been seriously ill for almost two years.[534]

Only from the sixth cultural epoch onwards will it become possible for human beings to receive into themselves the spiritual forces of imprints of the etheric body of the Luke Mary (and, subsequently, also of her astral body) in full consciousness, that is, also *after* the onset of sexual maturity. And the highest archetype of such an instance of someone being taken hold of in full consciousness by the forces of the divine etheric body— thus enabling a supersensible connection with the entire macrocosm to be maintained in complete serenity—was manifested in human history by the *Mary of St Matthew's Gospel*. For through the exceptional purity and selflessness of her astral body, qualities which were further strengthened by her deep suffering,[535] she was, according to the spiritual–scientific research of Rudolf Steiner, able—at the moment of Jesus' union with the cosmic Being of the Christ at the Baptism in the Jordan—to experience

---

* More will be said about these special qualities of the etheric body later in this chapter.

the penetration into her being from the higher worlds, even to her *etheric body*, by the spiritual being of the Luke Mary. In the lecture of 11 January 1910, given in Stockholm,[536] Rudolf Steiner speaks about this event as follows: 'At the Baptism in the Jordan ... the mother principle experiences a re-birth in that the pure *etheric body* of the Nathan mother descends and permeates the other mother. Now she is again a virgin, and a deep connection is formed between Christ and the mother.'[537] From the standpoint of the forces working in the cosmos, this means: while at the moment of the Baptism in the Jordan the spiritual forces issuing from the highest point of the zodiac, from the region of the *Ram*, were uniting with Jesus of Nazareth, at the same moment the cosmic forces from the zodiacal region of the *Virgin* were, *through the mediation* of the etheric body of the 'Nathan Mary', uniting with the Mary of St Matthew's Gospel, permeating her own etheric body and working on in a transforming way right into her physical body. For the zodiacal region of the Virgin is the source of all the forces of virginal purity in our cosmos.

This can also be expressed as follows: At the moment of the Baptism in the Jordan, the being of Jesus of Nazareth was transformed out of the cosmic forces of the Ram, and the being of the Solomon Mary was transformed out of the cosmic forces of the Virgin, as a result of which Jesus became the 'Lamb of God, who takes away the sins of the world' (John 1:29), and Mary the representative on Earth of the primordial forces of the most sublime virginal purity and chastity, the bearer of the forces of the *Virgin*-Sophia on the Earth.[538]

In the lecture of 3 July 1909 in Kassel, Rudolf Steiner characterises this transformation of the being of the Solomon Mary through to her physical body in the following words: 'At the same moment in which the Spirit of Christ descended into the body of Jesus of Nazareth and a transformation took place such as we have described, an influence was also exerted upon the mother of Jesus of Nazareth. This influence consisted in that at the moment of the Baptism she regained her virginity, that is to say, she reverted in her inner organism *to the condition of the female organism before puberty*. At the birth of the Christ, the mother of Jesus of Nazareth became a virgin.[539] These words, which appear in the tenth lecture of the cycle, *The Gospel of St John in Relation to the Other Three Gospels, especially that of St Luke,* are the first reference to this fundamental mystery of the 'transformation of Mary' in the life work of Rudolf Steiner.[540] In a remarkable, and at the same time a thoroughly right way, the very first revelation of this profound mystery is connected with the creative work of Novalis, not only because at the beginning of the lecture there are to be found what are perhaps the most meaningful words that Rudolf Steiner ever uttered about the significance of the Baptism in the

Jordan for earthly evolution as a whole (see note 444), but above all for the reason that this tenth lecture of the cycle immediately preceded the morning gathering devoted to Novalis' work (4 July 1909). At this morning gathering Marie Steiner (at the time still von Sivers) recited Novalis' *Spiritual Songs* and *Songs of Mary*. Behind the first of these there stands the mystery of the Baptism in the Jordan, the mystery of the union of the cosmic Being of the Christ with the earthly sheaths of Jesus of Nazareth. Behind the second stands the mystery of the union of the two Marys.

Thus in these two cycles of poems the principal spiritual leitmotif of Novalis' entire life, 'Christ and Sophia', or—expressing this leitmotif in the language of the starry script—the sacrificial surrender of two human beings to the forces of the macrocosm which stream, respectively, from the cosmic regions of the Ram and the Virgin, finds its poetic reflection.

As has already been said, only from the beginning of the sixth cultural epoch, the epoch when the Sophia mystery or the mystery of the Holy Spirit will become generally known amongst mankind, will it become possible for an ever greater number of people not merely to receive imprints of the etheric body of the Luke Mary which has been permeated by the Sophia forces, but also to experience their working in full consciousness and, hence, to preserve their forces also into riper years. In other words, from approximately the beginning of the sixth cultural epoch it will, to a certain extent, become possible for human beings to attain that condition whose archetype was made historically manifest to mankind in the sublime figure of the Solomon Mary, whose etheric-physical organism became, at the moment of the Baptism in the Jordan (when she was about 45 years old), through the union of the forces from the cosmic region of the Virgin with her etheric body, again of like nature with 'the condition of the female organism *before* puberty'.[541] She became once again a 'virgin', that is, a human being who has been transformed by the cosmic forces from the zodiacal region of the Virgin, to the extent of her etheric-physical nature, and who from this moment enters into a fully conscious connection with them. This means that from this time her etheric body became a 'mirror' for the spiritual processes of the starry cosmos that surrounds our Earth and that the forces of the Divine Sophia, the heavenly wisdom, could begin to work directly within her soul and spirit. The Solomon Mary became from this moment the earthly bearer of the Sophia principle. This is why amongst the Apostles and later in the circles of esoteric Christianity, especially until the fourth century of the Christian era, the Solomon Mary was never called by her earthly name (see, for example, John 19:25) but always, in an esoteric sense, bore the name Sophia, this being the only name which directly refers to the fundamental mystery of her spiritual-physical being.[542] For she is, in Emil Bock's words, the female human being who 'follows to the end the path that leads to the rediscovery of the lost virginal purity', so that 'the earthly feminine aspect of her nature becomes ever more permeable to the rays of the eternal feminine.'[543]

This process, which is connected with the gradual approach to the high ideal represented by the Solomon Mary, will become accessible to human beings in full waking consciousness only in the sixth cultural epoch. Then it will be possible for the Sophia impulses to be spread universally amongst mankind, a fact which, in its turn, will be associated with the fulfilment of certain mysteries of Johannine or Rosicrucian Christianity. In the sixth epoch this process will *not*, of course, be connected with the difference between the two sexes. In its purely spiritual aspect it will work in a region higher than that of sexuality. However, the female organism will, so to speak, have a natural predisposition for it. On the other hand, those who in the sixth epoch will have a male organism will not by any means be excluded from this aspect of evolution, but will achieve this condition with considerably more effort and only with the help of intense spirit-pupilship in the respective mystery schools.[544] Although these difficulties will be of an altogether different kind, they are nevertheless, to a certain extent, comparable with those which people with a female organism have to overcome today if they want to take a full part in the development of modern civilisation, with its decidedly intellectually materialistic and anti-spiritual character.[545] In this respect one can say: *To be born as a woman in the sixth cultural epoch will be a special gift of destiny.* Novalis writes in anticipation of this future time: 'Charcoal and diamond are of one substance and yet how different—it is surely the same, is it not, with man and woman. We are alumina—and women are *world-eyes* and sapphires which consist of this same alumina.'

All this also sheds new light upon words which Rudolf Steiner spoke in the circle of doctors and medical students to the effect that the primary task of the male part of humanity is 'to keep the female world as healthy as possible . . . for it is through women that influences from beyond the Earth will then be drawn into the sphere of earthly processes.' For in her nature, 'woman has the inclination to unite herself ever more and more with extra-terrestrial processes. She tends increasingly . . . to be drawn up into the heavenly worlds.'[546] In the sense of what has been said in the present chapter, this means that the future of mankind depends upon whether the social structure of modern times, which has been created and directed principally by its masculine element, will be able to save from degeneration that womanhood towards which the mightiest destructive forces of modern times are directed, forces whose object it is to prevent the emergence of the sixth cultural epoch onto the stage of earthly evolution. Thus a decisive precondition for its coming into being will be that humanity's masculine element is able to protect the spirit-soul and physical being of woman and, hence, also the spiritual potential for the future that rests within her organism. This guarding of the spiritual forces that reside within the female organism will also be one of the most important tasks of Johannine Christianity in its Rosicrucian form. There is a prophetic reference to this high task of true modern Rosicrucianism, a task which is associated with the service of the divine purposes of Earth evolution, at the end of St John's Gospel in the scene of the hill of Golgotha, where Christ Jesus from the Cross unites His mother, the Matthew Mary, and John, His beloved disciple, as they stand beneath it, into a new spiritual whole. 'When Jesus saw His mother, and the disciple whom He loved standing near, He said to His mother: "Woman, behold your son!" Then He said to the disciple: "Behold your mother!" And from that hour the disciple took her to his own home.'[547] In entrusting him with this task, Christ Jesus makes his most advanced pupil, for all future times, *the guardian of the Sophia forces amongst mankind* and at the same time the great preparer of the sixth cultural epoch[548] and, through it, also of the future Jupiter condition—an imagination which John was later to depict in the twenty-first chapter of Revelation.

In the sixth cultural epoch the revelation of the spiritual forces of the Sophia will also be associated with the gradual preparation of that time when the propagation of the human race on Earth will take place in a far more spiritual way. This will to a certain extent already come about at the end of the sixth epoch, while in the seventh epoch it will become general amongst wider circles of mankind. However, in order that this may happen, *two* things are necessaary. In the first place, the Sophia forces must have attained a certain level of development through the union of imprints from the etheric body of the Luke Mary with the etheric bodies of an ever-growing number of human beings—which is to say that human individuals must, by that time, be to a sufficient degree in a position to develop a likeness to the high archetype which is represented in the historical evolution of mankind by the Mary of St Matthew's Gospel.

In other words, by that time a degree of selflessness and openness to the spiritual cosmos surrounding the Earth must have been attained by human individuals such as to enable the spiritual forces from the zodiacal region of the Virgin to work within the human organism through to the etheric body, and thereby also upon the physical body, as happened in the

191

case of the Solomon Mary at the moment of the Baptism of Jesus in the Jordan. This will then be the *first stage* on the path to the gradual fulfilment of that sublime imagination which is described at the beginning of the twelfth chapter of Revelation and which will be an essential part of the Sophia mysteries of the future. This is the imagination of the cosmic Virgin clothed with the Sun, with the Moon beneath her feet and a crown of twelve stars on her head. In this imagination we may discern a certain aspect of the Divine Sophia, giving birth to the higher Sun life which she has received from the divine Word or Cosmic Logos; through it we behold the fructifying of the Sophia by the World Spirit who calls forth the birth in our world of a new Sun Being.

According to the spiritual–scientific research of Rudolf Steiner, this imagination will become a full *physical reality* only when the Earth again unites with the Sun.[550] However, what will take place in the distant future as a great cosmic event must gradually be prepared amongst mankind through the microcosmic realisation of this imagination within human beings as the first anticipation of the future cosmic existence of mankind.

This is, however, only one aspect of what must be achieved by human beings in the sixth cultural epoch. The second aspect of the whole will have to be a particular development of the *word* and its capacities.

Approximately by the fifth millennium (that is, by the beginning of the second half of the sixth epoch), the capacity will again develop—albeit on a completely different plane—of exerting a *magical* influence upon the world through the word, a capacity which in the early stages of Atlantean times, and to a lesser degree even until the beginning of the third post-Atlantean epoch, had—in a completely different form—once been possessed by mankind in full measure.[551] By this time the human *larynx* will have become so spiritualised that the spirit-permeated word will again be able, to some extent, to influence the processes and beings of the surrounding world, awakening in human souls now no longer abstract thoughts, as is the case today, but wholly new, moral impulses. Thus the human word will gradually become a force that can serve as a new creative element in earthly evolution. It will then, in its effect, become truly akin to the influence of the Macrologos in our cosmos, *it will itself become a micrologos*.[552]

Just as in the Sophia mysteries the pupil is led to a real spiritual experience of the Imagination of the Virgin clothed with the Sun, so for developing within himself the capacity of working magically in the world through the word he will have to come to an equally real, supersensible experience of another imagination; he may be led towards

192

beholding such an imagination by mysteries of another kind, which we may call the mysteries of the Logos, or Word. This second imagination is also to be found in the Book of Revelation. John describes it in the first chapter as the cosmic vision of the Son of Man holding 'in His right hand the seven stars', whose face was 'like the Sun shining in full strength' and 'from whose mouth issued a sharp two-edged sword' (v. 16). Only if in the future this sublime imagination is experienced and gradually made an inner reality will man be transformed in such a way that the forces of the Spirit-Sun will shine forth within his purified astral body. He will then, in his will, be in a position to encompass the forces of the seven moving stars in his etheric body. This will change his physical larynx in such a way that, from it, the *word* will be able to work in the world, as the revelation of his higher ego, like a fiery, two-edged sword which unerringly divides good from evil in the moral sphere.

Thus the working of these *two kinds of mysteries*, the mystery of the Sophia and the mystery of the Logos, will lay the spiritual foundation for mankind's further evolution in the sixth epoch.

From our time onwards, however, this imagination will increasingly be placed before mankind from yet another, altogether different side. For just as the last purely spiritual experience of the human soul before birth, one which immediately precedes the prophetic vision of the future earthly life (see p. 181), is the imagination of the Virgin clothed with the Sun—the imagination of the personified *world wisdom* of our cosmos—so the first really spiritual experience of man after death, when the memories of the earthly life that has passed have left him together with his etheric body which has dissolved in the far reaches of space, will be the sublime imagination of the Son of Man.

Since ancient times, and approximately until the end of the dark age of the Kali-Yuga in 1899, the figure that the human soul encountered after death immediately prior to entering Kama-Loka was that of Moses, judging all the person's thoughts, feelings and deeds in his past earthly life *according to the cosmic law*. Of our times, however, Rudolf Steiner has the following to say: 'As the influences of the supersensible Christ increasingly pervade the souls of men, the figure of Moses will be replaced after death by that of Christ Jesus. This means that our karma will be linked with Christ; Christ will enter into an ever closer union with our own karma.'[553] Thus from the twentieth century onwards, simultaneously with the new appearance of Christ in the etheric realm and with His becoming the Lord of Karma,[554] the judgment of souls after death will, in accordance with an inexorable cosmic law, be gradually replaced by a judgment of Christ, the *judge of the highest cosmic love*. This means: 'That when in the future we have found our way to Christ our

193

karmic account may be balanced out, that is, inserted into the cosmic order in such a way that the process of compensating for our karma may serve the greatest possible good of mankind, for the rest of human evolution: this will be the concern of Him who from our time onwards will be the Lord of Karma; it will be the concern of Christ.'

The imagination of the Son of Man which we find at the beginning of the Book of Revelation is a prophetic reference to Christ as the Lord of Karma, who in place of the figure of Moses now meets the human soul after death before it enters Kama-Loka and judges it according to the *law of cosmic love*. His face shines like the new Sun of *love*; in His right hand are the forces of the seven planets, an indication that man's etheric body will by this time have completely dissolved in the far widths of space, and that the cosmic forces working within it will have returned to the planetary world;[555] while from His lips there comes the fiery, two-edged sword of the creative power of the Sun-Logos, a power which *indicates* to the human ego *the direction* for all the time that it will subsequently spend in the spiritual world. This is the fiery sword of the judgmentary love of the Cosmic Word, which shows the soul the path through Kama-Loka into the higher spiritual spheres 'so that the process of compensating for our karma may serve the greatest possible good of mankind for the rest of human evolution . . .'

Thus these two sublime imaginations of the Son of Man and the Divine Sophia stand in all their stupendous cosmic reality ever and again before the human soul: the one as its first really spiritual (that is, free from everything earthly) experience after death and the other as its last really spiritual experience before birth.[556] In other words, they appear to the human soul as the cosmic imaginations of *immortality* and *prebirth*. Hence the mystery of the Logos and the mystery of the Sophia referred to above can also be called *the mysteries of immortality and the mysteries of prebirth*, in contrast to the corresponding pre-Christian mysteries of death and birth.[557]

Only the future working together of these two mystery streams will enable humanity gradually to prepare for the final overcoming of birth and death which have arisen as a result of the division into two sexes and of the need that the procreation of the human race be continued in the manner that it is at present.[558]

The possibility of a more spiritual way of procreating the human race will arise when, through the working of the mysteries of immortality (or of the Logos), the human larynx is transformed into a new higher organ of reproduction, when the human word—permeated by spiritual will— is able to become creative even to the extent of physical substances, a stage which in Rosicrucian schools has always been marked by the symbol of the fiery, two-edged sword or the lance of light. Simultaneously with this, the human heart, too, undergoes a complete transformation through the working of the mysteries of prebirth (or of the Sophia). First it becomes an organ for the conscious perception of the cosmic forces of the spiritual cosmos surrounding the Earth, and then it is transformed into a new spiritual organ of reproduction.[559] In the imagination of the cosmic Sophia this comes to expression in that, at the radiant centre of the solar disc in which she is arrayed, the heart appears like an invisible etheric chalice, receiving and bearing within itself the light of the Spiritual Sun.[560]

And so in the distant future, when a more spiritual condition of the Earth has become a reality, and the final goal of both these mysteries is attained, the human being will, *through the working together* of the transformed larynx and heart, be able to give birth, out of himself, to beings of like nature to himself.

This high ideal of a future, purely spiritual means of reproduction, that is, in the highest spiritual sense, of 'immaculate conception', was from the early Middle Ages always represented in the mysteries of esoteric Christianity through the image of the Holy Grail. In later times, the knowledge of this occult mystery, which has so fundamental a significance for the entire future evolution of mankind, passed over to the Rosicrucians. In their mystery schools the goal of human evolution, referred to above, was spoken of in the following words: 'See how the plant inclines its calyx innocently towards the Sun, how the sunbeam kisses its blossom. This was called the chaste kiss of the sunbeam, of the holy lance of love. In the chaste kiss of the sunbeam, the holy lance of love, to which the calyx of the plant opens, there was seen to be an indication of the ideal of a future age, when man will again lead the evolution of his organs towards the chastity of the plant. In our time, man is evolved to the stage where he is permeated with desires. His evolution will continue to unfold to the point where he has transformed his desires, where he is once again kissed by the spiritual sunbeam, where he brings forth his own kind at a higher level, where the power of reproduction is spiritualised; in the mystery school this was called the Holy Grail. The true ideal of the Holy Grail is an organ that man will have when his reproductive power is spiritualised.'[561]

This new organ of reproduction, called here the Holy Grail, will, however, as we have seen, be made up of the activity of two transformed organs: the heart and the larynx. Rudolf Steiner speaks about this as follows: 'There are within man organs of two different kinds, those which are on the way to becoming imperfect and will gradually fall away and those which are still in the process of formation. All lower organs, the sexual organs, will fall away. *The heart and the larynx*, on the other hand, are organs which will be perfected and find their full development only in the future.'[562] In another lecture he speaks about this with full clarity: 'Above all there will be a transformation *of the larynx and the heart. In future, they will be the organs of reproduction.*'[563] The heart and the larynx are the new spiritual organs of reproduction whose interaction, in the far future, 'will bring forth beings similar to man.' It is they that are engraved, as symbols of the future evolution of a humanity which has overcome earthly birth and death, in the imagination of the Sun chalice and the lance of love, the transformed heart and larynx.[564]

Thus from out of the Grail Mysteries,[565] of which the Rosicrucian Mysteries of modern times represent the continuation, there shines this sublime ideal of the distant future. This will be a time when the experiences of immortality and prebirth unite for man into a continuous span of consciousness; death and birth in their present-day form will be finally overcome, and man himself will pass on to far more spiritual forms of existence. By this means, the Earth will be fully ready to unite once more with the Sun. Rudolf Steiner speaks about this event as follows: 'The Earth will then be ready to unite with the Sun ... The forces of the Moon will be overcome. At this stage man can unite with the Sun. He will live in the spiritualised Earth and at the same time be united with the power of the Sun; and he will be the conqueror of the Moon.'[566]

However—and this is clear from the above quotation—before this condition of complete spiritualisation (the union with the Sun) can come about in earthly evolution, mankind will have to endure a battle and overcome the retardant Moon forces, which will enter into earthly evolution with particular power from the seventh millennium of the Christian era onwards, that is, in approximately the second half of the seventh cultural epoch, when, in accordance with what has been imparted through spiritual science, the Moon will again unite with the Earth. Rudolf Steiner speaks about this event, which will so radically change the spiritual–physical situation on the Earth, as follows: 'Then a time will come in the seventh millennium ... Women will become barren; an altogether different kind and manner of earthly life will begin. It will be the time when the Moon is again approaching the Earth, when it again unites with the Earth.'[567]

As a consequence of the separation of the Moon from the Earth, there took place, at the beginning of the Lemurian epoch, the division of mankind into two sexes,[568] and, with it, the necessity of earthly birth and death and also the final loss of the forces of immortality. By the seventh–eighth millennium, with the re-union of the Moon with the

Earth, a new stage in human evolution will begin which will lead to the gradual overcoming of dual sexuality, that is, to the overcoming of birth and death in their present form, the final disappearance of which will, it is true, take place only when the Earth unites with the Sun.[569]

But what will eventually also be manifest in an outward physical way must first become a reality within human beings. If, therefore, mankind is to find the *right* relationship to the union of the Moon with the Earth which is to take place in the seventh–eighth millennium, and that means to *overcome* all its harmful and seductive influences, it must, by that time, have been able—even if only to a certain extent—to make the imagination of the Divine Sophia referred to above (see p. 182) an inner reality. For only if, at the moment of the outward physical union of the Moon with the Earth, mankind can *inwardly realise within itself* the imagination which represents the future union of *the Earth and the Sun* will it be able to receive the forces of the Moon in such a way that they can work for the good and not for the ill of subsequent earthly evolution; that this can happen will be the concern of the Sophia Mysteries, especially from the sixth cultural epoch onwards.

However, through the fact that modern spiritual science has paved the way to a purely spiritual knowledge of the Christ Being, it is, to a certain extent, possible to approach these Sophia Mysteries of the future already in our time. And if, as a result of intense meditative work, man succeeds in experiencing the first of the two apocalyptic imaginations described above as he falls asleep, he will as he awakes eventually be able to experience also the second imagination and, therefore, gradually approach the mysteries of the Sophia. This will be the path from Christ to Sophia.

Novalis took this path. He began with the experience of Christ in the spiritual world, or the 'world of night', and ended with a premonition of the fundamental mystery of the Earth's future evolution:

> Established in eternity's domain,
> In love and peace now ends the strife and pain,
> The age-long dream of sorrows now is over,
> *Priestess of hearts, Sophia is forever.*

*

In these considerations, the attempt has been made to approach, in some small way, the future mysteries of the Divine Sophia, lightly to lift the veil that hides her secrets. In our time the content of these mysteries cannot as yet be openly disclosed to humanity, for the majority of human beings are today completely incapable of bringing to the highly meaningful secrets which they contain an appropriate feeling of reverence and an inner purity of heart. In our present epoch the feelings that are necessary for such a development to take place exist only as a very rare exception. Novalis was one such exception. As no one else, he was—in prophetic anticipation of the fundamental spiritual impulses of the sixth cultural epoch—able to approach the Sophia Mystery *in his personal spiritual experience.* It is for this reason that, in a book which is devoted to his karmic biography, these future mysteries could become the subject of our considerations.

We now return to the riddle of the etheric body of Sophie von Kühn. Although in her everyday consciousness the 12-year-old Sophie von Kühn knew nothing about the forces of the imprint of the Luke Mary's etheric body that worked within her own etheric body, nevertheless these forces rayed forth everywhere around her. Not even Novalis could solve the profound and seemingly contradictory mystery of his bethrothed's enigmatic nature with his ordinary consciousness.[570] But what his powers of reason could not explain was felt in all fullness by his heart, deeply imbued as it was with the mysteries of the spiritual world.

In his unfinished novel, *Heinrich von Ofterdingen*, Novalis expressed his inner yearning for this imprint of the etheric body of the Luke Mary, not in the form of dry concepts, but through a tender and highly poetic image, the image of the 'blue flower', in whose calyx is revealed the radiance of her tender, divine countenance: 'But what most strongly drew his attention was a tall, light blue flower that stood close by the spring and touched him with its broad, shining leaves . . . He saw nothing but the blue flower and watched it for a long while with an ineffable tenderness. At last he wanted to approach it, when all at once it began to move and change its shape; the leaves became shinier and nestled around the growing stem, the flower inclined itself towards him, and the petals took on the appearance of a blue, extended collar wherein a tender face hovered.'

As has already been fully described in the chapter entitled 'Novalis' Sources of Inspiration', he was able to approach this purely spiritual experience because he bore an imprint of the astral body of the Nathan Soul in his own *astral body.*

Since the early Middle Ages, such an astral body that was purified from all lower desires was, in Christian-Rosicrucian esotericism, denoted with a quite definite symbol. An unpurified astral body bore a different symbol.

According to Rudolf Steiner, who in his descriptions drew upon this tradition, the expression of a human astral body that is still permeated by passions and desires is the red colour of the blood. On the other hand, the purified and light-filled astral body was, in these esoteric circles, always symbolised through the image of the *rose*, which unites in itself the red colour, as an expression of the individual ego principle which lives within man's astral body, and the complete lack of lower desires and passions that is characteristic of the plant world.[571] Of such a nature was the astral body of the Nathan Soul (Jesus of Nazareth), an imprint of which Novalis bore within his soul. This higher astral body, this spiritual rose within him, led him to the 'heart-knowledge' of the blue flower or spiritual lily in the etheric body of Sophie von Kühn.

Thus in a remarkable way that profound mystery of human evolution which in the occult language of esoteric Christianity can be called the *spiritual marriage of the rose and the lily*,[572] an event which had formerly been no more than indicated through the images of tales and legends, came once more to fulfilment in modern times, at the end of the eighteenth century. In the words of the hero of the novel, *Heinrich von Ofterdingen*, Novalis would have been able to say of himself: 'but the blue flower is what I long to behold. It is ceaselessly in my mind, and I cannot write poems or think about anything else.' Thenceforth, Novalis aspired with all his soul forces towards this imprint of the etheric body of the Luke Mary which was permeated by the cosmic forces of the Divine Sophia.

This mystic marriage of the rose and the lily which is accomplished during the life of Sophie von Kühn on Earth extends its influence to the life after death. Thus three days after death the etheric body of Sophie von Kühn dissolves in the far reaches of the world ether, freeing the imprint of the etheric body of the Luke Mary which had been woven into it 'in the life' of Sophie von Kühn on Earth. Upon becoming free in the spiritual sphere surrounding the Earth, this etheric imprint then aspires towards its archetype in the cosmic region of the constellation of the *Virgin*! And because of the mystical wedding which had taken place on the Earth, Novalis is in a position to *follow* this etheric imprint with his soul into the higher spiritual worlds, in the direction of the constellation of the Virgin, the all-embracing cosmic sphere of the Sophia.

We find an allusion to this inner process in the following brief diary entry of Novalis, probably made in July 1798: 'A marriage is a union that extends beyond death and gives us a companion for the night [that is, for the spiritual world].' This inner connection with the cosmic sphere of the Sophia that blossoms like a magic flower within the soul of Novalis only gradually forms and becomes a conscious experience for him. At first his perception of her is still interwoven in his soul with earthly memories of

Sophie von Kühn, through which, however, the features of the cosmic archetype appear with ever greater strength and clarity.

Numerous letters, diary entries and, of course, the poetic works of Novalis testify to this. Thus in the letter to Caroline Just which he wrote on the fifth day after Sophie von Kühn's death, he writes: 'Only the heavenly eye that strikes me with its indescribable sublimity and mildness—this alone draws me forever away from all other vistas. How often I now consider that an open mind should long have surmised that her destiny lies with heaven . . . She appears so innocent, so calm—as though she had no place in this world. Do you not also think that she was too good for me . . . How inexpressibly happy I would be even now if she were to appear before me now and then . . . I still have not given up this hope . . . Her image shall and will be my better self—the wondrous image which is illumined within me by an eternal lamp and which will surely rescue me from so many assaults of the evil and impure . . . She shall be an example to me . . .'

Then Novalis goes on to describe in some detail—and this is in no way merely a poetic comparison, but corresponds precisely to the actual spiritual processes in his own soul—how out of this 'bethrothal in the higher sense', which we have represented as a mystical marriage of rose and lily, there gradually crystallises his higher calling on the Earth, his principal task amongst mankind: 'Who am I, that I lament in so earthly a way? Ought I not to thank God that he brought tidings of my calling for eternity so early? Is it not a calling worthy of an apostle? Can I in all earnestness bewail Sophie's fate—Is it not a privilege for her—Is not her death, and my dying at night after her, *a betrothal in the higher sense*? God has preserved me and you from the creeping infection of meanness (i.e. the commonplace); He has wanted to bring her to a higher place of learning, to *transplant this tender flower beneath a better heaven* and leave me, the strong, rough man, to ripen in the earthly air. Should not God now demand from me genuine exaltation, manly perfection, a deep trust in His love, looking steadfastly towards heaven and my higher calling, an eternal vow of virtue and a belief in the seminal ideas of innermost human nature? Thus it is that just these ideas enter my consciousness with an unaccustomed warmth—I feel what I might become, but God sees how frail and weak I am.'

Novalis' soul being now aspires all the more strongly to the higher world of the beyond, following this imprint of the higher etheric body that worked within Sophie von Kühn during her life on Earth. 'I must forget the whole of my former existence,' he writes nine days after Sophie von Kühn's death to Rachel Just. His principal task now consists in 'the calling to the invisible world', in 'coming really close to God and to all that is most sublime in human life'.

'If I live wholly within her, and eternally long for her'—is not the same mood manifest in these words, which are indeed directed towards the spiritual world, as is evident in the yearning of the hero of his novel for the blue flower? '. . . but the blue flower is that I long to behold. It is ceaselessly in my mind, and I cannot write poems or think about anything else.' And in the letter to Frau von Thümmel Novalis writes: 'She is around me all the time. Everything that I do I do in her name. *She was the beginning; she will be the end of my life.*' In a letter to Woltmann: 'It is certainly not passion. I feel it to be too incontestable, too cold, too close to my whole being, that she was one of the noblest, most ideal figures that have ever been, and will be, on the Earth. The fairest of human beings must have been like her. There is a picture of Raphael which, in its physiognomy, has the closest resemblance to her of any that I have yet seen, although it is certainly not a completely perfect picture of him.'*

This comparison of Sophie von Kühn with the picture of Raphael can acquire a quite particular significance for us if, at this point, we once again recall the special nature of the etheric body that the great painter bore within him.

As we have already seen (p. 46), after the profound shock caused by the death of Sophie von Kühn, there began, almost at once, to stir within Novalis' soul the forces of the imprint of the astral body of the Nathan Soul that resided in the depths of his own being. These forces of the mystic rose in his soul, which then, in the manner described, aspired to union with the forces of the lily in the spiritual worlds (the etheric body of the Luke Mary), gradually embraced also the sphere of his ego. Thus after Sophie von Kühn's death, the higher man, the inner awareness of his immortal ego, began step by step to awaken within Novalis. At first quite imperceptibly, like the first shy rays of a rising spiritual Sun, Novalis felt its activity in himself as the awakening of a *new power*. 'But I know that there is a power in man which, with careful tending, can develop into energy of a singular kind,' he writes in a letter to Just ten days after Sophie von Kühn's death. And two weeks later, in a letter to Friedrich Schlegel, even more decisively: '. . . it is already quite clear to me what a heavenly chance of fortune her death has been—*a key to everything* . . . a simple mighty power has entered my awareness.' And on the following day, in a letter to Woltmann: 'I am wholly content—the power that

---

* Novalis speaks here of the famous self-portrait of Raphael from the year 1506 (see Plate 4), an engraving of which was to be found in the book to which he refers.

assumes superiority over death is one that I have newly won—my being has acquired unity and form—*a future existence is springing up within me.*'

It is hard to say whether Novalis was fully aware as he wrote these last words that only 30 days were to separate him from that mighty initiation-experience—from the supersensible birth of his higher ego, from the 'future existence within [him]'—through which he was to pass on 13 May 1797 at the grave of Sophie von Kühn.

We have already spoken at some length in this chapter about this experience, which Rudolf Steiner once described as an 'initiation bestowed on him through grace.'[573] Here it is only necessary to add what directly relates to the theme of the Sophia. For Novalis himself this 'initiation' was the fully conscious awakening of his higher ego, which, because of the yearning of all his soul-forces for the etheric body of the Luke Mary, was able to follow this etheric body on its path into the spiritual World of Archetypes.

Already in his 'letter of lament' to Woltmann, of 14 April 1797, Novalis had written, as though sensing the imminence of this higher supersensible meeting: 'How delighted I shall be to tell her, *if I now wake and find myself in the old, long-familiar land of my origins*, and she stands before me, "I dreamed of you: I would have loved you on the Earth—*you bore your own likeness even in earthly form*—you die—and, after an anxious few moments, then I followed you."'

'*You* bore *your own* likeness even in earthly form'—in these words, which seem at first so enigmatic, Novalis approaches more closely than perhaps ever before the central mystery of Sophie von Kühn's etheric body, namely, its likeness to its heavenly archetype. Now the awakened higher ego of Novalis follows this etheric body towards the zodiacal region of the Virgin. 'If I now wake and find myself in the old, long-familiar *land of my origins, and she stands before me*'—it is not the soul of the dead Sophie, but the all-encompassing cosmic archetype that stands before his 'awakened' ego in the 'long familiar world of [his] origins'. *At this moment his ego-consciousness becomes open to the cosmic sphere of the Sophia*, to the all-encompassing sphere of night, the personification of which, in the higher worlds, is the spiritual being of the Luke Mary.

At the end of the first 'Hymn to the Night', Novalis describes this mystical 'meeting' in the following poetic words: 'Praise to the world Queen, the high herald of sacred worlds, the fostering nurse of blessed love; she sends you to me, tender beloved, lovely Sun of the night.[574] Now I wake, for I am yours and mine; you have proclaimed to me the night as life and made me human. Consume my body with spirit-fire, that I may ethereally co-mingle with you more intimately and that the bridal night may then last for ever.' Novalis goes on to make this experience still more concrete, connecting it, at the end of the third 'Hymn to the Night', directly with his initiation experience by the grave of Sophie von Kühn: 'The place around me gently rose aloft; and over the region hovered my released, new-born spirit. The hill became a cloud of dust, and through the cloud I saw the transfigured features of my beloved. In her eyes reposed eternity. I grasped her hands, and my tears became like a glittering, unbreakable chain. Millennia disappeared into the distance, like storms. Upon her neck I wept ecstatic tears unto the new life. It was my first dream in you. It passed, but its reflection remained, an everlasting, immutable faith in the heaven of the night and in its Sun, the beloved.'*

That the passage quoted has to do with the supersensible meeting, in the higher worlds, with the spiritual being of the Luke Mary is made plain by the following lines from the fifth 'Hymn to the Night', where Novalis uses deeply personal expressions (similar to those in the above quotation) to describe his relationship to the Luke Mary:

> To you, Mary, are turning
> A thousand hearts as one;
> In shadow-life are yearning
> For you and you alone.
> With joy of expectation
> They hope for healing's rest—
> If you, their blessed salvation,
> Will clasp them to your breast.[575]

In the prose part of the fifth Hymn there follows the merging of both motifs into the higher unity of 'Christ and Sophia':

> The Mother soon hurried after You [Christ]—in heavenly triumph. She was the first to be with You in the new home. Long ages have swept by since then, and Your new creation has been arrayed in ever greater radiance. Thousands have followed after You, out of griefs and torments, full of faith, yearning and loyalty; they hold sway now with You and the heavenly Virgin in the kingdom of love, serve in the temple of heavenly death, and are unto eternity Yours.[576]

And, finally, this twofold motif concludes the whole cycle of the *Hymns to the Night*, the final verse of which begins thus:

* The ending of the hymn is given in accordance with the original, handwritten version.

> Come down to the bride of sweetness,
> To Jesus the Beloved . . .[577]

As he follows the 'blue flower', this wondrous etheric body permeated with the forces of the 'eternally feminine', in the spiritual worlds to where the cosmic forces of the constellation of the Virgin have their influence, Novalis has by this time finally completed the transition from the reflection to the archetype, from the earthly 12-year-old girl, Sophie von Kühn, to the personified representative of the forces of the Divine Sophia in earthly evolution. And the transition that Novalis makes in this poem comes over with such power and directness that it was—although without any clear understanding of its deeper spiritual meaning—also evident to academic research. Thus, for example, the well-known Novalis scholar, Richard Samuel, wrote the following about this poem in one of his books on Novalis.[578] 'The elevation of Sophie [von Kühn] to Mary probably came about before Novalis had become aware of the analogy with the Catholic cult . . .'

To all that has been said hitherto regarding Novalis' relationship to the sphere of Mary–Sophia, one further experience of his should be added which is associated with Raphael's *Sistine Madonna*, a work which he saw for the first time in August 1798 in Dresden. Later, in recollection of it, he wrote in one of his Fragments: 'Glory of melodies, like Angels round the Madonna? *I am you.*' In his book about Novalis, Friedrich Hiebel comments as follows about this observation: 'In this "I am you" Novalis was referring to the "open mystery" [see Novalis' words on p. 56] which remains eternally unfathomable, because it is an experience of the most individual kind, and yet would ideally be possible for every man to grasp [:] ". . . In the bosom of the heavenly bride, Sophia, the birth of the Christ Spirit comes to pass within the human soul." ' In the above statement, as in the two 'Songs of Mary' written in the year 1800, Novalis makes, as never before, a direct connection in his inner experiences with his former earthly incarnation as Raphael. Rudolf Steiner refers to this relationship at the end of his lecture of 22 December 1908: 'No wonder that, as he stood before the Madonna, there arose (in the one who had the first word today*) the most beautiful, most glorious memory of that life of which this present life of his was itself the memory, and who thereby germinated within himself all the beautiful feelings and wonderful sensitivity that the mystery of humanity depicted in this painting could

---

* At the beginning of the lecture Marie Steiner (at the time she was still von Sivers) recited the sixth Hymn from the *Spiritual Songs*: 'Wenn alle untreu werden . . . ('When all are faithless growing . . .'). At the end of the lecture she recited the 'Songs of Mary'.

awaken; no wonder that, within him, these feelings streamed on from there to the being from whom Christ was born, to the figure who brought forth the bud, the calyx, from which sprang the blossom that could allow the seed of the new God to ripen.'

Indeed, what Raphael portrayed in the *Sistine Madonna*—depicting as it does the Mary of the Luke Gospel, who was wholly permeated by the forces of the cosmic Sophia, bearing the Nathan Jesus child in her arms— Novalis brought once more to expression, though now through the medium not of painting but of poetry, in the two 'Songs of Mary' referred to above.[579] But the deeper reason for this remarkable 'coincidence' lies not in the outward expression by Novalis in verbal form of the fact that he had seen Raphael's painting in Dresden, but on the contrary (as follows from what has been already said) in the kinship and direct continuity of the mystical experience of both, in the sphere of the Sophia.

This particular circumstance opens up one further question, the answer to which closes the present chapter. This question runs as follows: What is the source of this direct connection with the sphere of the Sophia which exists equally with Raphael and Novalis, not merely in their creative work, but above all in their real mystical experience?

Looking once more to the events of the Turning-Point of Time as they are presented in modern anthroposophically orientated spiritual science, we must, in order to answer this question, emphasise especially *four* of them, which may be characterised as follows. In the course of roughly three seven-year periods, four events took place, in the case of each of which two different beings were united into a single whole.

In the twelfth year of the Christian era there took place the union of the two Jesus boys, described in St Luke's Gospel in the scene where the 12-year-old Jesus is found in the temple at Jerusalem (2:41–52), when the ego of the reincarnated Zarathustra left the body of the Solomon Jesus and entered that of the Nathan Jesus. Through this sacrificial deed, Zarathustra sacrificed all the forces of his exceptional physical body, the birth of which, amongst the Hebrew people, had been prepared over the course of forty-two generations.[580] This event was the 'physical precondition for the Mystery of Golgotha; for through it the earthly body of Jesus of Nazareth received everything that it had to receive in order that it might subsequently become the vessel for the Christ Being.

The second event took place on the etheric plane, and led to the soul of the Luke Mary, which had by that time long since passed over into the spiritual world, to unite with the soul of the Solomon Mary at the Baptism in the Jordan, as described in the Gospel of St Matthew.[581] This union—in Rudolf Steiner's words—took place in such a way that,

205

simultaneously with it, the etheric body of the Luke Mary—which had been preserved in the spiritual worlds—was able to permeate the etheric body of 'the other Mary' and imbue it with the forces of the cosmic Sophia to such a degree that she (the Solomon Mary) again became a virgin (see p. 187), and from this moment 'a deep connection' was formed 'between Christ and the Mother'.[582] This event was the second, 'etheric' precondition for the Mystery of Golgotha.

The third event, in this ascending series, was the awakening of Lazarus in Bethany and his 'initiation' as John, 'the disciple whom the Lord loved' (John 13–23), in the course of which he was overshone from above, from the spiritual world, as far as the consciousness soul, by the entelechy of John the Baptist, which was then to remain connected with him throughout his subsequent earthly life.[583] This third union was the 'astral' or soul precondition for the Mystery of Golgotha.

Finally, the fourth event was the *final* union of the macrocosmic Ego of Christ with the physical body of Jesus of Nazareth. This gradual process of the union of the cosmic principle with the human, which had begun with the Baptism in the Jordan and continued for three years, reached its culmination and highest tension in the scene of the prayer about the cup in the Garden of Gethsemane, where the macrocosmic Ego of Christ was, for the first time, able fully to penetrate the physical body of Jesus of Nazareth even to its skeletal structure.[584] This means that from this moment the physical body of the 'Son of Man' becomes spiritualised to such an extent that the cosmic impulse can gradually withdraw from it and enter into its immediate spiritual surroundings. If until this point there had been a gradual 'contraction', 'curtailing', 'self-restriction' of the cosmic forces of the Christ-impulse—His ever greater assimilation to the earthly man—Jesus, now, after passing through what could be thought of as the nil-point of complete union with the skeleton, with the hardest, mineral components of the physical body, there begins the process back to a spiritual expansion. The Christ-impulse, His macrocosmic Ego, gradually begins to enter the supersensible surroundings of Jesus of Nazareth and to form a supersensible aura that hovers around him like a radiant cloud.

Rudolf Steiner describes this process in detail in the penultimate lecture of the cycle devoted to the study of the Gospel of St Mark. There he says: 'We can still see the cosmic element present, but less and less connected with the Son of Man . . . What could they [the people who came with Judas to Gethsemane] seize, what could they condemn, and what could they nail to the Cross? The Son of Man. And the more they did this, the more did the cosmic element that had entered earthly life as a youthful impulse withdraw. It withdrew. And to those who sentenced

Him and carried out the judgment there remained the Son of Man, around Whom *only hovered* what was to come down to Earth as a youthful cosmic element. No Gospel, other than that of St Mark, tells how only the Son of Man remained, and that the cosmic element *only hovered* around Him [after the event in Gethsemane].'[585]

In other words, from the moment when Christ Jesus was taken prisoner, we must—from a spiritual point of view—imagine Him as being approximately as He was immediately after the Baptism in the Jordan:[586] outwardly the form of an earthly man, but supersensibly surrounded by a mighty spiritual aura which was as yet only very loosely connected with him, the aura of the cosmic Ego of the Christ. Thus the change in the relationship between the Son of Man and the Ego of Christ after the event in the Garden of Gethsemane can be seen as the fourth, 'ego' precondition for the Mystery of Golgotha.

With the description of these four steps that preceded the Mystery of Golgotha itself we are now, at the conclusion of our studies, ready once more to place the event on the Hill of Golgotha—in its *twofold*, physical-earthly and spiritual-supersensible reality—before our inner eye.

On the Earth, in the physical world, we behold the figure of the crucified Son of Man and, standing beneath the Cross, the 'Mother of Jesus' and the 'disciple whom the Lord loved' (John 19: 25–26). From above, from the Cross, sound the words: 'Behold, your mother—behold, your soul!,' signifying the forging of a new spiritual union, the creation of a higher archetype for all subsequent mystical unions between rose and lily. The mystical marriage of the two spiritual principles—whose representatives are the 'mother of Jesus' and the 'beloved disciple'—is being accomplished. From the heights of the Cross, like a higher priestly blessing, this union between the Sophia-impulse living in the *soul* of the 'mother of Jesus' and the impulse of the 'I am', which John has borne in his *spirit* since his initiation as Lazarus, shines forth for the entire future evolution of the Earth.

That is the picture of what took place in the earthly sphere. In the spiritual sphere that immediately adjoins it, however, the following picture opens up before our inner eye. Before us there appears the spiritual being of the Luke Mary, who overshines the 'other Mary' from above, from the higher worlds, and is thereby supersensibly present at this moment on the Hill of Golgotha. Then we see the entelechy of John the Baptist, who overshines the 'beloved disciple' beneath the Cross from above, from the spiritual surroundings.[587] Both these spiritual beings, the being of the Luke Mary and the entelechy of John the Baptist, are enshrouded by and immersed in the mighty aura of the Cosmic Christ which, like a radiant, supersensible cloud surrounding the crucified Son of Man, unites them in a higher mystical union. And from this radiant cosmic aura there sounds at this moment—no longer in human language but in the language of spiritual archetypes—what in its echo in the lower world becomes earthly words on the lips of the Son of Man: 'Behold, your son—behold, your mother!'588

Here, too, in the supersensible surroundings of the Hill of Golgotha, the higher marriage of two spiritual beings, two world spheres, takes place. For the words that follow, which relate to the earthly events, 'And from that hour the disciple took her to his own home' (19:27), have significance for both worlds.*

So we see at what moment the connection arises, in the spiritual worlds, between the entelechy of John the Baptist and the Luke Mary—the personified bearer of the Sophia forces in the supersensible sphere surrounding the Earth—a connection which continues to live as a vital source of higher inspirations in the deepest regions of John the Baptist's soul, when he again returns to Earth, first as Raphael and then as Novalis.

Among Raphael's many works there is one picture where, through the veil of a traditional religious subject, the master's latent memories of this supersensible scene, which was enacted in the spiritual surroundings of the Golgotha Hill, appear with perhaps the greatest clarity. This is the picture entitled *The Betrothal of Mary*. Rudolf Steiner speaks about its significance—not only in Raphael's creative output, but in world art as a whole—in the following words, first citing the views of the well-known art historian, Herman Grimm: 'Herman Grimm makes us aware that the work which gives us such delight today in Milan, the 'Betrothal of Mary', stands like a totally new phenomenon in the evolution of art and has no direct connection with anything in the past.' Giving further emphasis to this opinion of Herman Grimm, Rudolf Steiner adds: 'one could say that Raphael's soul has, as though *out of the unchartered depths of a human soul*, given birth to something which, *out of these depths*, has entered into spiritual evolution as something completely new.'589

We have already referred to the spiritual content of these 'unchartered depths' of Raphael's soul as the artist's subconscious memories of his own mystical marriage with the Sophia-sphere, at the Turning-Point of Time, in the supersensible surroundings of the Hill of Golgotha. These memories are also the source of many of his inner experiences, the most

* In the original version of Emil Bock's translation [into German] of this passage, the phrase '. . . so that she was completely one with him' follows the words just quoted. And this addition relates not only to what was taking place at that moment on the physical plane, but, in an even greater measure, to what we have described as happening in the spiritual sphere.

perfect artistic expression of which is the *Sistine Madonna*,[590] a painting which at the same time points towards profound spiritual secrets of both macrocosm and microcosm that are assocaited with the all-encompassing future mysteries of the Divine Sophia. In the lecture of 6 October 1923, which is devoted to a description of the cosmic aspect of the Christmas imagination, or in other words, to how 'this image of Mary with the Jesus child . . . arises out of the cosmos itself',[591] Rudolf Steiner refers with full clarity to the direct connection that exists between this cosmic imagination and Raphael's *Sistine Madonna*.

The features of Mary's face, he says, and especially her gaze, as portrayed in the picture, bear within them the revelation of the lofty secrets of the *starry* cosmos; the child in her arms is like a newly-risen *Sun*, illuminating the entire surroundings with its light; and the broad folds of her garment express, through their downward movement, the whole dynamic of the *Moon*–Earth forces. Not out of the descriptions in the book of Revelation, but out of a direct spiritual vision was Raphael able to communicate, in artistic form, the cosmic imagination of the Sophia, the heavenly *Virgin* clothed with the Sun, with a crown of stars around her head and the Moon beneath her feet, shining through the figure of the Mary of the Luke Gospel.[592] Thus we can say, in Rudolf Steiner's words, that, truly, we have here to do with 'a picture that has its origin in the divine-spiritual world.'[593] It not only brings great macrocosmic relation-ships to expression, but is at the same time a reflection of the most inward and intimate processes of the human soul, processes which transform it in such a way that the possibility gradually opens up before man of himself gaining clairvoyant insight into the sphere of the Sophia. Rudolf Steiner describes these processes in the following words: 'What is this human being who gives birth to the higher man within man, a man who represents a small world within the wider world, who is it that gives birth to the true, higher man out of a pure soul? He can be characterised only by what we call clairvoyance. If we try to form a picture of the soul that gives birth to the higher man out of himself, out of the spiritual universe, we need only call to mind the picture of the Sistine Madonna, the wonderful child in the arms of the Madonna. Thus in the Sistine Madonna we have before us a picture of the human soul as it is born out of the spiritual universe; and, springing from this soul, the highest that a human being can bring forth—his spiritual birth, *the re-engendering of the creative activity of the world* that lies within him as a potential.'[593] To the extent and in the manner that this was possible in his time, Raphael passed through such an experience, and its consequence was that he painted the *Sistine Madonna*. As we have seen, Novalis also passed through a similar experience (see p. 56), and its consequence was his composition of the

'Songs of Mary'. Thus both these experiences through which the two personalities passed, almost three centuries apart from one another, clearly focus our attention upon the future task of the *one* individuality who stands behind both of them, upon this individuality's leading role in the Sophia Mystery of the future, which will arise within mankind in the sixth cultural epoch.

The mystery of this inner connection of the individuality of John the Baptist–Raphael–Novalis with the future mysteries of the Divine Sophia, whose source is the experience of the entelechy of John the Baptist in the spiritual surroundings of the Hill of Golgotha, was well known in the Slavic East of Europe from the very beginning of the spread of Christianity.

As though out of a profound sense of anticipation of its own spiritual future, at the spiritual-compositional focus of the Orthodox iconostasis, in the principal row of icons (called the 'Deesis', which is to say, 'Intercession'), there was—in all Russian churches without exception—the following arrangement of the central figures.[594] In the centre is the figure of Christ as the new spiritual ruler of 'all cosmic forces on the Earth', seated on a throne illumined by an oval aura that embraces the entire surroundings of the Earth and by a double 'quadrangular' aura—sometimes with the symbols of the Bull, the Lion, the Eagle and the Angel (as an indication of the future sheaths of the Christ-impulse amongst mankind: see p. 127) in its corners—which stretches to the four quarters of the world.[595] On either side of Him stand: at His right Mary, and on His left, John the Baptist. Then follow two Archangels: Michael, the Spirit who was most especially connected with John the Baptist in his previous incarnation as Elijah, and Gabriel, who proclaimed the birth of the Nathan Jesus to Mary.*[596]

Approximately from the second quarter of the seventeenth century, the first Rosicrucian influences gradually began to penetrate into Russia (mainly from Central Europe), and in the middle of the eighteenth century they were significantly strengthened in connection with the frequent visits to Moscow and St Petersburg of Count Saint-Germain, the last exoterically-known incarnation of Christian Rosenkreutz.[597] This

---

* The two Archangels—unlike John the Baptist and Mary, who once actually lived on Earth in physical incarnations—work amongst mankind only as *astral* Beings, so if rightly viewed clairvoyantly they would appear to spirit-vision, in accordance with the laws of the astral world, as though in a mirror. Thus the Archangel Gabriel, who was actually more connected with Mary, is in the 'Deesis' placed beside John the Baptist, and the Archangel Michael, who was more connected with John, beside Mary.

Rosicrucian influence also found its reflection in Russian icon-painting, and in the seventeenth and eighteenth centuries called into being the so-called 'mystical-didactic' style, one of whose central subjects at once became the theme of 'the Sophia, the divine wisdom'.

It is remarkable that this subject, which is fairly complex in its mystical symbolism, became unusually widespread and popular even amongst simple folk. Not for nothing have most of the icons on this theme that have come down to us now had their origin not in the principal centres of icon-painting in Moscow, Kiev or Novgorod, but most frequently deep in the provinces.

These icons of the Sophia which were created under the influence of Central European Rosicrucianism have as a rule a threefold form. Above, in the first part of the icon, is God the Father, holding a globe of the world in His hand, surrounded by six or nine Hierarchic (Angel) Beings, sometimes with the Holy Spirit issuing from His lips in the form of a dove with a golden halo.* Below it, in the second part, is God the Son, Christ, surrounded by a radiant Sun aura which blesses what is taking place in the lower, third part of the icon. In this lower and, in a compositional sense, central part, the Sophia is portrayed sitting on a throne,[598] with a sceptre or scroll of parchment in her hands, the golden crown of wisdom on her head, the wings of an Angel and, in certain icons, a face of a fiery red colour and—around her—a mighty cosmic aura. At her side, sometimes standing on the Earth, sometimes in the clouds, are the Luke Mary, bearing the Nathan Jesus beneath her heart, on the right, and John the Baptist on the left. With his right hand he points towards the sphere of the Sophia, and in his left hand he holds a scroll of parchment which bears the words: 'Behold the Lamb of God, who takes upon Himself the sins of the world' (John 1:29) or 'Repent, for the Kingdom of Heaven is at hand' (Matthew 3:2).

Thus in Russian icon-painting this subject is a living testimony of the direct participation of the Luke Mary and John the Baptist in the Sophia sphere, the former as the individualised representative of the Sophia in earthly evolution, and the latter as the future guide of humanity into her sphere (which is why he points towards her with his right hand).[598] The images of these icons, taken as a whole, form a kind of synthesis of almost all the principal motifs of the present work: the Book of Adam, as the symbol of the primal revelation, the guidance of man and humanity by the Hierarchies, the grace-bestowing revelation of the Christ Being (the

* In certain 'Sophia icons', there is, in the upper part, instead of the Father God, an altar with a book lying on it, which in an exoteric sense is a Bible but which in an esoteric sense is an allusion to the heavenly Book, or Book of Adam (see Appendix 1).

Damascus experience), and, finally, the connection of the entelechy of John the Baptist with the Luke Mary, the Nathan Soul and the future mysteries of 'the Sophia, the divine wisdom', the central mysteries of the sixth, Slavic cultural epoch.

At the end of the Stockholm cycle of 1910, which has been entitled 'The Gospel of St John and the Three Other Gospels'[599] and which is associated with the first proclamation of the new advent of Christ in the etheric sphere, Rudolf Steiner places the following picture before his listeners. First he refers to that distant time in the history of human evolution when, as the Bible tells us, the sons of God descended to the daughters of men, with the consequence that a great egoism spread over all the Earth.[600]

Rudolf Steiner then contrasts this Biblical picture with a picture of the future, when '. . . as a consummation of the ages, the sons of men will once again find the daughters of God and will ascend to them.' But this can (in his words) only happen 'when human wisdom has been sacrificed for divine wisdom, for then we shall again find the daughters of the Gods, *the divine wisdom* [Sophia]. Then will the sons of men ascend to the daughters of the Gods. And with this begins the second half of earthly evolution.'

To these daughters of the Gods, these creative forces of the world wisdom working in the cosmic sphere of the Sophia, the whole of humanity must ascend in future, a future whose first harbinger is the individuality of Novalis, this truly *eternal individuality*.

In Place of an Epilogue

Not only for Rudolf Steiner himself but also for many of those who, in accordance with the will of the karma of the Anthroposophical Movement, were to form his most immediate surroundings in the last years of his earthly life, the inner connection with the individuality of Novalis played a highly significant role. In conclusion, we shall cite three such examples.

Marie Steiner. In her tireless service to the word, through her artistic recitations from the autumn of 1908 until practically the end of her earthly life, she introduced the poetry of Novalis into the Anthroposophical Society, which through her activity became its inalienable property. But hers was a decisive part, not only in the realm of art, but also in that of Rudolf Steiner's spiritual–scientific research with regard to the individuality of Novalis and his karmic past. Thus through pointing out to Rudolf Steiner during the Holy Nights of 1908 the spiritual connection between Novalis and Raphael, she enabled him three days after their conversation, on 6 January 1909, to speak to all anthroposophists about this individuality's spiritual biography, about his spiritual connection, not only with Raphael, but also with John the Baptist and the prophet Elijah.[601]

Albert Steffen—in whose work, germs and seeds of the new truly Christian art are to be found everywhere—lived for many years in a very intimate way with the poems of Novalis, which were the secret source of inspiration for many of his own poetic works. However, not only the works of Novalis, but above all the 'living spiritual image' of the great poet-seer found its highest and most artistically perfect expression in Albert Steffen's essay, 'Die Botshaft von Novalis' ('The Message of Novalis') (1945), which became the heart of the collection of his essays entitled *Wiedergeburt der Schönen Wissenschaften* ('Rebirth of Belles-Lettres') and which is, in truth, amongst the best of all that has been written about Novalis in world literature.[602]

Ita Wegman. After she had received from Rudolf Steiner, in the autumn of 1924, an indication regarding the mystery of the working together on Earth, and especially in the spiritual worlds, of the 'two streams of Michael'—the leading individuality in the second of which was from the outset that of Elijah—she searched for many years afterwards, with a deep inner intensity, for inner ways of uniting spiritually with the

213

'second' stream, inasmuch as this was the most important task placed by Rudolf Steiner before all anthroposophists in his 'Last Address' of 28 September 1924.[603]

All three—Marie Steiner, Albert Steffen and Ita Wegman—were called by Rudolf Steiner at the Christmas Conference of 1923 to join the original Vorstand of the newly founded Anthroposophical Society. And they were called not only as individuals who were karmically connected with Rudolf Steiner himself, but above all as representatives of the principal karmic streams *which sought their union in the Anthroposophical Society* so as to prepare together on Earth for the culmination of the Anthroposophical Movement at the end of the twentieth century.

And in his 'Last Address', which truly bears the character of a last testament, Rudolf Steiner, in turning directly to the entelechy of Novalis in the spiritual worlds, speaks of how all anthroposophists will sooner or later meet this individuality in order to prepare with him for the further evolution, also in the super-earthly sphere, of the work of Michael-Christ at the end of our century. These words of Rudolf Steiner relate in the first instance to his closest colleagues, each of whom sought in their previous earthly life, in their own way, a connection with the spirit of Novalis.

Thus we should now see the three above-named closest colleagues of Rudolf Steiner, and the souls connected with them, as being in very close harmony with one another and the individuality of Novalis, who is the *mediator* in the spiritual worlds for so many spiritual streams (see Chapter 10).

This spiritual community, led by him who in his last earthly life bore the name of Rudolf Steiner, works in the higher worlds like a kind of mighty spiritual council, extending over the whole twentieth century and uniting in itself the many and varied human individuals who, in one way or another, are connected with the central stream of Michael.

Whether the culmination—predicted by Rudolf Steiner—of the Anthroposophical Movement at the end of our century will also take place *on the Earth* does, however, depend quite decisively upon the extent to which the Anthroposophical Movement is able to become a real reflection and conscious instrument of what is happening now in the spiritual worlds, in the supersensible stream of Michael, which is to say, to bring about in its midst what Rudolf Steiner in one of his lectures characterised in the following words: 'Apart from the fact that as modern souls we belong to the fifth post-Atlantean cultural period, where we develop in a wholly individual way . . . we must in addition become conscious of a higher community, founded upon *free, brotherly love*, which is like the breath of magic that we breathe in our working groups.'[604]

And in another context Rudolf Steiner expressed this thought in an even more radical way, indicating that, while for certain other streams in present-day humanity brotherhood is a desirable element, *for the Anthroposophical Movement brotherhood is the fundamental condition for its very existence on the Earth*: 'Anthroposophy demands that a truly human brotherliness becomes a reality even to the very depths of the soul . . . Anthroposophy . . . flourishes only on the ground of brotherliness and cannot grow in any way other than out of brotherliness, which arises out of a situation where one individual gives to another what he has and what he can.'[605]

As a true forerunner of modern anthroposophically oriented spiritual science, Novalis felt, with a particular intensity in his soul, the need for such a universal brotherhood of all spiritually striving human beings. This yearning he had borne in his soul since the time of his supersensible participation in the events of the Turning-Point of Time, when he worked from the spiritual worlds as a higher group-soul, a uniting guardian spirit, in the innermost circle of the disciples of Christ Jesus, a circle which, in its twelvefoldness, is the archetype of the new humanity of the future.[514]

Novalis expressed this high ideal—also for our time—in poetic words which, for all their apparent simplicity, have within them great occult depths.

With these words, which by the end of our century *should have become the destiny* of the Anthroposophical Movement in the modern world, we would bring this book to an end:

> Within your cells awaken,
> You children of the past;
> Your resting-place abandon,
> The morning comes at last.
>
> Your threads I am now spinning
> Into one single thread;
> Gone are the days of feuding,
> *One* life shall now you wed.
>
> Each one will live in others,
> And all in everyone.
> *One* heart within you surges,
> Through life-breath of the One.

APPENDICES

Appendix I

Concerning a Poem by Novalis

There is a further poem by Novalis, written at the beginning of the year 1800 and dedicated to his friend Ludwig Tieck, which for its particular bearing on our theme we should now like briefly to consider. It begins with a description of the lonely wanderings of a child—in whom it is not difficult to recognise Novalis himself—who has been 'driven out' from his spiritual home into the earthly world, but who nonetheless retains a memory of 'olden' times and remains faithful to them. After a long search in the 'desolate garden'—an allusion to the state into which the Garden of Eden entered after the Fall (see the fifth Hymn to the Night)—the child finds a remarkable book:

> An ancient book with golden claspings,
> Whose words no man had ever heard.

As he reads this book, he becomes aware of 'an inner sense':

> And like the Springtime's tender sproutings,
> An inner sense in him unfurled,

which enables him to behold a 'new [that is, a spiritual] world' as though in a magic 'crystal'. From this spiritual world a venerable old man with the features of a child appears before him in a vision. And the child recognises him as 'the high spirit of the book', who shows him the way back to the dwelling-place of the heavenly Father. Then the old man speaks to the child of how he (the child) is destined, in the future, to become the inheritor of everything that he (the old man) possesses ('the heir of my possessions') and the bearer of a high divine revelation: 'God's deepness will be known to you.' He also explains to the child how, in his youth, he himself was able to contemplate this 'heavenly book':

> And through this gift I then was able
> All living creatures to behold,

219

as a result of which the fundamental mystery of Christianity, the deep mystery of the New Covenant, was revealed to him:

> Before my eyes stood clearly open
> The ark of the New Covenant.

The poem ends with four verses in which the old man puts before the child's [Novalis'] inner eye a picture of his future spiritual mission amongst mankind:

> The time has come, no longer hidden
> Shall be life's awesome mystery.
> In this great book the morn has broken
> Into our age so mightily.

> Proclaimer of the ruddy dawning
> The harbinger of peace you'll be.
> I shall inspire you with my breathing,
> Like flute's and harp's soft melody.

> God be with you, in yonder places
> Go wash your eyes with morning dew,
> Be true to the book and my own ashes,
> And bathe in the eternal blue.

> You will proclaim the last dominion,
> A thousand years it shall endure;
> You'll find there multitudes of beings,
> And Jacob Boehme see once more.

On account of the last line, the figure of the old man is usually identified by modern students of Novalis with the German mystic and theosopher Jacob Boehme, and the book which the child finds with his work, *Aurora or Dawn in the Ascendant*, with which Ludwig Tieck had made Novalis acquainted. (In the first line, of the second of the four verses quoted above, Novalis also uses the word 'Morgenröte', the particular word for 'dawn' employed by Boehme.) Behind this outward fabric of the poem, however, there is actually a profound mystery which, if we seek to fathom it, can help us to shed new light upon the very foundations of Novalis' spiritual being.

The following words of Rudolf Steiner about Jacob Boehme may serve as a starting-point for our investigation: 'Jacob Boehme once made us aware that he would speak of past epochs of human evolution—*say, of the figure of Adam*—as though these experiences had been taking place immediately around him, and he said: Many might ask: Were you then present when Adam walked the Earth? And Jacob Boehme answers unequivocally: Yes, I was present.'[1] Here Rudolf Steiner has in mind a reply which Jacob Boehme gave in the face of the attacks of one of his many opponents and which is to be found in his book, *The Great Mystery, or Interpretation of the First Book of Moses*: 'To him let it be said that in my soul's and life's essence, in that I was not yet I *but was Adam's essence, I was indeed there*, and that I forfeited my glory in Adam. Because, however, Christ has restored it to me, I may see in the Spirit of Christ what I have been in Paradise, and what I have become in sin, and what I shall again become.'[2] Thus we see from these words that Jacob Boehme had the faculty (and Rudolf Steiner goes on to confirm this in the lecture referred to) of reading in the Akashic Chronicle of what had still lived *before the Fall* as divine knowledge in the spirit of the first man, Adam. Boehme writes as follows about this divine knowledge of Adam: 'But as, at the time when God created Heaven and Earth, there was as yet no human being who could have seen this, one must conclude that Adam knew of it in the spirit, before his Fall, when he still abided in a deep knowledge of God; and then when he fell and was established in a state of outward birth, he lost this knowledge and preserved it only as a memory, as a dim and secret story which he passed on to his descendants.'[3]

It was this primal knowledge of Adam which was then handed down through all subsequent generations to Moses, who inscribed it in his 'Genesis': 'Moses writes of this in his first Book as if he had been present and had seen it for himself: without doubt he received it in writings *from his ancestors*, although, perhaps, he learnt somewhat more about this in the spirit than his ancestors.'[4] In the last few words, Boehme is referring to the special initiation of Moses.

According to ancient Hebrew esoteric tradition, the whole all-embracing cosmic knowledge which Adam possessed before the Fall was then preserved in the Akashic Chronicle, and from the very beginning had as its symbol the so-called 'Book of Adam'. Regarding this 'Book of Adam', which was given to Adam in Paradise at the behest of the God Jahve by the Archangel Michael, a certain ancient Hebrew legend has this to say: 'A holy Book of seventy-two characters was given to Michael the Angel, he who is lord over the seven Princes who serve the King of all Kings. And Michael imbued Adam, the first man, with the foundations of knowledge, and handed the Book on to him. Thus Adam became wise and knew to give names to all the beasts and also to all birds, fishes and reptiles. And Adam read in the Book, learnt to revere it with all his strength and cultivated in himself purity, chastity and humility. He gained insight into the spirit of wisdom and comprehended the golden words of the Book.'[5] There then follow words of which the corresponding lines from Novalis' poem are virtually an exact repetition, although one can be quite sure that Novalis could not have had any outward knowledge of this tradition: 'All things became clear to him, and he understood everything through the Book of the Holy Spirit.' (Compare with the lines, 'All living creatures to behold', and—in the manuscript version—with the line from the last verse of the poem which runs '. . . you will see things as they began . . .'

From this we may see that Jacob Boehme belonged to those few who, being spiritually identified with the 'essence of Adam' in the Akashic Chronicle, was able to read in the 'Book of Adam' ('but as I was Adam's essence, I was indeed there'). He then set forth the results of this 'reading' in his *Aurora* and in his other works, the acquaintance with which was for Novalis the outward cause for the awakening within him of the hidden memories of the 'Book of Adam' which had formerly been the property of the first man, Adam. Thus, through his works, Jacob Boehme became for Novalis a guide to the spiritual memory of his oldest incarnation on the Earth. So, turning once more to Novalis's poem, we can say: the 'heavenly Book'—which arouses in him 'an inner sense', leads him into a 'new world' and makes it possible for him 'all living creatures to behold'—is indeed the 'Book of Adam', while the old man with the features of a child, the 'high spirit of the Book', is none other than the personified memory of Adam himself, as it was awakened in Novalis through his studies of Jacob Boehme. Today, on the grounds that in the manuscript version Novalis calls the old man who appears to him in the spirit a 'child' ('a high divine child with grey hair'), even outward research has come to the conclusion that what is meant by these words is his connection with the primordial 'golden age', the paradisaical condition of humanity.[6]

Certain other images in the poem also bear witness to this. The line, 'I shall inspire you with my breathing', is reminiscent of one of the stages in the creation by the God Jahve of the first man Adam.[7] And the line, 'Be true to the book and my own ashes', calls for faithfulness towards the 'Book of Adam' and 'On my bare grave you make oblations' towards the grave of Adam, with which are connected so many significant occult legends and traditions telling of the special tree that grew on Adam's grave from three seeds of the heavenly Tree of Life which he took with him when he was driven out of Paradise.[8] Hence in the manuscript version of the poem we find a twofold reference to the element of life. In the original version the last two lines of the ninth verse were:

And with this gift [the heavenly Book] I then was able
To walk in cheer the path of *life*.

While the original version of the first line of the concluding verse ran as follows:

A new *life* will you give foundation.

And another variant of the same:

You'll help the realm of *life's* foundation.

The stream of Melchizedek (see p. 5 and Note 13) is also referred to in this poem:

Proclaimer of the ruddy dawning,
Harbinger of peace you'll be.

Thus in the imaginative picture of Novalis' meeting with the old man we have, in a certain sense, his supersensible encounter with himself in his oldest incarnation. And this vision of his oldest incarnation in the astral light awakens within Novalis an awareness of his future mission amongst mankind: that of bringing to it the new tidings of the 'Book of Adam', transforming what in the works of Jacob Boehme was like a tender dawn into the mighty radiance of day:

The time has come, no longer hidden
Shall be life's awesome mystery.
In this great book the morn has broken
Into our age so mightily.

This revelation of the Mysteries of the 'Book of Adam' will be the return of that cosmic knowledge which humanity had possessed before the Fall, an event whose beginning is now being marked by modern spiritual science or Anthroposophy. Novalis himself calls this the coming of the primal or (which is the same thing) the final condition of existence:

You will proclaim the last dominion,
A thousand years it shall endure.

But Novalis does not only want to be the proclaimer of this higher knowledge—he also wants to take part in the fashioning of the 'new world' of the future. Thus we find, in the manuscript version of the last verse, the following variant:

> You'll help the realm of life's foundation,
> If full of meekness you'll endure,
> Where eternal love finds affirmation
> And Jacob Boehme you see once more.

Only through remaining unshakably true to the primal spiritual impulse of human evolution (see the first verse of the poem) will it be possible again to establish 'the realm of life' as the result of a conscious ascent into the etheric cosmos: 'And bathe in the eternal blue' (in the manuscript version it says, 'Thus rests your head in the radiant blue'). For the establishing of this new realm or dominion could be regarded as the source of a kind of counter-pole to the Fall. The foundation for accomplishing this task is, for Novalis, that spiritual fire of the Resurrection (see p. 81) which he bears within his soul.

> Inflamed by golden shafts of godly fire—

This is how it was expressed in the original version of one of the last lines of the poem.

The image of the 'Book of Adam' as an imagination of the highest primal revelation that was given to mankind also appears in the tenth chapter of the Apocalypse, where the 'Book' is spoken of which John the Evangelist is to eat in the vision.[9] It is also depicted on the icon of St Sophia, lying on the heavenly altar of the Father God. (See Chapter 12 and Plate 9.)

Appendix II

Novalis and Rudolf Steiner's *Philosophy of Freedom*

> *'We cannot . . . take the concept of man to its conclusion without arriving at the* free spirit *as the purest mark of human nature.'*

> *'Each of us is called to become a* free spirit, *just as every rose-bud is called to become a rose.'*
> Rudolf Steiner, *The Philosophy of Freedom*

> *'Freedom and love belong together, as I have already shown in my* Philosophy of Freedom.'
> Rudolf Steiner, 19 December 1920

If we turn to the early part of Novalis' life, to the time of his studies at the School of Mining in Freiberg, we can detect a certain parallel between his general interests in this period and the interests of the youthful Rudolf Steiner. Friedrich Hiebel, in his article entitled 'Novalis and his place in the earliest foreshadowings of Anthroposophy', refers to this parallel in the following words: 'If one considers the subjects— mathematics, geometry, chemistry, physics and mineralogy—that Novalis chose at the School of Mining in Freiberg alongside his studies in philosophy, one may observe an identical tendency towards the same scientific disciplines as those of the young Steiner at the Technical College in Vienna.'[10] In order to become fully convinced of the appropriateness of these words, it is suff"cent to compare them with the following observation of Rudolf Steiner about the subjects that he studied at the Technical College: 'Officially I studied mathematics, chemistry, physics, zoology, botany, mineralogy and geology.'[11]

It should also be said that the young Rudolf Steiner had—already from his fourteenth year—made an intensive study of Kant, and somewhat later of *Fichte*, Schelling and Hegel. This was also the time of his meeting, and subsequent friendship, with Karl Julius Schröer, who was the first to open to him the world of Schiller and, most especially, of Goethe.[12] For Novalis there followed, at roughly the same age, his acquaintance with the works of Kant and then a thorough and detailed study of *Fichte*, whom he also knew personally, as he did Schiller, whose lectures he attended at

Jena University. Somewhat later he got to know the artistic works and natural-scientific publications of Goethe. Moreover, it was Novalis who, in accordance with the will of destiny, 'was the very first to understand the natural-scientific endeavours of Goethe and to pay wholehearted tribute to them.'[13] Thus at the end of 1798, or the beginning of 1799, Novalis wrote of Goethe the scientist (or, as one said at that time, the 'physicist'): 'His [Goethe's] studies of light, of the metamorphosis of plants and insects represent a confirmation, and at the same time the most convincing proof, that a perfect discourse of learning belongs to the realm of the artist. One may also in a certain sense maintain with some justification that Goethe is the first physicist of his time, and indeed has made great strides in the history of physics'; and somewhat later in the same fragment: 'As Goethe the physicist relates to other physicists, so does the poet to other poets.'

However, there is in these words not only a complete recognition of Goethe as a scientist, but also—hidden behind them—an ever-growing inner yearning to continue Goethe's work in (as we can now say with full conviction) the direction of Anthroposophy. 'Goethean treatment of the sciences—my project,' he writes. And when we read these lines today, our inner eye turns at once towards the introduction that Rudolf Steiner wrote to Goethe's scientific writings and also to his two books: *Grundlinien einer Erkenntnistheorie der Goetheschen Weltanschauung* and to his later work, *Goethes Weltanschauung*.[14] For what had already crystallised in Novalis' soul as a general spiritualisation of the sciences 'in accordance with Goethe's method'—which, however, in the course of his short life remained no more than a 'project'—was later realised by Rudolf Steiner through the founding of Goetheanism, the chief elements of which were included in the books referred to, but which he later developed and intensified in his many lectures.[15]

'In many ancient writings there beats a mysterious pulse, which is a point of contact with the invisible world—a coming to life. Goethe is to become the liturgist of this physics—he understands completely the service in the temple.' With these words, Novalis refers to his understanding of the further evolution of the natural sciences and the role of Goethe's genius in this evolution. To find in science the 'point of contact with the invisible world' means to embark upon the path towards that situation whereby—in Rudolf Steiner's words—the laboratory bench becomes an altar and the carrying out of experiments becomes a religious rite which, in its turn, will be associated with a general spiritualisation of all sciences: 'A spiritual chemistry, a spiritual physics is what will come in the future.' As is evident from a great number of instances in his works, and especially from many of his fragments, this was a future about which Novalis had a deep inner premonition.[16]

In the year 1922, during his visit to the Hague, Rudolf Steiner was asked by Walter Johannes Stein about the historical–philosophical sources of Anthroposophy. At that time he mentioned two names: Fichte and Aristotle. He said: 'I have brought together two elements. From Johann Gottlieb Fichte I learned of the ego-activity that is withdrawn from the outer world. But from Aristotle I took the fullness of an empiricism that embraces everything. Only he who is able to supplement Fichte with Aristotle finds the total reality and that was my path.' These words were preceded by an earlier remark of Rudolf Steiner's in the same vein, which he made to Stein in 1914: 'If you develop Aristotle further through Fichte, you come to anthroposophy.'[17]

It follows from these two observations that Anthroposophy was in a certain sense born on Earth out of a higher spiritual synthesis of the spiritual streams represented by these two philosophers. Fichte—pre-eminently amongst all philosophers—places the *ego-principle* at the centre of his system, and made it the sole foundation of his whole view of the world. Aristotle, as the father of empiricism, which finds its concrete expression in scientific observation and experimentation, became thereby the ancestor of the *scientific method* as such. Historically, the stream of Aristotle entered into European spiritual life as a counter-force to a *one-sided* Platonism. And if the latter leads in the end to Kant and to his insurmountable 'frontiers of knowledge', a rightly understood Aristotelianism evolves through Thomas of Aquinas to Goethe and his phenomenological approach to the world of appearances.[18]

Thus in this case too we may discern a deep inner affinity between the historical roots of the chief aspirations of the young Rudolf Steiner and Novalis. For what Fichte and Aristotle were for the one, Fichte and Goethe were for the other. In Fichte, attention is concentrated solely on man's inner being, on his ego, the experience of which is accessible only to a thinking which is intuitively grasped, while in Aristotle there is a scientific empiricism which finds its continuation in the phenomenological observation in nature according to the method of Goethe, where attention is focused above all on the world-processes in man's natural environment.

Both these standpoints form, with respect to one another, two diametrically opposite poles, while each on its own manifests a certain onesidedness. Thus Fichte in his philosophy is purely centripetal and, hence, is unable to find the transition from the human ego back to the world; while Goethe is in his relationship to the world and to nature

227

essentially centrifugal and for this reason is unable to find the individual human being (the ego) in his picture of the world.[19]

These two extremes, which can also be contrasted with one another as the polarities of the centre and the periphery of a circle, I and world, subject and object, must be brought to a higher synthesis in a theory of knowledge that corresponds to reality. This is what Rudolf Steiner achieved in his *Philosophy of Freedom*. With the principal conclusions of its first part, regarding the refusal to recognise any limits to the cognitive process, arising as it does out of a higher synthesis of 'concept' and 'percept', through the union of which—as a result of the inner activity of the human ego—man comes to an experience of a higher reality, the foundation was laid for the spiritual path which, in its further development, leads directly to Anthroposophy.

Already in Rudolf Steiner's previous work, *Truth and Science*, which he wrote as a 'Prelude to a "Philosophy of Freedom"', we have, even in its very title, an indication of such a synthesis. Here, the 'Philosophy of Freedom' springs as the only real philosophy of the future out of a union of 'truth', in so far as it is revealed within the human ego through pure or intuitive thinking and 'science', the foundation for an experiential, empirical relationship to the world. Thus it is indeed the case that the initial philosophical foundation of Anthroposophy springs from a union between Fichte and Aristotle, or Goethe.

Something similar, though in a different form, takes place in the second half of the *The Philosophy of Freedom*, where the theme is no longer the theory of knowledge as such, but its actual implications and significance for the moral world of man. While in the sphere of knowledge the aim is to attain a true experience of reality, in the moral sphere the aim becomes the realisation of the inner state which Rudolf Steiner characterises as 'ethical individualism'. This, too, arises out of a union, or higher synthesis, of two poles: an 'individualism' which is the focus of the bringing about of an individual grasp of 'moral concepts' within the ego, and then their influence upon man's outward conduct and actions, which leads to an 'ethical', that is, a free outpouring of this intuitively grasped inner content through imprinting it upon the outer world.

Only out of a union of these two spheres of human activity, inner and outer, rooted as they are in self-knowledge and knowledge of the world, and out of an experience of their complete equilibrium in man's relationship to himself and to the world, can the first steps be taken towards the *real inner experience and realisation of freedom*.

In all that has been said, a path may be found which leads from *The Philosophy of Freedom* to Anthroposophy. Or, as Rudolf Steiner has put it from the opposite viewpoint in one of his lectures: 'Anthroposophy leads in a direct line back to what was sounded—though of course in a philosophical way—in my *Philosophy of Freedom*.'[20] For when the content of this book is translated from the realm of intellectual study to that of *spiritual observation*, the activity of real supersensible beings is simultaneously revealed behind the two extremes referred to above.

Thus behind the outer world of perceptions the activity of ahrimanic beings, and behind the inner world of thinking the activity of luciferic beings, is revealed to the spiritual investigator. From a more psychological viewpoint one can say: Lucifer is more connected with the human faculty of making mental pictures and conceptual thinking, and Ahriman with the 'relationship of the will to the outer world'[21]—and to this sphere of man's will-activity his faculty of perceiving the outer world also belongs.[22]

Something similar can also be observed in the moral sphere. There Lucifer tries to entice man into a hypertrophic development of his individuality, into using all its forces for purely egoistic ends. Ahriman, on the other hand, tries to influence the outer manifestations of the human will (actions), and seeks to impress upon them a character that is at variance with the world as a whole, with the result that such actions can no longer be regarded as free or moral (ethical).

It follows from this that, as in the sphere of knowledge, so also in man's practical activity, it is mainly a question of overcoming both extremes through penetrating to *true reality*; this is achieved through, on the one hand, a union of concept and percept and, on the other, the development of *ethical individualism*. Such a striving to overcome onesidedness then leads man to a middle or central path, which is the only Christian path. When the state of equilibrium between these two extremes has been achieved, man attains, on his spiritual path, to an experience of the *supersensible reality of the Christ* and, through this, to a capacity to work out of freedom in the world as an ethical (moral) individual. He then acts out of that middle sphere of human nature which lies between the two poles that have been referred to. This middle sphere within man has its physiological foundation in his rhythmic system and, when viewed from the standpoint of human consciousness, in the spiritual or *imaginative* sphere that is associated with it—that sphere where man is alone able to be free (in that he derives the motives for his actions solely from impulses of *moral imagination*).[23]

This imaginative sphere, which is connected with the 'middle man' (with his rhythmic system), is also that region where the Christ-impulse works within man's being, holding the balance between the luciferic beings of the head and the ahrimanic beings of the metabolic-limb system.[24]

Thus only such an equilibrium—established through the Christ-impulse—between the opposing powers working from above and below, which comes to expression in the working of *moral imagination from the middle sphere*, can make a man truly man, endowing him with an experience of 'true humanity'. In our time, man can receive such an experience only from Christ. Hence Rudolf Steiner speaks of 'the growing together of the experience in and with Christ and the experience of real and true humanity'. And he continues: ' "Christ gives me my humanity"—that will be the fundamental feeling which will well up in the soul and pervade it.'[25] And in another context he speaks of how we should never call to mind the concept of freedom without first associating it with the Deed of Christ on Golgotha.[26]

Thus to be in the fullest sense human signifies none other than the attainment of such a state of equilibrium: 'We can only bring about this state of equilibrium by permeating ourselves ever more and more with the Christ-impulse, which calls forth the state of balance between the Luciferic and the Ahrimanic elements.' For: 'It is part of our human nature that we permeate ourselves with the Christ-impulse.'[27]

This is, however, what true Anthroposophy is, Anthroposophy that is experienced in man's inner being: 'Anthroposophy is really none other than that Sophia, that is to say, that content of consciousness, that element of inner experience within the human soul, *which makes a man a full-fledged human being*. The right interpretation of the word Anthroposophy is not 'wisdom of man' but 'awareness of one's humanity.'[28]

Man's being is placed in the world in such a way that the forces of the Sophia or cosmic wisdom are constantly working in all three systems of his physical organisation. In the present cycle of evolution, however, this cosmic wisdom is, in his head system, appropriated to some extent by Lucifer and in his limb-metabolic system by Ahriman.[29] Only in the middle realm do these forces of cosmic wisdom remain untouched by the opposing powers, which is why the Christ is able to enter it.

This is the knowledge which lies behind Rudolf Steiner's indication that 'behind' the sculptural Group, which portrays the state of equilibrium that the Representative of Humanity establishes out of the middle sphere between the luciferic and the ahrimanic powers, the sleeping Isis, the new Sophia, is concealed.[30] And this new Sophia, the focal point of Anthroposophy, must be *awakened* through 'man becoming conscious of his true humanity'.

All that has just been said can be seen as a description—albeit from a somewhat different point of view—of what Novalis, as the motto of his life, sought to define through the words 'Christ and Sophia'.

*

If we now turn directly to the work of Novalis and especially to his Fragments, we can find a striking confirmation of how Novalis, at the end of the eighteenth century, anticipated the fundamental ideas of Rudolf Steiner's *Philosophy of Freedom* and the path leading from there to Anthroposophy. Already in the Fragments of 1798–9 we often find allusions to the necessity of uniting the two fundamental elements in the process of cognition: those of outer and inner, object and subject, percept and concept, although the words and concepts that Novalis chooses for elucidating his thoughts differ at times in their form from the more clearly defined and more consistent formulations of Rudolf Steiner.

'When our intelligence and our world are in harmony—then are we like God.' In this Fragment the need for a union between human concepts (intelligence) and the realm of percepts (the world) can already be discerned. 'Now do the so-called transcendental philosophy—the referring back to the subject—idealism, and the categories—the connection between object and mental picture—appear in a completely new light.' This is the same motif, now more clearly defined as 'the connection between object and mental picture.' And he goes on: 'Knowledge—the contemplation and experimentation (moral help) of God is the true source of life.' 'Contemplations of God—and experiments of God.' This 'referring back to the subject' mentioned above refers to the human ego as the centre through which a synthesis is made between percept and concept, or in Novalis' words between 'object and mental picture' or 'experiments of God and 'contemplations of God'.

Moving further along the path of what we could here—in the words of the motto of Rudolf Steiner's *Philosophy of Freedom*—describe as 'observing the human soul as natural science observes nature',[31] on the quest for words to express his inner experiences, Novalis speaks of the 'power of Imagination', by which he means that higher activity of the human spirit whereby man can, through uniting percept and concept ('materiality and understanding'), attain to true reality.[32] 'The power of Imagination is made up of materiality and understanding—when both are united they shall be a creative and formative force.' 'Materiality and understanding correspond most exactly with one another—because they are one in the third.' And in another context: 'Beholding—mental picturing . . . the power of imagination is the connecting intermediate member—the synthesis—the power of alternation.'

As we have already seen, all perception or contemplation of the outer world of the senses is associated with the unconscious activity of the human will. Hence in this case one can also speak of the antithesis between 'willing and mental picturing', faculties which must be united by means of the ego, and in its higher synthesis this is to a certain extent itself also the ego: 'Ego is action and product at the same time. Willing and mental picturing are in mutual alternation—the ego is none other than willing and mental picturing.' Only an ego which is able to unite in a higher synthesis 'willing and mental picturing'—in Novalis' language the moral idea (mental picture) and the moral action—does he call a 'complete ego'; this can be achieved only through intense inner work. 'Being a complete ego is an art—one can do, and is, what one wills. One is more or less an ego according to how one wills.'

Finally, here are two more utterances of Novalis where he comes so close to the principal formulations of the first part of *The Philosophy of Freedom* that his words almost sound like quotations from it:

Novalis: 'Each thing is a whole, consisting of beholding and mental picturing—One of these two alone is the half of the reality of the thing. The more reality I place in the one half, the less do I in the other—which becomes the negative dimension. Each thing has a positive and a negative dimension.'

Rudolf Steiner: 'The percept is therefore not something finished and self-contained but is only one side of the total reality, the other side being the concept. The act of knowing is the synthesis of percept and concept. Only the percept and concept together constitute the whole thing.'[33]

In the second utterance there also appears the thought that the reason for the division of the world into concept and beholding (percept) or object lies simply in our human organisation and that it can be removed only through the activity of the ego in the cognitive process.

Novalis: 'The law of the concept and the law of the object must be one—separated only in reflection—conceiving and beholding are one when they are related to the ego, divided when one reflects upon both without relating them to the ego.'

Rudolf Steiner: 'Our whole being functions in such a way that from every element of reality the relevant aspects come to us from two sides, from perceiving and from thinking. How I am constituted for gaining knowledge of things has nothing to do with the nature of the things themselves. The division between perceiving and thinking exists only in the moment that I, as thinking observer, confront the things.

'It is only when our egohood has united for itself the two elements of reality—which are actually indivisibly united . . . that the ego again arrives at the reality.'[34]

No less remarkable is the correspondence between some of Novalis' fragments and the second part of *The Philosophy of Freedom*. There Rudolf Steiner speaks of how, as distinct from all other objects and beings in the world, in the case of man 'his true concept as a moral being (free spirit)'[35] does not at first correspond to any concrete percept. 'The intellectual life overcomes the two-fold nature [of concept–percept] through cognition; the moral life overcomes it through the *actual realisation of the free spirit*'— through such endeavours alone can the only percept that corresponds to him be united with the concept of man! And this can be achieved only by each human individual himself, through a conscious development of his spiritual predispositions towards the fullest possible realisation in earthly life of the 'concept of man', that is, the full realisation of his earthly destiny as a *free* and *moral* being. Rudolf Steiner continues: 'This he can do only if he has found the concept of the free spirit, that is, the concept of his own self.' In other words, the true philosophy of freedom should not be a preaching of morality or the establishing of ethical norms and laws, but a *description* of one's own concept of man as a moral (free) being. For *without* such a concept man will never be able to become a moral and free being. This description is given in the second part of *The Philosophy of Freedom*, where it forms its focal point.

Novalis, too, struggles to find such a 'concept of man' as is in accordance with his spiritual being and his higher purpose, in full awareness of the difficulty of this task in our time: 'Hence to describe human beings has hitherto always been impossible, because one has not known what a man is—if one could only know what a man is one would be able to describe individuals in a truly genetic way.' However, Novalis does not evade these difficulties. He searches further, approaching ever more closely to a solution of the mystery, to an answer of the *central question*, 'What is man?' 'Ethics. Regarding the moral law. With complete self-knowledge and knowledge of the world, with complete determination in self and world, the moral law disappears and the description of the moral being stands in place of the moral law.' We see that, according to Novalis, a man who is a 'moral (free) being' (second part of *The Philosophy of Freedom*) can give rise to a 'complete determination of self and world' only out of a 'complete self-knowledge and knowledge of the world' (first part of *The Philosophy of Freedom*). And this means: 'I determine the world in that I determine myself—and so indirectly myself and vice versa.'

Novalis also knows about the indivisible oneness of morality and freedom described by Rudolf Steiner (see 'moral human being = free spirit' above) as the fundamental characteristic of the 'concept of man'. He writes: 'Moral feeling is a feeling of absolute creative power, of productive freedom, of boundless personality, of the microcosm, of our own particular divinity in us.'

And the path to this comprehension of the 'idea of man' lies in the *development of thinking*, in its transformation into what Rudolf Steiner calls '*pure* thinking', to which Novalis also refers: 'Freedom grows with the training and skill of the thinker. (Degrees of freedom. Freedom and love are one.)' By 'love' in these words is meant the central source of all morality. 'Freedom and love are one'—that is the shortest definition of the 'concept of man', whose realisation is at the same time the highest goal of earthly evolution (see p. 166).[36]

If man acts in the world out of *such* a 'concept of man', his will is free, because it has become in the highest sense one with the will of God. In other words: at the moment when man acts in the world out of his innermost, primordial being, his own will becomes the will of God. And then man acts in the world not as an earthly, but as a cosmic (divine) being. Novalis writes of this as follows: 'Morality, rightly understood, is the real life-element in man . . . Our pure moral will is the will of God. In that we carry out his will, we enliven and expand our own existence, and it is as though it had been our own will alone that we thus acted out of our inner nature.' To this observation of Novalis we would only add the concluding words from *The Philosophy of Freedom*: 'Such an act of will therefore has its grounds only in man himself. Man is then the ultimate determinant of his action. He is free.'

However, like Rudolf Steiner, Novalis does not stop at this philosophical description of the 'concept of man', but tries to make it a reality within himself. 'To become man is an art,' he says. And this 'becoming of man' signifies for him none other than a direct and fully conscious growing into the spiritual world, a return to man's true home. The precondition of this for Novalis, as for Rudolf Steiner, is that mood which permeates the whole thought structure of *The Philosophy of Freedom*, for only a soul-attitude of *such* a kind can lead man in our time to a perception of 'true revelations' from the higher worlds: 'I am convinced that one is more likely to attain to *true revelations* through a cold technical understanding and a calm, moral sense than through fancy, which would simply appear to lead us into the realm of spectres, to this antipode of the true heaven.'

For Novalis, the first real revelation on this path is the inner need to find a spiritual balance between the two extremes described above, for only in the balance of these forces can the true 'concept of man' as a free and moral ego-being be realised, of man as a being who derives the motives for his actions only from the impulses of 'moral imagination' or, in Novalis' terminology, from the impulses of 'productive imagination.'[37]

'All knowledge should bring about morality—the moral impulse, the impulse towards freedom, should give rise to knowledge. To be free is the propensity of the ego—the capacity of being free is the *productive imagination*—*harmony* is the condition of its activity—of *hovering between opposing forces*. To be at one with yourself is, therefore, the basic condition of the highest purpose—of being, or being free. All being, being in general, is none other than being-in-freedom—*hovering between extremes* which need to be united and need to be separated. From this focus of hovering, all reality streams forth—everything is contained within it—object and subject arise through it, not it through them. Egohood or *productive imagination, hovering*, determines, produces the extremes, that between which the hovering is happening. This is an illusion, but only in the realm of common understanding. In other respects it is something that is absolutely real, for *hovering*—its cause, is the source, the mother of all reality, reality itself. *Regard the nature of this hovering.*'

This condition of 'hovering' between two extremes is the necessary condition for the free moral development of the ego and, as we have seen, is the central nerve of *The Philosophy of Freedom* and at the same time the path which leads from it to the central focus of Anthroposophy, to the experience of the Christ-impulse, which brings about a balance between the opposing powers in the cosmos and in man's being:

'Morality must be the kernel of our existence, if it is to be for us what it would be. The destiny of the ego is an infinite *realisation of being*. Its striving would be ever more to be. From the I am, the path of evil goes downwards, the path of the good upwards. The highest philosophy is ethics. Therefore all philosophy begins from the I am. The highest principle of knowledge must be the outward expression of all knowledge as a means of establishing a reality which relates to the purpose of the ego. This is to be attained, or aimed at, through knowledge in the widest sense, as existence in the sense-world—that is, [the purpose of the ego] *complete freedom of being*. The ego seems to be caught in an inner contradiction where one does not know the nature of its activity, the activity of *productive imagination*, in that the attainment of its purpose would appear to be frustrated by the means that have been chosen—but for this very reason it acts in harmony with itself, and therefore I would say that it must act in such a way through its very nature—that is, because it is nothing other than *a hovering* etc. and hence only brings forth, and only can bring forth, what it seeks to bring forth. Unless it acts in this way it cannot bring forth anything—for all generation is concerned with being, and *being is hovering* etc. That which is must seem to contradict itself in so far as one—so to speak—breaks it up into its component parts, which, through the very nature of the faculty of reflection, one is in a sense forced to do. [See Novalis' words on p. 232] *To be, to be I, to be free and hovering are synonymous*—one expression is related to the next—all refer to the same reality. All are merely predicates of the one concept "I"—though here, concept and reality are one. "I" is a concept that cannot be grasped, because in that it exists it is its own concept. Through its existence, its uniquely possible concept is given.[38] Here one thinks of events and actions commonly as of something that is going on in time or has been. The event in question here must, at all events, *be thought of purely spiritually*—not on its own—not in time—quasi *as a moment which embraces the eternal universe*, which includes within itself an infinite reality, in which we live, weave and are, which happens wholly in every moment—*like a genius that works ever onwards*—"I"-existence.'

And in another Fragment, where he again turns to the process of 'hovering between opposing forces', Novalis, in order to characterise it more precisely, uses the same word that Rudolf Steiner was also to employ—'balance' or 'equilibrium': 'Strength is replaced by balance—and in balance every man should remain—*for this is indeed the condition of freedom.*'[39]

This realisation of the freedom that stems from the attainment of 'balance' is the fulfilment of man's true destiny, as a being who fulfils in the world deeds out of his higher or, in Novalis' expression, 'infinite ego': 'In every moment when we act in freedom there is such a triumph of the infinite ego over the finite, for this moment the not-I is utterly vanquished—though not for material existence.'

If this stage is attained, the moral will is then no longer an indeterminate and mysterious force that rises dimly out of the depths of bodily existence, but a new cognitive organ for a higher reality which will have a clarity that would otherwise belong only to thinking: 'The active use of organs is nothing other than magical, miraculous thinking or voluntary use of the physical world—for *will is nothing other than a magical, vigorous capacity of thinking.*' This is a further important characterisation of *free* will given by Novalis: the will is free when it is inwardly experienced by man as 'a magical, vigorous capacity of thinking'.

Thus in all we may say: the experience of 'the concept of man' in the sense of Rudolf Steiner's *Philosophy of Freedom*—as has been considered in this Appendix—can indeed be seen as the entry of Anthroposophy into earthly evolution. This experience is in its inner nature identical with what Novalis indicates by means of the following image:

> One achieved it—he lifted the veil of the Goddess at Saïs—
> But what did he see? He saw—wonder of wonders—himself.

In these words we have a testimony of Novalis' laying hold of man's higher being, of his primal divine idea, so that he can say with complete justice: 'The most wonderful, the eternal phenomenon is one's own existence. The greatest mystery is man himself. The solution of this infinite task is, indeed, world history.'

He gains an ever deeper insight into the mystery of man's true being: 'What is man? A perfect metaphor of the spirit.' And what is the world? According to Novalis: 'The world is macro-anthropos.' This means that 'the world is a universal metaphor of the spirit—a symbolic picture of the same.' This is indeed *the birth of Anthroposophy in his soul*, where man is recognised as a pure spirit and, at the same time, as a key to all the mysteries of the world order.

Thus a new path of all-embracing knowledge lights up for Novalis, one which opens up inexhaustible sources of 'moral imagination' for man's practical life and activities and which leads him to take hold of the spirit within the self as a still incipient but nevertheless wholly real experience of the *Spirit-Self*.

In the following words, which as though sum up in one brief characterisation the whole of Novalis' life's path and creative work, Rudolf Steiner refers to the experience of the Spirit-Self which he (Novalis) attained in his last earthly life:[40] 'Novalis feels and experiences himself as having his being within the higher spirit-nature. What he expresses he feels through his innate genius as the revelations of this *very spirit-nature*.'

*

In conclusion, there remains to be considered one further aspect of *The Philosophy of Freedom*, which enables one to see the extent to which this remarkable book is a spiritual gate to the sixth cultural epoch.

The fundamental significance of this book for the further evolution of mankind stems from the fact that the full realisation of 'ethical individualism', that is, of that *ideal of man* which arises from its theory of knowledge, is indeed none other than the fulfilment within man of the impulse of the Spirit-Self.

In the 'Hague conversation' referred to above, Walter Johannes Stein asked Rudolf Steiner: '"What will be left of your work in a few thousand years' time?" He answered: "Nothing except *The Philosophy of Freedom*. But everything else is contained within it. If someone makes the act of freedom that is described there a reality, he will find the whole content of Anthroposophy."' For 'through the *Philosophy of Freedom*, man rises to a perception of the human being as a purely spiritual being.'

In the ninth chapter of *The Philosophy of Freedom*, Rudolf Steiner observes: 'Freedom of action [and, in a spiritual sense, freedom as a whole] is conceivable only from the standpoint of ethical individualism.' If this freedom is to a certain extent attained, if a man has really evolved to the stage of the 'ethical individual', he thereby enters a higher circle of human beings where there reigns only the greatest harmony and peace in human relationships, for a 'moral misunderstanding', a clash, is impossible between people who are morally free. Only the morally unfree who follow their natural instincts or the conventional demands of duty antagonise their fellow men if they do not obey the same instincts and commands as themselves. Such a time will be the dawning of that 'holy age of eternal peace' of which Novalis speaks at the end of 'Christendom or Europe'.

Thus 'the inner disposition, the attitude of soul', that stems from ethical individualism will form the foundation of that universal human brotherhood of free (moral) individuals, where differences of opinion, disagreements and other anti-social manifestations will be impossible: 'It is only because human individuals *are of one spirit* that they can live out their lives in close proximity to one another.' For through the spiritual evolution of the individual principle within his own being, man will in time be able truly to experience himself as a being belonging to the *One Spirit* who unites the whole of humanity—the Christ Spirit. 'The free individual lives in confidence that all other free human beings belong with him to *one spiritual world* and that their intentions will harmonise with his. A free individual does not demand agreement from his fellow man, but he expects to find it because it is inherent in human nature.'[41]

The fulfilment of the ideals of *The Philosophy of Freedom* will lead mankind to a real and fully conscious growing into the spiritual world, a world which is one for all men. The fruit of this growing will be the spreading of a 'free spirituality' amongst mankind, a spirituality which excludes any element of unfreedom in the spiritual sphere, for human life on Earth will then be permeated by the spirit, will become an expression of the supersensible: 'The standpoint of free morality . . . sees in free spirituality . . . the final stage of human evolution.'

In what has been said above, we may recognise the three chief characteristic traits of the sixth cultural epoch of which we spoke in the seventh chapter:

1. Universal brotherhood. Disagreements between those who work in the world out of impulses of true love are impossible: 'To live in love

towards our actions, and to let live out of an understanding of the other person's will, is the fundamental maxim of free human beings.'

2. Absolute freedom in spiritual life, which is associated with the realisation of 'free spirituality'.

3. Pneumatosophy, as the consequence of a conscious ascent into an objective spiritual world which is the same for all men.

In our time, the ideal of *The Philosophy of Freedom* as described here is attainable for only a few people. In the sixth epoch, however, its fulfilment will become a necessity for the whole of humanity if it is to attain that stage in its evolution which the higher spiritual powers have destined for it.

'Human individuals, with the moral ideas belonging to their nature, are the prerequisites for a moral world order.' The realisation of the new 'moral world order' referred to in these words will be the most important task of the sixth cultural epoch. However, the foundation for it must be laid in our time through the awakening of an awareness that 'the human individual is the source of all morality and the centre of earthly life'. Only Anthroposophy can give mankind such an awareness in our time.

That the ideal of man in the sense of *The Philosophy of Freedom*—as expressed in these words by Rudolf Steiner—is at the same time also the ideal of the sixth cultural epoch can be seen from what he says in the following words:[42] 'The human being then rises in the next cultural epoch to Manas or the Spirit-Self . . . This will have its beginning when men start to feel that the innermost kernel of the human being is at the same time the most universal. What is at present looked upon as an individual human blessing is not as yet an individual blessing on a higher plane. That people quarrel and have different opinions is considered today to have a great deal to do with man's individuality, with his personality . . . Just because they want to be independent, they must hold different opinions, but that is an inferior point of view. Men will be most peaceful and harmonious when they, as separate persons, become most individualised. As long as men are not yet fully overshone by the Spirit-Self, there will be opinions that differ from one another. These opinions are not yet experienced in the true, innermost part of man's being.'

And he goes on: 'It will be Manas culture when the sources of truth are ever more experienced within the strengthened human individuality, within the human personality, and when, at the same time, what is experienced as higher truth has a similar measure of agreement between one man and another as is accorded to mathematical truths . . . Then the truth that is found within one soul will tally exactly with the truth in the other, and there will be no strife. That is the guarantee for true peace and true brotherhood, because there is but one truth, and this truth has to do with the Spiritual Sun . . . Thus when in the course of the sixth cultural epoch the Spirit-Self enters into human beings, there will indeed be a *Spiritual Sun* to which all men will incline and in which they will find harmony.'

Rudolf Steiner's *Philosophy of Freedom* may be seen as the first heralding rays of this rising spiritual Sun of the Spirit-Self.

Appendix III

The Festival of the 'Intercession of the Virgin' and the Spiritual Future of Eastern Europe

In Eastern Europe, the Festival of the 'Intercession of the Virgin'* occupies a place of quite particular importance amongst the principal annual festivals. In Russia it is not just one of the so-called 'great festivals',[43] but is the *only* great Christian festival that is not directly connected with the Gospel story, in that it has as its source an event which took place in the middle of the tenth century in the suburbs of Constantinople in the church of Vlacherni, where a cloak of the Virgin was kept which had been brought there from Palestine in the fifth century.

At the time, Constantinople was under threat of attack by the Saracens, and services in its churches took place more frequently than normal. On Sunday, 1 October, during the evening service and when the church was full of people, St Andrew Yuròdivy (Andrew the holy fool) experienced, in the fourth hour of the night, a vision of the Mother of God appearing before him, surrounded by Angels and a host of saints, martyrs, apostles and evangelists. Ahead of all, on either side of the Mother of God, were John the Baptist and John the Evangelist, who were later to become the most beloved and most revered saints in Russia.[44] The holy Virgin approached the altar and, on bended knee, began to pray for all Christian people. She begged her divine Son to accept the prayers of all who confess His holy Name. After remaining for a long time in prayer, she took off her wide, mantle-like veil, which had also covered her head, and spread it over all who were present in the church to protect them from enemies visible and invisible.

Andrew and his pupil Epiphanias contemplated the wonderful vision for a long while until the Mother of God, having finished her prayer for the world, disappeared in shining glory. And as she left, the mantle that she had spread over the people became invisible.

A further element in this story which is of particular significance is

---

* 'Pokròv Bogoròditsy' ('the Protecting Veil of the Mother of God'), 'episkepsis', is celebrated on 14 October (old style), that is, on 1 October according to the new calendar.

that, according to tradition, the Andrew who had this vision was a man of Slavic descent. In his younger years he had been taken prisoner and had been sold in Constantinople to Theognost, an inhabitant of the locality. After being given his liberty, he was baptised and then had lived ever since at the church of Vlacherni. Thus even in its origins this supersensible event had a definite connection with the Slavic East of Europe.

When Russia was Christianised in the year 988, the legend of St Andrew's vision—together with the principal 'Biblical' festivals—spread remarkably quickly amongst the Russian people, even to the extent that less than two centuries after the Christianising of Russia a special festival was established in memory of this event. In the year 1165 on the River Nerl, not far from the town of Vladimir, the first church to be named in honour of the Festival of the Intercession was erected. Shortly afterwards, at the end of the twelfth century, a monastery was founded in Novgorod in honour of the 'Intercession of the Virgin'. In the centuries that followed, churches and monasteries dedicated to it spread throughout Russia. For example, in Moscow a church consecrated in memory of this festival was built in the middle of the sixteenth century (this is now generally known as 'St Basil's Cathedral').

Despite the fact that, as regards its origins, this festival goes back to a vision which was experienced not in a Slavic region but in Constantinople, it nevertheless acquired its full significance *only amongst the Russian people*. Neither the Greek Orthodox nor—still less—the Catholic Churches know of it. The reasons for the very close relationship of the Russian people to the spiritual content of this festival have deep occult foundations and have to do with the future mission of Eastern Europe in the sixth cultural epoch.

This future mission of the Slavic East does, however, include a further occult tradition, of which it is necessary to have a clear grasp if one is to gain insight into the mystery of the transition from the fifth to the sixth cultural epochs and also if one is to understand the latter. This tradition is connected with the image of the Palladium. Its history is briefly as follows. Exoterically, the Palladium is a particular sculptural representation of Pallas Athene, esoterically it is an *imagination* of the most ancient clairvoyant wisdom of humanity.[45] Thus the legend tells us that it first appeared in ancient Troy having 'fallen from the heavens', which indicates from the outset that we have here to do with the clairvoyant wisdom which in former times gave mankind direct access to the spiritual world.

In Troy the Palladium served as a force of protection and connection with the Gods. As long as it was present, the city would not be conquered. Thus if he was to conquer the city Odysseus had to steal the Palladium.

Odysseus is no longer a bearer of the ancient clairvoyant forces of mankind. He is under the special protection of the Goddess Athene, who had the task, in the fourth post-Atlantean period, of leading mankind from the old clairvoyance to the new, more intellectual culture which was subsequently to find its highest manifestation in Greek philosophy.[46] According to another version of the legend, Aeneas rescued the Palladium from the burning Troy, and took it with him to the Rome which he was later to found.

If we then turn to Roman history, we see how the remnants of the old clairvoyant wisdom are finally lost. There is a reference to this in one of the versions of the legend, where it says that the Emperor Constantine did not take the Palladium itself from Rome to Constantinople but only a 'copy' of it. Historically this is confirmed by the fact that Constantine was not initiated in the Mysteries[47] and, hence, did not have any direct connection with the higher worlds.

Thus the total disappearance of the ancient clairvoyant wisdom, by the time the Palladium was brought from Rome to Constantinople, comes to expression in that the original Palladium can no longer be found on Earth—the ancient wisdom no longer flows into earthly evolution.

However, the Palladium legend ends with a description of how this wisdom will eventually be again accessible to humanity, and how the newly found Palladium will be brought from Constantinople to the North, 'to a Slavic town'.[48]

From the standpoint of a spiritual–scientific view of history one can say: the bringing of the Palladium from Troy to Rome corresponds to the transition from the third post-Atlantean epoch to the fourth. Its subsequent removal from Rome to Constantinople corresponds to the transition from the fourth epoch to the fifth. The fifth epoch is associated with the deepest immersion of mankind in matter, which is why it is in Constantinople that all 'historical' knowledge of the Palladium is finally lost. Its future transfer from Constantinople to the Slavic East of Europe will correspond to the historical transition from the fifth cultural epoch to the sixth. During this period, the Palladium will again—albeit in a wholly different form—descend to Earth, which is to say that mankind will once more gain access to the primordial clairvoyant wisdom and will again—though now in full consciousness—enter the spiritual world. This will be the beginning of the true culture of the Spirit-Self.

In ancient Greece the Goddess Athene guided the transition from the old clairvoyance to the 'earthly wisdom' that was to replace it. The wisdom of the mysteries, arrayed in the garment of the most richly inspired human concepts (as is the case in Greek philosophy), was her gift to humanity.[49] For this reason, the Greek philosophers always regarded Athene as their protector and inspirer. In a more esoteric sense this means that, through the figure of Athene, the impulses of the cosmic wisdom of the Sophia still permeated Greek culture, although they were not perceived directly but only through the delicate web of the human concepts that were gradually being engendered.

When translated into Russian, the word 'Palladium' means a place or a source of 'virginity'. It refers to those cosmic forces which flow into earthly evolution from the constellation of the Virgin (from the sphere of the cosmic Sophia). *Pallas* Athene—the Greek Goddess of Wisdom—is thus a definite Being of the spiritual world who is 'clothed' with the Sophia forces, with the forces of cosmic virginity. She is the bearer of the Sophia forces in the pre-Christian epoch of human evolution.

In the Christian epoch, an altogether new relationship to the Sophia forces in our cosmos needed to arise. This new relationship appears before us historically in a different image, which is in a certain sense a higher metamorphosis of all previous evolution. Rudolf Steiner refers to this as follows: 'Pallas Athene, too, is a Maja, a Mary; but Pallas Athene is that Maja who still reflects wisdom from out of her own being, who out of herself enables wisdom to shine forth before men. The great step forward consists in that this same Maja, this same Mary is fructified by the cosmos and a new wisdom is born. Pallas Athene was the representative of wisdom. The Christ-impulse is the Son of the Maja, of Mary, of the virginal representative of wisdom and the cosmic-divine, cosmic-intelligent powers of the world.'[50]

The difference between these two images is that the Virgin Pallas Athene was mankind's guide on the path from cosmic wisdom to human wisdom, while Mary Sophia will be its guide on its return from human wisdom to cosmic wisdom, from an inspired thinking to a new clairvoyance. This ascending cycle of evolution, where mankind will again find access to the virginal wisdom of the cosmic Sophia, will be associated with the diffusion, in the sixth epoch, of those Mysteries which were spoken of in Chapter 12.

The general line of evolution outlined here can be made somewhat more concrete if we take the following into consideration. After the decline of ancient Greece, its spiritual culture fructified the entire life of the Roman Empire. Many Romans who had had a Greek education and considered themselves to be friends of Greek philosophy sought to emphasise this in their dress. Thus in contrast to other Romans, who wore a toga, they preferred to wear a special garment which they called a 'pallium' or 'philosopher's gown'. Through this name they wished to emphasise their affinity with Greek philosophy and with its patron, *Pallas* Athene. Tertullian, for example, wore a pallium in Carthage, and this led to his having to defend his right to wear this garment before the other citizens of the town.

The female equivalent of the pallium in ancient Rome was a garment called the palla. It consisted of a broad rectangular cloth which covered the whole body, including the head.

In early Christian art the Mother of God was often portrayed wearing a palla. This tradition lived on in the world of art. For example, the Mother of God is clad in a palla in almost all Russian icons. Raphael's *Sistine Madonna* is also a classic instance of the same phenomenon. If at this point we recall that early Christian art still had its source wholly in the old clairvoyance and therefore tried to transmit something of the *spiritual aura*[51] surrounding man even in the forms and colours of garments, we must say: the very name 'palla', which is a last echo of the memories of the Virgin Pallas Athene, is indicative of the cosmic forces of the Sophia or the 'virginal wisdom' which surround the earthly figure of Mary like a mighty radiant aura.

According to the testimony of modern spiritual research, these cosmic forces of the 'virginal wisdom' or the Sophia are related in their substance to the fifth principal of man's being, his *Spirit-Self*. This is why Rudolf Steiner says: 'The fully fashioned Manas . . . is wisdom, Sophia, the Mother.'[52] And the figure of Mary clothed with the palla is indicative of the aura of Manas or the Spirit-Self that surrounds her.

Christ, who united at the Baptism in the Jordan with Jesus of Nazareth, bears through this act a still higher principle into earthly evolution, the principle of the Life-Spirit or the substance of cosmic love. Rudolf Steiner refers to this in the following words: 'In Greece men called Buddhi "Christos", and this is today present in most men only in its initial stages.' And he goes on: 'Through the Holy Spirit Manas is developed, through Christ the sixth principle [Buddhi].'[53]

In the scene of the Annunciation, as it is described in St Luke's Gospel, the Archangel says to the Luke Mary: 'The Holy Spirit will come upon you, and the power of the Most High will overshadow you (1:35).' From this moment, the forces of the Holy Spirit work within her whole being, 'developing' the Manas principle within it throughout the 12 years that preceded her early death. Then from the spiritual world, during the Baptism of Jesus in the Jordan, she immerses this Manas principle in the astral body of the Solomon Mary—who, as a result of this, becomes one who is 'clothed in a "palla"', that is, the bearer of a higher, spiritual aura through which she is directly connected with the forces of the Sophia in our cosmos.

At first, however, the substance of the Spirit-Self still works in her without her conscious knowledge. The Manas-impulse is already working within her being, but it is not as yet grasped by her consciousness to such an extent that she would have been able thenceforth to become a conscious witness of the three-year period while the divine Christ Being was on the Earth.

Such an awakening of the Manas forces that were already essentially contained in her aura, *within her waking consciousness*, takes place as a result of the influence upon her being of the higher principle of Buddhi, whose bearer on the Earth is Christ Jesus. In the first miracle described in St John's Gospel, which took place at the Wedding at Cana of Galilee, we have an allusion to this awakening. It can be found in the words with which Christ Jesus addresses His Mother: 'Woman, what have you to do with me? (John 2:4).' This is the awakening influence of Christ's Life-Spirit upon the Spirit-Self of Mary,[54] an influence which enables her to raise the Manas substance—which connects her with the cosmic sphere of the Sophia—to consciousness in order that, from this moment onwards, she might accompany Christ Jesus with full *understanding* on the paths of His cosmic-earthly destiny.

The imagination of the transformation of water into wine through the Sun forces of Christ bears witness to this. Water does not have any direct influence upon the human consciousness. However, when it is transformed by the forces of the Sun into the juice of the vine, it is able to exert such an influence. Through receiving the 'spiritual wine' (the Buddhi forces) from Christ Himself in an act of supersensible communion, the Solomon Mary awakens to a fully conscious life in Manas, she becomes indeed a conscious representative of its forces on the Earth.

Thus all that we have said about the spiritual significance of the miracle at the Marriage at Cana of Galilee has implications for its particular prophetic relationship to the sixth cultural epoch. Rudolf Steiner refers to this relationship in the lecture of 30 May 1908: 'Picture to yourself the seer of that age. He experienced . . . how mankind is gradually being prepared to receive the Spirit or Spirit-Self, Manas, in the sixth epoch. And he experienced this in an astral pre-vision. He experienced the marriage between humanity and the Spirit.' And he continues: 'The writer of the Gospel of St John points out that it is not merely a question of an actual event, but that it is at the same time a great, mighty prophecy. This marriage expresses the great marriage of humanity which occurred on the third day of initiation . . . On the third day [there occurred] what will happen when mankind passes over from the fifth to the sixth cultural epoch.'[55]

These words of Rudolf Steiner are further confirmed by the presence, in the description of the miracle, of the Marriage at Cana of Galilee, of a certain occult number symbolism. Thus the *six* stone water-vessels (2:6) refer directly to the sixth cultural epoch, while what is said about their capacity: 'each holding two or three measures', speaks of those members of man's being which will exert an influence in that epoch. Two of them will still be connected with the Earth (the physical and etheric bodies); when he departs from them *at night* during sleep, man will no longer abide with his astral body and ego in the spiritual world in a state of complete unconsciousness but, through being clothed in the Manas sheath, will be able to work there in full consciousness. In other words: the conscious connection with the spiritual world will become a reality in the sixth epoch through the fact that man will consist not of two and two members, but of two and three! This means that in the sixth epoch man will, to a certain extent, be able to experience, *even during incarnation on Earth*, what he would otherwise experience only after his death, before entering Kama-Loka: 'For what he now delivers up to the world ether as his etheric body, he clothes in what we have called the Spirit-Self. That is in a certain sense now an outer member. An undefined ether presses towards him, and envelops him with a kind of Spirit-Self.'[56]

· The Solomon Mary, who was clothed in the spiritual sheath (palla) of Manas at the moment of Jesus' Baptism in the Jordan, will be the archetype of such an experience for mankind.

This 'being clothed with the Spirit-Self' will give the sixth cultural epoch its *moral character*.[57] We can best understand this if we take the following into consideration. In the spiritual world after death, the Spirit-Self forms man's outer sheath during the Kama-Loka period. According to Rudolf Steiner, it forms the 'driving-force' which leads a person to an experience of what those who were connected with him have inwardly lived through as a result of his words and actions in the previous earthly life. All suffering that has been inflicted upon *other* people, whether wilfully or involuntarily, is now experienced by the human soul as its own suffering. And it is the sheath of the Spirit-Self, in which it is now clothed, that impels it to this.[58] This is the other aspect of the future working of the Spirit-Self amongst mankind in the sixth epoch.[59]

This influence will, however, be felt not only through man's experience of his own mistakes and omissions, but will gradually be extended to an all-embracing sense of responsibility for *all* earthly evolution, so that 'those who are at the heights of culture in the sixth post-Atlantean cultural period will feel the suffering of others as their own suffering.'[60]

The Gospel of St Luke also offers a prophetic indication of this particular quality of the sixth epoch in the words which old Simeon addresses to the Luke Mary: 'And a sword will pierce through your own soul also; the thoughts of many hearts will be revealed [to you] (2:35).' This future capacity of an all-embracing compassion, and of voluntarily taking upon oneself the sufferings of others, was imparted by the Luke Mary to the Solomon Mary together with the substance of the Spirit-Self.

We shall now return to the miracle at the Wedding at Cana of Galilee and consider one further aspect of it. As we have already seen, the awakening of the Manas *consciousness* in the Solomon Mary, which took place then, is a prophetic anticipation of its awakening within mankind as a whole in the sixth cultural epoch. But as this awakening of the Manas culture takes place only through the influence upon it of the higher Buddhi principle, this means that in the sixth epoch not only the forces of wisdom (Sophia) but also the forces of cosmic love will be at work amongst mankind.[61] One can also say: the Spirit-Self will descend to Earth permeated by the impulse of cosmic love. Thus despite the fact that the Manas-impulse will, in the first instance, be connected with the substance of cosmic wisdom, it is at the same time the foundation for the great community of brotherly love which will embrace the whole of mankind.

'This sixth epoch will be a very important one, because it will bring peace and brotherhood through a common *wisdom*. Peace and brotherhood, because the higher self will *descend*—at first in its lower form as Spirit-Self or Manas—not only to certain chosen human beings, but also to that part of humanity passing through a normal evolution.'[62] And in another lecture Rudolf Steiner speaks of this even more clearly: 'Only gradually will humanity be able to evolve out of the small communities into a great *community of love* which will become a reality precisely through the implanting of the Spirit-Self.'

In order the better to understand this process, we must take the following into consideration. According to the spiritual–scientific research of Rudolf Steiner, the descent of the Spirit-Self into mankind will take place in the sixth epoch and the descent of the Life-Spirit in the seventh.[63] Just as in the forming of the essential character of the present epoch, the consciousness soul—albeit without most people's conscious knowledge—is stirred into action by the Spirit-Self (the Sophia),[64] so in the sixth epoch the conscious mastery of Manas will be brought about from still higher spiritual worlds by the Life-Spirit, the full experience of which, however, will in the sixth epoch (as with the Spirit-Self in the fifth) be attainable only by an initiate or by those who have already embarked upon the path of true spirit-pupilship. This means that that impulse of cosmic love which is revealed through Buddhi and which will descend to the Earth only in the seventh epoch will in the sixth epoch be working amongst mankind *in a preparatory way through the mediation of Manas.*

This Manas substance which is permeated with Buddhi forces will, in the Philadelphia epoch, serve as the foundation for a universal human brotherhood. While in the seventh epoch, when the Buddhi substance descends directly into humanity, this latter substance will be released out of the sphere of Atman or Spirit-Man, as a result of which the impulse of love will not merely be a means of uniting people in a brotherly way, but will enable the Spirit-Will of our whole cosmos to work through this impulse, so that love becomes a creative power of the highest order which engenders something altogether new in earthly evolution.[65]

Rudolf Steiner referred to this whole process when he directed his attention to the archetypal picture of the events of the Turning-Point of Time: 'How Christ entered the world can be recognised as follows: The sixth principle, Buddhi, is born out of the fifth when the latter has attained to its full stature out of the Spirit-Self or Manas, or as the Greeks called the fifth principle at that time, out of the Sophia. All Gnostics who acknowledged the truth of St John's Gospel called the mother of Jesus "Sophia". Through the appearance of Jesus, the sixth principle is brought to the Earth. The union of the Life-Spirit with mankind is fulfilled. For this the Sophia had first to become wholly mature [in the sixth epoch]. When the Life-Spirit unites with mankind [in the seventh epoch], mankind is Sophia. In the Wedding at Cana this is explained to us in a parable.'[66]

In the spiritual–historical sense this means that before the Buddhi principle descends to humanity in the seventh epoch, Manas must come to maturity during the sixth epoch, or, in other words, *humanity itself must become Sophia.*

This is the principal task of the sixth epoch, the archetypal image of which was given at the Wedding at Cana of Galilee: 'We may call this a spiritual marriage—and this is what the union of the human ego with Manas or the Spirit-Self was always called in Christian esotericism.'[67]

The historical progress of humanity which we have been considering will also be connected with the further evolution of Christianity as *a living spiritual impulse.* Rudolf Steiner refers to this as follows: 'Christianity will evolve into the future, quite other things will be offered to mankind, and Christian evolution and Christian attitudes to life will arise in a new form: the transformed astral body will appear as the Christian Spirit-Self, the transformed etheric body as the Christian Life-Spirit.'[68] In an occult sense this means that the seed which through the Mystery of Golgotha has been laid into the Earth, the seed of its becoming the new *moral Sun* of our cosmos, will gradually become accessible to the direct supersensible perception of human beings: 'The Deed on Golgotha has permeated the Earth with an astral light which will gradually become etheric and then physical light.'[69]

But mankind will, from the sixth epoch onwards, be able not only to *behold* this light, but also consciously to *participate* in the Earth's shining forth into the cosmic expanses. At present such a participation is possible only indirectly,[70] and only later will it mature into a *conscious* participation. Then in the seventh epoch humanity will participate directly in uniting the etheric light with the astral, and still later, after the great catastrophe of the 'war of all against all', also in uniting the physical light with the etheric.

The sixth cultural epoch will have a quite particular significance for the Earth's gradually becoming a new Sun. 'This sixth epoch will be a very important one', as Rudolf Steiner says.[71] For it is during this epoch that the *beginning* will be made in humanity's participation in this process, which will become possible through the 'descent' to the Earth of the substance of the Spirit-Self or, to express the same thing in a more imaginative language, of the spiritual aura or 'Palla' of the Sophia, her supersensible mantle, whose bearer at the Turning-Point of Time was the Solomon Mary. And what has here been described objectively as the descent of spiritual substance will, in a subjective sense (that is, from the standpoint of human beings themselves) signify their fully conscious ascent into the spiritual world, their re-union with the primal wisdom of mankind.

In other words: this descent of the spiritual palla of the Sophia into humanity in the sixth epoch, an event whose geographical focus will be Eastern Europe, is none other than the *return of the Palladium from the spiritual world to the Earth*, its initial rediscovery amongst the largest of the Slavic peoples and then throughout all mankind.[72]

The central imagination of the Russian Festival of the 'Intercession of the Virgin' ('the Protecting Veil'), is indeed a prophetic indication of this time in the distant future.

In the year 869, at the eighth Ecumenical Council in Constantinople, the spirit was abolished.[73] This was a direct testimony of the fact that the forces of the ancient Palladium which had been brought to Constantinople had finally forsaken earthly humanity. Thus the question of its rediscovery, upon which so much in the further evolution of the Earth depends, presented itself in all acuteness as a spiritual–historical necessity. And the spiritual–historical answer to this question came already in the following century in the form of the prophetic vision of St Andrew in the church at Constantinople, of the rediscovery of the Palladium, of its descent from heaven in the sixth epoch, in the image of the palla of the Sophia coming down to the Earth.

The fact that the legend of the vision of St Andrew was spread only amongst the people of the Slavic East and that then a great festival in its honour was established in Russia confirms *historically* not only the indication in the legend that the Palladium will indeed be brought from Constantinople to Russia but also that there are forces living in the spiritual depths of the Russian people which testify to their capacity to have an unconscious premonition of this future and, in the Festival of the 'Intercession', to anticipate the future descent of the Spirit-Self to humanity.[74]

The vision of St Andrew includes two individualities who will make a particular contribution towards this descent. These are the two Johns, John the Baptist and John the Evangelist, who will in future take a central part in transforming mankind into 'Sophia'.

In addition to them, St Andrew in his vision sees around the Mother of God and the Angelic Beings apostles, evangelists, holy women, and Christian martyrs of all periods and races. This is an Imagination of all these human souls who, as a result of receiving the Christ-impulse into themselves, will thereby be able to become true servants of the work of Christ amongst mankind in the sixth epoch.[75] For the supersensible appearance of the saints of all nations and countries of the Earth before Andrew's clairvoyant gaze has in an occult sense the same meaning as the Apostles' clairvoyant vision at the Turning-Point of Time of the feeding of the five thousand. According to the spiritual–scientific research of Rudolf Steiner, this vision of the Apostles was none other than a supersensible contemplation of those human souls who will incarnate in the fifth cultural epoch to serve the Christ-impulse.[76]

In a similar way, St Andrew beholds the great brotherhood of all those who will be permeated with the Christ-impulse in the sixth cultural epoch, the all-embracing community of love of the future Philadelphia: 'There hovers before us, as a high ideal, a form of community that will so encompass the sixth cultural period that civilised human beings will quite naturally meet each other as brothers and sisters.'[77] For 'the Spirit-

Self is to descend, but it can only descend into a human community that is permeated with brotherliness.' These words of Rudolf Steiner correspond precisely with the vision of St Andrew, which later became the foundation of the Russian Festival of the 'Intercession'; for in the middle of the tenth century he beheld the great brotherly community of Philadelphia, a community which embraces the *whole* of humanity and which is therefore ready to receive the new Palladium, the spiritual aura or palla of Sophia, descending from the spiritual worlds as an imagination of the substance of the Spirit-Self descending from the heights.

Rudolf Steiner also calls this Spirit-Self descending to the Earth a 'spiritual aura' which is borne and nurtured by 'Spirits of the higher Hierarchies': 'It needs the conscious nurturing of that *spiritual aura* which still hovers over us, cherished by the Spirits of the higher Hierarchies, and which will flow into the souls of men when they live in the sixth cultural epoch.'

Turning in the same lecture directly to anthroposophists, Rudolf Steiner refers to the task of anthroposophical groups, which already feel the Spirit-Self 'hovering over them', as that of being forerunners of the great brotherly community of Philadelphia: 'We want to call together human beings who resolve to be brothers and sisters, and above whom there hovers something that they strive to develop by cultivating spiritual science and by feeling the good spirit of brotherliness hovering over them.'

*

Everything that we have said here has also found its reflection in Russian art. There are a number of icons on the theme of the Festival of the 'Intercession', or the 'Protecting Veil', some of which have—quite apart from their high artistic merit—considerable occult significance.

Through the example of one such icon, it can be shown what mysteries of the future evolution of humanity the Russian icon-painters and their inspirers were already able to foresee.[78] This icon of the 'Intercession of the Virgin' from the Novgorod School, was painted at the beginning of the fifteenth century[79] (see Plate 10).

In this icon we see the inner view of a Russian church with imperial gates leading to a centrally positioned altar. In the right-hand group at the bottom is St Andrew, drawing his pupil Epiphanias' attention to the vision of the Mother of God, while the latter stands next to him holding an open copy of the Gospel. All the other images of saints and Angels in the various parts of the icon are also part of Andrew's vision.

Behind this outward aspect of the picture, however, a knowledge of certain occult truths is hidden which comes to expression primarily in the composition and in the number-symbolism of the icon. Thus the group of people in the bottom left corner represent the four Evangelists together with John the Baptist, who is at the front with a scroll of parchment in his hand. Their number—*five*—refers in the first instance to a particular aspect of man's *physical body*. This is his five sense-organs, of which John the Baptist represents sight, and the four Evangelists, respectively, hearing (John), taste (Luke), smell (Mark), and touch (Matthew).

In the second group, at the bottom right, are *four* people. Their number refers to a particular aspect of the *etheric body*, which consists of four kinds of ether: warmth, light, sound and life. Here, the two human beings incarnated on the Earth—St Andrew and Epiphanias—represent the two lower kinds of ether, which were to a certain extent enveloped by the forces of the Fall, while the two saints on the right, who form part of the supersensible vision, represent the two higher kinds of ether, those which remained untouched by earthly forces.[80] On the other hand, the etheric body is the first supersensible member of man's being and can only be perceived clairvoyantly. This is why Andrew and Epiphanias, who beheld the vision of the Mother of God, form part of this group.

In the next group, at the top left, there are *three* holy men in white robes. Their number refers to a fundamental mystery of the *astral body*. They represent man's purified thinking, feeling and will.

Finally, in the fourth group (above right), there are *two* Angels, who are associated with a certain mystery of the human *ego*. Of course, the ego of each man is guided by only one Angelic Being or Guardian Angel. However, what is being referred to here in the imagination of the *two* Angels is another aspect of the ego, its connection with the heights and depths of the world, its principal task of finding the balance between the forces of heaven and Earth. For this reason, the imagination of the human ego in the Apocalypse is a *two-edged* fiery sword that issues from the lips of the Son of Man.[81] Its 'two-edgedness' can in the imaginative world also appear in the form of *two* 'fiery' Angels.

At the centre of the icon we see just *one* Mary-Sophia figure, standing on a cloud, with her divine palla spread over both her and the world and supported on either side by two Archangels, Michael and Gabriel—an imagination of the substance of the Spirit-Self or the new Palladium, the *fifth* member of man's being, gradually descending to the Earth. (In certain older icons, she holds the palla in her own hands, while the Archangels merely support it at either end.

The entire number-symbolism of the icon is directed towards this mystery of the Spirit-Self that is to come; its various individual groups express the following numerical pattern, which is at the same time the path of spiritual ascent to the Spirit-Self:

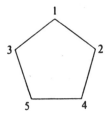

Or: physical body, etheric body, astral body, ego and, in the centre (at the top), Mary-Sophia, the representative of the Spirit-Self at the Turning-Point of Time. The Sun and Moon Archangels above her reveal to mankind the mysteries, and indicate the path to a clairvoyant experience of, respectively: the future (Michael) and the past (Gabriel).[82] Still higher, in the sphere of the *cosmic present*, we see Christ as the Bearer of the world focus of the Life-Spirit, blessing from above the descent to the Earth of the Spirit-Self, the new Palladium.

The icon is completed from above by means of five churches, four small and one large: these again refer to the four lower members of man's being and to the *fifth* (or first) and highest member, which mankind will come to possess in the sixth epoch.*

Thus we see how in the icon that we are considering almost all the principal aspects of the sixth cultural epoch of which we have spoken hitherto indeed find their artistic-occult expression.

All that has been said also has a direct relationship to the creative work and to the individuality of Novalis. For there is probably no-one in the history of the spiritual life of Western and Central Europe who has—in his inner experience—so directly approached the deep mystery of the historical evolution of mankind which finds its expression in the imagination of the palla, or the veil, of the Sophia.

Through his supersensible experience of Christ in the 'Damascus event', Novalis is in a position to become a true forerunner of the sixth cultural epoch, and at the same time a participator in the process of its gradual preparation amongst mankind, or—to say the same thing in more imaginative language—a bearer of the 'veil of the eternal Virgin':

* This fivefold principle lies at the foundation of the outward aspect of the traditional Russian church, where a large cupola, raised in the centre, is as a rule surrounded by four small cupolas.

If I only have Him,
Then the world is mine,
Blessed as a child of Heaven,
Who doth hold the Virgin's veil.
Lost in contemplation,
Never need I fear the Earth's dominion.

In this imagination of the 'virgin's veil', many features of the future condition of humanity come together for Novalis: the faculty of a new conscious clairvoyance, the 'true revelation of the higher world', and above all the possibility of attaining a certain level of *perfection*, both in one's creative work and in one's life: 'All that is perfect speaks not of itself alone—it expresses a whole world of kindred things. Thus around every kind of perfection there hovers the veil of the eternal Virgin— which the gentlest touch dissolves in a magical fragrance that becomes the cloud-chariot of the seer. It is not antiquity alone that we see—it is the sky, the telescope—and the fixed stars all at once—and, in addition, a true revelation of a higher world.'

Do not particularly the words about 'the cloud-chariot of the seer' represent Novalis' dim memory of 'the fiery chariot of Elijah' (2 Kings 2:11), the great seer of the pre-Christian epoch? And do we not in the imagination of 'Elijah's mantle' have an indication of the age-old connection of his whole being and his spiritual mission with the 'veil of the eternal Virgin'? For from an occult point of view this 'mantle of Elijah' is none other than a microcosmic reflection of what otherwise works in the world macrocosmically as the forces of the Divine Sophia.

Rudolf Steiner calls Elijah one who is filled with the Holy Spirit,[83] with that same Holy Spirit who, as we have seen, brought about the forming of Manas within the soul of the Luke Mary. This openness to the Manas-forming activity of the Holy Spirit is brought to expression in the imagination of the 'mantle of Elijah',[84] this being an allusion to his higher being, which was at that time as yet unable fully to descend from the spiritual worlds into his body and, hence, enveloped him only very loosely from without like a special, spiritual aura.[85]

Novalis, too, has a feeling for this higher spiritual aura, the aura of the Spirit-Self, experiencing it as a 'spiritual atmosphere', a 'touching of the earthly spirit . . . by a heavenly, extraterrestrial Spirit', or as a 'living, moral space' around himself: 'Christianity will thereby be raised to the rank of the foundation, the projective power, of a new world-building and [a new] humanity—a true emblem of chastity—a living moral space.'

'A new world-building and [a new] humanity'—do not these words

255

remind one of the principal goal of all true Rosicrucians throughout the centuries: of building the great spiritual temple of humanity?[86] 'The veil is for the Virgin what the Spirit is for the body', writes Novalis in 'Christendom or Europe'. From the standpoint of anthroposophical terminology we could say: '. . . what the *Spirit-Self* is for the body.' And then he continues: '. . . her most essential organ whose folds are the letters of her sweet proclamation; the endless play of folds is a musical code, for language is too wooden and too brash: her lips open only in order to sing.'

The highest spiritual organ of the Virgin-Sophia is her aura, her mantle, whose folds form the individual letters of the higher proclamation, that 'occult script' which all men will be able to read in the sixth epoch. This higher proclamation is heard by Novalis already in our time 'as the solemn call to a new majestic gathering' to the forming of the great brotherly community of love of Philadelphia: 'To me, it [the veil of the Virgin] is none other than the solemn call to a new majestic gathering, the mighty wing of a passing Angelic herald. These are the first labour pains; all should make ready for the birth!'

The most important spiritual fruit of the historical evolution of Western and Central Europe is the possibility of a truly Christian experience of *freedom*, as described by Rudolf Steiner in his *Philosophy of Freedom*. Towards it—from Eastern Europe—shines the imagination of the Festival of the 'Intercession', which is a premonition of the future *community* of Philadelphia that will come to embrace the whole of humanity.

Both of these elements come together in the personality and creative work of Novalis as a prophetic vision of the entry of humanity into the new age of light, the future realm of light: 'Transcending *freedom* and *community* in the realm of light—that is dynamic indeed.'

Appendix IV

Christ's Appearance before the People by Alexander Ivanov

One of the most important paintings in nineteenth-century Russian art is *Christ's Appearance before the People* by Alexander Ivanov (1806–58).* The very fact that the artist worked on it for 20 years,[87] with the result that this work became for him a long-sustained meditation—brush in hand— on the most important problems of Christianity, is itself worthy of particular attention.

Alexander Ivanov, who spent almost half his life on a stipend from the Russian Academy of Arts in Italy (where he also painted this picture), turned again and again throughout this time to the question of the significance and destiny of Russia, as a Christian country, for the future evolution of mankind. Such thoughts as he had regarding the higher calling of Russia and its spiritual mission, thoughts which in course of time took on the character of a real mystical premonition, he endeavoured to incorporate in his picture.

There were two sources whence emanated influences which were decisive for the artist's creative development and personality: a book by the early German romantic W.C. Wackenroder entitled *Herzenergiessungen eines kunstliebenden Klosterbruders*,[88] which fell into his hands while he was still a young man, and the works of Raphael.

The first source served as a gate whereby Ivanov was able to attain to a new understanding of the role of art in the spiritual evolution of mankind. What had lived in his soul—until his acquaintance with the book of the German romantic—as no more than a dim presentiment of the supersensible origins of art and of the high calling of the creative artist as one who fulfils and furthers the divine will which has made all things visible, now entered his consciousness with full force and became the foundation for all his subsequent artistic and moral endeavours.

The other, no less important source, which nourished his creative work throughout his life, was that of the paintings of Raphael. On his way to Italy in 1830, Ivanov specially makes a stop in Dresden in order

* At the present time the painting hangs in the Tretyakovsky Gallery in Moscow. See Plate 7.

to see Raphael's *Sistine Madonna* with his own eyes. The painstaking pencil copy of the faces of the two central figures which he made directly from the original testifies to the considerable impression that this picture made upon him. In a letter to his father of 13 September 1830 he wrote: 'Here for the first time I have been deeply moved by the effect of painting, the effect of the refined brush of Raphael. I sought by looking attentively to find even one imperfection in the head of this beautiful form, and the more I exerted all my forces to discern traces of the human hand the stronger this effect became. In my despair at retaining what I had seen in my memory, I made every effort to make a sketch of this perfection, and then I realised that I would have to copy from Raphael; however, my drawing is no more than a monument to my weakness when compared with this great work.'

Thus what Wackenroder stated in a more theoreteical way in his book was for Ivanov here fully embodied in life. Also during the subsequent longer period of his residence in Italy, the work of Raphael remained for the artist a high, unattainable ideal, an indisputable testimony of the divine forces working within art. To this devotion to the work of Raphael the artist remained faithful throughout his life.

It was out of such a higher understanding of the role of art in the spiritual evolution of mankind that Ivanov chose as the theme of the principal work of his life 'The Appearance of Christ before the People', a subject which represents an illustration of the following words from the beginning of St John's Gospel: 'The next day John saw Jesus coming towards him, and said: "Behold the Lamb of God, who takes upon Himself the sins of the world! This is he of whom I said: 'After me comes a Man who ranks before me, for He was before me.' I myself did not know Him; but for this I came baptising with water, *that He might* be revealed to Israel."' (1:29–31)

Regarding the subject of the picture, which in his notebooks he described as 'universal', Ivanov wrote the following in one of his letters from Italy in November 1834: 'If it had pleased God at this moment to take away this life of mine, I would thank Him for giving me the glory of finding the prime subject in the world!'

The unusual significance which the artist attached not only to his future picture but simply to its overall conception is connected with the fact that its motif of the appearance of this highest of divine Beings before mankind, His recognition by His chosen prophet and His reception by all the people, was for the artist at the same time an unconscious premonition of the spiritual future of Eastern Europe, of its future receiving of the 'Christian Spirit-Self'.[89] This latter event will take place historically only in the sixth cultural epoch, which will begin approximately in the middle of the fourth post-Christian millennium. Only then will the Slavic peoples finally become sufficiently mature to make their contribution to the further evolution of humanity as a whole. Until this time, that is during the next one and a half thousand years or so, Slavic culture must remain a *culture of expectation*, expectation for the appearance in its midst of the higher spiritual principle of man's being.

Ivanov tried to incorporate in his picture this fundamental soul-mood of Eastern Europe of hope and expectation with regard to the future descent of the real substance of the spirit, and also of a wish and a readiness to receive it as a deed of sacrificial service on behalf of earthly evolution. Because of this his painting, despite his twenty years of working on it, remained unfinished. For what it was really intended to say to the world through the artistic fabric of its Biblical images could, in the last century of the dark age of the Kali-Yuga, not be expressed through the medium of earthly art. As far as the artist himself was concerned, his many years of work on the picture were at the same time an intense inner search for that future time which we today, on the ground of spiritual science, call the sixth or Slavic epoch.[90]

The central figure in the picture of *The Appearance of Christ before the People* is that of John the Baptist. As he is at once the last prophet of the Old and the first representative of the New Testament, he is both in a spiritual and in a compositional sense portrayed in the picture as standing at the boundary between two worlds, of the past and the future, while through the gesture of his hands and the expression of his face he would *proclaim*, and *awaken* mankind to receive, a new spiritual impulse.[91]

'Repent, for the Kingdom of Heaven is at hand!' (Matthew 3:2) The whole way that the figure of John has been conceived and executed by the artist in his picture can be seen as an artistic embodiment of this call of John the Baptist at the Turning-Point of Time. At this moment, John is truly the *representative of the conscience of humanity*. And as such he feels himself called to awaken this same call within other people, in order that they too might, through conscience as a new organ of knowledge, recognise and receive into their hearts the cosmic Being of the Christ descending to the Earth.[92]

In his picture, the artist has sought to show all the stages and all the nuances of this gradual *inner awakening* wrought amongst the multitude by the mighty call of John the Baptist. Particularly when one observes those people who can be seen in the area from the right-hand edge to the middle of the picture, this becomes clearly evident.

'One of them is looking at Jesus with wild curiosity; another is smiling disbelievingly at John's words, a third watches the whole proceedings with a hardened heart, while a fourth is ready to believe', Ivanov wrote in one of his letters to his father. Later the famous Russian writer and friend of the artist, Nikolai Gogol, referred, in an article on this work, to the fact that Ivanov shows in his picture 'the whole . . . course of man's turning towards Christ.'

Already in the compositional structure of the picture, the artist has tried with every means available to him to show this gradual awakening of human beings to an ever more conscious perception of the Christ-impulse through the impulse of conscience that John has stirred within them. Two human streams, associated respectively with the past and the future, with the pre-Christian and the Christian epochs of human evolution, clearly divide the whole area of the picture into two parts.

On the right are the representatives of the world that is passing away: the Roman soldiers looking in a sceptical, mocking way towards the approaching Jesus and the scribes and Pharisees who, in their repudiation of the Messiah, are turning away. Neither the one nor the other *want* to listen to the *conscience*-awakening voice of John. They want to live their lives as before according to the letter of the law: the Romans according to the *ius civile* and the scribes and Pharisees according to the Torah of Moses.

On the left-hand side of the picture, as a contrast to this group on the right, are the future disciples and followers of Christ Jesus standing behind John: John son of Zebedee,[93] behind him Peter (?), then Andrew and on the far left Nathaniel. They are the representatives of future evolution who, through the impulse of conscience that has been awakened in them by John, are ready immediately to receive the approaching Christ so as to become His disciples.

But this is not all that is to be said about the composition of the picture. For if we look more closely we see that the people who are standing on the right are bunched together as one dense mass of humanity. The separate individuals are barely distinguishable. These people still belong to that period of human evolution when the words 'I and father Abraham are one' ruled all circumstances of life.

In the group of John's disciples, on the other hand, each is shown at full length, as the bearer of a sovereign, self-contained ego-individuality. This is in harmony with what Rudolf Steiner says about conscience being able to work only within those who have a strong feeling for the individual ego.[94]

Past and future, group and individual principles, dense and free groupings of figures—these are characterisations of the two principal human streams, of which one (on the right) slowly descends the hill, while the other is already preparing for a new ascent. Is not this artistic contrast of the two streams a picture of the whole of human evolution, embracing as it does the path from the spiritual heights down to the realm of matter, of unfreedom and law, and the possibility, called forth by the entry of the Christ-impulse into earthly evolution, of a new ascent into the higher worlds founded upon the forces of the free ego-individuality, an ascent which the disciples of John the Baptist were, through their readiness to become disciples of Christ Jesus, called to begin?

Both streams—the descending and ascending—are, in the picture, united into a single whole by the central figure of John. We see how, under the influence of his words and also of the gesture of his hands which point forcefully towards the approaching Jesus, the people—crowded together on the right—gradually begin to awaken; their faces become lighter and more conscious, while nearer to the centre of the picture the crowd enters into movement—some are standing up and looking round, turning in the direction indicated by John's hand, namely towards Jesus. Others, still sitting on the ground, seem to be listening to the mysterious new voice that is beginning to speak within them and which reveals to them the cosmic mystery of the human figure approaching from afar.[95]

This strong movement, which arises in the middle of the picture and which is (so to speak) framed on both sides by two more static groups, enables one to divide the whole composition as regards its meaning into *three* interrelated parts. This leads one to see a further, highly important aspect of the inner content of the painting, namely, that it is in a certain sense a picture of *the whole of humanity* as a single spiritual–physical organism.

In the group on the right are the heirs of the ancient cultures of the East, the last bearers of the primordial *wisdom* of earthly evolution, those who, even in our time, have still not really received the Christ-impulse into their spiritual and religious life.[96] In the group on the left we find the youthful peoples of Europe. They do not have a fund of inherited wisdom, but instead bear within themselves a powerful, future-orientated *will*, into which they want to receive the Christ-impulse.[97] These are the two principle poles of man's being: the wisdom of the head, and the aspirations of the will which work in the limbs.

In the central part of the picture, where everything is *in movement*— thus compositionally uniting the right and left parts into a single whole— there is a kind of reflection of man's rhythmical system, the focus of which is the figure of John the Baptist, who is the true *heart* of the whole composition, the representative of that future organ in man's being for perceiving the Christ, the organ with whose etheric forces He united after He had passed through the Mystery of Golgotha.[98]

261

This entry of the Christ-impulse into man's middle, 'rhythmic' system, the gate of which is the heart, is depicted with a remarkable artistic mastery in the painting's general composition.

In the human organism, the rhythmic system is primarily the physical expression of the working of the forces of the etheric body. Its focus— the physical heart—is merely a projection on the physical plane of the *etheric heart*, man's most important spiritual organ.

On the other hand, the etheric body is also the bearer of the impulse of conscience in man's being.[99] Thus, for example, in the Russian language one often says not 'do as your conscience tells you' but 'do as your *heart* tells you'. Hence for the genius of the Russian language the words 'conscience' and 'heart' (of course not in its physical aspect, but as an etheric organ of perception) are to a certain degree synonymous. This points towards an important mystery of earthly evolution, which also comes to expression in the position of the figure of John the Baptist in the picture. For although he is in an artistic sense clearly its focus—and in a spiritual sense its heart—John the Baptist is, as regards the composition, somewhat to the left of the transverse axis of the picture, a fact which emphasises his future connection with that historical stream of humanity, of which we said that it develops conscience out of the forces of the individual ego from amongst the youthful European peoples.

Moreover, it is John who is their representative and forerunner at the Turning-Point of Time, for his recognising and receiving of Christ on the Earth can be seen as a prophetic anticipation of the European people's subsequent receiving of Christianity out of the forces of conscience.[100]

Thus we can say: probably nowhere in the world of art is the chief characteristic of John the Baptist, that of being the bearer of the impulse of conscience, an impulse which he aroused within mankind as an organ of cognition for the Christ Being, brought to expression with such artistic conviction and inner strength as in the painting of Ivanov that we are considering. And it is not by chance that so exact and intuitive a perception and so thoroughly artistic an embodiment of this central task of John the Baptist at the Turning-Point of Time appears in the work of a *Russian artist*—for the forces of conscience belong to the Russian people to a far greater extent than those of knowledge or will-activity. 'Conscientiousness'—this magic word has a completely different significance for Slavic man than for the people of Central or Western Europe.

And if Rudolf Steiner speaks of how, from our time onwards and throughout the course of the next three thousand years (that is, until approximately the middle of the sixth epoch), the forces of conscience amongst mankind will gradually be transformed into a new higher faculty of etheric clairvoyance, into the faculty of perceiving the Etheric

Christ in the spiritual world in full consciousness,[101] is it not the most important task of the Russian people, the 'Christ-people',[102] to become, *in the next few centuries*, the forerunners of the whole of mankind on this path, just as John the Baptist was once the forerunner and preparer of the physical appearance of Christ on Earth?

The two principal impulses of earthly evolution, which have been moving towards one another throughout the entire history of humanity, emerge from two opposite poles: the Christ-impulse from the East and the impulse of conscience from the West: 'We see the Sun of the Christ-nature rise in the East; and we see how the Christ-eye within the human conscience is being prepared in the West in order that it may understand the Christ.'[103]

These two impulses meet historically at the Turning-Point of Time, on the bank of the River Jordan, in Jesus of Nazareth, who received the Christ-impulse into himself, and John the Baptist, who as the first amongst the whole of mankind to *recognise* Christ on the Earth embodied the impulse of conscience with his entire personality.

We live today in an epoch when to a certain extent—although in a completely different form—the spiritual constellation of the Turning-Point of Time is being repeated. Again, from two opposite sides, two new impulses are coming towards one another which are to meet at a definite point of earthly evolution, now no longer at a certain geographical region of the Earth but within human consciousness, man's soul: the impulse of the Etheric Christ; and the faculty of perceiving it with the help of a human conscience that has passed through a higher metamorphosis and has again become clairvoyant. The only difference is that now both these impulses pass through humanity not in the same but in the opposite direction when compared with their way of working at the Turning-Point of Time.

Rudolf Steiner describes this highly important spiritual event of the nineteenth century which preceded the new resurrection of Christ in the etheric environment of humanity in the twentieth century as a kind of supersensible repetition of the Mystery of Golgotha, one that is associated with a second Crucifixion of Christ, but which is on this occasion not in the physical world but in the spiritual world nearest to the Earth. In his words, this deeply tragic event was called forth by those 'seeds of earthly materialism' which souls of materialistically inclined human beings, after their death, brought into the spiritual world in the period between the sixteenth and the nineteenth centuries: 'The seeds of earthly materialism, which since the sixteenth century have been introduced into the spiritual world in ever greater measure by the souls that have passed through the gate of death and have brought about an ever-intensifying darkness, formed the "black sphere of materialism". This black sphere was received by Christ into His Being—in the sense of the Manichaean principle—in order that He might transform it. The result was that it brought about a "spiritual asphyxiation" in the Angelic Being through whom the Christ Being has revealed Himself since the Mystery of Golgotha. This sacrifice of Christ in the nineteenth century is comparable to the sacrifice on the physical plane in the Mystery of Golgotha, and can be regarded as the second Crucifixion of Christ on the etheric plane. This spiritual asphyxiation, which led to the extinction of the consciousness of that Angelic Being, is a repetion of the Mystery of Golgotha in the worlds which lie immediately behind our own, so that a resurrection of the Christ-consciousness, which had formerly remained hidden, can take place in the souls of men on Earth. This resurrection becomes the clairvoyant faculty of mankind in the twentieth century.

'Thus the Christ-consciousness can be united with the earthly consciousness of humanity from the twentieth century onwards; for the dying of the Christ-consciousness in the sphere of the Angels in the nineteenth century signifies the resurrection of the direct consciousness of Christ in the earthly sphere—that is to say, Christ's life will, from the twentieth century onwards, increasingly be felt in the souls of men as a direct personal experience.'[104]

Throughout the historical period referred to here, which was the time of the fullest extent of the diffusion of materialism amongst Western humanity, Eastern Europe was to a significant degree kept away from the centre of these developments.[105] Thus the human souls which through their materialism brought about this 'spiritual asphyxiation' of the Christ-consciousness in the spiritual sphere nearest to the Earth were, to an overwhelming extent, the souls of those who had incarnated in the course of the period between the sixteenth and the nineteenth centuries in the *Western* world (in Western and Central Europe)—the historical area where materialism arose and was then developed further.

This fact leads us directly to a conclusion of the greatest importance which has considerable significance for the subsequent spiritual evolution of mankind. This conclusion is as follows: just as at the Turning-Point of Time the Crucifixion and Resurrection of Christ Jesus took place *in the East,* so did the second Crucifixion and resurrection of Christ in the supersensible worlds which came about during the nineteenth and twentieth centuries take place—in a spiritual sense—'*in the West'*.[106] Just as at the Turning-Point of Time the impulse of conscience came *from the West* like a 'world-eye' that was able to behold Christ as He entered historically into earthly evolution, so now towards the Etheric Christ, though moving in a reverse direction, the *transformed faculty of conscience,* the new organ of clairvoyant perception (though now no longer of the physical, but of the Etheric Christ), will in the course of the coming centuries appear *from the East*.[107] And this will also be associated with the principal task of the Slavic peoples of Europe, with their spiritual contribution to the further, onward flow of human evolution.[108]

If, in conclusion, we turn again to the painting of Alexander Ivanov and consider it once more from the standpoint outlined above, we can say that Alexander Ivanov, taking his departure from the historical event of the Appearance of God before humanity at the Turning-Point of Time (Epiphany), developed, in the course of the twenty years while he was working on the picture, a clear premonition of what was to take place amongst mankind, namely, the spiritual repetition of this historical Event, though this time not as a physical, but as a *supersensible appearance of God*, as an etheric appearance of Christ to all the peoples of the Earth.

Notes

Except where indicated, all works referred to are by Rudolf Steiner. The *Gesamtausgabe** (GA) volume number is only listed where a published translation is not available. The full list of relevant German title GAs will be found on p. 376.

RSP   = Rudolf Steiner Press, England
AP   = Anthroposophic Press, New York
RSPC = Rudolf Steiner Publishing Co., London
APC = Anthroposophical Publishing Co., London

Unless otherwise indicated, notes are by the author.

1. See 'W.J. Stein (Rudolf Steiner: *Documentation* . . .', Dornach 1985), the so-called 'Hague conversation' of 1922.
2. See the lectures of 31 March 1924 (*Karmic Relationships*, vol. v, RSP 1984) and 16 April 1924 (*Karmic Relationships*, vol. vi, RSP 1989).
3. See the lectures of 6 February 1917 (*Cosmic and Human Metamorphosis*, Spiritual Research Editions, Blauvelt, NY 1989) and 2 December 1911 (*Faith, Love, Hope*, Steiner Book Centre, N. Vancouver, n.d.).
4. See *The Principle of Spiritual Economy*, AP 1986, also GA 109.
5. No notes from this lecture have been preserved.
6. The examples referred to are those of Aristotle and Alexander and of Hypatia (see *Occult History*, APC 1957). It should be added that the karmic connection between Elijah and John the Baptist has an especially great significance for humanity as a whole, in that it is the only example in the Gospels of Christ Himself speaking of the reincarnation of a human individuality (see note 49).
7. Lecture of 19 September 1909 (*The Gospel of St Luke*, RSP 1964).
8. Ibid., lecture of 18 September.
9. Ibid., lecture of 19 September.
10. Ibid., lecture of 18 September.
11. We may conclude from various statements of Rudolf Steiner that the original location of the 'Mother Lodge of the rulership of harmony' is to be sought in the sphere of the Sun. See in this connection the indications regarding the cosmic dwelling-place of the Nathan Soul in the lectures of

---

* The full catalogued works of Rudolf Steiner in the original German. Published by the *Rudolf Steiner Nachlassverwaltung*, Dornach, Switzerland.

30 December 1913 (*Christ and the Spiritual World and the Search for the Holy Grail*, RSP 1963) and 18 September 1909.

12. Lecture of 18 September 1909.

13. See the lectures of 28 September 1924 (*The Last Address*, RSP 1967) and 28 January 1924 (*Karmic Relationships*, vol. VI, RSP 1989).

14. The chief task of the Hebrew people—that of preparing the earthly sheaths for the incarnation on Earth of the Christ Being—was entrusted to their forefather Abraham in the imaginative picture of the bread and wine by Melchisedek, the 'priest of the most high God' (Genesis 14:18–20). According to indications of Rudolf Steiner, in the figure of Melchizedek we have to do with the last earthly incarnation of Manu, who for this incarnation made use of the etheric body of Shem (see the lecture of 4 September 1910, *The Gospel of St Matthew*, RSP/AP 1965, and *The Principle of Spiritual Economy*, AP 1986. The Apostle Paul refers to this mystery which lies hidden behind the figure of Melchizedek, the earthly incarnation of the greatest Sun Initiate of Atlantis and the ruler of its central 'Christ Oracle' (see *Occult Science—An Outline*, RSP 1984) in the following words, calling him 'king of righteousness' and 'king of peace': 'He is without father or mother or genealogy, and neither beginning of days nor end of life, but resembling the Son of God he continues a priest for ever. See how great he is! Abraham the patriarch gave him a tithe of the spoils' (Hebrews 7:2–4).

15. Lecture of 2 September 1910 (*The Gospel of St Matthew*, op. cit.).

16. Lecture of 24 June 1909 (*The Gospel of St John in Relation to the Other Three Gospels*, AP New York 1982).

17. Numbers 25:10–12 and the lecture of 22 September 1912 (*The Gospel of St Mark*, AP 1986).

18. See the lecture of 20 September 1909 (*The Gospel of St Luke*, RSP 1964, and that of 14 December 1911 (*Turning-Points in Spiritual History*, Spiritual Science Library, Blauvelt, New York, 1987). Rudolf Steiner speaks about this special task of Elijah with regard to the revelation of Jahve in, for example, these words: '. . . throughout all human evolution it is precisely those forces, which are of greatest power and intensity, that operate in obscure and secret fashion. From what has been said it is clear that through the influence of the prophet Elijah, man was raised to a higher spiritual level and became more and more imbued with Jahve's thoughts and concepts. We also realise that the life and deeds of that great patriarch, when viewed in the proper manner, must be regarded as forming an epoch of supreme importance to humanity' (lecture of 14 December 1911). Rudolf Steiner returns to this theme several times in this particular lecture.

19. Lecture of 14 December 1911.

20. 1 Kings 17. See also the lecture of 14 December 1911 and that of 17 September 1912 (*The Gospel of St Mark*), op. cit.

21. The reason why Moses was unable to enter the 'Promised Land' and could only lead the Hebrew people to its boundary was that the experience of

the 'I am' was for him no more than the outward revelation of Jahve in the fire of Sinai. Hence the inner experience of the 'I am' remained hidden from him, for he was not able to come to a knowledge of the Christ Being who was working *through* Jahve and was approaching the Earth (see Numbers 20:12 and the lecture of 12 July 1914, *Christ and the Human Soul*, RSP 1984). On the other hand, it was just this knowledge which, as an irrefutable inner reality, was the foundation of the entire soul life of the prophet Elijah. Rudolf Steiner refers to this as follows: 'In his soul is the knowledge: "As a prophet of Jahve I must above all things proclaim *that in Jahve there lives the Christ* who later on fulfils the Mystery of Golgotha . . ."' Elijah proclaimed the Christ-filled Jahve' (lecture of 31 December 1913, *Christ and the Spiritual World. The Search for the Holy Grail*, RSP 1963). (See also note 72). We may understand this still more clearly if we recall that the supersensible experiences of Moses had their source in the etheric body of Zarathustra, which he bore in his inner organisation, while Elijah worked more out of the forces of *his own ego*, which had the capacity of being directly open to inspirations from higher sources.

22. Lecture of 14 December 1911, op. cit.
23. Rudolf Steiner speaks about the relationship of the Bodhisattvas to the Moon Teachers of Wisdom in the lecture of 28 August 1923 (*The Evolution of Consciousness*, RSP 1991): 'But these Beings [the Moon Teachers of Wisdom] have had *successors* of the Beings now entrenched on the Moon.' This should be compared with the corresponding words quoted on p. 160 regarding the relationship of Elijah to the Moon Teachers of Wisdom. In each case the descriptions correspond even to the extent of the expressions that are employed. Thus Rudolf Steiner says of the Bodhisattvas: 'And the life of the Bodhisattvas is passed *in community* with these Beings who live in the cosmic fastness of the Moon'; while in the 'Last Address' we read: '. . . how he [Elijah] comes into association here with the Spirits who live in the Moon-sphere. . .' Then in the former lecture: 'There [in the sphere of the Moon Teachers] lie the springs of their strength, the sources of their thoughts,' that is, it was from there that their thoughts were *inspired*. And in the 'Last Address': '. . . [these] are the spiritual individualities of the great original leaders of mankind, by whose wisdom Raphael, as Elijah, had been deeply inspired.'

Particularly if we compare the descriptions of Bodhisattva-hood and the being of Elijah, as given in the lecture cycle on the Gospel of St Luke, we may speak of the 'Bodhisattva-like' nature of the latter. In both cases the theme under consideration is 'incomplete incarnation' and 'being overshone by the Holy Spirit'. Thus in the lecture of 20 September 1909 we find the following characterisation of Elijah: 'What we described as being necessary in the ancient Indian epoch, also as the special nature of the Bodhisattva, *had to be repeated again and again in the Hebrew people too*: there had to be individualities who were not wholly contained in the human personality; one part of their being was in the earthly personality and the other in the spiritual world. Elijah was an individuality of this nature. Only part of his being was present in his personality on the physical plane; the egohood of Elijah could not penetrate fully into his physical body. He must therefore be called a personality "filled with the spirit".' And earlier in the same lecture Rudolf Steiner speaks about the incarnation of a Bodhisattva: 'part of his being [the being of a Bodhisattva] was obliged to remain in the spiritual world; he could send only part of himself into the physical body . . . The fact that some men lived with part of their being in the spiritual world was known to all religions and conceptions of the world. It was known that there were Beings destined to work on the Earth for whom human embodiment was too restricted to contain the whole individuality. In the religious thought of Western Asia this kind of union of a higher individuality with a physical body was called "being filled with the Holy Spirit". This is a quite definite, technical expression. In the language of those regions it would have been said of a Being, such as a Bodhisattva while incarnated on Earth, that he was "filled with the Holy Spirit"—meaning that the forces and powers possessed by such a Being were not fully contained within his human organism and that something spiritual must work from outside. Thus it might with truth be said that the Buddha, in his previous incarnations [as a Bodhisattva], was "filled with the Holy Spirit".' This comparison can, however, be sensed more concretely if we contrast it with the following words of Rudolf Steiner from the same cycle: 'All the *prophets* and forerunners, however exalted, even when they descended [to Earth] as *Bodhisattvas*, were obliged to use faculties transmitted by way of the seed [the physical body]' (lecture of 26 September 1909). And there is, finally, a further fact which indicates the connection between Elijah and the Bodhisattva principle, namely, that this individuality will be amongst those who in the far future will be the inspirers of the Maitreya Buddha: 'Thus does he prepare for a great event. This will be as follows: The old ego passes out and another ego then enters. And this may be such an individuality as Moses, Abraham, *Elijah*. This ego will then be active for a certain time in this body; thus can that take place which must take place in order to prepare the Maitreya Buddha. For the rest of his life he lives with this [new] ego which enters at that moment' (lecture of 5 November 1911, *Esoteric Christianity and the Mission of Christian Rosenkreutz*, RSP 1984).

Despite this, however, the Elijah individuality is only a 'Bodhisattva-*like*' being. For there is a fundamental difference between him and a Bodhisattva, the goal of whose development is the attainment of *Buddha-hood*—after which he no longer returns to Earth in a human incarnation.

In the case of a Bodhisattva one is therefore speaking of an *individuality* for whom the individual incarnations in which he appears on Earth as one or another historical *personality* do not have any special importance. By contrast, in the succession of incarnations of Elijah–John–Raphael–Nova-lis it is not only the *single* individuality standing behind them who is of significance, but rather it is all those concrete *personalities* in whom he is incarnated. For this individuality's goal is, in contrast to that of a Bodhisattva, not liberation from Earth existence and the cycle of incarnations but rather *to unite ever more with the evolution of the Earth* for the sake of its future spiritualisation. This high significance which is impressed upon the individual personality in the course of human evolution is the most important fruit of the working within it of the Christ-impulse.

For this reason Rudolf Steiner, in a whole series of lectures (2 May 1912, *Earthly and Cosmic Man*, Garber Publications, Blauvelt, NY 1985 and 8 May 1912, *Anthroposophical Quarterly*, 18:1, GA 143), represents, as a definite *polarity* in earthly evolution, the Eastern tradition of the Bodhisattvas and the Western teaching of reincarnation in its Christian form; and he explains this by means of the example given, in that it presents with full clarity the significance not merely of the individuality himself, but of all those concrete personalities through whom he has worked on the Earth.

24. Lecture of 17 September 1912 (*The Gospel of St Mark*, op. cit.).
25. Ibid.
26. Genesis 2:7 and the lecture of 1 April 1907 (*Festivals of the Seasons*, APC, London 1928).
27. Michael's direct participation in the 'creation of man' may be deduced primarily from the fact that before the Mystery of Golgotha he worked in the cosmos as the *Countenance of Jahve*, as the mediator between him and evolving humanity (see the lecture of 22 November 1919, *The Mission of the Archangel Michael*, AP 1980). Moreover, Rudolf Steiner refers to the quite particular nature of Michael's participation in the 'creation of man' in a lecture of 1 November 1904 (unpublished) and in the article of 1924, 'The World Thoughts in the Working of Michael and in the Working of Ahriman' (*Anthroposophical Leading Thoughts*, RSP 1973). Numerous legends and folk-traditions also testify to this. See *Die Sagen der Juden*, Frankfurt am Main 1962, and *Aus Michaels Wirken*, collected by Nora Stein-von Baditz, Stuttgart 1967.
28. See the lecture of 22 November 1919, above.
29. Regarding the initiation of Elijah, see the lecture of 14 December 1911 (*Turning Points in Spiritual History*, op. cit.).
30. Lecture of 20 September 1909 (*The Gospel of St Luke*, op. cit.).
31. From the aspect of the fourfold structure of man we may imagine the working of these two Hierarchic Spirits in the beings of Elijah in the following way: The ego of Elijah has, because of his only partial incarnation in the physical body of Naboth (see note 23), so unegoistic a nature that his astral and etheric bodies remain, in the course of this particular incarnation, to a significant degree 'transparent' for the higher Beings who would work through them, which is why they are able to serve as 'tools' for the inspiring influences of the Moon Elohim, Jahve, and the Sun Archangel, Michael. In this respect, Jahve works only through the

spirit of Elijah, while Michael works through his spirit *and* soul; and, finally, his own ego extends its influence to the physical body.— Regarding the original connection of the individuality of Elijah, as the reincarnated *Adam*, with these two Hierarchic Beings, see note 27.

32. According to the spiritual–scientific research of Rudolf Steiner, the Nirmanakaya of Buddha worked within the astral body of Jesus of Nazareth before his twelfth year, and Zarathustra's ego between the twelfth and thirtieth years. See further in *The Gospel of St Luke*, op. cit., and *The Fifth Gospel*, RSP 1968).

33. See *The Principle of Spiritual Economy*, op. cit., and *The Gospel of St Matthew*, op. cit.

34. Lecture of 20 September 1909 (*The Gospel of St Luke*, op. cit.). For this reason Elijah appears beside Moses in the scene of the Transfiguration.

35. Lecture of 20 September 1909.

36. Ibid. Somewhat earlier in the same lecture Rudolf Steiner speaks of this as follows: 'The Nirmanakaya of Buddha worked as an inspiration into the ego of John the Baptist . . . And the preaching of John the Baptist was to begin with the re-awakened preaching of Buddha.' To this it should be added that the union (that has been referred to) of the various spiritual streams in the individuality of John the Baptist, as preparation for their eventual merging in Christ Jesus, was preceded even earlier—albeit in a more outward way—by the first stage of their union in the person of Moses, when he was initiated first into the Egyptian Mysteries and then, as a result of his meeting with Jethro, the priest of Midian, into the Mysteries of other peoples (Exodus 2:16–21). See also the lecture of 22 September 1912 (*The Gospel of St Mark*, op. cit.).

37. Mark 1:2–3. Regarding the particular Angelic Being who worked through John the Baptist, see also the lectures of 25 February 1911, GA 127 (*The Work of the Ego in Childhood—A Contribution towards an Understanding of Christ*, AQ 21:4) and 6 December 1910 (*Background to the Gospel of St Mark*, RSP/AP 1968).

38. Lecture of 20 September 1909 (*The Gospel of St Luke*, op. cit.).

39. Lecture of 25 February 1911, as above.

40. Rudolf Steiner speaks as follows regarding the working of the Nirmana-kaya of Buddha upon John the Baptist: 'Thus it was the Nirmanakaya of Buddha which now stirred the ego-force of John into activity, having the same effect as the spiritual forces that had formerly worked upon Elijah' (lecture of 20 September 1909).

41. Lecture of 16 September 1909 (*The Gospel of St Luke*, op. cit.). In the same lecture Rudolf Steiner confirms the testimony of the Gospel that in the scene where the news is given to the shepherds in the field the appearance of the *Angel* preceded that of the Nirmanakaya of Buddha.

42. Mark 1:3.

43. Lecture of 6 December 1910 (*Background to the Gospel of St Mark*, RSP/AP 1968).

44. Ibid.
45. *Michaelmas* (APC 1957); *The Festivals and their Meaning* (RSP 1981). Lecture of 18 May 1913.
46. Ibid, lecture of 20 May 1913.
47. In the lecture of 18 May 1913 Rudolf Steiner speaks of him as follows: 'Now not all the Beings who belong to the Hierarchy of the Archangels are of the same nature or of the same rank . . . But the highest in rank, as it were the *chief*, is the one who takes over the leadership in our age— Michael. Michael is one of the order of Archangels, but he is from a certain aspect the *most advanced*. Now there is, as you know, evolution; and evolution embraces all Beings. All beings are in an ascending evolution, and we live in the era when Michael, the chief of those of the nature of the Archangels, passes over into the nature of the Archai.'
48. In the present work it is only possible to touch briefly upon the profound mysteries of the spiritual life that are associated with the activity of this particular Angelic Being. The reader may find a more detailed examination of his development from the earliest stages of human evolution until his participation in our time in the new appearance of Christ in an etheric body in another of the author's books, *The Cycle of the Year as a Path of Initiation leading to an Experience of the Christ Being*, Temple Lodge 1991, part XII, the chapter entitled 'The Vidar Mystery'.
49. It is this 'shift' in the Hierarchic Beings who inspire John which renders him incapable of recalling his previous incarnation as Elijah. And this is indicated with remarkable precision in the Gospels. Thus in the Gospel of St John we read: 'And they asked him, "What then? Are you Elijah?" He said, "I am not"' (1:21). Christ does not merely know this secret of the reincarnations of Elijah, but also tries to draw it to the attention of His disciples. Thus in the Gospel of St Matthew he says to them directly: 'And if you are willing to accept it, he [John] is Elijah who is to come. He who has ears to hear, let him hear' (11:14–15).
50. *The Mission of the Individual Folk Souls in Relation to Teutonic Mythology* (RSP 1970), evening lecture of 12 June 1910.
51. Ibid.
52. See the lecture of 24 December 1918 (*How Can Mankind Find the Christ Again?*, AP, 1947).
53. As note 50.
54. Ibid.
55. John 1:6–8 and 33, also 3:28. Regarding John the Baptist as the 'forerunner' see especially the lecture of 19 September 1912 (*The Gospel of St Mark*, op. cit.).
56. Mark 1:2. This emissaryship of the Angel who worked through John the Baptist is also confirmed by Christ Himself (Matthew 11:7–10). The following words spoken by Christ also refer to this Angel: 'Truly, I say to you, among those born of women there has risen no-one greater than John the Baptist; yet he who is least in the Kingdom of Heaven is greater than

he' (verse 11). 'Those who are least in the Kingdom of Heaven' are the Angels.

57. John 3:28.
58. John 3:30.
59. Lecture of 12 December 1910 (*Background to the Gospel of St Mark*, RSP 1968).
60. John 1:33.
61. In *The Threshold of the Spiritual World* (together with *A Road to Self-Knowledge*, RSP 1975) Rudolf Steiner also calls Him the 'true Ego'.
62. Regarding the descent of Christ to the Earth with His Spirit-Self, see the lecture of 27 August 1924 (*Karmic Relationships*, vol. VIII, RSP 1975). Regarding the principle of the Spirit-Self as the bearer of the Holy Spirit principle in man, see for example the lecture of 25 April 1907 (GA 96). It should be added that these words from the Gospel are an exact reflection of the nature of the inspirations of the aforesaid Angelic Being. For on the one hand the Angels, as the bearers of an evolved Spirit-Self, are themselves the representatives of the Holy Spirit in the spiritual sphere nearest to the Earth (see the lecture of 20 February 1917, *Cosmic and Human Metamorphoses*, op. cit.), and on the other, as has been said, the proclamation of the birth on Earth through the Baptism in the Jordan of the cosmic Ego of Christ—as the new spiritual impulse capable of penetrating every human ego—was the principal mission of this particular Angelic Being at the Turning-Point of Time. Finally, the very expression, 'but he who sent me to baptise with water', also refers to an Angelic Being, who would have been particularly associated with the element of water and whose precepts John would have been able to heed because of his Waterman initiation (see the lecture of 6 December 1910, *Background to the Gospel of St Mark*, op. cit.).

So as to avoid misunderstandings, one needs to bear in mind that the spiritual impulses that have been described have their source in far higher spiritual spheres than the realm of activity of the Angels. The Angel is in this case simply the mediator or emissary of higher powers. The beginning of St Mark's Gospel (1:2) refers to these higher powers working through the Angel in words which Rudolf Steiner translates as follows: 'Lo, the bestower of egohood sends his Angel before you to whom egohood is to be given' (lecture of 12 December 1910, ibid.).

63. See the lecture of 20 February 1917, as above.
64. Lecture of 19 September 1909 (*The Gospel of St Luke*, op. cit.) Luke 3:22; Mark 1:11. The very fact that these words sound at the moment of the Baptism testifies to the participation in this event of the Hierarchic Being *who was being prepared to become* the 'leader of *exoteric* Christianity'. For the Baptism by John was a metamorphosis of certain procedures of the ancient mysteries that had been brought forth onto the plane of outer history (see note 82). Moreover, the fact that the Baptism of Jesus took place amidst a great throng of people is an indication of the influence of this Spirit.

However, the character of his new mission is manifested with even greater clarity in the conversation of Christ Jesus with the *Greeks* who had come to see Him. Christ Jesus ends this conversation with the following words: ' "Now is my soul troubled. And what shall I say? Father, save me from this hour? No, for this purpose I have come to this hour. Father, glorify Thy Name." Then a voice *came from heaven*: "I have glorified it, and I will glorify it again." The crowd standing by heard it and said that *it had thundered.* Others said, *"An Angel had spoken to Him."* Jesus answered, "This voice has come *for your sake,* not mine." ' (John 12:27–30.) This scene has three aspects. Firstly, it was initiated by the encounter with the Greeks, for the Archai who was being active in that moment was formerly the Archangel of the Greek people. Secondly, the reference to the connection with the sphere of the Father indicates that the 'Angel' of which the people speak belongs to the rank of the *Archai* (who have their physical body in the element of *lightning* and *thunder*). Thirdly, the words of Christ about the voice from heaven being 'for your sake' (i.e. for the people) are an indication of how this Spirit works as the inspirer of *exoteric* Christianity. (Regarding the relationship of the Archai to the sphere of the Father, see the lecture of 20 February 1917 (*Cosmic and Human Metamorphoses*, op. cit.).

In connection with a further utterance of John the Baptist, Rudolf Steiner also points to his direct relationship to the ruling Time-Spirit of that epoch: 'At the time when Christ Jesus appeared on Earth, *His forerunner,* John the Baptist, characterised the Spirit, whom one could describe as the Time-Spirit, with these words: "Change your attitude of mind, for the Kingdom of Heaven is at hand." ' (Lecture of 7 June 1910, *The Mission of Folk Souls,* op. cit.) The words of John the Baptist in this quotation have significance for various levels of world existence. Rudolf Steiner draws upon them in his lectures in order to characterise the most diverse spiritual situations. Hence what is said here is not at variance with the description quoted on p. 21 of the transformation, within the soul of John the Baptist, of cosmic conscience into human conscience, but merely testifies to how this transition was accomplished in his soul with the participation of the Time-Spirit of that age, who until then had been the Folk-Spirit of ancient Greece—in that culture where, under his rulership, there appeared for the first time an *understanding* of conscience and a verbal expression for it.

65. John 1:34.
66. *The Christ-impulse and the Development of Ego Consciousness* (AP 1976), lecture of 2 May 1910.
67. In the lecture of 2 May 1910 (see above) Rudolf Steiner speaks as follows about the potential for ego-development amongst the various peoples before the Turning-Point of Time: 'The Egypto-Chaldaean people waited to develop the ego in the consciousness soul; the Graeco-Romans developed it in the intellectual soul; in Northern Europe it was prematurely developed in the sentient soul.' Thus from these words we

may see that by the Turning-Point of Time the ego-impulse was most intensively developed within the Graeco-Roman peoples, a circumstance in which we may discern the fruits of the activity of the ruling Time-Spirit, first as the Archangel of the Greeks and then as an Archai. If from this standpoint we now consider the structure of man's being as described in *Occult Science—an Outline*, op. cit., we have in the transition from a ninefold to a sevenfold structure on the one hand an amalgamation of the consciousness soul with the Spirit-Self and, on the other, of the sentient soul with the sentient body, while at the centre, the intellectual or mind soul remains unchanged as the bearer of the individual human ego. In this respect the latter member occupies a truly central place in man's being, in that it establishes *through the ego* an intellectual soul as a connection with the consciousness soul and, as mind soul, with the sentient soul. From this it becomes possible to understand why the incarnation on Earth of the Christ Being as World-Ego could occur only in the fourth post-Atlantean epoch which stood under the sign of the evolution of the intellectual or mind soul, and which was also the only epoch not subject to the law of repetition (the third epoch is repeated in the fifth, the second in the sixth, and so on): 'That was the period . . . in which the ego descended among men. Hence the Christ-event had also to happen in that epoch, because, with him, the ego made its descent in a special way' (lecture of 3 December 1911, *Faith, Hope, Love*, Steiner Book Centre, Vancouver 1986).

John the Baptist was the bearer of such a fully developed intellectual or mind soul (more will be said later about his deep connection in particular with this member of man's being). Thus although he does not belong to the Graeco-Roman peoples, he is nonetheless, like them, the bearer of a fully evolved ego in the intellectual or mind soul, a position which he attains as a result of the influence of the 'Greek Time-Spirit', who, being an Archai, has as his lowest member one that corresponds to the human ego (lecture of 2 June 1907, *Theosophy of the Rosicrucian*, RSP 1966). Moreover, this influence of the ruling Archai of his age upon John the Baptist was able to strengthen the impulse of the individual ego within him, to such an extent that, in seemingly generating a superfluity of forces in his intellectual soul, this individual ego also awakens his consciousness soul. As a result of this, John the Baptist appears before us as a man who already, in the fourth cultural epoch, bears within himself *to some extent* an awakened consciousness soul and who therefore, according to the occult teachings of the ancient Hebrews, can be called a 'Son of Man' (see Matthew 16:13–14). Rudolf Steiner speaks in the following way about such 'Sons of Man', who are at the same time 'leaders of humanity': '. . . normally developed men had as yet nothing of the 'Son of Man' in them. But there must always be some who are in advance of their generation, who already bear within them, in an earlier epoch, the knowledge and potentialities of a later one. In the fourth epoch—when normally only the intellectual or mind soul had developed—there would always have been some among the leaders of

275

men who, although their outward appearance was similar to that of others, had already unfolded the seed of the consciousness soul into which the Spirit-Self sends its radiance. And there were indeed such 'Sons of Man'. Hence it behoved the disciples of Christ Jesus to recognise and learn to understand the nature of these leaders' (*The Gospel of St Matthew*, op. cit., the eleventh lecture).

68. John 1:7–10.

69. Ibid. v. 15.

70. Regarding the connection of the impulse of conscience with the evolution of the ego, see the lecture of 2 May 1910 (*The Christ-Impulse and the Development of Ego Consciousness*, op. cit.) where we learn that the voice of conscience could at that time be heard only by an especially strongly developed ego. In the case of a weakly developed ego, a man would have experienced through his astral body not an inner voice but a vision of the spiritual Beings of the Eumenides, Furies and so forth who were pursuing him.

71. Regarding the Ten Commandments and their relationship to the human ego, see the lecture of 14 December 1908 (GA 108).

72. According to the Old Testament, Elijah has a quite special relationship to the substance of fire, for it is in fire or warmth that the ego dwells within man (see the lecture of 31 December 1923, *World History in the Light of Anthroposophy*, RSP 1977). This is why he frequently appears as the lord of lightning or 'heavenly fire' (1 Kings 18:38 and 2 Kings 1:9–14). His ascension into heaven also comes about through this substance, that is, through the forces of his ego: he was taken up by 'a chariot of fire and horses of fire' (2 Kings 2:11). In Russian apocryphal literature the functions of the chief Slavic God, Perun, the lord of lightning and thunder, the possessor of the thunderbolt and the enchanted axe, are transferred to Elijah shortly after the Christianising of Russia (988), and Elijah subsequently also takes on many of the characteristics of the 'dragon-slayer' of Russian folk-tales (thus emphasising his more Michaelic aspect). Perun is the Slavic equivalent of the Teutonic god Thor or Donner and is, according to Rudolf Steiner, the representative of the ego-impulse (lecture of 14 June 1910, *The Mission of Folk Souls*, op. cit.). The connection between the Slavic Perun and the Teutonic Thor, quite apart from the special relationship of both to thunder and lightning, can also be discerned from the fact that in Baltic and Slavic mythology *Thursday* is reckoned to be the 'day of Perun', and from the name of one of the most ancient sanctuaries of Perun found beneath Novgorod, 'Peruni', the ancient Gothic equivalent of which is 'fairguni' ('the rock') and the ancient Icelandic 'Fiorgyn', the name of the mother of Thor, the thunder god. Thus the lightning-flashes over which Perun–Elijah rules in the macrocosm correspond in man, as microcosm, to the ego working in his blood, while the thunder is connected with the ego-substance of thinking. (See ibid. and GA 264, pp. 232–3.) For this same reason Jahve, the God of the

'I am', manifests himself to Moses only in lightning and thunder (Exodus 19:16) and through the element of fire (Exodus 19:18 and 24:17).

If one is to sense to what extent the ego-impulse became in Elijah an inner experience in comparison to what it was in Moses, it is necessary to compare the descriptions of the spiritual meetings of these two with Jahve. Thus Jahve says to Moses that he cannot see his face and remain amongst the living (Exodus 33:20). This is why at the moment of his highest revelation he 'covers Moses with his hand', with the result that Moses is able to see him only 'from behind' and not face to face (33:22–3). Elijah, on the other hand, experiences this revelation in an altogether different way. In his case, Jehovah does not reach out his hand so as to shield him from beholding the highest revelation. It is rather the case that Elijah, in preparing himself for it, 'wrapped his face in his mantle and went out, and stood in the entrance to the cave' (1 Kings 19:13). This 'mantle' with which Elijah covers his face in this scene is the imagination of his own higher supersensible being that has not fully united with his physical body, and which surrounds him like a mighty aura. With the help of this 'mantle' Elijah calls forth in his pupil Elisha the future prophet (1 Kings 19:19–20), and subsequently transmits to him, from the spiritual world, part of his spiritual power (2 Kings 2:13–15). According to the Bible, when Elijah ascended before the inner eye of Elisha in the fiery chariot (that is, through the power of his mighty ego) into a higher spiritual sphere, Elisha was left with only his mantle: 'only the mantle fell upon him, that is, the spiritual power with which he now had to envelop himself' (lecture of 14 December 1911, *Turning Points in Spiritual History*, op. cit.).

And so we see that in order that he might experience the highest revelation of Jahve, Elijah 'came out of the cave', that is, out of his physical body (while Moses is put by Jahve 'in a cleft of the rock' (Exodus 33:22), which signifies that he cannot leave his body completely), and then 'his face', that is to say his earthly consciousness, he 'covers with his mantle'— meaning that he is united with the forces of his spiritual aura. In other words, his consciousness is at this moment shifted to the sphere of his higher being that is not incarnated in a physical body, to that aspect of his being where he can experience the reflection in the Moon-sphere of the World-Ego of the Christ approaching the Earth. And here something remarkable happens. To Moses, Jahve had revealed himself from without, in the substance of fire; while Elijah, as a result of his initiation, bears this fiery impulse of the ego within his soul. Thus Jahve manifests himself to him in a revelation proceeding not from without but *from within*, not in a raging fire but in 'a still small voice': 'And he [Jahve] said: Go forth, and stand upon the mount before the Lord. And behold, the Lord passed by, and a great and strong wind rent the mountains, and broke in pieces the rocks before the Lord, but the Lord was not in the wind; and after the wind an earthquake, but the Lord was not in the earthquake; and after the earthquake a fire, but the Lord was not in the fire; and after the fire a still small voice' (1 Kings 19:11–12). In a certain sense one can say that in this first inner revelation of the ego-impulse we also have the first appearance in human evolution of the impulse of *conscience*. Thus Elijah becomes not—like Moses—the bearer of the *wisdom* of the ego but the bearer of the *power* of the ego, '. . . the directing force, that which points the direction, that which gives the impulse' (lecture of 26 June 1908, *The Apocalypse of St John*, RSP 1977). A reflection of this polarity can also be found in the Old Testament (see Malachi 4:4–6). And just as John the Baptist after his death became the group-soul of the Apostles (lecture of 20 September 1912, *The Gospel of St Mark*, op. cit.) so did Elijah, the father of the prophets of the ancient Hebrews, become after his death the inspirer of all the prophets that followed him, helping them in the course of their incarnations amongst the ancient Hebrew people to *remember* the initiations which they had experienced amidst other peoples in their past incarnations. 'One may say that, *beginning with Elijah* . . . the prophets appear before us in wondrous majesty' (lecture of 16 September 1912, ibid.). For according to the testimony of Rudolf Steiner, the souls of the Old Testament prophets, coming as they did from other peoples and then incarnating amongst the ancient Hebrews, are united in this new incarnation with the soul-spiritual atmosphere created beforehand by Elijah, who 'comes before us as a soul who belonged in a quite special way to the ancient Hebrew people', so that 'what had remained from Elijah was blended, as in a mighty harmony or symphony, with what the souls of other peoples had to impart through the other prophets who incarnated in the people of the Old Testament' (lecture of 20 September 1912, ibid.).

It was from the supersensible inspirations of Elijah, the representative of the soul of the people of the Old Testament, that all the Old Testament prophets were to derive the strength for their battles against the Sibyls and the subconscious impulses of the soul, so that the impulse of the individual ego entered in the right way into the midst of the ancient Hebrew people and, in a wider sense, into humanity as a whole (see the lecture of 1 January 1914, *Christ and the Spiritual World. The Search for the Holy Grail*, op. cit.).

73. Genesis 3:24.
74. Lecture of 2 December 1911 (*Faith, Love, Hope*), op. cit. Later in the same lecture Rudolf Steiner speaks of how from our time onwards the place of Moses, in this imagination, comes to be taken by Christ, as the Lord of Karma, who gradually leads mankind to directly contemplating the consequences of deeds not only after death (before Kama-Loka) but already during earthly life. Rudolf Steiner concludes his description of this altogether new spiritual situation with a reference to the significance which the renewed call of John the Baptist consequently acquires in our time: 'Change your state of soul, for the time is coming when new faculties will awaken in men' (ibid.).
75. The '*flaming sword*' in the hands of the Cherub (the Russian canonical translation of the Bible has here a word to the effect that it 'turns about

itself', that is, that it is 'two-edged') is an imagination of the human ego, which after death is handed over to the cosmic conscience (the Cherub). See Revelation 1:16 and the lecture of 25 June 1908 (*The Apocalypse of St John*, RSP/AP 1977). According to Rudolf Steiner, the two-edged sword in the Apocalypse was depicted on the first apocalyptic seal as *flaming* (see GA 284, and *Art Inspired by Rudolf Steiner*, Mercury Arts Publications 1987).

76. Lecture of 27 January 1910 (*The Reappearance of Christ in the Etheric*, AP 1983).
77. 1:17.
78. In these words of John about his being 'of the Earth' there is a subconscious recollection of Adam, of whom the Bible says: 'And the Lord God formed man of the dust of the Earth . . .' (Genesis 2.7).
79. John 3:28–36.
80. Lecture of 17 September 1912 (*The Gospel of St Mark*, op. cit.).
81. Ibid. John the Baptist had already been prepared for this process of 'transmitting part of the spirit of Elijah' to other human beings, in his previous incarnation. However, this was at that time not possible with regard to an entire people on the physical plane, but only in the spiritual world with respect to his closest pupils. Thus after his physical death the prophet Elijah transmitted part of his spiritual power (that is, the forces of his ego) to the prophet Elisha (see Kings 2:1–15, and the lecture of 14 December 1911, *Turning Points in Spiritual History*, op. cit.). Subsequently, Elijah also accomplished this with respect to other Old Testament prophets, for example Daniel and Malachi, the latter of whom was supersensibly inspired by Elijah to foretell his future appearance on Earth at the Turning-Point of Time.
82. Ibid. See the description of the process of baptism in the lecture of 17 September 1912 and the lectures of 29 and 30 June 1909 (*The Gospel of St John in Relation to the Other Three Gospels*, AP 1982).
83. This process of baptism does, however, have an additional meaning. We have already seen (p. 10) that John the Baptist, through his connection with the Zarathustra stream on the one hand and, on the other, with the Buddha stream, was in a sense the forerunner and preparer of the world-historical union of these two streams in the Mystery of Christ Jesus. In a similar way, John anticipates, through his baptism, something that Christ Jesus was to accomplish as an event of world-historical significance. For the process of baptism as carried out by John, where the person was brought through a total immersion in water to the border between life and death (and thereby to the partial separation of the etheric body from the physical), was akin to an initiation-process of the ancient mysteries that had been brought out into the open.

In this sense, the Baptism by John was in a certain way an anticipation of the raising of Lazarus, with the difference that John led men to an experience of the World-Ego of Christ approaching the Earth, while in the raising of Lazarus, Christ Himself works already on the Earth. The result of the latter was, moreover, not the contemplation of the approaching World-Ego, but His direct penetration into man (in this case into Lazarus).

To what has been said here regarding the Baptism by John it should still be added that he had made preparations for his mission in his previous incarnation through the raising of the widow's son (1 Kings 17:17–24), and through transmitting part of his spiritual power to the prophet Elisha, who with his help was able to raise the son of the rich woman (2 Kings 4:17–37). Finally, John prepared himself, in his incarnation as Elijah, for his future task even from a 'geographic' point of view. For he experienced his initiation, which Rudolf Steiner describes in detail in the lecture of 14 December 1911 (*Turning Points in Spiritual History*, op. cit.) in a locality not far from the River Jordan. In the Old Testament we read of it as follows: 'And the word of the Lord came unto him, saying: "Get thee hence and turn thee eastward and hide thyself by the brook Cherith, that is, before Jordan"' (1 Kings 17:2–3). 'Turn thee eastward' means in this context 'turn to the spiritual world'. Subsequently, after his death, the soul of Elijah again turns to this place of his future earthly activity. Thus according to the Old Testament, he carries out the initiation of his favourite pupil, Elisha, when the latter is 'on the bank of the Jordan' (2 Kings 2:6–9). See also note 81.

84. Matthew 3:7–9.
85. Ibid. v. 10.
86. Christ Jesus also says: 'I have come not to abolish the law and the prophets, but to fulfil them' (Matthew 5:17).
87. John 10:41.
88. Matthew 14:1–12. That in the story of the relationship between Herod and Herodias was more involved than the outward violation of the Old Testament law can be adduced, for example, from the fact—familiar from several apocryphal legends (including some of Slavic origin)—that, at the time of the events referred to, the husband of Herodias, Philip, was already dead. Emil Bock speaks of certain deeper *spiritual–historical* causes of the conflict between John and Herod in his book, *Cäsaren und Apostel*, Urachhaus, 1983. In the present work, however, we wish to emphasise principally the spiritual–psychological causes.
89. Lecture of 3 February 1912 ('Consciousness and Astonishment as Indications of Spiritual Vision in Past and Future', *Golden Blade* 1967).
90. Lecture of 17 September 1912 (*The Gospel of St Mark*, op. cit.).
91. Lecture of 20 September 1912 (above). Rudolf Steiner speaks of this as follows: 'The soul of John the Baptist, the soul of Elijah, becomes the group-soul of the Twelve; it lives and continues to live in the Twelve.
92. Lecture of 28 September 1924 (*The Last Address*, RSP 1967). See also the elucidations of Dr Noll and Dr Kirchner-Bockholt in the German edition of 1981.
93. Lecture of 10 September 1910 (*The Gospel of St Matthew*, op. cit.).

94. The two fish are the supersensible forces of the physical and etheric bodies, and the five loaves are the forces of the astral body, ego, Spirit-Self, Life-Spirit and Spirit-Man (see note 92).—This participation of the entelechy of John in the scene of the *multiplying of the loaves* and the feeding of the five thousand testifies to the relationship of this individuality to a certain spiritual stream that was from the beginning connected with the mysteries of the 'Bread of Life' (John 6:35). The leading representative in the Old Testament of this stream, who imparted to Abraham and, hence, to the ancient Hebrews as a whole the high mission of preparing the sheaths for the descent of Christ, the heavenly 'Bread of Life, to the Earth, is Melchizedek', 'the priest of the most high God' (Genesis 14:18–20). He was the last earthly incarnation of Manu, the leader of the great 'Mother Lodge' of the rulership of mankind (see note 14). As an individuality who was directly connected with the Mother Lodge, Elijah also works amongst the ancient Hebrews as a direct furtherer of its impulses. His connection with the 'stream of Melchizedek' is manifested with full clarity in his previous incarnation as Phinehas. Subsequently his belonging to this stream comes to be expressed in his incarnation as Elijah in the scene with the widow and the barrel of meal (1 Kings 17:8–16). The continuation of this is the miracle with the loaves wrought by his favourite pupil, Elisha (2 Kings 4:42–44), to whom Elijah transmitted part of his spiritual strength and, through this, the connection with the 'stream of Melchizedek'. The crowning, and final, manifestations of these mysteries is the incarnation on Earth of the Christ Himself and the feeding by Him of the four thousand and the five thousand, and also the transformation of bread and wine into spiritual forces during the Last Supper—a cultic act which, according to the Apostle Paul, He accomplished as a 'high priest after the order of Melchizedek' (Hebrews 5:10 and Psalm 110).

Amongst the manifold meanings which the symbols of bread and wine have in an occult sense, there is one which has a particular significance for us here. This is the connection of the symbol of 'bread' with the destiny of the earthly primal man, Adam, and of the symbol of 'wine' with the destiny of the heavenly primal man, the Nathan Soul. In the parable of the grain of wheat: 'Unless a grain of wheat . . . dies . . .' (John 12:24), we already find an indication of this destiny of earthly humanity, whose ancestor was Adam. This path of descent into the realm of matter and death in all its inner tragedy is also imprinted in the words of the macrocosmic 'Our Father' (see *The Fifth Gospel* RSP, 1968, and *Guidance in Esoteric Training*, RSP 1977), where in the fourth line there is a reference to 'bread' as an image of the most characteristic feature of man incarnated in a physical body; and then, when Christ transforms the macrocosmic 'Our Father' into its microcosmic counterpart (the lecture of 6 October 1913, *The Fifth Gospel*, op. cit.). He indicates thereby to all the descendants of the earthly Adam—that is, to all mankind—the new path from below upwards, back into the spiritual world (see for further details *Rudolf Steiner and the Founding of the New Mysteries*, RSP/AP 1986, Ch. 3). Another path is reflected in the image of 'wine', the symbol of the purest etheric forces (of water) which unite in the vine ('I am the true vine,' says Christ, John 15:1) with the cosmic forces of the Sun. This is a symbol of the heavenly destiny of the Nathan Soul. (It is for this reason that 'wine' is not mentioned in the 'Our Father', which relates to the descendants of the *earthly* Adam.) The first 'miracle' performed by Christ at the Marriage in Cana of Galilee (John 2:1–11) also relates to this mystery of the Nathan Soul or 'heavenly humanity'.

In the mysteries of Melchizedek–Manu, which are connected with the Mother Lodge of the rulership of humanity and at the same time with Adam and the Nathan Soul, both streams, with their symbols of bread and wine and their mysteries of the earthly Adam and his heavenly 'sister soul', had been gradually preparing already since ancient Atlantis for their union, the foundation for which was subsequently laid by Christ Jesus in the events of the Turning-Point of Time.

95. John 6:35.
96. Lecture of 18 September 1909 (*The Gospel of St Luke*, op. cit.).
97. Lecture of 19 September 1909 (ibid.).
98. Lecture of 5 October 1913 (*The Fifth Gospel*, op. cit.). In the same lecture Rudolf Steiner refers to how, in the course of one of the conversations between Jesus and John, Jesus has a direct clairvoyant experience of John's previous incarnation as Elijah.
99. Lecture of 17 September 1912 (*The Gospel of St Mark*, op. cit.).
100. Rudolf Steiner says to this: 'Can one not feel that what hovered like an aura around Elijah–John also surrounded Raphael, so that Raphael had something about him that was similar to the other two, something which, one could say, was too great to be contained in one personality, but which hovered over the individual concerned *in such a way that the revelations that this physical personality received had the force of illuminations? This was how it was with Raphael*' (ibid.). And a little further on he puts it more clearly. 'And they [the words of Herman Grimm about Raphael] would seem to express the notion that Raphael had something like a great aura that hovered over him, in the same way that the spirit of Elijah hovered over Naboth.'

We have in addition a very similar testimony from a contemporary: 'Raphael was of a very noble and tender complexion, so that his life seemed to be attached to his body by no more than a thread; for he was wholly spirit' (quoted by W. Keller, *Raphael von Urbino*, Stuttgart 1979). These words are remarkably in tune with some other words spoken about Novalis by his friend Ludwig Tieck: 'He [Novalis] was a man of the truest kind, the purest and dearest embodiment of a high immortal spirit' (GA IV page 558). Nonetheless, Novalis was only partially incarnated in his physical body, though not so incompletely as Raphael.
101. See the description of the *Sistine Madonna* given by Rudolf Steiner at the end of the lecture of 22 December 1908 (*The Christmas Mystery: Novalis as*

Seer, Mercury Press 1985) and in the lecture of 8 May 1912 (GA 143), and also the reference to it in the lecture of 6 October 1923 (*The Four Seasons and the Archangels*, RSP 1968), as a direct artistic reflection of the cosmic imagination of Christmas. That Raphael painted his pictures of the Madonna and Child out of inner clairvoyant experiences has been frequently attested. See further regarding this in notes 293 and 325.

102. Lecture of 15 February 1909 (*Christianity in Human Evolution*, AP 1979).

103. See the lectures of 7 March and 6 April 1909 (*The Principle of Spiritual Economy*, op. cit.).

104. In *The Principle of Spiritual Economy*, op. cit., Rudolf Steiner refers on several occasions to how an embodiment of this kind in human sheaths, of impressions of the etheric or astral bodies of the Nathan Soul, has often been called forth (naturally always only where the karmic conditions are right) by some sort of tragic experience or shock experienced in childhood or youth. For although the embodiment of such impressions has already taken place before birth in the spiritual world, a certain stimulus from without was nevertheless needed in order that the higher spiritual forces contained in these impressions might become active in, respectively, the etheric or astral body. Such an event in the life of Raphael, which brought the forces associated with the impression of the etheric body of the Nathan Soul into movement within him, was a series of deaths in his family, which took place at the time when his own etheric body was being developed (from his seventh to his fourteenth year). When he was 8 years old, in the space of one month his grandmother Elisabeth, his 'angel-like' mother [Kelber] and his sister all died, and when he was eleven his father also died.

105. Lecture of 6 October 1923 (*The Four Seasons and the Archangels*, RSP 1968).

106. This fairly long poem of Raphael, which is one of the few that have come down to us, has, despite its poetic imperfection, much in common as regards the nature of its imagery with many poems of Novalis, especially from his poetic cycle, *Hymns to the Night*. It is sufficient that we direct our attention to the following lines by Raphael:

> Midnight's hour has come.
> One Sun had long gone down,
> When that *other* Sun appeared to me,
> Of words nigh bereft, but with such power of action!

(Compare with Novalis' words about 'another Sun' on p. 5).

> Or Yet all my labours and you, glorious grief,
> Awaken my beleagered spirit,
> Showing it new paths, letting it sense the heights.
> Whither now a way for my heart opens.

Rudolf Meyer, in his book on Novalis, has already referred to the complete inappropriateness of understanding this poem merely as a 'love-poem' in the ordinary sense of the word.

107. GA 292. See also note 475.

108. See the lecture of 10 September 1910 (*The Gospel of St Matthew* op. cit.), and *Rudolf Steiner and the Founding of the New Mysteries*, op. cit., Chapter 3. According to Rudolf Steiner, the spiritual archetype of the human etheric body has its abode on Devachan.

109. See the scheme that is elaborated in note 177.

110. The special connection between Raphael and his mother is borne out by the fact that Raphael's father painted a fresco in the child's room which depicted them together as Madonna and Child. She appeared to her contemporaries as a 'young, warm-hearted woman with the tenderness of a madonna' [Kelber].

111. See the lectures of 7 and 13 October 1923 (*The Four Seasons and the Archangels*, op. cit.) In his lectures devoted to the subject of Raphael, Rudolf Steiner again and again emphasises the fact of his having been born and having died on Good Friday as an indication that he 'stands in a special way with regard to the spiritual world' (lecture of 8 May 1912, GA 143, see AQ 18:1). Reflected in this fact is not only what has been already described regarding his connection with the Archangel Raphael, but also his experience of the Mystery of Golgotha, when the supersensible being of John the Baptist was, through his union with Lazarus–John, able to be spiritually present (see the lecture of 28 September 1924, *The Last Address*, op. cit.).

112. See the lecture of 18 September 1909 (*The Gospel of St Luke*, op. cit.).

113. That the individuality of Raphael the artist had already been connected in his previous incarnations with the Archangel of healing is supported by the fact that in another version of the story about righteous Tobit it is not the Archangel Raphael who is sent from the spiritual world to heal him but the prophet Elijah.

114. Lecture of 22 August 1924 (*True and False Paths in Spiritual Investigation*, RSP 1985). In the lecture of 18 August 1924 Rudolf Steiner refers *three times* to the fact that the previous rulership of the Archangel Raphael amongst mankind lasted from the ninth to the fifteenth century, that is, it came to an end approximately at the time of Raphael the artist's birth on Earth. In individual human development this historical epoch corresponds to the period from seven to fourteen years, when the development of the *etheric body*, the source of the healing forces of man's earthly organism, takes place (see note 104). What is surprising about this description is that Rudolf Steiner places the time of Raphael's rulership immediately *before* that of Gabriel, omitting the rulership of the Archangel Samael that took place between them (1190–1510). However, this could be understood as meaning that, exceptionally, the Archangel Raphael still retained, during the epoch of Samael's rulership, a certain influence over some areas of the spiritual life of mankind—an influence which finally came to an end only

with the beginning of the epoch of Gabriel's rulership (1510), that is, some ten years before the death of the artist. In this connection, the following words spoken by Rudolf Steiner about Raphael's *birth* acquire a particular significance: 'In a manner of speaking it can be said that he 'let himself be born' on Good Friday in order to indicate his connection with the Mystery of Golgotha' (lecture of 2 May 1912, *Earthly and Cosmic Man*, op. cit.).

115. This sequence of pictures, which consists for the most part of Raphael Madonnas and which Dr Peipers prepared for the patients of his clinic in Munich, was approved by Rudolf Steiner for its therapeutic effects. The reason for this healing influence of the pictures of the Madonna is that those spiritual forces work within it in a metamorphosed form which in olden times were connected with the cosmic sphere of the Virgin Sophia, the representative of the forces of cosmic healing (see the lectures of 4 and 5 August 1908), *Universe, Earth and Man*, RSP 1987). Rudolf Steiner refers to this mission of the images of the Madonna—in so far, of course, as they correspond in a spiritual and artistic sense to their heavenly archetype, as was the case in the art of Raphael and of certain other artists—in the following words: 'And so we may see what continues to live in that wonderful symbol of the Virgin Mother with the child which, as we can say with full confidence on the ground of spiritual science, has been preserved in the healing properties of the Madonna picture. For the Madonna picture is a means of healing' (5 August 1908). Hence the spiritual impulse of the Archangel Raphael must have worked within the artist Raphael with a quite particular strength for him to have made this most therapeutic of themes in the pictorial arts the *very heart* of his creative work. To this should be added that, of all Raphael's Madonnas, Rudolf Steiner especially singles out the *Sistine Madonna* and remarks upon its therapeutic influence, not only for expectant mothers, but for all people who are suffering from psychological or physiological disturbances of whatever kind.

116. Lecture of 28 September 1924 (*The Last Address*, op. cit.).

117. Lecture of 30 January 1913 GA 62 (Z 27, Typescript: *The Mission of Raphael*).

118. The zeal with which Raphael devoted himself to leading excavations and restorations of the architectural monuments of ancient Rome cost him his life. In the course of the excavations, on which he spent many days, he contracted a fever which was the outer cause of his premature death. As a result, his contemporaries attested '. . . that everyone took him for a divine Being from heaven, who had been sent in order to restore the eternal city to its former glory. For all that, there was not a trace of arrogance in him, and he simply became even more friendly towards all men . . .' (Quoted by R. Meyer, *Elias*, Stuttgart 1964).

119. This is not at variance with what was said earlier (see p. 7) as to how the Jahve-impulse, which Moses had perceived in a more spiritually outward way, was experienced by Elijah within his soul. For this impulse working

285

'within the soul of Elijah' remained for him no more than a 'higher inspiration' which only in his next incarnation, as John the Baptist, could to some extent become *a power of his own* that was united with the content of his ego. Rudolf Steiner refers to this as follows: 'I do not propose to go into further details now, but will only say that, in the light of occult knowledge, Elijah was one who proclaimed with power and deep intensity that the primal, original form of what humanity may call the divine can be glimpsed only in the innermost centre of man's being, in his own ego. Thus if we would characterise the great prophetic message of Elijah as a whole, we could say: *from him there went forth the recognition* that everything the outer world can teach us is mere semblance and that knowledge of the true nature of man can arise only within his own ego. However, Elijah could not as yet recognise the power and significance of the individual ego, but he conceived of a divine ego which was, so to speak, external to man [as did Moses also]. Man had to recognise this divine ego, he had to recognise that *it rays into the human ego.*' (Here we have an indication of the particular task of Elijah, and also of the inner evolution which this represented in comparison to that of Moses.) And then in the same lecture, in characterising the task of John the Baptist in connection with his summons, 'Change your state of soul . . .', Rudolf Steiner continues this thought thus: 'That is to say, the phase of development has come when, in very truth, the ego [of man] can find the divine within itself. And we may see [in John the Baptist] that *the form in which Christianity was heralded by Elijah has changed with the course of time*' (lecture of 2 May 1912, *Earthly and Cosmic Man*, op. cit.). Rudolf Steiner speaks in further detail about the nature of this 'heraldship' and about the spiritual progress of John the Baptist with respect to Elijah in the lecture of 17 September 1912 (*The Gospel of St Mark*, op. cit.) where he describes how, as a result of the preaching and baptising of John, the group ego of the people of the Old Testament, as represented by Elijah, gradually became differentiated and entered into the souls of individual human beings as an impulse of the *individual ego*: 'That this spirit [Elijah] which had, as it were, [formerly] hovered over mankind and human history would now be able to enter more and more into each individual breast, was the great fact now made known by Elijah–*John* . . .' This means that, as a result of the activity of John the Baptist, the spirit of Elijah could bring about the awakening within human beings of the principle of the individual ego, this being the most important prerequisite and the fundamental condition for receiving the impulse of the World-Ego, which was to be brought to the Earth by Christ, in the right way.

This extraordinarily complicated process of the inner evolution of the spiritual being of Elijah–John—that he attained on Earth the principle of the individual ego, and also that he brought tidings of the gradual approach of the World-Ego—is characterised by Rudolf Steiner again and again from many different aspects. For example, in the lecture of 8 May 1912

286

(GA 143, AQ 18:1) he describes the spiritual progress which Elijah achieved in comparison to Moses: 'He [Elijah] was not able to bring an awareness of the whole significance of the human ego, he represents a *transitory stage* in ego-recognition between the Mosaic idea of Jehovah and the Christian idea of Christ.' The next step in this sequence is John the Baptist's bringing to all mankind tidings of this 'Christian idea of Christ'. Rudolf Steiner speaks of this as follows: 'He [John the Baptist] has clearly indicated what impulse was to come into being through Golgotha: that a wholeness, a spiritual essence, can be found within the human ego, that the Christ Ego shall enter ever more and more into the human ego, and that the impulse to achieve this is nigh' (ibid.). Thus in the spiritual progress which Elijah achieved in comparison to Moses, and which John the Baptist made in comparison to Elijah, there is revealed a kind of archetype of human evolution in its relationship to the ego-principle, whose most important representative is the individuality of Elijah–John.

120. See further in *The Cycle of the Year as a Path of Initiation*, Part II, op. cit., the chapter entitled 'The Final Week of Advent. The Temple of Higher Knowledge'.

121. *Knowledge of the Higher Worlds: How is it Achieved?* (RSP, 1969), the chapter entitled 'Changes in Dream Life'.

122. This occult tradition of 'building a hut' in the spiritual world—'The pupil must seek out some place which he has thoroughly explored and take possession of it spiritually. In this place he must establish a spiritual home for himself and relate everything else to it' (ibid.)—also finds expression in the Gospels. Thus in the scene of the Transfiguration (Matthew 17:4), Peter says to Christ Jesus: 'Lord, it is well that we are here; if you wish, I will make three booths [the original Greek word at this point means 'tents'—Translator's note] here, one for you and one for Moses and one for Elijah.' (In the astral light Peter sees everything in an inverted form. It is actually a question of 'building huts' for the three Apostles as a means of furnishing their souls with a foundation for the spiritual experiences to come).

123. Lecture of 26 October 1908, GA 108. At the end of this lecture, Rudolf Steiner describes what Novalis was able to read and perceive in the 'astral light': 'Thus Novalis was able to gain an insight into these times when the Gods dwelt amongst men, when everything had a spiritual foundation and the spirits and souls [of men] had not yet descended into earthly bodies'— this is a description of that spiritual state in which the Nathan Soul had abided in the spiritual worlds from the very beginning and until its first incarnation at the Turning-Point of Time. 'And so he was able to see the transition: how death entered into the world, and how the men of those times depicted death in its earthly, shadowy aspect, and how they sought to beautify it through fantasy and through art. But death remained a riddle.' Here we have a reference to the process of the 'Fall' and its consequences for the future earthly existence of Adam and of humanity as

a whole. 'Then something of universal significance took place. And Novalis was able to behold the universal significance of what was happening in the world at that time. Souls had descended . . . [into the] Kingdom of Nature . . . The memory of the spiritual origins of existence had been lost, though a particular spiritual Being lived on in this *universal womb* whence everything had descended'—that is, the Nathan Soul. This reference to it in connection with the description of Novalis' 'initiation' comes almost exactly a year before the detailed account of the mysteries of the Nathan Soul in the lecture cycle *The Gospel of St Luke*, op. cit. 'One Being was held back for a time; it stayed above, meanwhile only sending down its gift of grace . . .' By this we are principally to understand the three heavenly deeds of the Nathan Soul during Lemuria and Atlantis, of which Rudolf Steiner spoke for the first time in the lecture of 30 December 1913 (*Christ and the Spiritual World and The Search for the Holy Grail*, RSP 1963), and also its supersensible participation in many of the post-Atlantean mysteries (see *The Bhagavad Gita and the Epistles of Paul*, AP 1971). Rudolf Steiner continues: '. . . in order then, when mankind would be in greatest need, to descend into the earthly sphere. The Being of spiritual light, that Being who was concealed behind the physical Sun, remained aloft in the sphere of spirit. He abides in the heavenly spheres and descends, if mankind should so need, in order that human beings might again be borne up into the spiritual worlds.'

Here the impression arises that Rudolf Steiner's spiritual vision, in investigating the spiritual experiences of Novalis, is directed at one and the same time towards the Nathan Soul and the Christ Being, for in the three cosmic preparatory stages of the Mystery of Golgotha they worked together, these being for both the stages of their gradual approach to the Earth (see the lecture of 30 March 1914, GA 152). However, in the words that follow the difference between these two Beings is presented with absolute clarity; and they make it clear that the Being referred to is indeed the Nathan Soul: 'And [this being] descended when at the time of the Mystery of Golgotha the Christ appeared in a physical human body. One comprehends this Being of the Christ in His universal aspect if one traces what lived in Jesus of Nazareth back to his spiritual origin, to that spiritual light.' (Rudolf Steiner speaks about the connection of the Nathan Soul with the spiritual light and its new, 'light-filled' revelation in the lecture of 1 January 1913 (*The Bhagavad Gita and the Epistles of Paul*, op. cit.). And only because Novalis was—in the sense of the above question—able to some extent to behold in the astral light the heavenly and earthly destiny of the Nathan Soul in its constant service of the Sun Being of the Christ, only for this reason was the fundamental mystery of the whole of earthly evolution, the Mystery of the death on Golgotha, also revealed to him: '. . . that life has won the victory over death and a new impulse has been given to mankind . . . this Novalis was able to see . . . Then the whole significance of Christ's death became clear to him. Then was the riddle of death, the riddle of Christ, unvailed to him in the night of soul-existence. It was indeed so that this particular individuality learnt to know this most significant event that anyone is called upon to know—namely, the Mystery of Golgotha—*through his memories of previous lives*' (lecture of 26 October 1908 (GA 108—not translated).

In these concluding words we have what is essentially a reference to Novalis' memory of the supersensible presence—as a result of its spiritual union with the individuality of Lazarus John—of the entelechy of John the Baptist at the death of Christ Jesus on Golgotha and His subsequent Resurrection.

To what has been said in this note regarding the relationship of Novalis to the Nathan Soul it should still be added that Rudolf Steiner also compares Novalis' supersensible experience of Christ with what Paul experienced before Damascus (see p. 37)—which is to say that, like Paul, Novalis experienced in his 'Damascus event' the manifestation of *two* Beings: for Christ appeared clothed in a radiant aura of light, which was none other than the Nathan Soul (see the lecture of 1 January 1913, *The Bhagavad-Gita and the Epistles of Paul*, op. cit.).

124. This and the next two quotations from Rudolf Steiner are taken from his lecture of 22 December 1908 (*The Christmas Mystery: Novalis as the Seer*, AQ vol. 12, no. 4, Winter 1967, and Mercury Press, Spring Valley, 1985).

125. Lecture of 1 October 1911 (*The Etherisation of the Blood*, RSP 1985); the quotations that follow are taken from the same source. See also R. Meyer, *Novalis*, Stuttgart 1972.

126. Regarding the heart as a new higher organ of knowledge, see the lectures of 29 and 30 March 1910 (*Macrocosm and Microcosm*, RSP 1968) and the article, 'At the Dawn of the Michael Age' *Anthroposophical Leading Thoughts*, RSP 1985).

127. See the lecture of 17 December 1906 (*Signs and Symbols of the Christmas Festival*, AP 1969).

128. See the article, 'At the Dawn of the Michael Age', and the following note.

129. In the lecture of 9 November 1914 (GA 158, *The Connection of Man with the Elemental World: Finland and the Kalevala*, Typescript Z 144), Rudolf Steiner says: 'This event of the appearance of Christ, as Theodora has intimated, can only be brought about if Michael's rulership is able to spread more and more widely.' And in his article, 'The World Thoughts in the Working of Michael and in the Working of Ahriman' (*Anthroposophical Leading Thoughts*, op. cit.) he refers to the essential goals which Michael would wish to attain through humanity during the time of the present period of his rulership: 'Therefore it is his intention that the Intelligence shall flow in future through the hearts of men, but that it shall flow there as the self-same force which it was in the beginning, when it poured forth from the divine-spiritual powers . . . And when he pervades intellectual powers it becomes manifest that these can equally well be an expression of the heart and soul as of the head and spirit . . . Consequently he does not convey to

289

the intellect anything that is soulless, cold, frosty, but he stands by it in a manner that is full of soul and inwardly warm.' And it is like a microcosmic reflection of this macrocosmic process that the intellectuality of Novalis comes before us now, for even in the smallest fragments that he has written there is expressed a complete, harmonious merging of the forces of head and heart, of intellectuality and morality.

130. Lecture of 25 January 1910 (*The Reappearance of Christ in the Etheric*, op. cit.). Regarding the new appearance of Christ in the etheric realm see further in *The Spiritual Guidance of Man and Humanity*, AP 1970, and the lectures contained in *Esoteric Christianity*, RSP 1984 and GA 152 [several of which are translated though not collected in any one volume—Translator's note].

131. See the lecture of 14 December 1911 (*Turning Points in Spiritual History*, op. cit.) and also note 72.

132. GA 127 and *Faith, Love, Hope*, Steiner Book Centre 1986.

133. In the lecture of 2 December 1911 (see above), John the Baptist is not mentioned in the course of the description of the *second* call, but Adam, his earliest incarnation, is spoken of at some length.

134. Regarding the connection of the individuality of Elijah–John–Raphael–Novalis with the Bodhisattva principle in general and with the Maitreya Bodhisattva in particular, see note 23.

135. Lecture of 1 October 1911 (*The Etherisation of the Blood*, op. cit.).

136. In these two lines Novalis refers in poetic form to 'a great mystery' which is associated with the life of Christ on the Earth which is known to us only through spiritual science. Thus in the lecture of 3 July 1909 (*The Gospel of St John in Relation to the Other Three Gospels*, AP 1982) Rudolf Steiner speaks of how, through the union of the Christ Being with the physical body of Jesus of Nazareth, this body was the first in the whole evolution of humanity to be permeated by the new spirituality even as far as its bone system.

137. In speaking of the new appearance of Christ in the etheric realm, Rudolf Steiner often refers to how an experience of the Etheric Christ can arise as a result of human beings being prepared for it through receiving spiritual knowledge of Christ *while still on Earth* (see, for example, the lecture of 14 October 1911, *From Jesus to Christ*, RSP 1991). For it is only the preparation for this event that has to take place on Earth; the meeting with the Etheric Christ itself can, under certain conditions, also take place in the spiritual world after death, as was the case with Novalis.

138. Further details about this etheric sphere of Christ may be found in *The Cycle of the Year as a Path of Initiation*, part IX, the chapter entitled 'The Three Stages of Christ's Union with the Sphere of the Earth . . .'

139. No notes have been preserved from this lecture.

140. From this first lecture on the theme of the etheric advent of Christ, only a brief report by Marie Steiner, covering half a typewritten page, has been preserved.

141. The conclusion of this lecture expresses with particular clarity the direct connection between the individuality of Novalis and modern spiritual science—or Anthroposophy—with their spiritual inspirers, the Masters of Wisdom and of Harmony of Feelings. See further in Chapter 11.

142. Although from the first of these, that of 12 January 1910, only a very brief report, in which there is no reference to the call of John, has been preserved, the author is nevertheless convinced that this call was indeed mentioned.

143. Lecture of 25 January 1910 (*The Reappearance of Christ in the Etheric*, AP 1983). See also the lectures of 27 January 1910 and 18 April 1910 from the same volume, the lecture of 20 February 1910 (GA 118, Typescript Z 295), that of 2 December 1911 (*Faith, Love, Hope*, op. cit.) and many others. In all these lectures there are many references to the great importance of the renewed call of John the Baptist for preparing mankind for the new advent of Christ, and of particular importance in this connection are the words of this call in the context of the lecture of 23 January 1910 (GA 125, Typescript EN 46), where they come immediately before the *spirit* of Novalis is mentioned as being connected with the *spirit* of modern spiritual science and with the *spirit* of the Masters of Wisdom and of Harmony of Feelings.

144. Lecture of 18 April 1910 (contained in *The Reappearance of Christ in the Etheric*, op. cit.).

145. *Anthroposophical Leading Thoughts*, op. cit., the article entitled 'Michael's Mission in the Cosmic Age of Human Freedom'.

146. In this line Novalis anticipates in a remarkable way the fundamental mystery of our time: that Christ has, from the twentieth century onwards, become the 'Lord of Karma' (see regarding this event the lecture of 14 October 1911, *From Jesus to Christ*, op. cit., and that of 2 December 1911, *Faith, Love, Hope*, op cit.).

147. Lectures of 2 May 1912 (*Earthly and Cosmic Man*, op. cit.) and of 16 May 1912 (GA 143, Typescript NSL 184). The questions that follow are taken, respectively, from the lectures of 8 May 1912 (GA 143, AQ 18:1), 16, 8 and 2 May 1912, *Earthly and Cosmic Man*, op. cit.

148. After the visit of Elisabeth to Mary, as described in the first chapter of the Gospel of St Luke, Mary never visited her relative again. On the other hand, Elisabeth, Zachariah and their son on several occasions visited the family of the Nathan Jesus in Nazareth after John the Baptist had been born. Such visits took place especially during those years while the family of the Solomon Jesus was still in Egypt. It is the latent memory of these visits and the short periods of the two families' life together in Nazareth which finds its reflection in a number of Raphael's 'Madonnas' where Mary is depicted with two boys, Jesus and John the Baptist, and sometimes also with Elisabeth (for example, in the pictures entitled *Madonna Canigiani, Madonna dell' Impannata* and *Madonna Franz 1*). These pictures, if one takes into account the memory of his past incarnation as it lived in the

depths of the artist's soul, are a far more trustworthy historical witness than many a supposition that outer science has made in this regard. Moreover, at least one of these visits took place at a time when the family of the Solomon Jesus had already returned to their native land and had settled in Nazareth close by the other family. The memory of this later visit was incorporated in the *Madonna Terranuova*, where Mary is depicted with three boys: the two Jesuses and John the Baptist (see also p. 79).

This means that these meetings of the two families took place largely in the *first seven-year period* of both boys (Jesus and John); for the return of the Solomon family from Egypt came about when the Matthew Jesus was five or six years old. Rudolf Steiner speaks about the numerous meetings and conversations that subsequently took place between John the Baptist and Jesus when they had grown up in the lecture of 5 October 1913 (*The Fifth Gospel*, op. cit.).

149. Rudolf Steiner sets, *as a general guideline*, certain historical limits both with regard to the incorporation into man's being of an imprint of the etheric body and of the astral body of the Nathan Soul. Thus in connection with the incorporation of its etheric body Rudolf Steiner particularly singles out the time from the fourth until the twelfth centuries AD, and in connection with the incorporation of the imprints of its astral body the time from the eleventh until the fifteenth centuries (lecture of 15 February 1909, '*Christianity in Human Evolution*', AP 1979). However, in the case of the individuality with whom we are concerned, there is an exception to this general rule, even though it is not really a contradiction but rather an affirmation of it. Such an exception is possible because in this case we are concerned with the reincarnations of Adam, that is, the earthly 'brother' of the heavenly being of the Nathan Soul, who [i.e. Adam], like the Nathan Soul, was directly—albeit in a different way—connected with the Mother Lodge of the rulership of humanity and with its leader, Manu (compare the lecture of 19 September 1909, *The Gospel of St Luke*, op. cit.). This also sheds light upon the fact that Novalis received an imprint of the astral body of the Nathan Soul by way of his intellectual or mind soul. For according to the testimony of spiritual science, the Nathan Soul was the bearer of the primordial, unfallen *etheric* forces of humanity to which the whole being of the 'earthly Adam' aspired (see p. 27 and p. 46); while the intellectual or mind soul in man represents the forces of the etheric body which have been transformed and, in a certain sense, raised to consciousness (see the lectures of 7 and 9 June 1910, *The Mission of the Individual Folk Souls in Relation to Teutonic Mythology*, op. cit.).

150. Lecture of 15 February 1909 (see previous note).

151. Lecture of 6 April 1909 (*The Principle of Spiritual Economy*, AP 1986). The quoted words that follow are taken from the lecture of 15 February 1909.

152. See note 123.

153. Lecture of 26 October 1908 (see note 123).

154. At this point one should recall those forces of primal youth which, having streamed forth from the astral body of the Luke Jesus until his twelfth year, united in the spiritual world with the Nirmanakaya of Buddha and led to the spiritual *renewal* of Buddhism (see the lecture of 18 September 1909, *The Gospel of St Luke*, op. cit.). Subsequently these forces of youth, which had worked not only in the astral but also the etheric body of Jesus of Nazareth, were further strengthened as a result of the three-year presence of the Cosmic Christ-Being in his sheaths.

155. These words of Novalis bear a striking resemblance to the words spoken by Rudolf Steiner on 24 December 1923 in his introductory address to the Christmas Conference, that event in the history of the evolution of the Anthroposophical Movement on Earth which can, perhaps, indeed best be characterised as a 'world-renewing feast'. Thus Rudolf Steiner says in this address: 'And how, my dear friends, is one in the true sense in the Anthroposophical Society? If one has an inkling for what is welling up today from spirit depths for both young and old [that is, regardless of age] as a *cosmic youthfulness* that *renews* every area of our lives.' [An English version of this address may be found in *The Christmas Conference*, AP 1990.]

156. Lecture of 3 June 1913 (*The Occult Significance of the Bhagavad Gita*, AP 1968).

157. Compare note 123.

158. Lecture of 21 August 1924 (*True and False Paths in Spiritual Investigation*, RSP, AP 1969).

159. Ibid., likewise the quotations that follow.

160. Ibid.

161. Lecture of 20 February 1917 (*Cosmic and Human Metamorphoses*, op. cit.). The quotations that follow are from the same source.

162. Rudolf Steiner says of Novalis in this connection: 'Thus do the worlds of night, the true spiritual worlds, open up before Novalis, and so night becomes precious to him from this point of view' (lecture of 26 October 1908, GA 108). This is the source of Novalis' glorifying of death as the 'elder brother' of sleep and night.

163. Lecture of 20 February 1917 (see above).

164. This relationship of Novalis to night, as a poetic image for a conscious awakening in the spiritual world nearest to the Earth (the astral or Moon sphere), also derives from the influence which the imprint of the astral body of the Nathan Soul that was incorporated in his astral body had upon his soul. This connection between the astral body of the Nathan Soul and the awakening of a 'nocturnal' perception of the spirit world nearest to the Earth is referred to in the Gospels in the scene of the feeding of the five thousand, which the Apostles experience in the imaginative world of night. According to Rudolf Steiner, the Apostles were then able to say to themselves: 'Then we become aware of how, through the power of Christ, what we may call the *night* Sun, the Sun which is [physically] invisible during the *night* . . . sends the heavenly food into our souls . . . And in our

nocturnal imaginative state of clairvoyance we are made aware . . . of what applies to the immediate future, to the fifth thousand [for the fifth cultural epoch]!' (lecture of 10 September 1910, *The Gospel of St Matthew*, op. cit.). This scene which takes place 'at night' (that is, in the astral world) is directly followed by another which also occurs 'at night'—that of the walking on the waters (Matthew 14:25). Both of these accounts testify to the revelation to the disciples of 'the power of imaginative, astral vision' (ibid.), and *are the result of the union of Christ with the astral body of Jesus of Nazareth*. (See further in *The Cycle of the Year as a Path of Initiation*, part IV, op. cit.).

165. Novalis tries ever and again in many other of his Fragments to express this relationship of the two 'egos', the higher and the lower, sometimes in a more pictorial and at other times in a more philosophical form. In the earlier Fragments this theme frequently appears only as a general premonition and sometimes as a question; while in the later ones, on the other hand, the spiritual experience behind the words appears with greater clarity. 'How does the ego absolute become an empirical ego? . . . The ego absolute goes from the infinite to the finite; the mediatory ego from the finite to the infinite. But how does the ego absolute enter into the realm of the finite, where it then becomes a mediatory ego which functions according to its own laws?' 'The pure ego we see always outside—the pure ego is the object. It *is* in us and we see it outside in one and the same moment.' 'The accidental or single form of our ego ceases to be only for this single form—death sets an end only to egotism. The single form is retained for the whole only in as far as it has become a general [form]. We speak of "I" as of one when they are two that are completely different from each other—and yet absolute correlates.'

In these lines there can still be sensed an echo of Novalis' studies of Fichte. In the later Fragments, those written after the death of Sophie von Kühn, the effects of what he has personally experienced come more to the fore. 'The highest task of one's inner development is to make oneself master of one's transcendental self [in anthroposophical terminology we could now say 'Spirit-Self'], and one's ego the equal of its ego.' Or in another Fragment: 'We are not yet "I", but we can and shall become "I". We are the embryos of true ego-development. We are to transform everything into a "you", into a second ego, for only in this way will we rise to the great ego which is *one* and at one level with everything.' These Fragments of Novalis have a profound, spiritual content. If they are used as material for meditation, they can offer the one who meditates a considerable degree of help in understanding the relationships and the interweaving of the higher and lower ego within man's being.

166. AP, New York 1973 (the chapter entitled 'The Age of Kant and Goethe').
167. See note 1.
168. *Knowledge of the Higher Worlds: How is it Achieved?* (RSP 1919).
169. For further details about this mystical process, which is the most important

element of the mysteries of esoteric Christianity, see the lecture of 31 May 1908 (*The Gospel of St John*, op. cit.).

170. Lecture of 23 January 1910 (GA 125, 'Extract of a lecture given at the "Novalis" Branch', Typescript EN 46).

171. In his story from the unfinished novel, *Heinrich von Ofterdingen*, Novalis introduces at the beginning the somewhat enigmatic figure of the 'fable', which is really none other than a personification of the faculty of higher supersensible knowledge. Such knowledge streams forth not in abstract concepts but in *imaginations*. 'You will be the soul of our life', Sophia says to her at the beginning of the new 'spiritual' aeon of evolution.

172. Lecture of 26 October, GA 108 (see note 107).

173. Lecture of 20 February 1917 (*Cosmic and Human Metamorphoses*, op. cit.).

174. The connection with the Angelic Being gradually becomes for Novalis such a concrete experience that in one of his fragments he was enabled to characterise with, one could say, spiritual–scientific precision the difference between the consciousness of a man and that of an Angel: 'Withdrawing into ourselves for us means to abstract ourselves from the outer world. For spirits [Angels], earthly life signifies inner contemplation, entering into oneself, an immanence of activity [this means: when Angels think, their thoughts are the spiritual foundation of our visible world, of 'earthly life']. Thus earthly life issues from a primal reflective deed [of the Angels], a primitive [i.e. 'primal'] entering or gathering into oneself which is as free as our reflective deeds.' In another fragment the same theme appears, though expressed more simply: 'What corresponds to human existence in yonder regions? The daemon, or genius, to whom the body is what the soul is to us.' That is to say, one is speaking of Angels or Geniuses who have, as their outer sheath, what in man corresponds to his soul or astral body. And this means that Novalis already has a glimmer of an awareness that in the fifth post-Atlantean epoch the Angel works in the human astral body (see further in the present chapter).

175. Lecture of 22 December 1908 (*The Christmas Mystery: Novalis as Seer*, op. cit.). In the context of this lecture the words that have been quoted are a direct expression of that spiritual knowledge of Novalis which was the immediate consequence of the 'Damascus event' in his life.

176. In the words of Rudolf Steiner which were quoted on p. 44, and also in many of his lectures that are devoted to the various aspects of the life and work of the Elijah–John–Raphael–Novalis individuality, Rudolf Steiner again and again calls this individuality 'the *herald* of Christianity' in effectively all his incarnations. It follows from the observation of Novalis that has been quoted that the word, 'herald', that is so often used by Rudolf Steiner, refers at once to Novalis himself *and* to his Guardian Angel, who has the task of preparing the individuality of Novalis for that all-embracing world-task which he will have in the future. More will be said about this later.

177. If we would bring together all that has been said in the present work

regarding the *Hierarchic aspect* of the incarnations of the individuality of
Elijah–John–Raphael–Novalis, we can arrive at the following picture:*

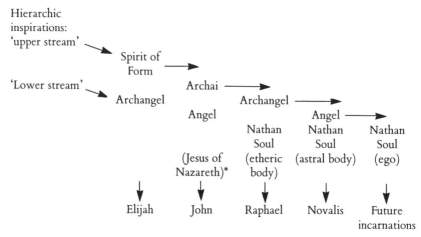

178. Albert Steffen, *Die Botschaft von Novalis* (Dornach 1972).
179. Regarding the Spirit-Self as a reflection of the impulse of the Holy Spirit
   within man, see the lecture of 25 March 1907 (*Festivals of the Seasons*, APC/
   AP 1928).
180. Revelation 3:8 and 12. It is indeed the case that these words are essentially
   a characterisation of the spiritual qualities of the sixth cultural epoch (see
   the lecture of 20 June 1908, *The Apocalypse of St John*, op. cit.) although this
   also signifies that they can be applied to any of its true representatives or
   precursors, as Novalis was. Regarding Elijah's role as one of the spiritual
   pillars in the 'temple of the New Covenant', which at the end of earthly
   evolution will pass over into Jupiter, see the lecture of 26 June 1908 (ibid.).
   There are various legends in Christian tradition about the individuality
   who will come to represent the second column. Some say it will be Moses,
   others Enoch, he who, like Elijah, was 'borne up into heaven' (see the so-
   called 'Gospel of Nicodemus', ch. 26).
181. Rudolf Steiner also speaks in various places about the being of man in
   words such as these. See for example in his article, 'The Way of Michael
   and what preceded it' (*Anthroposophical Leading Thoughts*, op. cit.): 'Man is
   spirit. And *his* world is that of spirits.'
182. In these words of Novalis, 'we would be inspired at once by ourselves and
   the spirit', the expression 'by ourselves' refers to the forces of the astral
   body of the Nathan Soul working within his soul, while the expression 'by

* It is here that there takes place the first and more outward association between the
individuality of John the Baptist and Jesus of Nazareth (the Nathan Soul). In a certain
sense one can say that this was their first meeting on Earth since Lemurian times. See
also note 148.

the spirit' refers to the Spirit-Self who inspires him and, hence, to the Angelic Being who is its bearer (see note 179).

183. Regarding the three fundamental qualities of the sixth cultural epoch, see the lectures of 15 June 1915 (*Preparing for the Sixth Epoch*, AP 1957) and 9 October 1918 (*The Work of the Angels in Man's Astral Body*, RSP 1973). The sayings of Novalis that correspond, respectively, to the three qualities may be found on the following pages:

   69, 70, 71, 75, 77, 78, 89, 97, 98, 116, 215
   84, 88, 89, 90
   60, 61, 63, 96, 97

   See also Rudolf Steiner's words about Novalis on pp. 56, 57, 103, 130, 131, 146, 153.

184. Lecture of 9 October 1918 (see above).

185. Rudolf Steiner says about this evolution in the realm of the Angels: 'The Beings [Angels] who guided the old Egypto-Chaldean culture were not under the direction of the Christ. It is only since that period that they have placed themselves under His guidance. Their progress consists in that they may now guide our fifth post-Atlantean cultural period under Christ's influence; they are following Him in the higher worlds' (*The Spiritual Guidance of Man and Humanity*, AP 1970, ch. 3).

186. Ibid., as with the following quotation.

187. Lecture of 2 May 1912 (*Earthly and Cosmic Man*, op. cit.).

188. Lecture of 22 December 1908 (*The Christmas Mystery: Novalis as Seer*, op. cit.).

189. *The Spiritual Guidance of Man and Humanity*, op. cit., ch. 3.

190. Ibid. Rudolf Steiner speaks as follows of how these Angelic Beings have, from our time onwards, become the guides to a new experience of Christ in the etheric realm: 'And as in our time the same great teachers [Angels] who have already guided mankind through the Egypto-Chaldean culture are working, so also in the twentieth century it will be these same teachers who will lead men to behold the Christ as Paul beheld Him. They will show mankind how the Christ not only works upon the Earth but also spiritualises the whole solar system' (ibid.).

191. Lecture of 9 October 1918, *The Work of the Angels in Man's Astral Body*, op. cit.; the next two quotations are from the same source.

192. In the same lecture (see note 184) Rudolf Steiner also speaks of how the Angels will be forced to transfer their activity from men's astral bodies to their etheric bodies if by the year 2000 this work of theirs in the astral bodies of human beings is not perceived by them in a conscious way (if not clairvoyantly then at least through the communications of spiritual science). Such a step would eventually lead to the arousing of new and extremely harmful instincts within human beings. Rudolf Steiner refers to *three* kinds of such instincts, which will work particularly in the sexual realm, in the realm where the medicinal properties of certain substances

are used in an instinctive way, and in the realm of a new technology which will arise from the merging of human soul-forces with the soulless activity of mechanical devices. If we now consider the creative work of Novalis from this point of view, we find everywhere the rudiments of those faculties of spirit and soul which mankind will need in order to withstand the growth of these instincts of such devastating power. Against the enticements of sexuality—his lofty ideal of love as a creative cosmic power; against the use of medicine that is directed solely towards the satisfaction of personal egoism—the principle of *healing art*, which we encounter in the forms and colours of Raphael's paintings, and which appears again in a different form in Novalis' art of the word: 'And now we behold the wonderful artistic power of Raphael appearing again in the poetry of Novalis, which so stirs and enraptures the heart. Everything which human eyes have seen through Raphael, with this could human hearts be permeated when it surfaced again in Novalis' (lecture of 28 September 1924, *The Last Address*, op. cit. Novalis' views about medicine, with which he began seriously to concern himself in the last years of his life, also bear witness to this: his endeavour to place *man* at the centre of all research, not merely as a physical but principally as a being of soul and spirit; to restore to medical science its deeper spiritual meaning and moral foundations; and to regard the process of healing as one of bringing man's being, as a microcosm, into harmony with the forces and especially the rhythms of the macrocosm. Despite the fragmentary character of his observations, these and many other thoughts of Novalis have a far greater significance for the future of medicine than it would appear at first glance (see W. Holtzapfel, *Die Sprache der Krankheit*, Dornach 1986, ch. 4 and M. Schad, *Novalis, Grundriss einer Menschenkunde in seinen Fragmenten*, Stuttgart 1986). And finally, if we cast our eye over everything that Novalis has said about the natural sciences and especially about physics, astronomy and mathematics, we may gain an impression of a relationship to nature and technology which is such as to be able to help mankind to deal also with the third kind of destructive instincts. For a relationship to nature such as Novalis bore within himself makes it possible for the spiritual *truly* to be discerned in all material phenomena: 'Through the magical idealism of his poetry, he can make the most insignificant material thing live again *in all its spiritual light and glory*' (ibid.). Of course, much that lived in Novalis was still in the earliest stages of its development, which is not to deny that his entire creative work shows us the *direction* in which mankind must evolve in the future if the dangers that have been referred to are to be avoided. And this is also the direction in which this individuality will subsequently seek ways (possibly in a completely different form) of fulfilling his mission of healing amongst man.

193. Lecture of 9 November 1914 (GA 158, *The Connection of Man with the Elemental World. Finland and the Kalevala*, Typescript Z 144).
194. Lecture of 28 September 1924, *The Last Address*, op. cit.

195. Lecture of 26 October 1908, GA 108.
196. In the lecture of 20 May 1912 (*Earthly and Cosmic Man*, op. cit.) Rudolf Steiner refers to the connection that exists between the beginning of the activity of the Spirit-Self principle within man and the new appearance of Christ in the etheric realm: 'I have often intimated how entry into the Spirit-Self will come about. I have said that in the course of the next three thousand years an increasing number of people will experience the appearance of the Christ-impulse, that human beings will gradually become capable of experiencing the Christ-impulse in the spiritual worlds. But the experiencing of the influences streaming in from the spiritual world will have to be something with which men become more and more familiar in the times that lie ahead.'
197. Lecture of 9 November 1914 (see above). The quotations that follow are from the same source.
198. Albert Steffen, *Die Botschaft von Novalis*, Dornach 1972.
199. If, in accordance with the law of spiritual reflection set forth by Rudolf Steiner in the lecture of 17 February 1918 (*The Mission of the Archangel Michael*, AP 1980), we take as mid-point the *beginning* of the sixth cultural epoch, corresponding approximately to the thirty-fifth century after the birth of Christ, we arrive on the one hand, if we deduct fifteen centuries, at the twentieth century, which is immediately preceded by the ending of the dark age of the Kali-Yuga (1899); while if we add a further fifteen centuries to the thirty-fifth century, we reach the fiftieth century after Christ's birth, corresponding to the beginning of the last third of the sixth cultural epoch, which is separated from our time by roughly three thousand years. This time will, according to Rudolf Steiner, be the beginning of that 'golden age' of which Novalis had a premonition (see p. 68). Thus according to the law of spiritual reflection, everything which takes place amongst men during the twentieth century, by way of the development and the spreading of modern spiritual science or Anthroposophy, is none other than the foundation for the future 'golden' or 'moral' epoch. For everything that we sow in our time as a seed of spiritual knowledge in the evolution of humanity will then rise up and bear its fruits, though not in the form of thoughts but of a higher magic.
200. Regarding Michael's participation in the creation of the first man by Jahve-Elohim and the spiritual connection that has existed since that time between the sphere of Michael and the individuality of Adam, see p. 8, where more will also be found about the relationship of Michael, as the supersensible leader of the people of the Old Testament, to the prophet Elijah.
201. This observation derives from the fact that, according to the law of spiritual reflection (see note 199), the Mystery of Golgotha, which took place in the fourth post-Atlantean age, is with respect to the *temporal* centre of earthly evolution the spiritual–historical counter-pole of the Fall, which occurred approximately in the middle of the Lemurian age (see

the lecture of 14 October 1911, *From Jesus to Christ*, RSP 1973). This means that our fifth post-Atlantean cultural epoch corresponds to the paradisaical condition that preceded the Fall of mankind.

202. Rudolf Steiner says about the sixth cultural epoch and its relationship to the concluding seventh epoch, when mankind will approach the great catastrophe in real earnest: 'But we, in that we speak today on the basis of Anthroposophy, are able to say in full consciousness what is to happen, that the Christ will gradually reveal Himself to ever higher powers in human beings. . .' This is the thought which, though expressed in different words, stands behind the following observation of Novalis: 'In Christianity one has eternities to study. Everything becomes ever higher, more manifold and more magnificent.' And then Rudolf Steiner continues: '. . . [and we] are able to say how *the teachers*, who up to now have taught only individual peoples and individual men . . .'—this relates at once to the Maitreya Bodhisattva and his incarnation as Jeshu ben Pandira and also to the individuality of Novalis in his three incarnations amongst the people of the Old Testament with which we are familiar—'will become the interpreters of the great Christ-event *for all men* who are willing to listen. We are able to speak of how, through the dawning of the age of love [the sixth cultural epoch], the conditions for this age of morality are prepared. And then will come the last great period [the seventh cultural epoch] . . . Then, strengthened through the power *that flows from the Mystery of Golgotha and from the age of morality*, men will take into themselves forces of hope. This is the most important gift that they need in order to face the catastrophe and to begin thereafter a new life, just as the post-Atlantean age also ushered in a new phase of life' (lecture of 3 December 1911, *Faith, Love, Hope*, op. cit.).

In these words we have a further confirmation that the 'moral' or 'golden' age will begin in the sixth cultural epoch. Nor did Novalis limit human evolution to this 'golden age' or think of it as a *final* goal, when he says: 'The world becomes to the living ever more infinite—thus there can never be an end to the binding of the manifold, there can never be a condition of inactivity for the thinking ego. Golden ages may come—but they do not bring an end of things—the goal of man is not the golden age. He shall exist eternally and be and remain a well-ordered individual—this is the tendency of his nature.'

203. Lecture of 14 October 1911, *From Jesus to Christ*, op. cit.
204. Lecture of 3 December 1911 (see above). (The next quotation is from the same source.)
205. The particular connection between the individuality of Elijah–John–Raphael–Novalis and the future Maitreya Buddha has already been spoken of in the present work. See p. 41 and note 23.
206. Lectures of 3 December 1911 (*Faith, Love, Hope*, op. cit.) and 20 November 1911 (*Esoteric Christianity and the Mission of Christian Rosenkreutz*, RSP 1984).
207. The phrase, 'magical idealism', encompasses not only the epoch of

'magical morality', as the final goal of a certain cycle of evolution, but also the epoch of 'aesthetic impulses' or 'emotions' which precedes it (lectures of 18 November 1911—see previous note—and 14 January 1912, GA 143), to which the word 'idealism' refers.

288. Behind this reference to the New Jerusalem we may sense an echo of the Novalis individuality's memories of his spiritual connection with Lazarus–John while the latter was passing, on the island of Patmos, through that initiation into the future destiny of the Earth and of humanity, the results of which he later set forth in the Book of Revelation.

209. Lecture of 3 December 1911 (see above). The quotations that follow are from the same source.

210. Lecture of 29 June 1908 (*The Apocalypse of St John*, RSP 1977).

211. See *Occult Science—An Outline*, op. cit) the end of the chapter entitled 'Present and Future Evolution of the World and of Mankind'. In an unpublished lecture of 21 October 1907 in Berlin, 'White and Black Magic', Rudolf Steiner refers to the 'first principle' which 'holds good of modern white magic' in the following words: 'Love for the whole of mankind, the widening of the sphere of one's love . . .' And he goes on: '. . . through white magic the Earth will be brought ever closer to Sun-nature'. However, the beginning of this process of the gradual spiritualisation of the Earth is the formation of the new Etheric Christ-sphere in its spiritual surroundings (see note 138).

212. See the lecture of 31 December 1922 (*Man and the World of Stars and The Spiritual Communion of Mankind*, AP 1963).

213. Lecture of 27 February 1917 (*Cosmic and Human Metamorphoses*, op. cit.).

214. *Esoteric Christianity and the Mission of Christian Rosenkreutz*, lecture of 4 November 1911 (RSP 1984).

215. In many of his lectures Rudolf Steiner speaks of how the spiritual work that is accomplished in anthroposophical groups and branches is a direct preparation of mankind for the sixth cultural epoch. After all that has been said above concerning the relationship of Novalis to the Angelic Being who guides him in the principle of the Spirit-Self, the following words of Rudolf Steiner acquire a particular significance in this connection: 'We may therefore picture to ourselves that through uniting in brotherliness in working groups, something hovers invisibly over our work, something that is like the child of the forces of the Spirit-Self—the Spirit-Self that is nurtured by the Beings of the higher Hierarchies in order that it may stream down into our souls when they are again on Earth in the sixth cultural period. In our brotherly working groups we perform work that streams upwards to those forces that are being prepared for the Spirit-Self' (lecture of 15 June 1915, *Preparing for the Sixth Epoch*, AP 1957). In the same way, the anthroposophical deepening of the fundamental truths of Christianity, an endeavour whose first messenger was Novalis, with his purely spiritual understanding of the Christ-impulse, is already the beginning of mankind's transition from the fifth to the sixth cultural

epoch: 'We have now almost reached the moment . . . when men must of necessity form a connection with the spiritual aspect of Christianity, with what Christianity should really be, in order that its true spiritual content may be drawn forth. This will come about through the anthroposophic deepening of Christianity. When we direct the insights of Anthroposophy towards Christianity, we are following the world-historical necessity of preparing for the . . . Christian epoch which livingly anticipates the in-streaming of Manes in the sixth epoch' (the first of the two lectures of 30 May 1908, *The Gospel of St John*, op. cit.).

216. See the lecture of 6 October 1911 (*From Jesus to Christ*, op. cit.).
217. Lecture of 26 October 1908, GA 108 (see note 123).
218. Lecture of 20 July 1924 (*Karmic Relationships*, vol. VI, RSP 1971).
219. Lecture of 28 September 1924 (*The Last Address*, op. cit.).
220. Ibid.
221. Quoted by Albert Steffen in *Die Botschaft von Novalis*, Dornach 1972.
222. That Novalis here mentions 'Hindustan' represents an echo of the last great deed of the Greek Archangel, which he accomplished under the guidance of the Time-Spirit, Michael, and which came to expression in Alexander's campaigns to spread Greek culture *even* in India.
223. In this extract from Novalis' letter to Fr. Schlegel one can—where he speaks of the union of the Greek world (antiquity), which lived primarily in a consciousness of space, and Christianity, which lives in a conscious experience of the stream of time—also sense an echo of the supersensible connection of the entelechy of John the Baptist with John the Evangelist, who united the Greek doctrine of the Logos with the fundamental concepts of Christianity, in particular, in the prologue of his Gospel. In another connection Rudolf Steiner once referred to how, in the Gospel according to John, the inspirations and the entelechy of John the Baptist are especially strongly in evidence until the chapter about the raising of Lazarus, so that it would actually be possible to speak of a *dual* authorship of the first twelve chapters of this Gospel (see the lecture of 23 May 1908, *The Gospel of St John*, op. cit.).
224. See L. Kleeberg, *Wege und Worte. Erinnerungen an Rudolf Steiner aus Tagenbüchern und aus Briefen*, Stuttgart 1990.
225. The full wording of this extract from Novalis' letter runs as follows: '. . . surely, dear Sir, you will grant that I am right in this, and in any event pardon my youthful zeal: but an error of whole generations—at the cost of the ordinary faculty of human good sense—which concerns the desecration of our dear ones could entitle one to have the fiery zeal of an Elijah, he who had the prophets of Baal slaughtered by the Kidron brook in a right Jewish way.'
226. See also note 72.
227. Lecture of 11 April 1909 (*The Festivals and Their Meaning; Easter*, RSP 1981).
228. Lecture of 27 August 1924 (*Karmic Relationships*, vol. VIII, RSP 1975).

229. Lecture of 31 December 1913 (*Christ and the Spiritual World and The Search for the Holy Grail*, RSP 1963).

230. In one of his lectures Rudolf Steiner says that the formation and increase in the number of spots on the Sun (that is, its gradual dimming), which has now been observed even by ordinary astronomy, testifies to the 'fall' of the Sun, and is in a spiritual sense called forth by Christ's departure from it (lecture of 8 August 1924, *Karmic Relationships*, vol. III, RSP 1977). The extract from Novalis' writings that has been cited is like an echo of the Gospel words: 'The Sun will be darkened and the Moon will not give its light' (Mark 13:24; Matthew 24:29).

231. Lecture of 11 April 1909 (*The Festivals and Their Meaning; Easter*, op. cit.).

232. Lecture of 22 December 1908 (*The Christmas Mystery: Novalis as Seer*, op. cit.).

233. Lecture of 29 June 1909 (*The Gospel of St John in Relation to the Three Other Gospels*, op. cit.).

234. Lecture of 30 June 1909 (ibid.).

235. See the lecture of 17 August 1924 and *The Spiritual Guidance of Man and Humanity*, op. cit., ch. 3.

236. Lecture of 11 April 1909 (see above).

237. See 1 Kings 19:19–20, and also note 72.

238. See 2 Kings 2:13–15 and also the lecture of 14 December 1911 (*Turning-Points in Spiritual History*, op. cit.) from which the two quotations that follow are taken.

239. In a remarkable way something of a similar kind is repeated in the case of John the Baptist. What through the event of Damascus was for Paul the fundamental experience which he was to express in the words, 'Not I, but Christ in me', John had already experienced—albeit in a form appropriate for the time *before* the Mystery of Golgotha—when he felt within himself the influence of the 'particular Angel' whose task it was to prepare the incarnation on Earth of the Christ, the Bearer of the principle of the World-Ego. Thus John the Baptist at the Turning-Point of Time is, from this point of view, also the precursor and preparer of the Damascus-event for Paul and for many other disciples and disseminators of Christianity, particularly in the first centuries after its founding. Rudolf Steiner refers to this mutual relationship as follows: 'And while he [man] formerly received the Angels, so today must he, through devotion to the Christ-Being, receive the Christ. While John was still able to say: Not I, but the Angel in me has been sent and uses me as a tool in order to prepare, so must the man of today say with Paul: "Not I, but Christ in Me." He shall learn to understand Christ in such a way as spiritual science teaches him' (lecture of 25 February 1911, GA 127, Typescript AQ 21:4).

240. The ancient Hebrews regarded Jahve as their group-soul. See the lecture of 19 June 1908 (*The Apocalypse of St John*, RSP/AP 1977).

241. See further regarding the initiation of Elisha by Elijah in the lecture of 14 December 1911 (*Turning Points in Spiritual History*, op. cit.).

242. Lecture of 1 January 1913 (*The Bhagavad Gita and the Epistles of St Paul*, AP 1971).
243. Lecture of 26 October 1908, GA 108 (as note 123).
244. Ibid.
245. Numbers 25:12–13.
246. Genesis 14:18 and Hebrews 7:2.
247. See note 94.
248. Regarding the repetition of the Mystery of Golgotha in the supersensible worlds which preceded the new appearance of Christ in an etheric body, see the lecture of 2 May 1913 (*Occult Science and Occult Development*, RSP 1966). [The passage in question is not to be found in the English edition, which appeared before the German edition, where the relevant passage is included, was published.]
249. Lecture of 22 December 1908 (*The Christmas Mystery: Novalis as Seer*, op. cit.).
250. See *The Spiritual Guidance of Man and Humanity*, op. cit., ch. 1.
251. Revelation 21:5. See also *The Apocalypse of St John*, lectures of 29 and 30 June 1908 (op. cit.).
252. Although from a somewhat different viewpoint, the 'creation' of man from 'the dust of the Earth' by the Moon-Elohim, Jahve, may be seen as an indication of the connection between the paradisaical condition of mankind and the forces of the Moon (see the lecture of 25 August 1910, *Genesis*, RSP 1982).
253. It follows from indications given by Rudolf Steiner in the lecture of 2 October 1913 (*The Fifth Gospel*, op. cit.) regarding the eclipse of the Sun which took place on Maundy Thursday, that at the moment when Jesus was taken into custody the Moon was full.
254. Mark 14:51–52.
255. Lecture of 23 September 1912 (*The Gospel of St Mark*, op. cit.).
256. Mark 16:5.
257. In the esoteric lesson of 16 January 1908 (GA 245) Rudolf Steiner speaks of how any true experience of the past, which since the Fall has been connected with an inner sensing of the activity of irregular Moon-forces within the soul, calls forth in man a feeling of shame, while any experience of the forces of the future and especially of the future Jupiter-condition awakens a feeling of fear, terror. This is why the Gospel of St Mark speaks of how the women who came to the grave were 'terrified' when they saw there the Risen One in the form of a youth (16:5). 'And they went out and fled from the tomb; for trembling and dread had come upon them. And they said nothing to anyone, for they were afraid' (16:8).
258. The final resurrection in supersensible bodies through the mitigation of the new Holy Spirit that proceeds from Christ—in the etheric body after the 'first death' and in the astral body after the 'second death'—leads directly to the transition to the new spiritual aeon of Jupiter (lecture of 30 June 1908, *The Apocalypse of St John*, op. cit.).

259. In the lecture of 7 March 1914 (*Pre-Earthly Deeds of Christ*, Steiner Book Centre, N. Vancouver 1976) Rudolf Steiner speaks of how the Egypto–Babylonian–Chaldean epoch was in a sense a repetition in the post-Atlantean age of the Lemurian period, which for its part was a small-scale repetition within the confines of the Earth incarnation of the Old Moon condition, just as the Hyperborean and Polarian periods were miniature repetitions, respectively, of the Old Sun and Old Saturn incarnations of our planet.

260. Lecture of 17 June 1910 (*The Mission of Folk-Souls*, op. cit.). The fact that in the passage quoted Novalis has in mind not so much the Nordic Gods as those of Greece, Egypt and even India (see 'Materials for "The Novices as Saïs"', part four, and also Novalis' words quoted on p. 79) does not materially affect the issue that there is an inner connection between the words of Novalis and Rudolf Steiner. For in the passage quoted above Novalis points above all to *the reality of the actual spiritual process taking place in the higher worlds*, employing for this purpose those concepts and images of the ancient Gods which were most accessible to him. For his part, Rudolf Steiner often speaks of how both Nordic and Greek Gods belonged to one and the same etheric stream on ancient Atlantis (see, for example, the lecture of 4 August 1908, *Universe, Earth and Man*, RSP 1987).

261. See *The Spiritual Guidance of Man and Humanity*, op. cit., ch. 3.

262. Ibid. See also Rudolf Steiner's words quoted on p. 85.

263. John 8:58.

264. Revelation 10:6.

265. Rudolf Steiner, in the lecture quoted on p. 92, continues as follows: 'All the forces opposed to Odin and Thor, everything which has developed as a counter-force, will once again be visible to the human soul in a mighty tableau. But the human soul would not progress, it would not be able to defend itself against harmful influences, if it were subject solely to the forces known to the old clairvoyance.' Novalis also refers to these forces of opposition, in his inspired poetic vision, in the quoted section from the fourth 'Hymn to the Night' (lines 25–32). Here he also speaks of how only as a result of the inner connection of the human soul with the Christ-impulse (lines 33–36) do 'the resistance' (28) and 'the frenzy' (32) of the opposing powers become 'in vain' (31).

266. Rudolf Steiner speaks about the 'race of Michaelites' in the lecture of 3 August 1924 (*Karmic Relationships*, vol. III., op. cit.), and about Novalis as 'a radiant forerunner ... [of the] Michael-stream' in the lecture of 28 September 1924 (*The Last Address*, op. cit.).

267. See Appendix 1.

268. Address given at the Laying of the Foundation Stone of the First Goetheanum, 20 September 1913 (*Guidance in Esoteric Training*, RSP 1972).

269. See the lecture of 30 December 1913 (*Christ and the Spiritual World. The Search for the Holy Grail*, op. cit.).

270. Address of 20 September 1913, see above.

271. Ibid.
272. Matthew 18:3, then 18:4–5, 11:11.
273. Lecture of 11 February 1911 (GA 127, Typescript AQ 22:2).
274. Matthew 18:10.
275. John 3:3–6.
276. *The Spiritual Guidance of Man and Humanity*, op. cit., ch. 1. See also the lectures of 11 and 25 February 1911, GA 127 (respectively, Typescript AQ 22:2 and Typescript AQ 21:4).
277. See *The Spiritual Guidance of Man and Humanity*, ch. 1. The quotation that follows is from the same source.
278. Ibid, as with the quotation that follows.
279. Lecture of 26 September 1909 (*The Gospel of St Luke*, op. cit.).
280. Lecture of 25 February 1911, see above.
281. See Matthew 16:13–16 and the lecture of 11 September 1910 (*The Gospel of St Matthew*, op. cit.).
282. Lecture of 25 February 1911.
283. Lecture of 11 September 1910 (*The Gospel of St Matthew*, op. cit.).
284. Lecture of 25 February 1911.
285. Lecture of 8 May 1912 (GA 143, AQ 18:1).
286. Lecture of 11 February 1911 GA 127. In the lecture of 25 February 1911 Rudolf Steiner says of this process: 'It follows from the needs of the Christianising process—from the living out of St Paul's dictum, "Christ in me"—that we say: we must permeate ourselves with the transformation of what lives in us in earliest childhood, for then is Christ in us.' Paul the Apostle was able to experience the Damascus-event only because he had a natural karmic predisposition which came to expression in his *premature birth* (see 1 Corinthians 15:8 and the lecture of 7 July 1909, *The Gospel of St John in Relation to the Other Three Gospels*, op. cit., and, associated with this, in the awakening of the spiritual forces of early childhood in his later years.
287. Lecture of 1 January 1911 (*Occult History*, op. cit.).
288. Novalis speaks of children, childhood and the various aspects of a child's life in a number of places in his works and fragments. See, for example, his words quoted on pp. 69–70, 90, 99, 105 of the present work. It should also be emphasised that, when speaking of children, Novalis never has in mind a sentimental relationship to them but always a purely *spiritual* relationship to the cosmic forces which are active within them in the early years of childhood. The following words, for example, may serve as an illustration of his completely objective relationship to children: 'Not all children are children.' And in another fragment: 'When Christ says, become like little children, he means children who have not lost their freedom, and not the spoilt, pampered, mawkish children of today.'
289. Quoted in Novalis' *Collected Works* (German edition), vol. 4, pp. 639–640.
290. The whole verse runs as follows:

Now burns with mighty power that hidden fire—
My ancient being—deep in the structure
Of the Earth: You shall be a priestly
Sacrificer, singing the song of the return.

In this verse, as Ritter-Schaumberg demonstrates convincingly in his book about Novalis (see note 504), the first two lines relate to Novalis and the last two to Schlegel, 'who, as no-one else, was in a position to recognise Novalis' special being, and his unusual possibilities' (ibid.). In the poem quoted above ('Der sterbende Genius'), Novalis compares himself with the higher genius who must shortly leave this world and is handing over his priestly initiation together with his spiritual powers to his friend and pupil so that he may further his earthly task as 'priestly sacrificer' and sing 'the song of the return' of humanity to its original divine state.

In a similar way, Schlegel also experiences his relationship to Novalis as one of a pupil to a future teacher. In a letter of 2 December 1798 he writes to Novalis: 'Probably *you* have a greater talent for being a new Christ [that is, a new teacher of a higher Christianity], one who finds in me his gallant Paul.' And then, more decisively: 'Maybe you have the choice, my friend, of being either the last Christ, the Brutus of the old religion, or the Christ of the new Gospel.'

This relationship of the two personalities, and also the handing over by the one to the other of the wherewithal to continue his task, is in a remarkable way reminiscent—even though admittedly in a completely different time and in quite different spiritual circumstances—of the relationship between the prophet Elijah and the prophet Elisha as this is portrayed in the Old Testament (see note 72 and p. 85).

Here this parallel can only be indicated outwardly; a consideration of its karmic foundations lies quite beyond the scope of the present work.

291. See note 239.
292. See p. 30 and note 106.
293. There is a tradition associated with how Raphael painted the *Sistine Madonna*. Most of the works of his later period were not painted by Raphael alone but with the help of numerous pupils. Usually he made a preliminary sketch, discussed the general features of the composition, together with the colours to be used, and then left the task of execution to the pupils, resuming his own work on the painting only in the final stages and, as a rule, finishing it with his own hand. The *Sistine Madonna* was painted in an altogether different way. Already before beginning the task Raphael was for some time in a particularly festive mood. Then, having sent all the pupils away and having ordered that he be brought a meagre quantity of food twice a day to be left outside by the door, he shut himself up in his studio. Thus for some weeks, without any preliminary sketches or drafts, he painted this mysterious picture in complete solitude and without interruption. But those of his pupils whose task it was to bring him

his food twice a day saw from afar, through the half-open door, the radiant face of their teacher and the 'unearthly light' which filled the room where he was working. And so the opinion soon spread amongst the pupils that the heavenly Queen herself with her holy child had appeared to Raphael in a vision in order that he might, like St Luke, the patron of all true artists, engrave her heavenly features in line and colour for all generations to come (see also note 325).

294. Lecture of 8 May 1912, GA 143 (Typescript AQ 18:1).

295. *The Spiritual Guidance of Man and Humanity*, op. cit., ch. 1.

296. Lecture of 25 February 1911 (GA 127, AQ 21:4). At this point it should be added that Rudolf Steiner distinguishes very clearly between the forces of the Nathan Soul and those of Christ within man. The former represent that 'region' within the human soul with which alone the Christ-impulse can unite and out of which it can work. The following words of Rudolf Steiner offer a very precise indication of this: 'The Christ-power must unite with the best forces of the child-nature in man. It may not link itself with the faculties that man has corrupted, with what derives from a wisdom that is born merely from the intellect, but rather with what has remained from the child-nature of primeval times. That is the best; it is this that must be reinvigorated and thereafter fructify the other parts of man's nature' (lecture of 26 September 1909, *The Gospel of St Luke*, op. cit.).

297. According to Rudolf Steiner (see the lectures of 15 March 1910, *The Reappearance of Christ in the Etheric*, AP 1983, and 4 September 1910, *The Gospel of St Matthew*, op. cit.) it was Melchizedek who initiated Abraham into the mystery of the 'I am'. Through this initiation he was able clairvoyantly to penetrate into the spiritual sphere of activity of Jehovah, without which his covenant with the Moon–Elohim would have been impossible.

298. Abraham's wife, too, as one who participated in his covenant with Jahve-Elohim, received the name Sarah instead of her former name of Sarai (Genesis 17:15). From the standpoint of the ancient Hebrew language, this change of Abraham's name (and to some extent also that of Sarah) came about through adding the sound ה, the holiest letter of the Hebrew alphabet and that with which the word 'Jehovah' (יהוה) begins. Thus in this change in the Patriarch's name we have a reflection of the bond concluded by him with the God Jahve. Such a change in a person's name, as a means of showing that the person concerned has reached a certain level of initiation where he receives an altogether new task of life, we encounter not only in the Old but also in the New Testament. Thus, through his meeting with Christ, Simon becomes Peter; the initiated Lazarus becomes John, the Evangelist and writer of the Book of Revelation (see *Christianity as Mystical Fact and the Mysteries of Antiquity*, RSP 1972 and *The Gospel of St John*, op. cit.; and finally, Saul, as a result of the event of Damascus, becomes Paul.

299. At this point the Old Testament text is in an occult sense particularly

exact. Thus the writer goes on to speak of how one of the three men (Angels) remained talking with Abraham (18:22–23) while the other two made their way towards Sodom (18:22; 19:1), which is a way of referring to the special connection of Abraham with that Angel who initiated him into the mysteries of the physical body. Hence, in the conversation with this Angel, Abraham says that he is but 'dust and ashes' (18:27), words which refer to the mysteries of the physical body; while the other two Angels rain upon Sodom 'brimstone and fire from heaven' (19:24), that is in a spiritual sense ('from heaven') they send down upon it destructive forces from the etheric (brimstone) and astral (fire) spheres. But Lot's wife, who—like his whole family—had been initiated by the two visiting Angels (19:1–17) only into the mysteries of the etheric and astral bodies, but not into the mysteries of the physical body was therefore, by her disobedience, turned into a pillar of salt (19:26).

However, the three Angels who presented themselves to Abraham in the spirit have a still deeper significance. For in an esoteric sense they are none other than the bearers of the spiritual forces which had poured forth during Lemuria and Atlantis into human evolution as a result of the three preparatory stages of the Mystery of Golgotha which had taken place in the spiritual worlds (see the lectures collected in GA 152 [several of which exist in English translation in the form of separate lectures]). These spiritual forces which had defended the human physical, etheric and astral bodies against the temptations of the opposing powers unite now in a particular form—represented by the three Angels—with the stream of heredity proceeding from Abraham, so as to prepare the central event of earthly evolution—the Mystery of Golgotha.

300. With his intervention, in the defence of the Jahve-impulse, Phinehas not only rescued the work of Moses amongst the Hebrew people but also renewed the covenant between Jahve and Abraham which had been concluded through the mediation of Melchizedek (see note 297). Thus Jahve has the following to say to Moses about Phinehas: 'Behold, I give unto him my *covenant of peace*: And he shall have it, and his seed after him, even the covenant of an *everlasting priesthood*' (Numbers 25:12–13). The allusion in these words to the 'covenant of peace' and the 'covenant of an everlasting priesthood' is a mark of how Phinehas is directly connected through his initiation with the stream of Melchizedek, who in the Old Testament is called the 'King of Peace' ('King of Salem', Genesis 14:18). The Apostle Paul also calls him 'a priest for ever' (see note 14).

301. Regarding Nathanael and his attainment of the fifth stage of the pre-Christian Path of Initiation, see the lecture of 23 May 1908 (*The Gospel of St John*, op. cit.) and the note that follows.

302. In the lecture of 23 May 1908, Rudolf Steiner characterises the Initiate who has attained this fifth stage of initiation thus: 'But the Initiate of the fifth degree had made a certain sacrifice, had stripped away his personality to the extent that he received the being of the particular folk into his own

personal nature. While other men felt their souls within the Folk-Soul, he had received the Folk-Soul into his own being, and this was because whatever belonged to his personality was of no importance to him, only the common Folk-Spirit. Therefore an Initiate of this kind was called by the name of his particular folk.' And in the lecture of 3 October 1913 (*The Fifth Gospel*, op. cit.) he characterises this degree of initiation as follows: 'In the fifth degree the person was ready for an extension of consciousness, giving him the power to become a spiritual guardian of the people to whom he belonged . . . We know that the peoples of the Earth are led and guided by those Beings of the spiritual Hierarchies known as Archangeloi or Archangels. An Initiate of the fifth degree was lifted into this sphere, *so that he participated in the life of the Archangels.* Such Initiates of the fifth degree were needed in the cosmos . . . In the souls of those who had been initiated in the fifth degree, the Archangeloi read what was needful for a particular people. To enable the Archangeloi to lead the people aright, there must be Initiates of the fifth degree upon the Earth. These Initiates are the mediators between those who are the actual leaders of a people, the Archangeloi, and the people itself. They as it were bear upwards into the sphere of the Archangeloi whatever is needed in order that the particular folk may be led in the right way.' Elijah possessed both of the spiritual qualities described in these words. To this testifies his activity as the representative of the Folk-Soul of the ancient Hebrews and also his direct connection with the Folk-Spirit, with the countenance of Jahve, the Archangel Michael, who was then the leader of the Hebrew people and who has already been spoken of at some length in the earlier part of this book (see Chapter 1). Rudolf Steiner refers, in the lectures of 7 and 8 June 1910 (*The Mission of the Individual Folk Souls in Relation to Teutonic Mythology*, op. cit.) to how the connection of the individual representatives of a people with the Archangelic Being who guides it is primarily through the forces of the *etheric body.*

303. Also at this point in the Old Testament the double nature of the danger threatening the etheric body of the ancient Hebrew people appears with complete clarity. For Ahab proposes to Naboth that he (Naboth) should either voluntarily hand the vineyard over to him in exchange for another (a Luciferic temptation) or sell it (an Ahrimanic temptation). See 1 Kings 21:2.

304. Hence in the scene where the spiritual bond is concluded between Abraham and Jahve–Elohim we find the following description: 'And He [Jahve-Elohim] brought him [Abraham] forth, and said: *Look now toward heaven and count the stars,* if you can number them. And He said to him: As many will be your descendants' (Genesis 15:5). The reference here to heaven and the stars is an expression of the connection which exists from this moment between Abraham and the entire astral cosmos, whence the forces of the astral body formed by Christ for His incarnation were, in time, to descend to the Earth. (The term 'astral body' denotes starry body

or body of stars.) It is to this fact, that this spiritual connection plays a highly important part in the future destiny of Abraham, and through him in the entire history of the Hebrew people, that the following words refer: 'Abraham believed in the Lord, and He counted it to him for righteousness' (6).

305. This process of the gradual incarnation amongst the ancient Hebrews of the forces of the macrocosmic astral body of the Christ is described by Rudolf Steiner in the lecture of 17 September 1912 (*The Gospel of St Mark*, op. cit.) where he says in particular: 'What was later to dwell in a single human being was in the case of Elijah still, as it were, the group-*soul* of the ancient Hebrew people. What was to descend as the individual *soul* into every individual breast at the time of John was as yet in the supersensible worlds.' But as this astral body was fashioned by the Christ Himself, it bore within itself, in the manner of a prophecy, a reflection of His Ego— the impulse of which He was, through His incarnation, to bring into earthly evolution as a whole. Hence Rudolf Steiner says in the same lecture that what worked in this way in the Folk-Soul of the ancient Hebrews was 'in a certain way the spirit of the Ego', that is, the future Christ-impulse, though not as yet directly but as if mirrored by the forces of the astral body. In a certain respect we could also think of the influence' of this cosmic astral body as being the influence of the *Sophia-forces* in Old Testament history.

306. Rudolf Steiner refers to this as follows: 'And now we shall consider the whole progress of evolution. On Saturn we have the *physical body* as the expression of the Logos. On the Sun the *etheric body* is added as an expression of the Life-Spirit: the Logos becomes life. On the Moon the *light-body* [astral body] is added: life becomes light! Here we have the story of the evolution of the human body [that is, its sheaths]' (lecture of 19 May 1908, *The Gospel of St John*, op. cit.). Thus we may say, in considering the historical activity of Phinehas–Elijah–John the Baptist: Phinehas stands before us as a personality who strictly and uncompromisingly preserved in his soul a trust in the spiritual *Word* of revelation which had formerly been entrusted to the Hebrew people. Elijah appears as a guardian of the *life* (the etheric body) of the ancient Hebrews, and John the Baptist as a purifier and awakener of *light* through the forces of his astral body.

307. The incarnation of the forces of this macrocosmic astral body takes place gradually in the whole of the ancient Hebrew people, though its quintessence is later united with the astral body of the Luke Jesus.

308. Thus in the Russian tradition of icon-painting the three Angels who appeared to Abraham in the grove of Mamre are called a 'Trinity', for these three Angels bear a relationship to the three earliest deeds of the Logos in world-evolution, which were accomplished out of the forces of the cosmic spheres of Father, Son and Spirit, respectively, on Old Saturn, Old Sun and Old Moon (see the lecture of 2 June 1907 (*Theosophy of the Rosicrucian*, op. cit.) and of which the three pre-earthly stages of the

Mystery of Golgotha represent a repetition in Earth-evolution (see note 299).

309. This relationship to the impulse of conscience of John the Baptist, as an individuality who at the Turning-Point of Time was its highest representative amongst mankind, also confirms our thought regarding his spiritual connection with the new appearance of Christ in the twentieth century. For the clairvoyant perception of this new appearance of Christ in the etheric body will, according to Rudolf Steiner, be a further metamorphosis of the forces of conscience amongst mankind (lecture of 8 May 1910, *The Christ-Impulse and the Development of Ego-Consciousness*, AP 1976). According to the spiritual law of the 'repetition of events' (see the lecture of 6 March 1910, *The Reappearance of Christ in the Etheric*, AP 1983) an individuality who has accomplished some particularly important deed or other in the evolution of humanity must at some future time repeat it, though in a different form, corresponding to the new stage reached by earthly evolution. Considering this we must say: just as John the Baptist was the most important earthly preparer of the physical appearance of Christ through his having developed within himself the forces of conscience, so is Novalis in the spiritual world the most important supersensible preparer of the etheric appearance of Christ through the help which he is now able to afford men in the inner transformation of the voice of conscience into the faculty of a new etheric clairvoyance. And just as John the Baptist formerly made mankind aware of the physically incarnated Christ, so the individuality of Novalis in the spiritual worlds is the most important *guide* of human souls towards an experience of the Etheric Christ (which comes about in the event of their entering the spiritual world as a result of a transformation of the forces of conscience or during their life after death). Rudolf Steiner also often speaks about the possibility of experiencing the Etheric Christ after death (for example, in the lecture of 14 October 1911, *From Jesus to Christ*, op. cit.).

310. Lecture of 1 November 1911 (*Occult History*, op. cit.).

311. Lecture of 2 May 1910 (*The Christ-Impulse and the Development of the Ego-Consciousness*, op. cit.).

312. According to the spiritual–scientific investigations of Rudolf Steiner, the impulse of conscience is rooted particularly in man's etheric body (see *The Education of the Child*, RSP 1975). The intellectual or mind soul is a partial transformation of the etheric body (see note 315). Hence it is within this member of man's being that the impulse of conscience arises in the fourth post-Atlantean epoch and, simultaneously with it, the impulse of the individual ego arises for the first time in earthly evolution: 'But at the same time it was the epoch in which the ego descended among men. The Christ-event also had to take place in this epoch, because, with Him, the ego made its descent in a special way.' Thus in the figure of John the Baptist, who possessed an unusually mature and powerful intellectual or mind soul, we have to do with a personality who united in himself at one and the same

time a highly developed impulse of conscience with an equally strong ego impulse; for the one impulse is, in a spiritual sense, inseparable from the other. Both these impulses also have a particular influence on man's life after death. Thus when the individual ego has been strongly developed in earthly life it enables man to attain a particularly clear level of awareness after death, and the impulse of conscience determines his further destiny in the spiritual world (see the lecture of 3 February 1912, GA 143). In this lies one of the reasons why John was able after death to become from the spiritual world the group-soul of the most intimate circle of Christ Jesus' pupils. What has just been said is not at variance with the indication quoted above (see p. 20) that the origin of conscience was in the sphere of the Cherubim. For as it is the partial transformation of the etheric body, the intellectual or mind soul is at the same time a partial anticipation of the future principle of the Life-Spirit (see note 315), the rudiments of which were formed within man's being by the Hierarchy of the Cherubim on Old Sun (see *Cosmic Memory*, Steinerbooks [Garber] Blauvelt, NY 1987).

313. Regarding the influence upon Raphael from the spiritual world of his father, Giovanni Santi (died 1491), who was also an artist, see the lecture of 23 May 1912 (*On the Meaning of Life*, APC 1928).

314. See note 293 and note 325.

315. According to Rudolf Steiner the intellectual or mind soul is the result of a 'preparatory modification' of the etheric body (see the lecture of 9 June 1910, *The Mission of the Individual Folk Souls*, op. cit.) and is at the same time 'a feeble foreshadowing, but nonetheless a foreshadowing', of the Life-Spirit (ibid., lecture of 7 June 1910).

316. John the Baptist, too, dies at an age between 30 and 33; Novalis dies in his twenty-ninth year—and so both of them died in that period of human life when the intellectual or mind soul is being developed.

317. See p. 29 and note 104.

318. Wilhelm Kelber, *Raphael* (Stuttgart 1979).

319. Quoted in Rudolf Meyer, *Elias* (Stuttgart 1964).

320. Lecture of 28 September 1924 (*The Last Address*, op. cit.). The quotation that follows is from the same source.

321. Jacobus de Voragine, *Die Legenda aurea*, Cologne 1969.

322. See further in the lecture of 19 September 1909 (*The Gospel of St Luke*, op. cit.). Here again it should be emphasised that the meeting of Mary and Elisabeth described in the Gospel of St Luke is the first *earthly* meeting of Adam with his 'heavenly archetype', the sister-soul from whom he had been separated since the time of the Fall of man; and between their two adjoining spheres of activity was placed the Cherub with the flaming sword, dividing the paths of the heavenly and the earthly Adam. This is also why, from this standpoint, the incarnation of this individuality as John the Baptist is the central and decisive incarnation for all his subsequent earthly lives. For his yearning for the Nathan Soul acquires, in precisely this incarnation, a *real* foundation for its later fulfilment, in that the karmic

connection between two beings can be *established only on Earth*, and only then carried forward in the spiritual worlds. It is for this reason that the motif of the friendship between John and the Luke-Jesus has played so great a part in works of art (in Raphael it merely attains its most consummate expression), for whole generations of artists have experienced in this image a prophetic anticipation of the future union of Heaven and Earth, of heavenly and earthly humanity.

323. Something similar also happens with John's father, who, like his mother, was also 'filled with the Holy Spirit and prophesied' (1:67) in recognition of his son's future mission: 'And you, child, shall be called the prophet of the Most High; for you will go before the Lord to prepare His ways, to give *knowledge* of salvation of His people' (1:76–77), that is, through the awakening within him of the impulse of conscience, the new organ of knowledge (see Chapter 3). The Apostle Paul later said about the connection that exists between the activity of the Holy Spirit within man and the impulse of conscience: 'I am speaking the truth in Christ, I am not lying; my conscience bears me witness in the Holy Spirit' (Romans 9:1).

324. Compare with the ending of the first and third of Novalis' Hymns to the Night.

325. The German eighteenth-century romantic, W.H. Wackenroder (1773–98), in a little work of his published anonymously in the year 1797 in Berlin under the title, 'Outpourings of an art-loving friar', includes a description—based on historical documents—of the spiritual experience whereby Raphael was enabled to find the path which led to the creation of his 'Madonnas'. In this book by Wackenroder, a German monk tells how, as he was looking amongst the manuscripts in his monastery, he found some writings by Bramante where the latter tells how he learnt from Raphael the secret of his wonderful Madonnas. Raphael had always wished that he could paint the Mother of God in all her perfection, but he had never succeeded. 'One night when, as had often happened, he had been praying to the Virgin in his dreams, he suddenly awoke with a start in a state of considerable distress. In the darkness of night his eyes were attracted by a bright light on the wall opposite his bed, and when he looked properly he became aware that his picture of the Madonna, which was hanging, as yet unfinished, on the wall, was illumined by a most delicate ray of light and had become a finished picture that was truly alive. The divine power in this picture so overwhelmed him that he broke out in tears. The image was looking at him in an indescribably moving way, and he even fancied that it had actually moved. What was most amazing was that it seemed to him as though this image was exactly what he had always sought, even though he had never had more than an obscure and confused idea of it. He was altogether unable to remember how he went to sleep again. On the following morning he arose like one newly born; the vision remained permanently and firmly imprinted on his mind and senses, and from then on he succeeded in portraying the Mother of God as she had

appeared before his soul. Ever since he felt a certain reverence for his own pictures.' Wackenroder is of the opinion that from these words it would be possible for anyone to understand what the divine Raphael intended when he wrote in his letter to the Countess Castoglione in the year 1515: 'As good judgement regarding beautiful women is something that is always lacking, I avail myself of a certain idea which comes to my mind (io mi servo di certa idea, che mi vienne nella mente)' (quoted from Wilhelm Kelber, *Raphael*, Stuttgart 1979). The prayer of Raphael that is mentioned in this account and which finally led him to a clairvoyant vision of Mary and the Child could be fully rendered in the following lines by Novalis:

> I long to serve you word and deed,
> You know so well my inmost need.
> O sweet Mother, now relent,
> Through sign of cheer show your intent.
> My being rests in you alone,
> Let for one moment my heart be your throne.

326. Lecture of 3 February 1912 (GA 143, GB 1967).
327. See Plate 5. The portrait is shown as it has been since restoration, where the element of wonder is much less evident than it was before. See also the Frontispiece.
328. Albert Steffen, *Die Botschaft von Novalis* (Dornach 1972).
329. *Knowledge of the Higher Worlds. How is it Achieved?*, op. cit., chapter 1: 'Conditions'.
330. That the capacity for reference and wonder, the point of departure for any true knowledge, has—in contrast to the impulse of conscience, which relates to man's life after death—its source in the spiritual life before birth, see the lecture of 3 February 1912 (see above). In this lecture, Rudolf Steiner puts this as follows: 'In the moment where dim feelings lead him [man] to say: "You face the rising Sun, the roaring sea, the growing plant, and are filled with wonder!" There is in this wonder the knowledge that all this has already been perceived in a way other than with bodily eyes. He has looked at all these with his spiritual eyes before he entered the physical world. . . . This was, and could only have been, before birth.' From this basic soul mood of Novalis, which in the sense of modern initiation-science could with full justice be called a *Parsifal-mood*, stems also his particular cognitive method, always beginning as it does with the putting of a question: 'The question clearly works as the stimulation and driving force of thinking, it allows the writer to enter into an inner conversation with himself which determines the path of investigation.' In connection with this essential quality of Novalis' thought process, H.J. Mähl shows in his introduction to the edition of his 'Fichte studies' that for him *all knowledge* began with a question, not with any kind of finished

demands or assertions, so that the process of knowledge unfolds as a kind of inner conversation with himself and the world. In his earlier fragments Novalis often tries to arrive at concrete answers, while in the later period he generally leaves most of the questions unanswered. For the immediate spiritual experience of 'veneration', of devotion to truth and knowledge', which has its outward reflection in a question that has been rightly put, was of far greater importance to him than a formal cognitive result (see H. Ritter-Schaumburg, *Novalis und seine erste Braut*, the chapter entitled 'Fichtes Lehre', Stuttgart 1986).

331. Lecture of 28 September 1924, *The Last Address*, op. cit.

332. Lecture of 22 December 1908 (*The Christmas Mystery: Novalis as Seer*, op. cit.) and see the lecture of 26 October 1908, GA 108 (as note 123). Rudolf Steiner also speaks of this as follows: 'This young man [Novalis], who at the age of twenty-nine left the physical plane and has given more to the German mind than hundreds and thousands of others, lived a life which was really the memory of a previous [earthly life].' Of course, in both cases the reference to the previous life (in this case that of Raphael) also includes the full content of his spiritual existence between the two incarnations, which Rudolf Steiner described so searchingly and meaningfully in the 'Last Address'.

333. Lecture of 30 May 1912 (*The Spiritual Foundation of Morality*, Steiner Book Centre, Vancouver, n.d.). Later in the same lecture, Rudolf Steiner defines the list of these qualities more precisely when he speaks of '. . . all moral acts of *wonder, trust, reverence, faith*, in short . . . everything, which *fashions the path that leads to supersensible knowledge.*'

334. Lecture of 3 December 1911 (*Faith, Love, Hope*, op. cit). Regarding the forces of faith, love and hope in their relationship to the fifth, sixth and seventh post-Atlantean cultural epochs, see also *The Cycle of the Year as a Path of Initiation*, part IV, op. cit.

335. Lecture of 2 December 1911 (*Faith, Love, Hope*, op. cit.).

336. Lecture of 8 October 1911 (*From Jesus to Christ*, RSP 1991).

337. How remarkably similar the lines in italics from this poem by Novalis sound when compared with the following four lines from Rudolf Steiner's 'Dance of the Planets':

> The soul is weaving—
> What raises our life
> From faith to vision
> With such great longing?

338. Lecture of 3 December 1911 (*Faith, Love, Hope*, op. cit.). The previous quotation was from the lecture of 2 December 1911. To this it is only necessary to add that although the 'sheath of faith' is reflected in human consciousness particularly in the fifth post-Atlantean epoch, nevertheless the power of faith as such will also continue to be the most important force

of the astral body in subsequent epochs, as its designation as 'faith-body' testifies. For however high the regions of the spiritual worlds that man may enter with his clairvoyant consciousness, there will always stretch out 'before' or 'above' him yet higher regions, and the path to these will consist in that the forces of faith working in the astral body will be permeated in the manner described by the moral will awakened out of the ego, thus raising human consciousness to a new spiritual plane.

339. Lecture of 2 December 1911 (see above). In the lecture of 14 June 1911 (GA 127, Typescript NSL 359), Rudolf Steiner speaks of how this soul-sickness, which is the consequence of the absence of the power of faith brought about through modern materialism, will lead in future also to the gradual sickness of the physical body, and in the end to the ever-increasing 'degeneration of humanity'.

340. Lecture of 18 November 1911 (*Esoteric Christianity and the Mission of Christian Rosenkreutz*, op. cit.).

341. Lecture of 13 April 1922 (*The Festivals and Their Meaning*, op. cit.).

342. Matthew 3:14–15.

343. Lecture of 22 December 1908 (*The Christmas Mystery: Novalis as Seer*, op. cit.). The quotation that follows is from the same source.

344. Lecture of 26 October 1908, GA 108.

345. In the motif of the 'recognition of Christ', which runs like a red thread through the entire poetic cycle of the 'Spiritual Songs', we have a very clear testimony of Novalis' semi-conscious memory of his participation in the events of the Turning-Point of Time.

346. Lecture of 30 May 1912 (*The Spiritual Foundation of Morality*, op. cit). The next quotation is from the same lecture. In this lecture only the mentioning of *Adam* can be seen as a reference to the individuality of Elijah–John–Raphael–Novalis. However, in earlier lectures of the same month, where the formation of the new sheaths for the Christ Being out of the forces of conscience, love, faith and wonder is described, this theme is on each occasion directly associated with the mystery of the four reincarnations of this individuality. See the lectures of 8 May 1912 (GA 143, Typescript AQ 18:1) and 2 May 1912 (*Earthly and Cosmic Man*, op. cit). In a further lecture on this theme, that of 14 May 1912, there is only a reference to Raphael, while in the next (20 May 1912) all four incarnations are mentioned (both contained in *Earthly and Cosmic Man*, op. cit.).

347. One could also say that, through the fact that by means of the Baptism in the Jordan he, so to speak, 'introduced' the cosmic Being of the Christ into the earthly sphere, John at the same time laid with this deed the foundation for the subsequent forming of the 'immortal Individual' amongst mankind.

348. Regarding this law, see also note 309. This law can work in the development of one and the same individuality on different levels. Here we are considering its *highest stage*, which encompasses virtually the whole of earthly evolution, while in the instance cited in note 309 we were concerned with its manifestation within the limits of several centuries.

349. In the lecture of 30 May 1912 (*The Spiritual Foundation of Morality*, op. cit.), Rudolf Steiner uses this expression of Goethe's for characterising and defining the goal of forming the new sheaths for the Christ-impulse amongst mankind.

350. Lecture of 14 May 1912 (*Earthly and Cosmic Man*, op. cit.). The next quotation is from the same source.

351. Genesis 3:17–19.

352. Lecture of 21 September 1911 (*From Buddha to Christ*, AP 1978).

353. Lecture of 26 June 1909 (*The Gospel of St John in Relation to the Other Three Gospels*, op. cit.).

354. Rudolf Steiner describes this fourth and highest category of Sun-Spirits as follows: 'The most advanced of these spiritual beings, who now [during the Earth-incarnation] adopted the Sun as their dwelling-place, were those beings who may be described in the true sense of the word as 'human archetypes', 'Spirit-men'. We should therefore imagine that amongst those spiritual beings who, during the Old Moon period, were to be found on the Sun as Bull-Spirits, Eagle-Spirits and Lion-Spirits there were some who had attained a higher level of development. They are the true Spirit-men, who now have taken up their abode on the Sun ... Up there [on the Sun], man did not evolve in the way that he lives on the Earth; what was evolving there was man's spiritual archetype, of whom modern man, as he confronts us in his present physical form, is merely a reflection' (lecture of 26 June 1909). There is also in the Book of Revelation a reference—albeit in a metamorphosed form—to the future working of the four primordial group-souls of humanity in the 'immortal Individual' in the image of the four beasts *around* the heavenly throne, which are full of eyes and ceaselessly glorify *Him that sits* on the throne (4:6–8).

355. Regarding Christ as the highest divine Ego of humanity, see the lecture of 24 June 1909 (see above). In a later lecture, that of 22 August 1924 (*True and False Paths in Spiritual Investigation*, op. cit.) the following words may be found: 'For it was as Cosmic-Man that Christ came from the Sun.'

356. *Occult Science—An Outline*, op. cit., the chapter entitled, 'Knowledge of Higher Worlds'.

357. For further details about these three stages of the supersensible preparation of Anthroposophy, see *Rudolf Steiner and the Founding of the New Mysteries*, op. cit., ch. 5.

358. See the lecture of 28 July 1924 (*Karmic Relationships*, vol. III, op. cit.).

359. In the '*Last Address*', op. cit., Rudolf Steiner says about this: 'This earthly personality of Raphael was completely yielded up and was only present through what Lazarus-John had given to this soul ...' These words fully correspond with the characterisation of Raphael given in note 100 from the lecture of 17 September 1912 (*The Gospel of St Mark*, op. cit.) of the incomplete incarnation of his entelechy in the physical body and also with all that has been said about this individuality as a 'Bodhisattva-like' being (see note 23).

360. In the lecture of 12 September 1924 (*Karmic Relationships*, vol. IV, RSP 1963) Rudolf Steiner says that the inauguration of the supersensible School of Michael took place already in the fourteenth century.
361. Lecture of 20 July 1924 (*Karmic Relationships*, vol. VI, op. cit.).
362. Lecture of 23 May 1912, *On the Meaning of Life*, op. cit.
363. Lecture of 28 September 1924 (*The Last Address,* op. cit.).
364. In the lecture of 19 July 1924 (*Karmic Relationships*, vol. VI, op. cit.), Rudolf Steiner at first speaks of how the supersensible cult took place in the spiritual world closest to the Earth 'at the beginning of the nineteenth and even already at the end of the eighteenth century', and then he makes the period of its influence more exact when he speaks of the supersensible cult as an event 'which took place in the first half of the nineteenth century.' Nevertheless, the influence of this cult in the spiritual world nearest to the Earth was so intense at the end of the eighteenth century that its effects were manifested directly on the Earth. Rudolf Steiner cites, as an example of such an influence, the 'Fairy-Tale' of Goethe (see the lecture of 19 July 1924), the first interpreter of which was Novalis. However, the influence of these supersensible events can clearly be sensed also in many of his own works, particularly through the character of his own initiation, as described in the *Hymns to the Night*.
365. See note 363.
366. As has already been observed (see p. 87), Rudolf Steiner says in the lecture of 31 December 1912 (*The Bhagavad Gita and the Epistles of Paul*, op. cit.) that a true 'Damascus experience', as a definite stage of inner development, always has within it a direct experience of *two* Beings, the Christ and the Nathan Soul (see in this connection *The Cycle of the Year as a Path of Initiation*, part XII, note 81a, op. cit.).
367. In the lecture of 2 December 1911 (*Faith, Love, Hope*, op. cit.), Rudolf Steiner says: 'The inmost kernel of our being [the ego] is enshrouded by our faith-body or astral body, by our love-body or etheric body and by our hope-body or physical body.' These words can become for us a further confirmation of what was elaborated in Chapter 9: that through his first meeting with Jesus of Nazareth (that is, the Nathan Soul) on the physical plane the forces of *conscience*, the new organ of cognition, were awakened for the first time within John the Baptist, and, years later, through his intercourse with Jesus of Nazareth and with various members of the Essene Order, the soul-forces of *hope* developed more and more strongly within him, hope that the Messiah, as foretold by the Prophets, would soon come. These hopes for His future arrival were cultivated especially strongly in the Essene Order (regarding the connection between the forces of conscience and the forces of hope see *The Cycle of the Year as a Path of Initiation*, part IV, ch. 6). Such were the principal *moral fruits* of the intercourse between John the Baptist and the Nathan Soul on the *physical plane*. Moreover, through the fact that, in his incarnation as Raphael, he received into himself an imprint of the etheric body of the Nathan Soul,

the faculty of *love* in his etheric body or 'body of love' could be strengthened in a quite unusual way. The etheric body is moreover connected with the impulses of art (see *The Education of the Child*, op. cit.). As the source of man's yearning for beauty, in the case of Raphael it stimulated him—in accordance with the spirit of the age—to transmute the forces of love that filled his whole being into works of art. And finally, through receiving into himself in his incarnation as Novalis an imprint of the astral body of the Nathan Soul, the faculty of *faith* within his astral body or 'body of faith' was strengthened to such an extent that these forces of faith could be transformed within him into forces of true clairvoyance, into a new, higher insight into the supersensible worlds.

368. Of course, this union with the imprint of Christ's Ego which is preserved in the spiritual world by the Nathan Soul does not have to happen *in full measure* in his next incarnation, but will quite possibly need not one but several earthly lives. For while the entry of the imprints of the etheric and astral bodies of the Nathan Soul into the corresponding human sheaths takes place in the spiritual world before a man's birth, the union with the imprint of the ego must be accomplished by *the human being himself* out of his *own inner forces* during earthly life. This means that the individuality of Novalis, who in his incarnation as Raphael—and to some extent even in his last incarnation in the eighteenth century—had not fully entered into the physical body (see note 100), will now, if he is to attain the next stage in his evolution, have to unite *fully* with it. However, there is one fact which will have a significant role to play in determining whether or not this will happen: will the individuality of Novalis find, in his next incarnation on Earth, a suitable physical body for the fulfilment of his task? (If such a body cannot be found, he will either wait in the spiritual world for more favourable conditions into which to incarnate, or, in the event of incarnating, shortly afterwards again leave the physical plane at a young age, before reaching age 35.) All in all, we have in these incarnations of Novalis since the Turning-Point of Time a kind of microcosmic reflection of that macrocosmic path which the Christ Being now and in the future will tread as the new Spirit of the Earth until the beginning of the new aeon of evolution (Jupiter). Rudolf Steiner refers to this macrocosmic development of the Christ-impulse amongst mankind in the following words: 'So we see how, starting from a physical man on Earth, the Christ who has descended to the Earth gradually evolves as Etheric Christ, Astral Christ and Ego Christ to become as Ego Christ the Spirit of the Earth who then rises to even higher stages [that is, to Jupiter] together with all mankind' (lecture of 21 September 1911, *From Buddha to Christ*, op. cit.).

369. Rudolf Steiner subsequently conceptualises this notion of 'Christ-bearer' more clearly, associating it more with the higher stages in the pre-Christian mysteries, and, as a designation for the corresponding stage in the New Mysteries, he introduces the concept of 'Christ-receiver', which characterises more directly and far more precisely the essential nature of

the occult process of receiving the 'ego' into the ego than can be conveyed by the word 'bearer'. (See further in *The Cycle of the Year as a Path of Initiation*, part V, ch. 2, op. cit.). The following lines from the Foundation Stone Meditation, coming from its second part, which especially concerns the mysteries of the Sun-sphere, also refer to the stage of 'Christ-receiver':

> Where the surging
> Deeds of the World's Becoming
> Do thine own I
> Unite
> Unto the I of the World.

370. Lecture of 31 May 1909 (*From Buddha to Christ*, op. cit.). Regarding the expressions 'Ego of Christ' and 'ego of Jesus of Nazareth', see note 374.

371. In the sense of what has been said hitherto in the present work (see p. 10 and note 21) regarding the relationship of Moses and Elijah to the revelations of Jahve–Christ, we should associate the words at the beginning of this quotation *to a greater extent* with Elijah than with Moses.

372. Lecture of 16 May 1909 (*The Principle of Spiritual Economy*, op. cit.). In connection with these words of Rudolf Steiner, it is necessary once more to recall that the transition from the fifth to the sixth cultural epoch, that is, from the epoch where the ego works within the consciousness soul to the epoch of the Spirit-Self, is at the same time a microcosmic anticipation of the future macrocosmic transition from the Earth-condition to that of Jupiter, which is to say, from the cosmos of wisdom to the cosmos of love, through the union of the human ego with the World-Ego of the Christ (see *Occult Science*, op. cit.).

373. *The Spiritual Guidance of Man and Humanity*, op. cit., ch. 2.

374. In the lecture of 28 March 1909 (GA 109), Rudolf Steiner speaks of this as follows: 'With the sixteenth century there begins a time when the imprints of Christ's Ego develop a readiness to intermingle with the egos of particular individualities. One of these was Christian Rosenkreutz, the first Rosicrucian. Due to this fact, an inner connection with the Christ became possible, as esoteric teachings reveal it to us.' By the words 'the imprints of Christ's Ego' in this quotation we may understand the reflection of Christ's Ego that has been preserved within the ego of Jesus of Nazareth (the Nathan Soul) and then multiplied according to the laws of spiritual economy. In the same lecture Rudolf Steiner explains this process further: '. . . the waiting imprints of Christ's Ego which Christ has formed through an impression within the body of Jesus. . .' (See also the note that follows.)

375. Rudolf Steiner speaks about Anthroposophy as the modern continuation of Rosicrucianism, and in an esoteric sense about himself as the furtherer of the work of Christian Rosenkreutz in the twentieth century, as follows: 'Thus through this anthroposophical–Rosicrucian spiritual stream we

again draw towards us what exists [in the spiritual world] by way of copies of the ego of Jesus of Nazareth. To the extent that his inner nature is like a seal-impression of the ego of Jesus, so will such a man receive the Christ-principle into his soul. Thus Rosicrucianism prepared something positive; Anthroposophy shall come to life, and the soul that truly receives it will gradually be transformed' (lecture of 16 May 1909). See also Friedrich Hiebel (*Time of Decision with Rudolf Steiner*, AP 1989), the chapter entitled 'Ending'.

376. Lecture of 7 March 1909 (GA 109, Typescript AQ 11:4).

377. See note 369.

378. See note 368.

379. Regarding Goethe's connection with Rosicrucianism, see *The Foundations of Esotericism*, RSP 1983. In the case of Novalis, on the other hand, one can only speak of a certain influence of the works of Jacob Boehme, who derived his wisdom from Rosicrucian inspirations.

380. Regarding the spiritual connection and occult succession of Rosicrucian-ism and Johannine Christianity, see the lecture of 24 June 1909 (*The Gospel of St John in Relation to the Other Three Gospels*, op. cit.).

381. Rudolf Steiner says, for example, in the lecture of 4 November 1904 (*The Temple Legend*, RSP 1985): 'This [the Cross encircled by roses] will become the symbol of the new Christianity of the sixth post-Atlantean epoch'; and then he says: 'This triangle [Atma, Buddhi and Manas], with all that it entails, will form the content of the renewed Christianity of the sixth cultural epoch. This is being prepared by the Rosicrucians...' At this point it is only possible to refer briefly to that mystery in the further evolution of humanity which is connected with the realisation of the so-called 'Temple Legend' of true Rosicrucianism in the sixth cultural epoch. For the founding and building of the spiritual Temple of mankind which is spoken of in this legend will be directly associated with a definite stage in the fashioning within man of the three sheaths for the Christ Being. Moreover, these sheaths will, *up to a certain point*, also form that spiritual Temple, the building of which true Rosicrucian sees as its most important task.

382. This new, exalted synthesis of spiritualised science, art and religion in the sixth cultural epoch will be associated with the beginning of the realisation of the 'mystery of the Golden Triangle' (see note 381) amongst mankind. The deep connection of the individuality of John–Raphael–Novalis with these mysteries is attested by the verbal explanation which Rudolf Steiner added to his 'Last Address' in response to Ita Wegman's question about the way in which the two Johns work together after the initiation of Lazarus (see the 'Appendix' to GA 238 in the German edition of 1981). There is also a version of the 'Golden Legend' which tells of how Adam, as he was being driven out of Paradise, took with him three seeds of the Tree of Life which after his death Seth planted on his grave, that is, they continued to be connected with the individuality of Adam even after his death (see the

lecture of 21 December 1909, *Festivals of the Seasons*, APC 1928). According to Rudolf Steiner, the two imaginations of the three seeds and the Golden Triangle refer to one and the same mystery of man's higher spiritual nature (see the lectures of 4th November 1904 and 29 May 1905, *The Temple Legend*, op. cit.). Subsequently, although in a different form, this motif of the 'three seeds' or the 'Golden Triangle' appears in the scene of the awakening of Lazarus. In this scene, the entelechy of John the Baptist, in uniting with him, endows him from the higher worlds with the principles of the *Spirit-Self*, *Life-Spirit* and *Spirit-Man*, so that in the person of Lazarus there stood before Christ Jesus a man 'who reached from the depths of Earth into the highest heights of heaven' and who 'bore within himself all members including those spiritual members of Manas, Buddhi and Atma which can be developed by all men in the distant future.' (From Rudolf Steiner's verbal elucidation of the 'Last Address', published in the second German edition of 1981.)

383. Lecture of 30 January 1913, '*The Mission of Raphael*' (GA 62, Typescript Z 27). 'The true spirit of God moralises. *John* is the moralist,' writes Novalis about John the Baptist in one of his fragments.

384. Regarding Novalis' religiousness, see the words of Henrik Steffens quoted in note 386.

385. In another fragment, Novalis speaks as follows about the all-embracing significance of 'rhythm', which is able to unite the natural and the moral principles in man and the world into a single whole: 'Seasons, days, life and destiny are all, remarkably enough, thoroughly rhythmical, metrical, measured. In all crafts and arts, all machines, organic bodies, throughout all our daily affairs: rhythm, metre, beat, melody. Everything that we do with a certain skill we do rhythmically, though we may not notice it. Rhythm can be found everywhere, it creeps in everywhere.'

386. In this last fragment what is of particular significance is the sequence of the transition from historical knowledge to mathematics, then to philosophy and thereafter to art and religion. For of such a nature is the new path of ascent which leads mankind from the present into the future (in contrast to the old, descending path leading from religion through art to modern science). Thus Rudolf Steiner began his spiritual activity from the foundation of a *science* of the spirit, whence the impulses for the deepening of art and the sphere of religion were then to proceed: 'Thus Anthroposophy begins in every case with knowledge, enlivens its concepts through art and ends in a religious deepening ... We must learn, on the anthroposophical path, to start with knowledge, raise ourselves to the level of art and end in the warmth of religious feeling' (lecture of 30 January 1923, *Awakening to Community*, AP 1974). What is of particular importance in the case of Novalis is, however, that he not only conceived of a higher unity of science, art and religion in a theoretical sense but represented it to a certain degree with his whole personality. As a testimony to this is, in the first instance, his strictly scientific upbringing,

which was further deepened and broadened through his philosophical studies; then his relationship to art as a divine calling and, finally, his profound religious feeling, of which the Scandinavian naturalist, Henrik Steffens, wrote in recollection of his meetings with Novalis: 'Indeed, Novalis was, in the deepest sense, a Christian and religious . . . In a religious respect Novalis was important to me as no-one else.'

Novalis, too, views the individual elements of this 'holy threefoldness' entirely in the spirit of this higher synthesis; of *science and religion* (for example mathematics, as the foundation of all sciences) he says: 'Mathematics is the life of the Gods. All godly ambassadors must be mathematicians. Pure mathematics is religion'; of *science and art* (for example poetry, as the highest of all arts): 'All science becomes poetry— after it has become philosophy.' And the same thought in other words: 'The poet is simply the highest degree of the thinker . . . The separation of poet and thinker is only apparent—and to the *disadvantage* of both. It is the sign of a sickness—and of a sick constitution'; and of *art and religion* (as exemplified by the priest, the man for whom religion is also a life's task): 'Poet and priest were originally one—only later times have separated them. The true poet is, however, always a priest, just as the true priest has always remained a poet—and should not the future bring about the return of the way things were before?'

387. In the lecture of 29 December 1912 (GA 143) Rudolf Steiner also calls Novalis a *mediator*.

388. Lecture of 20 November 1911 (*Esoteric Christianity and the Mission of Christian Rosenkreutz*, op. cit.). Thus in speaking about the etheric advent of Christ, especially in the lectures of 1910–11, Rudolf Steiner again and again mentions two individualities: Christian Rosenkreutz and Jeshu ben Pandira (see, for example, the lectures of 28 September and 20 November 1911 (ibid.); 1 October 1911 (*The Etherisation of the Blood*, op. cit.) and 14 October 1911 (*From Jesus to Christ*, op. cit.]. On the other hand, as a kind of leitmotif of all the lectures devoted to the theme of the new advent, Rudolf Steiner chooses words of John the Baptist, words which stir the conscience (see p. 74).

389. See regarding this activity of the Rosicrucians between the fourteenth and the nineteenth centuries: *Anthroposophical Leading Thoughts* (article of 6 December 1924, op. cit.). This is the source of both the present and the following quotation.

390. Rudolf Steiner refers to this highly important mystery, which began in the year 1879 with the new epoch of Michael, in the following words: 'The mark of Rosicrucianism is that its most enlightened spirits had a great longing to meet Michael. They were able to do this only as though in a dream. Since the end of the last third of the nineteenth century human beings have been able consciously to meet Michael in the spirit' (lecture of 13 January 1924, *Rosicrucianism and Modern Initiation*, RSP 1982). Rudolf Steiner tells of his own fully conscious experience—in accordance with

the new epoch—of the sphere of Michael from the age of 28 onwards in the lecture of 12 August 1924 (*Karmic Relationships*, vol. VIII, op. cit.). See further in *Rudolf Steiner and the Founding of the New Mysteries*, op. cit., ch. 2.

391. Ibid., ch. 3 and 5.

392. Ibid., ch. 4.

393. After the Christmas Conference Rudolf Steiner indicated in a private conversation that during the laying of the Foundation Stone on 25 December 1923 'Christian Rosenkreutz and his hosts' were spiritually present in the Schreinerei and took part in the proceedings (see Bernard Lievegoed, *Mystery Streams in Europe and the New Mysteries*, AP 1982, ch. 6; and Margarete and Erich Kirchner-Bockholt, *Rudolf Steiner's Mission and Ita Wegman*, published privately, 1977, the chapter entitled 'Rudolf Steiner's Mission').

394. The theme of Rosicrucian esotericism appears for the first time on 22 and 23 December, immediately before the day of the laying of the Foundation Stone, in the last two lectures of the cycle, *Mystery Knowledge and Mystery Centres*, which Rudolf Steiner gave before the Christmas Foundation Meeting, and in which he describes at some length the pre-Christian European Mysteries and their spiritual continuation in medieval Rosicrucianism. Especially in the lecture of 22 December, at the point where he speaks of the connection of the alchemists of the Middle Ages—through the mediation of gold—with the *Sun-Intelligence*, the invisible presence of the spirit of Michael can be discerned.

395. After the Foundation Stone Meditation, in its totality, had been spoken in three 'stages' for the first time on the day of the founding of the General Anthroposophical Society, 25 December 1923, there followed the gradual union of its substance with the earthly sphere in the *seven* so-called rhythms of the Christmas Foundation Meeting, which were concluded on the *seventh* day (1 January 1924) with a second *complete* reading of the words of the Meditation—though now not in parts but as a single whole. And after a further *twelve* days, on 13 January, its text was—with certain alterations—given to all anthroposophists through its publication. This took place when the 'permission' and also the 'blessing' of the seven planetary spheres and the twelve directions of the cosmic expanses for this step had been received.

396. 26 December 1923 (*The Christmas Conference for the Foundation of the General Anthroposophical Society*, AP 1990).

397. See note 373. There is a direct spiritual connection between the stream of 'modern esotericism' founded by Christian Rosenkreutz and what was accomplished at the beginning of the twentieth century in the Esoteric School of Rudolf Steiner, which was active from 1904 until 1914 (one of whose two *supersensible* leaders was Christian Rosenkreutz himself: see the 'Esoteric Lesson' of 1 June 1907, GA 264) and the three classes of the Esoteric School founded in 1924 out of the impulse of the Christmas Conference. Rudolf Steiner himself refers to this connection when on 24

December 1923 in the course of discussing no. 5 of the 'Statutes' he says that 'the three classes were already in existence in the Anthroposophical Society, albeit in another form, until the year 1914' (*The Christmas Conference for the Foundation of the General Anthroposophical Society*, op. cit.).

398. Lecture of 28 September 1924 (*The Last Address*, op. cit.).

399. From the complete (German) edition of Novalis' works, vol. 4, p. 559.

400. See note 398 and the quotation that follows.

401. All that has been said in this chapter regarding the *mediatory activity* of Novalis in the spiritual world between the various spiritual streams can be gathered together in the following way:

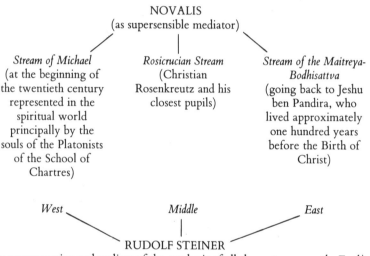

NOVALIS
(as supersensible mediator)

Stream of Michael	Rosicrucian Stream	Stream of the Maitreya-
(at the beginning of	(Christian	Bodhisattva
the twentieth century	Rosenkreutz and his	(going back to Jeshu
represented in the	closest pupils)	ben Pandira, who
spiritual world		lived approximately
principally by the		one hundred years
souls of the Platonists		before the Birth of
of the School of		Christ)
Chartres)		

West   *Middle*   *East*

RUDOLF STEINER
(the representative and realiser of the synthesis of all three streams *on the Earth*)

402. Regarding the seven rhythms of the Christmas Foundation Meeting as the seven stages of the Christian Rosicrucian Path of Initiation that is described in *Occult Science—An Outline*, op. cit., see further in *Rudolf Steiner and the Founding of the New Mysteries*, op. cit., ch. 5.

403. From the article of 13 January 1924, *The Life, Nature and Cultivation of Anthroposophy* (RSP 1976).

404. See *Rudolf Steiner and the Founding of the New Mysteries*, op. cit., ch. 5.

405. See the introductory words to the lecture of 18 July 1924 (*Karmic Relationships*, vol. VI, op. cit.).

406. See GA 258, 1981 edition, note to p. 35. (These lectures are published in English translation under the title of *The Anthroposophic Movement*, Collison 1933.)

407. Lectures of 28 December 1912 and 1 January 1913 (*The Bhagavad Gita and the Epistles of Paul*, op. cit.). In a similar way, Rudolf Steiner concludes the lecture on Novalis which he gave during the cycle with words in which he speaks not of 'the founding of the Anthroposophical Society', as at the

beginning of the lecture, but of 'the starting-point of the anthroposophical spiritual stream' (lecture of 29 December 1912, GA 143).

408. Lecture of 1 January 1913 (likewise the quotation that follows).

409. See further about this in *The Cycle of the Year as a Path of Initiation*, op. cit., Part XII, note 81a.

410. *The Spiritual Guidance of Man and Humanity*, ch. 3, op. cit.

411. Lecture of 29 December 1912 (GA 143): the quotations that follow are from the same source.

412. In this quotation, which is taken from the beginning of the lecture about Novalis, there appears—as with the description of the appearance of Christ to Paul before Damascus in the last lecture of the cycle—a *twofold motif*: that of the Christ-impulse and the shining light surrounding it (see note 409). This motif then becomes all the stronger when Rudolf Steiner, in comparing Novalis with Spinoza, Goethe, Fichte and Leibnitz, calls the latter the bearers of the light of the old, pre-Christian Yoga and Sankhya philosophy, that is—in the sense of the lecture-cycle as a whole—the light of Krishna, in contrast to Novalis, the bearer of the warmth and love of the Christ-impulse. This means that, when set before the Sun-impulse of the Christ which rises up within the heart of Novalis, the individualities referred to above can be seen as still belonging—to a significant extent— to the pre-Christian stage of human evolution or, in other words, they are connected more with the human principle of Jesus (Krishna) than with the divine principle of Christ. This impulse of love and warmth, Rudolf Steiner goes on to say, as it lives within the soul of Novalis, shall be united with and permeated by the light of Krishna, the light of the most ancient wisdom of mankind. John the Baptist referred to the need for such a union already at the Turning-Point of Time through his mighty call: 'Change your disposition, do not walk solely in the path of Krishna' (lecture of 5 June 1913, *The Occult Significance of the Bhagavad Gita*, AP 1968). 'Therefore,' Rudolf Steiner continues in the same lecture, again augmenting the original call of John the Baptist, 'it is just in our time that an understanding of the Christ-impulse must emerge: the path of Christ must be joined with the path of Jesus (Krishna).' And this means, in the sense of the lecture of 29 December, that the wisdom of Spinoza, Goethe, Fichte and Leibnitz must now be permeated by the Christ-impulse as it lives in the soul of Novalis.

413. Lecture of 28 September 1924 (*The Last Address*, op. cit.). The spiritual connection that was thus established between the founding on Earth of the Anthroposophical Society and the sphere of Michael in the higher worlds enabled Rudolf Steiner some four months later, when life in the newly founded Society had become rather more consolidated, to reveal to its members certain secrets associated with the activity of Michael in our cosmos. The first of these revelations was made in the lecture of 2 May 1913 in London (*Occult Science and Occult Development*, RSP 1966) and they then continued in the lectures of 4 and 9 May in Paris (not translated) and

of 18 and 20 May in Stuttgart (*The Festivals and their Meaning: Michaelmas*, op. cit.). In these lectures a position of particular importance was devoted to the study of Michael's mission in the Old Testament and the New Testament periods of human evolution, that is, *before* and *after* the Mystery of Golgotha, and also to his relationship to the new appearance of Christ in the etheric realm.

Thus we may say: while in May 1912 the theme of Novalis played a significant part (see note 494), in May 1913 it was the 'theme of Michael'. (It should further be noted that between the two lectures in Stuttgart, referred to above, a public lecture was given on 19 May entitled 'Raphael's Mission in the Light of the Science of the Spirit', GA 152, Typescript NSL 143.)

414. See note 425.

415. Lecture of 26 December 1909 (*Festivals of the Seasons*, APC/AP 1928); the quotations that follow are from the same source.

416. After all, did not Novalis himself, as a premonition of this important task of the modern science of the spirit, utter the following prophetic words?: 'Who has explained the Bible as complete in itself? Should the Bible not be understood as something that is still growing?'

417. See the esoteric lesson of 1 June 1907 (GA 264).

418. Lecture of 23 January 1910 (GA 125, Typescript EN 46). A similar motif, relating Novalis with the 'Masters of Wisdom and of Harmony of Feelings', appears in the lecture of 13 April 1913 (*The Inner Nature of Man and Life between Death and Rebirth*, APC 1959) at the inauguration of the Johannes–Raphael Branch in Erfurt. What is of relevance to the threefold Spirit who is referred to in the words that have been quoted is, however, that he is in his nature related to the Spirit who has already been spoken of in connection with what was said about the individuality of the prophet Elijah (see note 23).

419. The Gospel studies really began in 1906 (see also *The Course of My Life*, AP 1951, ch. 37), although essential elements of the spiritual–scientific approach to them had appeared already in the final lectures of the cycle, *Christianity as Mystical Fact* (24 lectures given in Berlin, between 19 October 1901 and 26 April 1902), which was then re-worked for the book with the same title (op. cit.). The principal cycles and individual lectures about Gospel studies which Rudolf Steiner gave before Christmas 1909 are to be found in GA 94, 97, 100: *The Gospel of St John*, op. cit.; *The Gospel of St John in Relation to the Other Three Gospels*, op. cit.; *The Gospel of St Luke*, op. cit.; and *Deeper Secrets of Human History in the Light of the Gospel of St Matthew* (RSP/AP 1957).

420. Lecture of 26 December 1909. See also note 419.

421. While there is a considerable amount of new information, almost all the basic themes contained in the previous studies of the Gospels of John, Luke and Matthew appear in this cycle again in a deepened form. See note 430.

422. This 'measure of the astral plane', which was to prepare the *right* entry of

the Etheric Christ into earthly evolution, is also connected with that event which can be described as a certain 'division' in the sphere of the 'Masters' which caused the separation of the streams of Eastern and Western esotericism. This was outwardly expressed in the final separation in May–June 1907 of the esoteric school founded and led by Rudolf Steiner from the esoteric school led by Annie Besant (see *The Course of My Life*, op. cit., ch. 32).

In the first esoteric lesson which was given immediately after this separation, that of 1 June 1907, Rudolf Steiner spoke as follows about this event and also about the need for all members of *his* school to choose between the two streams: 'What is given through me on behalf of the Masters of the West follows a path that is independent from what Mrs. Besant teaches at the behest of the Masters of the East . . . Each has its two Masters: Mahatma K(uthumi) and Mahatma M(orya); Master Jesus of Nazareth and Master Christian Rosenkreutz. The first of these schools is led by Mrs. Besant, the other by Dr. Steiner. However, one must come to a decision as to which one wishes to turn to' (GA 264).

In September of the same year, when he was at Barr in Alsace as a guest of Edouard Schuré, Rudolf Steiner gave his host an exhaustive, written reply regarding the occult foundations of the Theosophical Society and the intentions of the Eastern Masters in connection with it. 'They,' wrote Rudolf Steiner, '—these Eastern initiators—wanted to imprint *their* form of spiritual knowledge, which had been preserved through the ages, on the Western world . . . For the Eastern initiators must of necessity leave untouched the *Christ-principle* as the central *cosmic* factor of evolution . . . They could only hope for success within evolution if they were to eradicate the Christ-principle from Western culture. But this would be the same as eradicating the essential *meaning of the Earth* . . .' (*Correspondence and Documents*, 1901–25, RSP/AP New York, 1988, pp. 17–18). From these words of Rudolf Steiner it becomes understandable why from the very start the Theosophical Society of H.P. Blavatsky and H.S. Olcott bore so clearly an anti-Christian character (Rudolf Steiner speaks at some length about the anti-Christian impulses of Blavatsky in the lectures of 13 and 14 June 1923, *The Anthroposophic Movement*, Collison 1933). In contrast, 'the deepest aim' of the Western Masters was from the very beginning to work in the direction of '. . . knowledge and realising the intentions of the *living Christ*' (ibid.). It was out of such a knowledge and such an endeavour to do everything for their realisation that the aforesaid 'measure of the astral plane', which was to prepare the appearance of the 'living', that is of the *Etheric* Christ amongst mankind, was carried out during the first seven-year period of the twentieth century (between 1902 and 1909).

The Eastern Masters, however, *stood in opposition* to this 'measure', a circumstance which by the year 1907 had led to their total divergence from the Masters of the West and from the Western Rosicrucian esotericism which they inspired, an esotericism which is alone right and, moreover, wholly *necessary* for Western man. 'For,' in Rudolf Steiner's words, 'if it were to be lost, earthly humanity would come to renounce its meaning and true purpose' (ibid.). But these developments were not confined to the divergence of the two streams. For already in October 1909, as a kind of counter-weight to the 'measure of the *astral* plane', the foundations were laid in Benares (India) for a certain 'measure of the *earthly* plane' through the advancement of the Indian boy Krishnamurti as the physical reincarnation of the Christ. Then there began the so-called 'Alcyone affair'. That this was at any rate indirectly sanctioned by the Eastern Masters is borne out by the train of events that followed. After the scandal around Alcyone and his subsequent separation from the Theosophical Society at the beginning of the Thirties, this Society was so discredited in the eyes of the Western World as a whole that the Eastern Masters had to seek other channels for the attainment of their goals amongst the people of the West. That these goals have since that time not changed in any essential way, that (in other words) the general attitude of the Eastern Masters to the significance and place in the evolution of the Earth of the Christ-impulse has not become any different, is made apparent by, for example, the numerous works of their new 'medium', the American, Alice A. Bailey, who in the foreword to one of her books openly refers to the Master Kuthumi as her teacher and inspirer. Although Alice Bailey in her books hardly ever speaks about the Theosophical Society, which has become wholly discredited in the eyes of the West, and, moreover, does not mention the events connected with Alcyone, it is nevertheless the case that what she advocates with regard to the *physical* manifestation of Christ is not essentially any different from what Annie Besant advocated and tried to prove to the Western world forty years before. (See also—regarding Alice Bailey—the article by Jörgen Smit, 'Das Ereignis der Christus-Erscheinung in der ätherischen Welt' in the journal *Das Goetheanum*, 61st year, no. 19.)

423. This can be deduced from the fact that Rudolf Steiner, in the lecture of 26 December 1909 (*Festivals of the Seasons*, op. cit.) speaks about the impulses which had come to him from the spiritual world 'in the course of the last few years', while the first elements of the spiritual–scientific study of the Gospels appear in the lectures at the end of 1901 and the beginning of 1902 (see note 419).

424. Lecture of 26 December 1909.

425. That the Etheric Christ began to work amongst mankind in the year 1909 was spoken of by Rudolf Steiner in the lecture of 6 February 1917 (*Cosmic and Human Metamorphoses*, op. cit.) as follows: 'The occultist is able to point out that since the year 1909 or thereabouts what is to come is being distinctly and perceptibly prepared for, that since the year 1909 we have been inwardly living in a very special time. It is possible today, if we do

but seek Him, to be very near to Christ, to find Him in a quite different way than has been hitherto possible.'

426. This promulgation took place *twice* in Stockholm: first in a special lecture, not associated with the general course, for a smaller circle (12 January 1910), and then within the confines of the course itself, during the last lecture (15 January 1910) for all the participants (see also note 430).

427. Lecture of 23 January 1910 (GA 125, Typescript EN 46). The quotations that follow are from the same source.

428. The motif of the call of John the Baptist appears in one form or another in the following lectures from this period (the lectures cited here are only those of which a stenographic report was made and which have hitherto been published):

25 January 1910	Karlsruhe	*
27 January 1910	Heidelberg	†
2 February 1910	Berlin	†
6 February 1910	Kassel	GA 118
8 February 1910	Berlin	†
20 February 1910	Düsseldorf	(Typescript Z295)
9 March 1910	Berlin	†
15 March 1910	Munich	*
13 April 1910	Rome	GA 118
18 April 1910	Palermo	*
10 May 1910	Hanover	*

* *The Reappearance of Christ in the Etheric* (AP, New York 1983).
† *The Christ Impulse and the Development of Ego Consciousness*. See also note 429. (AP, New York 1976.)

429. *The Reappearance of Christ in the Etheric*, op. cit. We shall cite two further statements of Rudolf Steiner on this theme: 'Today one may say the same as was said then: Change your disposition of soul, so that you may find the Kingdom of Heaven that is approaching! Care must be taken that this hour shall not pass by unrecognised' (lecture of 6 February 1910, GA 118). 'The cry of John the Baptist, "Change the disposition of your souls", applies also to us today' (*The Christ Impulse and the Development of Ego Consciousness*, op. cit.). See also Rudolf Steiner's observation quoted on p. 43.

430. Novalis' participation in the preparation, in the spiritual world, of the new appearance of Christ in the etheric realm, together with his supersensible participation in the initial proclaiming of this event on Earth in January 1910 during the Stockholm cycle, 'The Gospel of St John and the Three Other Gospels' (not translated), is confirmed not only through the fact that the Stockholm cycle was framed on both sides by two lectures about Novalis (those of 26 December and 23 January) but above all by the inner composition of the cycle as a whole. Thus after three lectures of an essentially introductory nature, in the fourth lecture, which was given on

331

7 January, on the day after the Festival of the Appearance of God, Epiphany, the scene of the Baptism by John in the Jordan, together with the motif of John the Baptist's principal message to mankind, is placed at the centre of the themes under consideration. These *two* themes in their diverse aspects and variations then weave in one form or another through *all* the subsequent lectures (with the exception of the penultimate lecture, where Elijah is mentioned instead of John the Baptist). And on the morning of 12 January there follows Rudolf Steiner's *first* lecture about the advent in the etheric sphere. Evidently, it was given to only a small circle of people and bore the character of an esoteric lesson, in the course of which it was not permitted to take notes. This may serve to explain why the report that Marie Steiner made from memory after the lecture is significantly shorter than the rest of her reports of the lectures of this cycle.

The central theme of the next two lectures of the actual course, which were given on the evening of the same day (that is, at a time immediately after the first proclamation of the New Advent) and on the next day was that of the initiation of Lazarus. In both lectures, moreover, particular reference was made to the participation in this latter event of the entelechy of John the Baptist. Thus in the evening lecture of 12 January Rudolf Steiner speaks of how at the moment of the initiation of Lazarus— at the moment when the 'I am' of Christ, which had been awoken from the sleep of death, shone forth within him—the higher spiritual monad of man, Manas–Buddhi–Atma, united with Lazarus from the spiritual worlds. And it is known from Rudolf Steiner's verbal elucidation of his 'Last Address' that the individuality who served as the supersensible *means* for such a union of the higher spiritual monad with the initiated Lazarus was that of John the Baptist (see the introduction to *The Last Address*). In other words, from the moment of Lazarus' initiation in Bethany the individuality of John the Baptist worked within him as a 'Bodhisattva' (see Rudolf Grosse, *The Living Being of Anthroposophia*, Steiner Book Centre, Vancouver, 1986, ch. 3).

This motif of the spiritual union and subsequent working together of the Christ-initiated Lazarus and the entelechy of John the Baptist is also taken up in the next lecture of the cycle (that of 13 January), where Rudolf Steiner speaks of how the initiated Lazarus was able to unite in his initiation the principal fruits of *both* aspects of the Mysteries—the Southern and the Northern. His own awakening after a three-day, death-like sleep was in its nature more connected with the Southern or 'Egyptian' Mysteries (the descent into the microcosm); while through his being 'overshone' by the entelechy of John the Baptist the fruits of the Northern Mysteries (flowing from the macrocosm) also became accessible to him. In the lecture of 13 January Rudolf Steiner refers to this when he says that the receiving of the fruits of the Northern Mysteries was made possible for the initiated Lazarus through his clairvoyant beholding in the Akashic Chronicle of the scene of the Baptism in the Jordan.

However, such a supersensible beholding of an event at which Lazarus–John was not personally present, as with all the other events described in the Gospel of St John *before* the chapter about his raising from the dead, became accessible to his clairvoyant gaze only through being overshone in his soul by the entelechy of John the Baptist. Thus with regard to the first ten chapters of the fourth Gospel, one can in a certain sense speak of their *dual* authorship, that is, of the participation in their writing of *both* Johns: John–Lazarus and John the Baptist (see *The Gospel of St John*, op. cit., lecture of 22 May 1908).

Thus through his spiritual union with John the Baptist, John–Lazarus was able to receive into himself the totality of the latter's macrocosmic experiences in his life after death. But this is not all. For with the clairvoyant beholding of the scene of the Baptism, there also came before John–Lazarus an imagination of how the chief representative and highest Initiate of the Northern Mysteries, Zarathustra, had forsaken the sheaths of Jesus of Nazareth and passed into the spiritual world, that is, became united in that moment with the whole spiritual macrocosm. (For further indications regarding the connection of Zarathustra with the Northern Mysteries, other than those given in the lecture of 13 January of the Stockholm cycle, see also the lecture of 19 December 1910, *Background to the Gospel of St Mark*, RSP/AP 1968.) It should also be said that the possibility of beholding this deed was—in addition to the supersensible help given by the entelechy of John the Baptist—also furthered by the karmic connection between Lazarus and Zarathustra, inasmuch as the former had, as a result of the resolve of the world rulership, 'as though vicariously' to take the place of the latter in the immediate circle of the incarnated disciples of Christ Jesus (see GA 264).

The Stockholm cycle reaches its culmination in the concluding eleventh lecture (of 15 January), where Rudolf Steiner now, no longer in a smaller circle but before all those participating in the course, speaks for the first time completely openly about the Etheric Advent of Christ. Almost all the principal motifs of this proclamation as they were introduced for the first time in the morning lecture of 12 January appear again almost unchanged in the lecture of 15 January and are then once again repeated in the lecture of 23 January in Strasbourg, though now in connection with the theme of Novalis. In both these two lectures the motif of the renewed call of John the Baptist, the call which is now to be brought into the world through modern spiritual science, appears, too, as a summons to inner wakefulness and to a readiness to perceive the new Christ-event. (The author considers that there must have been a reference to the renewed call of John in the lecture of 12 January which, however, was not retained in the report.)

In connection with everything that has been said in this note, it is important still to mention the reference in the last lecture of the

Stockholm cycle to Raphael's *Sistine Madonna* as an example to elucidate the thought about the difference between the law of love given to humanity by Gautama Buddha and its actual *substance* as brought to the Earth by Christ Jesus. The very fact that Rudolf Steiner elucidates this difference through the example of the *Sistine Madonna* as the most perfect expression of the impulse of love in the fine arts can acquire a particular significance if we recall all that was said in the fourth chapter about the spiritual characteristics of Raphael's etheric body.

431. *The Gospel of St Matthew*, op cit.; *Background to the Gospel of St Mark*, op. cit., and *The Gospel of St Mark*, op. cit. Of course, there were also other spiritual individualities besides the entelechy of Novalis who participated in the engendering of these and the earlier Gospel cycles and also the individual lectures cited below.

432. For example, the lectures of 11 and 25 February 1911 (see, respectively, Typescripts AQ 22:2 and AQ 21:4).

433. Lecture of 3 May 1911 (*The Concepts of Original Sin and Grace*, RSP 1973).

434. The majority of the lectures on these themes can be found in *Earthly and Cosmic Man*, op. cit., GA 143 and GA 155 (the 1912 lectures of this latter volume may be found under the titles, *On the Meaning of Life*, AP, New York 1946, and *The Spiritual Ground of Morality*, op. cit. [Many of the lectures in GA 143 can be found in English translation in one place or another (mainly in Typescript form), but not all those relevant have been translated.—Translator's note.]

435. 16 May 1912 (GA 143, Typescript NSL 184).

436. See his unfinished poem, 'Die Vermählung der Jahreszeiten' ('The Marriage of the Seasons').

437. Words of Marie Steiner from the foreword to the first edition of the lecture in the year 1930. In the cycle, *The Bhagavad Gita and the Epistles of Paul*, op. cit., which was given alongside this lecture, virtually nothing is said about Elijah, John the Baptist, Raphael or Novalis (apart from the reference to Raphael in the first lecture); nor is there any mention of the renewed call of John the Baptist in its familiar form. However, at the very end of the last lecture, which, as we have seen (see p. 137), was a kind of spiritual legacy to the newly founded Anthroposophical Society, this call appears again—though in a completely transformed way—as a means of bringing together the entire content of the cycle. Thus the last lecture, and with it the whole cycle, ends with a reference to two principal tasks of Anthroposophy and the Anthroposophical Society: 'This Anthroposophy will lead us to the divine and to Gods.' And then: 'This can be a reminder to us that, through it, we seek above all things self-knowledge, self-instruction . . . self-education, self-discipline . . .' Here 'self-knowledge' and 'self-education' are none other than an adherence to the first half of the renewed call of John, 'Change your ways [your disposition of soul] . . .' while the path 'to the divine and to Gods' is a fulfilment of its

334

second half: '. . . for the human ego is nigh unto the Kingdom of Heaven' (see note 427).

438. Before the address of 29 December 1912, Marie Steiner recited poems 2, 3, 4, 8, 9 and 10 from Novalis' *Spiritual Songs*.

439. In this connection there is a particular significance in the fact that only with the proclamation of the birth of the Luke Jesus and John the Baptist is the Archangel Gabriel, who was sent to bring tidings of these events, referred to by name (1:19 and 26). At the proclaiming of the Matthew Jesus, only 'the Angel of the Lord' is mentioned (1:20 and 24).

440. Rudolf Meyer, *Novalis*, Stuttgart 1972.

441. See the end of note 412.

442. 17 December 1906 ('Signs and Symbols of the Christmas Festival', *The Festivals and Their Meaning*, op. cit.) and 25 December 1907 (*The Mysteries, A Christmas and Easter Poem by Goethe*, Mercury Press, Spring Valley, 1987).

443. This was preceded by the first lecture about Novalis, on 26 October 1908, GA 108. Both were accompanied by the recitation of his words by Marie Steiner; the first lecture by poems from the cycle, *Hymns to the Night*, the second from the *Spiritual Songs*. At the end of the lecture on 22 December, Rudolf Steiner also speaks about Raphael and the *Sistine Madonna* and refers to the spiritual continuity of the 'Mary theme' between Raphael and Novalis. The more sensitive reader might sense at this point that the mystery of the karmic biography of Novalis, which Rudolf Steiner was to unfold two weeks later in the lecture of 6 January 1909 in Munich, is beginning to sound for the first time. [The lecture of 22 December 1900 is published under the title of *The Christmas Mystery. Novalis as Seer*, op. cit. The lecture of 26 October 1908 is included in GA 108.—Translator's note.]

444. See note 425. The 'Novalis theme' also appears in the middle of this year in the lecture-cycle, *The Gospel of St John and its Relation to the Other Three Gospels*, op. cit., the most extensive of the Gospel cycles, the first lecture of which was given on St John's Day (24 June 1909). In this cycle, the most significant words which Rudolf Steiner ever spoke about the Baptism in the Jordan can be found at the beginning of the tenth lecture (that of 3 July): 'I beg you to realise from the outset that it is necessarily difficult to comprehend what actually occurred at the Baptism by John, *inasmuch as this was the greatest event of Earth evolution*.' And on the day after this lecture, in which the event of the Baptism by John occupies the central place, on the morning of 4 July, a morning gathering devoted to Novalis is organised by Rudolf Steiner at which Marie Steiner reads his *Spiritual Songs* and the *Marienlieder*.

This latter event is also connected with the fact that in the lecture given on the previous day (that of 3 July) Rudolf Steiner for the first time reveals to anthroposophists the mystery of the transformation of Mary when Jesus was baptised in the Jordan.

445. Of the lecture in Esslingen, apart from the title of its principle theme, no

notes have been preserved (Hans Schmidt, *Das Vortragswerk Rudolf Steiners*, Dornach 1978). The Christmas cycle of the year 1910, given in Stuttgart from 27 December 1910 until 1 January 1911, bore the title, *Occult History. Esoteric Studies of the Karmic Connections of the Personalities and Events of World History* (English translation published by APC 1957).

446. The lectures in question are those of 21 and 26 December 1911 (respectively, 'Christmas: a Festival of Inspiration' (*Festivals of the Seasons*, op. cit.) and 'The Birth of the Sun-Spirit as the Spirit of the Earth. The Thirteen Holy Nights' (*The Festivals and their Meaning*, op. cit.). In both of them it is referred to how until the fourth century of the Christian era the principal Festival of the birth of Christ in the earthly sphere was on 6 January (the Baptism in the Jordan). Only as Christianity became increasingly an outward force and as the deeper understanding of the actual events accordingly became lost was the Festival transferred to 25 December, which in a deeper sense signified a backward step from the Christ-principle to the Jesus-principle. Thus in both lectures Rudolf Steiner particularly emphasises, as an essential means of overcoming modern materialism, the need to arrive through spiritual science at a new understanding not only of the earthly birth of Jesus but *especially of the supersensible birth in Him of the Christ*. These two lectures for members of the Society were preceded by the public lecture given on 14 December: 'The Prophet Elijah in the Light of Spiritual Science' (*Turning Points in Spiritual History*, op. cit., 1987), where for the first time light was shed, from an occult point of view, upon the connection of the spiritual being of Elijah with his physical bearer Naboth, a connection which makes fully apparent his essential nature as a 'Bodhisattva-like' being.

447. Rudolf Steiner speaks for the first time about the three preparatory stages of the Mystery of Golgotha in the fourth lecture of the Christmas cycle of 1913 entitled *Christ and the Spiritual World. The Search for the Holy Grail*, op. cit., while in the next, fifth lecture Rudolf Steiner refers to the connection with them particularly of the prophet Elijah.

448. Hence it is not for nothing that Rudolf Steiner in the lecture inaugurating of the Erfurt 'Johannes–Raphael' Branch (on 13 April 1913, GA 150) speaks so very clearly of the help which he had on more than one occasion received from the souls of the dead in the course of his spiritual–scientific investigations.

449. As a 'motto' for 'the anthroposophical spiritual stream' Rudolf Steiner chose the poem by Novalis which he read at the end of the lecture, 'Wenn nicht mehr Zahlen und Figuren . . .', slightly adapting the final line. From the whole character of the lecture, and also from Rudolf Steiner's substantiation of the need for this change, the more sensitive reader may feel that this small change was directly inspired by Novalis himself from the spiritual world. For it was in such a way that Novalis wished to see the final line of his poem, a century after his death, as a 'motto' for the 'anthroposophical spiritual stream'.

450. To be more precise, this inspiration can be felt from Autumn 1919 onwards in the lecture cycle, 'The Mission of the Archangel Michael. The Revelations of the Essential Secrets of Man's Being' (see *The Mission of the Archangel Michael*, AP 1980; *The Michael Revelation* (GA 194), Typescript Z 415; and *The Mysteries of Light, of Space and of the Earth*, 1945, AP/RSPC, republished as *The Task of the English-speaking Peoples*, RSP 1992) where the motif of Michael's 'pre-Christian activity' as the Countenance of Jahve and the transformation of his mission as a result of the Mystery of Golgotha appears with considerable force. This theme is then repeated in the Christmas Day lecture of 1919 (*The Festivals and their Meaning*, op. cit.).

451. The cycle entitled *The Boundaries of Natural Science* (AP 1983).

452. See Novalis' *Mathematische Fragmente*.

453. Lecture of 25 December 1920 (*The Search for the New Isis*, Mercury Press, Spring Valley, 1983).

454. See the lecture of 9 April 1921 (*Materialism and the Task of Anthroposophy*, AP/RSP 1987).

455. Lecture of 25 December 1921 (GA 209, Typescript Z 22).

456. See the lecture of 24 December 1922 (*Man and the World of Stars. The Spiritual Communion of Mankind*, op. cit.).

457. John 3:30–31. In the same way one can feel in the last lecture of the cycle, given in the First Goetheanum on New Year's Eve on 'The Spiritual Communion of Mankind', the presence of the inspiration of Novalis, who strove to transform the whole of earthly life into a ceaseless consecrative act, into a purely spiritual process of higher, spiritual communion (see his words on pp. 87). Moreover, the inspiration of Novalis can also be felt in other lectures and cycles of the year 1923 which Rudolf Steiner gave at other festivals. For instance, in the Vienna cycle 'Anthroposophy and Human Feeling (Gemüt)' (*Michaelmas and the Soul Forces of Man*, AP 1946, formerly *Anthroposophy and the Human Gemüt*) where the theme of utter faithfulness to spiritual impulses, a motif with which Novalis concludes his work, *Christendom or Europe*, appears with particular force. And is not the whole character of the cycle reminiscent of that realm of spiritual–scientific truths which Rudolf Steiner, in a lecture of 17 September 1912 where he speaks about the deeds of Elijah amongst mankind, calls 'truths experienced in the realm of feeling' (17 September 1912, *The Gospel of St Mark*, op. cit.)? Finally, there is the reference in the lecture of 6 October 1923, which is devoted to a description of the cosmic imagination of Christmas, to Raphael's Madonna as the most perfect artistic representation of a higher spiritual reality (*The Four Seasons and the Archangels*, RSP 1968).

458. Similarly in Rudolf Steiner's last Christmas article (*Anthroposophical Leading Thoughts*, op. cit., p. 132), words are to be found which we may relate with full justice to Novalis, words about the need to introduce the principle of love into what is initially the cold, intellectual element of the consciousness soul (see note 412). And on the day after Christmas Marie

Steiner recites Novalis' *Spiritual Songs* in the Schreinerei [the old carpentry workshop which served as a hall after the fire of New Year's Eve, 1922—Translator's note].

459. *Festivals of the Seasons*, op. cit., lecture 6. Rudolf Steiner also speaks about the birth in the future of 'the great Easter Festival of mankind'—if the mood springing from an anthroposophically understood Christmas Festival is able to hold sway already today in all anthroposophical groups—at the end of the lecture of 27 December 1910 ('Yuletide and the Christmas Festival', GA 125, Typescript AQ 19:4). Here he refers in particular to two events which must take place if this transition from Christmas to Easter is really to happen in the manner described: 'So we look towards something that shines with the same certainty as the prophecy of the renewal of the vision of Christ given to us through Theodora in "The Portal of Initiation". With as great a certainty there lives within our souls the resurrection of the anthroposophical spirit in science, religion, art and in the whole life of humanity. The great Easter Festival of mankind stands before our anticipating souls.'

From these words of Rudolf Steiner it is evident that, from this standpoint too, the most essential elements of Novalis' future mission and the principal tasks of modern spiritual science are united together in a single whole: his service of the Etheric Christ and his aspiration towards the achievement of a higher synthesis between science, art and religion out of a truly Rosicrucian spirit. (See p. 135, and also note 386). Such an aspiration also connects the entelechy of Novalis with the First Goetheanum (an association of which more will be said later on in this chapter), which was a visible expression of this synthesis (see the lecture of 22 February 1923, *Awakening to Community*, AP 1974). Rudolf Steiner also speaks about the union of science, art and religion, as the most important task of the modern science of the spirit, at the laying of its Foundation Stone (*Guidance in Esoteric Training*, op. cit.).

460. GA 143, Typescript NSL 184.

461. At this point one should recall that in May, when the fate of the Johannes-Bau project in Munich was to be resolved, Rudolf Steiner spoke in his lectures again and again—more often than at any other time—about Novalis' karmic biography (see also note 494).

462. See p. 132. In so far as the transition from the fifth to the sixth cultural epoch is a microcosmic anticipation of the great transition from the incarnation of Earth to that of Jupiter, it is at the same time a preliminary (so to say) microcosmic fulfilment of the 'goal of the Earth's becoming', or at any rate a first, essential step in its direction.

463. This is why in the third part of the Foundation Stone Meditation, which has to do with the Third Hierarchy, are to be found the words:

Where the eternal *aims of Gods*
World-Being's Light
On thine own I
Bestow
For thy free Willling.

464. Regarding the connection of the Angels with the Moon-sphere, see the lecture of 15 April 1909 (*The Spiritual Hierarchies and Their Reflection in the Physical World*, AP 1970) and the lecture of 24 May 1924 (*Karmic Relationships*, vol. v, RSP 1984).
465. Rudolf Steiner speaks in many lectures of 1923 and 1924 about the Moon Teachers of Wisdom (see *The Evolution of Consciousness*, op. cit.; *Supersensible Man*, APC 1961; *Mystery Knowledge and Mystery Centres*, RSP 1973; *World History in the Light of Anthroposophy*, op. cit.; *Karmic Relationships*, vols v and vi, op. cit.). For example, in the lecture of 30 March 1924 (*Karmic Relationships*, vol. v) he calls them—as does Hilarius in his speech—'Spirit Beings'.
466. Lecture of 28 August 1923 (*The Evolution of Consciousness*, op. cit.).
467. In the lecture of 28 August 1924 (*Karmic Relationships*, vol. vi, op. cit.), Rudolf Steiner connects the Moon Teachers with the past of Earth evolution and the Beings above them belonging to the Hierarchy of the Angels with the future; in other words: the former with the ancient *wisdom* of humanity and the latter with humanity's future *purposes* (see the way in which the words 'wisdom' and 'purposes' are used in the speech of Hilarius).
468. Lecture of 28 September 1924 (*The Last Address*, op. cit.).
469. See the lecture of 20 September 1912 (*The Gospel of St Mark*, op. cit.). It is interesting that in the lecture cycle *The Gospel of St Luke*, op. cit., which actually contains the first communications from the Fifth Gospel, in the sixth lecture (that of 20 September 1909) the individuality of John the Baptist—together with his relationship to the mission of the ancient Hebrew people and to the spiritual streams of Zarathustra and Buddha—again occupies a central place. On the other hand, in the address at the laying of the Foundation Stone of the First Goetheanum on 20 September 1913 (of which more will be said later on in this chapter), Rudolf Steiner touches upon themes that are connected with the innermost yearnings of Novalis. This can be said especially of the first promulgation of the words of the 'Macrocosmic Lord's Prayer', which gives expression to the earthly path that mankind has to follow as a result of the 'Fall' of the first man, Adam, and to the great 'cry of longing of [modern] humanity for the spirit' to which this path leads, a cry to which spiritual science is now called to give an answer. The allusion at this end of the address to the need for a higher union of science, art and religion out of the sources of a new revelation of the spirit also bears a relationship to the same themes. Later on, Rudolf Steiner often said that the First Goetheanum as a whole, as a

total work of art, represented a way in which one could see this higher union *with one's own eyes* (for example, in the lecture of 22 February 1923, *Awakening to Community*, op. cit.).

470. See *The Fifth Gospel*, op. cit., especially the lecture of 5 October 1913, and also the lecture by Hella Wiesberger, 'Marie Steiner und die Novalisforschung Rudolf Steiners' (given on the 25th anniversary of her death). Published in *Beitrage zur Rudolf Steiner Gesamtausgabe*, nos. 43/44.

471. See further regarding the First Goetheanum in *Rudolf Steiner and the Founding of the New Mysteries*, op. cit., ch. 4.

472. Quoted by Wilhelm Kelber, *Raphael* (Stuttgart 1979).

473. Lecture of 5 May 1909 (GA 284/5, Typescript Z 147). Before giving a detailed description of the two pictures, Rudolf Steiner also spoke briefly about the problem of the two central figures in *The School of Athens*. What he said was that it is *not impossible* that these two figures could be Plato and Aristotle, although at the same time he emphasised that for a truly artistic understanding of the picture this purely intellectual element is of no significance. In the context of the whole lecture, the essential point for him was the fact that the figures in this picture are associated with the *pre-Christian* period of human evolution.

474. Ibid. In 1909 the word 'Theosophy' was used instead of the word 'Anthroposophy'.

475. See note 473. Rudolf Steiner's observation in the lecture of 5 May 1909 that the so-called *School of Athens* by Raphael—in contrast to his *Disputa*—depicted a scene from the *pre-Christian* period of human evolution would seem to be in complete contradiction with his later views. According to these later statements, the *School of Athens* portrays a scene out of the life of the Apostle Paul (Acts 17:15–34), with, for example, the group of people writing on the left representing the Evangelists, and so on—that is to say, we are concerned here with a depiction of the earliest times of the Christian era (see the lectures of 2 May 1912, *Earthly and Cosmic Man*, op. cit.; 13 April 1913, *The Inner Nature of Man and Life and Life Between Death and Rebirth*, op. cit.; the answer to the question after the lecture of 27 April 1913, *The Life between Death and Rebirth*, AP 1968; and the lectures of 1 November 1916 (Typescript R11, 'The History of Art') and 5 October 1917 (GA 292)).

Of course, there cannot really be any question that the true motive for Rudolf Steiner's change of opinion on this matter in later years was a mere feeling of inner protest against the profoundly inartistic nature of the traditional understanding of this picture as put foward in the guide of that time to the Vatican museums, the so-called 'Baedeker'. However, what appears to be a contradiction is resolved upon closer examination. The point is that in each of these two cases the attention of the spirit-researcher reading in the Akashic Record was directed towards two completely different aspects of this particular problem. For the *School of Athens* had *two* clearly distinguishable sources of inspiration. The first was connected with the especially powerful influence of the ruling spirit of exoteric Christianity in fifteenth–sixteenth century Rome where Raphael was working. As we have already seen (see p. 14), this spirit was in the past the Folk-Archangel of ancient Greece; then he ascended to the rank of Time-Spirit, and after the founding of Christianity took upon himself the rulership of its exoteric evolution, that is, principally that of the *Church*. Thus it is in the bosom of this high Hierarchic Spirit that we should seek the underlying impulse of the *Renaissance*, which aspired to unite the best achievement of ancient Greek culture with the forms of ecclesiastical or exoteric Christianity as they existed at that time. This spiritual aspiration was at that time the predominant one in Raphael's environment; antiquity and Christianity were the two pillars that bore the whole cultural evolution of that epoch.

Thus when Raphael painted these two pictures, the ruling Spirit of exoteric Christianity was working upon him with particular power from his whole surroundings (in that the Rome of that time and most especially the Vatican itself were indeed the focal point of the impulses of exoteric Christianity). This Spirit inspired Raphael *unconsciously* (to himself, that is) to paint the *two* pictures in such a form that one portrays, so to speak, the 'youth' of the aforesaid Hierarchic Spirit and the other his 'maturity'; or, in other words, so that they express to a remarkable degree of artistic perfection the whole character of the activity of this Spirit *before* and *after* the Mystery of Golgotha.

For this reason, in describing how these two pictures arose (in the lecture of 5 May 1909, Typescript Z 147), Rudolf Steiner makes it fully apparent that in the course of their creation the moods and impulses of Raphael's immediate environment were active within his soul. Rudolf Steiner goes on to describe these moods in the following words: 'For this was, indeed, what was experienced by a man who was able to grasp the meaning of evolution at that time [in the epoch of Raphael]. He looked back *to pre-Christian times*, when the sense world surrounded the human being as do the architectural forms of the first picture; and he perceived his own time, which through the coming of Christ Jesus had revealed a spiritual element to mankind, in the second picture. He felt part of his time; he felt his existence to be in complete correspondence with the existence of thousands. And so what was living in the souls of men had deeply imbued the imagination and the hand of the artist who painted these pictures, *so that what was living in the inner regions of the soul came to meet man in the outer world.*' From these words we may feel how in Raphael's soul, largely without his conscious knowledge, there worked the inspirations of the ruling spirit of exoteric Christianity, the former Archangel of the people of ancient Greece, striving in the age of the Renaissance to unite the culture of antiquity with Christianity. And the inspiring memories of the Spirit of exoteric Christianity regarding his connection with Greek culture were of such strength around Raphael that during the first decade after his death the names of the *Timaeus* of Plato and the *Ethics* of Aristotle were written on the two books which the central figures hold in their hands (5 October 1917, GA 292), and the words from St Luke's Gospel on the blackboard in the left part of the picture are replaced with a Pythagorean formula (5 October 1917, GA 292).

Thus in the course of his researches into the Akashic Chronicle in May 1909, Rudolf Steiner's spirit-vision was first and foremost directed towards that spiritually objective reality which found its expression in the *School of Athens*, towards that with which, independently of Raphael's will and his personal intentions, 'the hand of the artist had been deeply imbued'. This means that it was not the inner impulses working within Raphael's soul as his *conscious* intentions but the higher inspiring forces of the Hierarchic Spirit with which Raphael had been particularly connected in his previous incarnation that most especially interested Rudolf Steiner in the course of his researches into this matter in the Akashic Chronicle during the May of 1909.

However, this state of affairs soon changed altogether. For since the appearance of the Etheric Christ in the spiritual world and especially since the beginning of the public proclamation of this event amongst mankind in January 1910, the whole of Rudolf Steiner's attention was, in the first instance, directed towards the central spiritual event of our time and also towards those individualities in the spiritual world who were its preparers and progenitors. To these individualities Novalis also belonged, in that he prophetically anticipated the *modern* Damascus event not only in his last incarnation but, as we have seen (see p. 29 and note 106), in his incarnation as Raphael.

For this reason, from the moment indicated, the inner circle of the *spiritual experiences and intentions of Raphael himself* becomes for Rudolf Steiner the *sole* matter of importance. Not what unconsciously influenced Raphael from his spiritual environment, but what he strove *consciously*— as the central theme of his entire life—to embody in the *School of Athens* was now for Rudolf Steiner of decisive significance. From this time onwards, his inner eye was, in the course of his further investigations in the Akashic Chronicle, now directed exclusively towards the *inner world* of Raphael himself, and this is in itself a proof of Rudolf Steiner's direct spiritual connection with this individuality during those years. And his research in the Akashic Chronicle from this new point of view had as its result the revelation of the fact' . . . that [in the *School of Athens*] Raphael actually *wanted* to depict that moment when Paul appeared among the Greeks' (lecture of 2 May 1912, *Earthly and Cosmic Man*, op. cit.). Moreover, further investigations showed that the figure of Paul and his experience of Damascus was in a certain sense the *central* figure in Raphael's life of soul. For at this time ' . . . what lived in Paul, the vision, the Mystery of Damascus, and, hence, also the figure of Paul in general, had become a problem. For this reason, Raphael tried in his later course of development to comprehend the figure of Paul and to incorporate him in all kinds of different pictures' (lecture of 5 October 1917, GA 292). In other words, Raphael wanted with his whole soul '. . . to establish a Pauline vision of the world' (ibid.), he wanted to communicate to other men something of that Damascus experience through which, in prophetic anticipation of the future, he had himself passed. And it was this raying forth of the Damascus experience of Paul from within the soul of Raphael (and also, later on, within the soul of Novalis), together with his endeavours to bring his contemporaries closer to an understanding of it, that was for Rudolf Steiner of sole importance in all his subsequent occult investigations connected with the origin and sources of the *School of Athens* and in all that he said about it in his lectures from 1910 onwards.

476. Rudolf Steiner's address at the laying of the Foundation Stone of the First Goetheanum, 20 September 1913 (included in *Guidance in Esoteric Training*, RSP 1972).

477. In the lecture of 21 November 1919 (*The Mission of the Archangel Michael*, AP 1980), Rudolf Steiner speaks of how the spreading of the knowledge regarding the new 'trinity': the Christ-impulse maintaining the forces of Lucifer and Ahriman in a state of equilibrium, belongs to those fundamental impulses which in our time proceed directly from the *Time-Spirit*—Michael.

478. In our time the representative of this cosmic sphere for mankind is the Spirit of Michael. Hence Rudolf Steiner refers to the lecture of 2 April 1923 (*The Cycle of the Year as Breathing-Process of the Earth*, AP 1984) to Michael as the modern inspirer of the higher synthesis of religion, art and science, or, in the words of the Foundation Stone Meditation, of 'true life', 'true feeling' and 'true thinking'.

479. Lecture of 6 January 1918 (*Ancient Myths, Their Meaning and Connection with Evolution*, Steiner Book Centre, N. Vancouver, 1981).

480. As to how this deep inner yearning of Novalis to lift the veil of Isis, the Divine Sophia, was fulfilled as a real, occult act by Rudolf Steiner at the Christmas Conference of 1923/1924, see *Rudolf Steiner and the Founding of the New Mysteries*, op. cit., ch. 5.

481. See note 479.

482. In the Transfiguration on Mount Tabor, Christ revealed His high *Sun*-nature to His three chosen disciples, Peter, John and James. He manifested Himself to them not only as the most exalted Spirit of the Sun but also as the bearer of the spiritual light of the six leading Sun Elohim (see the lecture of 20 May 1908, *The Gospel of St John*, op. cit.). Through the Mystery of Golgotha, Christ united this substance of spiritual light, the seed of the Earth's becoming a new Sun, with the Earth's spiritual aura (John 1:4–5 and 9–10), and in this aura the Apostle Paul was able to behold it on the road to Damascus as a testimony that all the Old Testament mystery-teachings regarding the coming of the Messiah had been fulfilled.

If at this point we again recall that the figure of Paul, together with his

343

Damascus experience, stood at the centre of Raphael's soul life in the later period of his creative activity (see note 475), it will become still clearer to us why he chose as the theme of his last painting *The Transfiguration of Christ on Mount Tabor*. It is indeed the case that a profound secret of the karmic foundations of Raphael's biography lies hidden in the figures of this painting. For do not the two anonymous witnesses of this scene depicted above on the left remind us of the two Johns: of the incarnate Lazarus–John, immersed in shadow with his hands in a praying gesture, and of John the Baptist who, connected with the former, from out of the spiritual worlds, appears clad in a golden chasuble and freely reaches out towards the radiance of the spiritual Sun? This supposition is confirmed in a remarkable way by the conversation—contained in all three synoptic Gospels—which the three chosen disciples had on their way back from Mount Tabor. This conversation is reported with the greatest precision in the Gospel according to St Matthew: 'And as they were coming down the mountain . . . the disciples asked Him: "Then why do the scribes say that Elijah must first come?" Jesus answered: "Elijah must indeed come and put everything in order; but I tell you that Elijah has already come, and they did not know him but did to him whatever they pleased" (17:9–12).' After their experience on Mount Tabor the disciples of Christ Jesus ask not about Moses but about *Elijah*, and they receive an answer which refers them to the law of reincarnation, to the '*second*' coming of Elijah into the earthly world, and which at the same time testifies to the fact that Elijah has already been in the world but men did not recognise him. But this is not all. For this answer of Christ Jesus strengthens in the disciples the inspiration of that spiritual being who was a supersensible witness of the Lord's Transfiguration and, according to Rudolf Steiner, the new, accompanying 'group-soul' of the Apostles (see the lecture of 20 September 1912, *The Gospel of St Mark*, op. cit.). This being awakens in the disciples an *understanding* of what Christ Jesus actually meant by His answer: 'Then the disciples *understood* that He was speaking to them of John the Baptist (17:13). And so the entelechy of John the Baptist is at this moment awakening in the disciples an awareness of itself.

483. In the lecture of 9 March 1910 (*The Christ-Impulse and the Development of Ego-Consciousness*, op. cit.), Rudolf Steiner characterises Shamballa in the following words: 'Man's physical environment will present a totally different aspect in the course of the next 2500 years through the entry into his field of awareness of an *etheric realm*, which indeed is already here but which man must still learn to perceive.' And somewhat later in the same lecture he characterises it once again as a special 'realm of the Earth's orbit [which] is indeed there but only for the man who is able to behold it.' Is it not this 'realm of the Earth's orbit', the last vestige of memory of the primordial condition of mankind, that Novalis has in mind when he writes: 'Paradise has, so to speak, been *dispersed* over the whole Earth and has therefore become so unrecognisable—its dispersed features shall be

united—its skeleton shall be filled out. Regeneration of Paradise?' (Regarding the occult processes in the etheric environment of the Earth which stand behind these words of Novalis, see *The Cycle of the Year as a Path of Initiation*, op. cit., Part IX, ch. 1.)

484. Lecture of 9 March 1910 (*The Christ-Impulse and the Development of Ego-Consciousness*, op cit.). 'This is the land from which, at certain times, Initiates and Bodhisattvas ever and again draw their forces.'

485. Lecture of 16 March 1905 (GA 53, Typescript Z 231). And then Rudolf Steiner continues: 'Anyone who reads Novalis will feel something of the breath which leads one into this higher world. It is not expressed in the usual way, but there is something in him that charms or spells also have,' these having significance '. . .as much for ordinary, undeveloped people as they have for Initiates.'

486. Lecture of 22 December 1908 (*The Christmas Mystery: Novalis as Seer*, op. cit.).

487. Lecture of 9 March 1910, see above.

488. Lecture of 15 March 1910 (*The Reappearance of Christ in the Etheric*, op. cit.).

489. Lecture of 22 December 1908, see above.

490. Lecture of 14 October 1911 (*From Jesus to Christ*, op cit.).

491. Lecture of 30 May 1912 (*The Spiritual Foundation of Morality*, op. cit.).

492. Lecture of 14 May 1912 (*Earthly and Cosmic Man*, op. cit.).

493. Lecture of 8 May 1912 (Typescript AQ 18:1) and of 14 May 1912 (as above). Between these two lectures Rudolf Steiner gave only two 'esoteric lessons', both on 9 May in Cologne.

494. Typescript NSL 184. Thus we have the following picture of the evolution of the theme under consideration (in May 1912):

> 2 May — all four incarnations are spoken of,
> 6 May — about Raphael,
> * 8 *May* — about all four incarnations,
> *14 *May* — about Raphael,
> 16 May — about all four incarnations,
> *20 May — about Raphael and his father (John the Baptist is also mentioned as Raphael's former incarnation),
> 23 May — about all four incarnations (Raphael's relationship to his father is again described, and there is also a reference to the individuality of Adam).
> *30 May — the individuality of Adam is mentioned.

(The lectures of 2, 14 and 20 May are contained in *Earthly and Cosmic Man*; that of 23 May in *On the Meaning of Life*; that of 30 May in *The Spiritual Foundation of Morality*; those of 8 May and 16 May respectively in Typescripts AQ 18:1 and NSL 184; while that of 6 May is unpublished even in German.) On 6 May, apart from the lecture for members of the Society, a public lecture—entitled 'Christ and the Twentieth Century'—was also given, in which Rudolf Steiner, to the extent to which this was actually possible in an *open* lecture, speaks about the future possibility of a new clairvoyant experience of Christ in the twentieth century. Moreover, in the course of this month Rudolf Steiner on four occasions describes the process whereby new sheaths can be formed for the Christ Being out of human deeds of conscience, love and wonder (*), and on two occasions he speaks of how Christ Jesus looked in his physical appearance (dates in italics).

In the lectures of 7 and 16 May (GA 143; that of 7 May is contained in Typescript AQ 8:1; 16 May in NSL 184) Rudolf Steiner also refers to the newly published *Anthroposophical Calendar of the Soul* (this is mentioned for the first time in the lecture of 23 April, *Earthly and Cosmic Man*, op. cit.

495. Lecture of 14 May 1912 (*Earthly and Cosmic Man*).

496. This has its origin in the fact that the principal task of the fifth post-Atlantean epoch is to investigate the outer world of the senses and to enter with particular intensity into the world of matter, so that through such intimate knowledge of it the foundation for its future spiritualisation be established. However, if this immersion into the realm of matter is to serve the good rather than be to the detriment of earthly evolution, a new, conscious relationship to the Christ-impulse is needed, for this alone can lead mankind out of the realm of matter and death, which it has entered for the full development of its human ego-consciousness. On the other hand, in the sixth cultural epoch, the first anticipation of the future Jupiter condition, the principal task will be that of turning towards the working with the forces of the spiritual cosmos, that is, of consciously ascending into the sphere of the Sophia. For this reason, the Sophia mysteries must, at the time indicated, be united with the mysteries of the Christ.

497. One such preparer of the Slavic peoples for their future mission was one of the leading Initiates of post-Atlantean evolution, who in ancient times worked in the Northern part of the Black Sea region under the name of Scythianus (see the lecture of 9 November 1914, GA 158, Typescript Z 144).

498. Lecture of 19 February 1922 (*Old and New Methods of Initiation*, RSP 1991).

499. In the historical evolution of mankind this destiny of Goethe is remarkably akin to the destiny of Moses, who, like Goethe—albeit in completely different historical circumstances—also reached only the borders of the 'Promised Land', the place of the future physical incarnation and earthly activity of the 'I am that I am' impulse, and was unable actually to enter it.

500. That even Goethe attained consciousness soul development only in part and in many respects remained within the sphere of activity of the intellectual or mind soul was pointed out by Rudolf Steiner in the article entitled 'Michael's Suffering over Human Evolution before the Time of his Earthly Activity: Third Study' (*Anthroposophical Leading Thoughts*, op. cit.).

501. Goethe himself, in his conversation with J.P. Eckerman on 6 June 1831, referred to the difficulties that he had experienced in writing the concluding scene of *Faust* and the involuntary turning to 'ecclesiastical' symbolism that was associated with them: 'Moreover you will allow that the ending, where the immortal part of Faust's soul ascends to heaven, was very difficult to bring about and that where such supersensible, barely imaginable things are concerned I would have very easily got lost in vagaries had I not given my poetic intentions a necessarily circumscribing form and solidity through the sharply outlined figures and images of the Christian Church.'

502. Rudolf Steiner refers to the fact that with Novalis art and life were indissolubly one in the lecture of 9 April 1921 (*Materialism and the Task of Anthroposophy*, op. cit.). There he speaks of how—with respect to what he wants to say—in his search for 'some point or other' where 'in studying the realm of the artistic [he] might be able to enter into life', he was led as to 'something quite self-evident' to the figure of Novalis.

503. Lecture of 22 December 1908 (*The Christmas Mystery: Novalis as Seer*, op. cit.).

504. *Novalis und seine erste Braut*, Stuttgart, 1986.

505. One especially convincing confirmation of the characterisation of Sophie von Kühn that has been offered here is a fragment from her diary that embraces the period of two and a half months before her betrothal to Novalis (15 March 1795). Its particular characteristic, apart from the extreme poverty of the content and the grammatical mistakes, is the depressingly frequent repetition of the words: 'hardly anything happened [today]'; 'again hardly anything happened . . .' It is sufficient merely to compare this 'paltry' diary of the 13-year-old Sophie von Kühn with, for example, the letters of her contemporary, Bettina von Arnim (†1785) to have a feeling for the intellectual and spiritual abyss which separated Novalis from his first bride. In contrast, in his subsequent relationship to Julie Charpentier there is from the start a clear expression of a deep proximity of spiritual and intellectual interests and a wholly mutual understanding of two souls on all levels, an understanding which rapidly turns into an ardent and heart-felt bond. The following extract from a letter of Novalis to Karoline Just (of 5 February 1798) tells of the closeness of Novalis' interests to those of Julie and of the completely different character of the interaction between the two young people in Freiburg from those in Grüningen: 'You would get a clear idea of how I tend to be there if you had recently been a silent spectator of how I sat like an Eleusinian priest before them both [Julie and her sister] one evening in a large room where we were quite alone, inspired by their genuine attentiveness and expounding certain ideas about the future, nature and human life'.

506. These words are from a letter of Novalis—which has not been

preserved—to his brother Erasmus, and were quoted by the latter in his answering letter of 28 November 1794.

507. The actual description of the impression that Sophie von Kühn made on Goethe when he visited her in the September of 1796 in Dr Stark's clinic in Jena has not come down to us. However, there is a letter of Novalis to Prof. Woltmann (dated 14 April 1797) where he characterises Goethe's impression of her in the following words: '[Goethe's] devotion to the sublime image of Sophie has endeared him to me more than all his admirable works . . .' While Novalis' younger brother, Karl, describes Sophie von Kühn thus: 'Not long after he had come to Tennstedt, he got to know Sophie v. K. at a neighbouring estate called Grüningen, and the first sight of her settled his destiny for an eternity (as was the case with everyone who saw her). Sophie, too, was of so tender a disposition and so tall a figure that even then one could hardly fail to recognise in her thirteenth year one who was closely connected with the heavens.'

508. In the biography of Novalis that Ludwig Tieck wrote as a preface to the third edition of his works, we read the following about Sophie von Kühn: 'Even as a child, she gave an impression which—because it was so gracious and spiritually lovely—we must call superearthly or heavenly, while through this radiant and almost transparent countenance of hers we would be struck with the fear that it was too tender and delicately woven for this life, that it was death or immortality which looked at us so penetratingly from those shining eyes; and only too often a rapid withering motion turned our fear into an actual reality.'

509. Lecture of 23 January 1910 (GA 125, Typescript EN 46). The two quotations that follow are taken from the lecture of 26 October 1908 (GA 108).

510. If one were not to take into consideration what has been said here regarding the principal difference between the relationship of Novalis with Sophie von Kühn and Julie Charpentier, it would—after all that Novalis experienced in connection with Sophie von Kühn—seem to be almost inconceivable that, having become acquainted with Julie some nine months after the death of his first bride, he became betrothed to her in less than a year (in December 1798). Not even his closest friends were fully able to understand him at the time. For example, Ludwig Tieck perceived so rapid a betrothal to Julie as a kind of 'spiritual unfaithfulness' to the memory of Sophie von Kühn, and this led to a certain cooling of the relationship between the two friends during Novalis' visit in the summer of 1800 to the Tiecks at Weissenfels. However, one could not really speak here of any kind of 'unfaithfulness', for Novalis' relationships to these two female figures were developing on two completely different planes. This latter circumstance was to find its reflection in his novel (English translation, *Henry von Ofterdingen*, Frederick Ungar Pub. Co., New York 1964) where Julie Charpentier appears in the form of a completely real girl, Matilda, while Sophie von Kühn is transformed into the mystical

figure of Sophia, the representative of the Divine Sophia in the fairy-tale with which the first part of the novel ends.

511. Lecture of 26 October 1908 (GA 108).

512. Only through such an outer influence upon the astral body of the 12-year-old girl is it possible to explain the presence in 'Clarissa' of such observations as these: 'Her smoking of tobacco', 'She likes drinking wine' or 'A face full of obscenities'. The latter observation was in all probability connected with the presence in Sophie von Kühn's environment of Herr von Rockenthien, who was morally speaking a highly dubious individual.

513. This does not, however, exclude the possibility that the ego of Sophie von Kühn might also belong to a spiritual individuality of some significance. What is of importance for us here is simply the fact that at the time of her meeting with Novalis her ego was, for the reasons indicated, only to a very limited degree incarnated in her physical organism.

514. Ritter-Schaumburg further characterises this 'probing conscience' of Sophie von Kühn as follows: 'But what is it, this probing conscience? What does it probe? What criteria does it apply? It can hardly be meant by this that the young Sophie examined what was going on around her with criteria of the usual kind, somewhat along the lines of acceptable norms; this would not have affected Novalis. The criteria that Sophie applied must have been her own; she must have brought them with her. From where? Novalis, at all events, sensed that they derived from an archetypal standard of measure which slumbered in Sophie as an awareness of an eternal, ever-valid image of man . . . It was not really the girl Sophie that Novalis revered but this ideal that lived in the human being . . . As this was all still largely unconscious and at the same time quite self-evident to her, Sophie could certainly not appreciate what went on within Novalis, she could scarcely have any awareness of his estrangement from everything else, nor could she understand the exclusiveness of his attention to her . . .' The 'Sophia' who appears in the fairy-tale of Klingsor from the first part of the novel, *Heinrich von Ofterdingen*, and who is a kind of mystical, fairy-tale-like archetype of the essential character-traits of Sophie von Kühn (see note 510), adopts a similar role.

515. The words 'moral grace' or 'moral beauty' represent perhaps the best way of characterising this chief quality of the etheric body of the 12-year-old Sophie von Kühn; similarly Ritter-Schaumburg's reference to her 'probing conscience' (see note 514) as being the most essential trait of her character must be related to her etheric body, in so far as it is the etheric body which is the bearer of the impulse of conscience within man (see *The Education of the Child*, RSP/AP 1965).

516. Lecture of 26 May 1910 (*Manifestations of Karma*, RSP 1976).

517. Rudolf Steiner refers as follows to such a relationship between the fifth and sixth cultural epochs: 'We are living in the fifth cultural period . . . Its principal task is the conquest of the physical plane. The succeeding sixth

cultural epoch will have the task of leading outer culture again more towards the life of spirit. The banner-bearer for this is Anthroposophy' (lecture of 8 July 1906, GA 94). For this reason it is perfectly natural that in the Anthroposophical Movement there have, from the beginning, been more women than men (see the lecture of 26 May 1910), for this Anthroposophical Movement is in its inner nature a preparer and first harbinger of the future sixth cultural epoch (lecture of 15 June 1915, *Preparing for the Sixth Epoch*, AP 1976).

518. *Anthroposophical Leading Thoughts*, op. cit., the article entitled 'What is revealed when one looks back into former Lives between Death and a new Birth (Part Two)'.

519. Ibid.

520. Lecture of 21 April 1924 (*The Easter Festival in the Evolution of the Mysteries*, AP/RSP 1988).

521. *Occult Science—An Outline*, op. cit., the chapter entitled 'Sleep and Death'.

522. Rudolf Steiner uses this expression to refer to the highest point of the soul's ascent in the spiritual worlds between two incarnations. See his Fourth Mystery Play.

523. In the fifth 'apocalyptic seal' (see GA 284/285 or John Fletcher: *Art Inspired by Rudolf Steiner*, op. cit.), which depicts the Sophia imagination, the nature of this experience through which the human soul passes shortly before birth is elucidated through the representation of its lower part as a dragon with seven heads and ten horns symbolising the etheric and physical bodies, which in the course of incarnation become instruments for the working of the forces of Lucifer and Ahriman in the human organism on Earth. (See further regarding this in *Anthroposophical Leading Thoughts*, op. cit., the article entitled 'What is revealed when one looks back into former Lives between Death and a new Birth: Part Two'.) That the heads and horns of the beast refer to the etheric and physical bodies is borne out by the following words of Rudolf Steiner: 'The human etheric body actually consists of "heads", the human physical body of "horns" ' (lecture of 26 June 1908, *The Apocalypse of St John*, RSP 1977).

524. In the normal course of human evolution this working of cosmic forces in the etheric body of the female organism will be able to go beyond the boundary of the fourteenth year only with the advent of the seventh cultural epoch. Such a change will be associated with the process of the gradual 'becoming younger' of humanity, of which Rudolf Steiner speaks, for example, in the lecture of 13 May 1921 (*Materialism and the Task of Anthroposophy*, op. cit.). This process consists in that in our fifth post-Atlantean epoch the human being develops in his soul-spiritual organisation from nature only until the age of 28; whereas in the sixth epoch he will retain this faculty only until the age of 21, and with the arrival of the seventh epoch only until 14, that is, *before* the dawning of the age of sexual maturity (see with what is said on p. 196 and note 569).

525. See *The Education of the Child*, RSP 1975.

526. See the words of Novalis, and also of Rudolf Steiner, quoted on p. 177.
527. Lecture of 9 April 1921 (*Materialism and the Task of Anthroposophy*, op. cit.).
528. Lecture of 15 February 1909 (*Christianity in Human Evolution*, AP 1979).
529. For further details about this see *The Gospel of St Luke* (RSP 1975).
530. Emil Bock, *Kindheit und Jugend Jesu*, Stuttgart 1982.
531. See further in the lecture of 31 May 1908 (*The Gospel of St John*, op. cit.); and in appendix no. 2 to Rudolf Steiner's letter to Wilhelm Hübbe-Schleiden of 19.8.1902, published in the second volume of Rudolf Steiner's 'Letters' (Dornach, 1953). Regarding the sphere of activity in our cosmos of this second (as regards its significance) Avatar Being, see also note 538.
532. See note 530. In his book, *Kindheit und Jugend Jesu* (*The Childhood and the Youth of Jesus*—English translation in typescript only) Emil Bock points out that in the figure of the Luke Mary we have to do with a very young soul, whose destiny is to a remarkable degree a 'female' parallel to that of the Nathan Soul. For while in the case of the latter we are concerned with the incarnation on Earth of the primordial essence of Adam before the Fall, with the Luke Mary our concern is in a certain sense with the primordial essence of Eve before the Fall, whose entelechy was—like that of the Nathan Soul—preserved in the great 'Mother Lodge' of the rulership of humanity which was under the guardianship of Manu (see in this connection the lecture of 18 September 1909, *The Gospel of St Luke*, op. cit.
533. Of course, all that has been said is also directly connected with individual human karma.
534. In the history of eighteenth and nineteenth-century Russia, there is another such figure to be found amongst those surrounding the Russian saint Seraphim of Sarov (1759–1833), who lived at approximately the same time as Novalis. This is the figure of the simple country girl Maria, who at the age of 13 came with her sister to Saint Seraphim and then remained with him as a 'silent' nun. She died in her eighteenth year and Seraphim himself on more than one occasion called her 'a heavenly bride sent to him by God'. (See further in M. Voloschin, *Die grüne Schlange*, the chapter entitled 'Mysterium des Schweigens', Stuttgart, 1982). This simple country girl, too, bore within herself an imprint of the etheric body of the Luke Mary, while Seraphim was the bearer of an imprint of the astral body of the Nathan Soul, which, in his incarnation of that time, was active principally in his sentient soul.
535. See note 530.
536. The brief notes of the Stockholm cycle of 1910 have not as yet been published (see note 540). The lecture of 11 January 1910 to which reference has been made was given by Rudolf Steiner on the eve of his first proclamation of the New Advent of Christ in the etheric realm (12 January 1910), which took place in the small circle of the members of the then 'Esoteric School' who were present at the cycle.
537. The clear spiritual parallel between this mystery of the union of the two

Marys and the mystery of the union of the Cosmic Being of the Christ with the sheaths of Jesus of Nazareth at the Baptism in the Jordan is also made evident from the description of that aspect of this event which Rudolf Steiner gives at the end of the seventh lecture of the cycle, *The Gospel of St Luke*, op. cit. (the lecture of 21 September 1909). Here he first refers to how the mystery of the future descent to Earth of the Christ Being was already inherent in the esoteric teachings of Zarathustra, teachings which sprang from his direct connection with the Sun-sphere. For Zarathustra had already spoken of how '... also ... the divine, creative Word, Honover', was to descend to Earth. This latter event took place at the Baptism in the Jordan, when the divine Word did indeed descend into the *ether body* of Jesus of Nazareth: 'The divine Spirit-Word, which had been preserved since the Lemurian epoch, came forth from the ethereal heights at the Baptism by John and entered into the etheric body of the Nathan Jesus. And when the Baptism was over, what was it that had happened? The Word had become Flesh.'

538. In the lecture of 27 January 1908 (*The Influence of Spiritual Beings upon Man*, AP 1961), Rudolf Steiner—in the language of the starry script—describes the primordial sphere of activity of the Cosmic Christ or 'Mystic Lamb' as one which, in the circle of the zodiac, stretches from the Ram to the Scales. Correspondingly, the sphere of the Sophia reaches from the Virgin to the Fishes. See further in Part Two of the book, *The Twelve Holy Nights and the Spiritual Hierarchies*, Temple Lodge Press 1988.

539. Lecture of 3 July 1909 (*The Gospel of St John in Relation to the Other Three Gospels*, op. cit.).

540. This theme appears on three subsequent occasions in Rudolf Steiner's lectures: in the lecture of 19 September 1909 (*The Gospel of St Luke*, op. cit.) in the unpublished lecture of 11 January 1910 (cited above) and in the lecture of 6 October 1913 (*The Fifth Gospel*, op. cit.).

541. Lecture of 3 July 1909 (see above).

542. See the lecture of 31 May 1908 (*The Gospel of St John*, op. cit.).

543. See Emil Bock, *Kindheit und Jugend Jesu*, Stuttgart 1982.

544. The mystery schools of the sixth cultural epoch may be imagined as being in the form of a supersensible temple, whose Sun vault—as is depicted on the fourth apocalyptic seal (GA 284 or John Fletcher, *Art Inspired by Rudolf Steiner*, op. cit.)—will rest upon two pillars, which are actually the two spiritual streams of the revelations descending to the Earth from the sphere of the Christ and from the sphere of the Sophia. And each of these two streams will have two principal bearers of its wisdom; one bearer in the supersensible world and one in the earthly. The heavenly representative for the first stream will be the Nathan Soul, and the earthly, John, 'the disciple whom the Lord loved'; while for the second stream the heavenly representative will be the Luke Mary, and the earthly, the Solomon Mary. This will be the time of the complete fulfilment of the mysteries of *Anthropos-Sophia*, when the working together in the spiritual world of the

Nathan Soul—the primal human being of *Anthropos*, and the spiritual being of the Luke Mary—the individualised bearer of the *Sophia* forces, will find its reflection also on the physical plane.

545. See note 517. It should also be borne in mind that in the future, which has, however, already begun in our own time, female incarnations will acquire an ever greater significance for the further evolution of humanity. Rudolf Steiner refers to this as follows in one of his karma lectures: 'I stress the point here that I am not considering the female incarnations because, in the past, life as a man was more important. Incarnations as women are only now beginning to be of importance. *In the future it will be of quite particular interest to take precisely the female incarnations into account*' (lecture of 9 April 1924, *Karmic Relationships*, vol. VI, op. cit.).

546. Lecture of 8 April 1920 (*Spiritual Science and Medicine*, Steiner Books, Garber, 1989).

547. John 19:26–27.

548. This is also the esoteric significance of the words which the Risen One speaks about John the Evangelist: 'If it is My will that he remain until I come . . .' (21:22–23). See also note 381.

549. Like the imprints of the etheric and astral bodies of the Nathan Soul, the imprints from the etheric and astral bodies of the Luke Mary are preserved in the spiritual world in the Mother Lodge of the rulership of humanity, which is under the leadership of Manu (see note 532).

550. See the lecture of 26 June 1908 (*The Apocalypse of St John*, op. cit.).

551. In the book, *Cosmic Memory* (AP 1971), and in the chapter entitled 'Our Atlantean Forbears', Rudolf Steiner describes how the first sub-race of the Atlantean period was, through the word, able to heal human beings, influence the growth of plants and tame animals. In the figure of Orpheus, who tames wild beasts by playing his lyre, we have a testimony of the last remnants of this ancient faculty as it lived on in post-Atlantean times.

552. Rudolf Steiner refers on more than one occasion to this new faculty of the word—for which there is not as yet an appropriately formed larynx—in connection with observations regarding the mission of the future Maitreya Buddha, who will set about its fulfilment some three millennia hence. (See, for example, the lectures of 1 October 1911, *The Etherisation of the Blood*, op. cit.; 4 and 5 November 1911, *Esoteric Christianity and the Mission of Christian Rosenkreutz*, op. cit. and 14 October 1911, *From Jesus to Christ*, op. cit.).

However, this future activity of the Maitreya Buddha amongst mankind is only the *first stage* in the process whereby the human word, through the gradual mastery of its spiritual power, becomes the micrologos. In our fifth post-Atlantean epoch, as has been said, the word is merely the bearer of abstract thoughts, an instrument of the conscious *ego*. In the sixth epoch, with the streaming of the Spirit-Self into humanity, the power of the word will extend to the *astral body*. This will be a time when the Maitreya Buddha will, through the spiritual power of the word, be able to awaken new moral impulses in human souls. In the seventh cultural epoch, with the flowing of the Life-Spirit into mankind, it will become possible to have a direct influence upon the *etheric body*. Then will man, through the word, be able to influence, for example, the forces of growth and propagation in the plant world. And, finally, in the next epoch, after the 'War of All Against All', with the outpouring of the impulse of the Spirit-Man into humanity, the possibility will arise of directly influencing the *physical body* through the word, and, with it, also the physical processes of the surrounding world.

With this threefold evolutionary sequence will also go a corresponding gradual transformation of the human larynx, first in the astral sphere, then in the etheric and, finally—in the physical—into a new organ of reproduction. In other words, the arising in the epoch of the Spirit-Man of the possibility of working through the word into physical substances will also represent the *beginning* of the fulfilment of the ideal which Rudolf Steiner describes in the following words: 'In the future the larynx will not only bring forth words, but will be the creative organ of procreation which will bring forth beings similar to man' (lecture of 5 November 1907, GA 98).

553. Lecture of 21 September 1911 (*From Buddha to Christ*, op. cit.).

554. See in this connection the lecture of 14 October 1911 (*From Jesus to Christ*, op. cit.) and that of 2 December 1911 (*Faith, Love, Hope*, op. cit.) whence the following quotation is taken.

555. In His hand the Son of Man holds those planetary forces of the human etheric body which in the course of earthly life have been so transformed and purified through man's moral activity that they can be used by Christ for fashioning the so-called 'etheric-ring' around the Earth, a supersensible sphere where the Earth is, even now, being gradually transformed into a new Sun. (See further in *The Cycle of the Year as a Path of Initiation*, Part IX.) That in this imagination of the Son of Man an initiatory or *after-death* experience is being referred to is evident from the words: 'When I saw Him, I fell at His feet as though *dead*' (1:17).

556. Such an experience of these two imaginations is in our time also a path whereby mankind will in the course of the next three millennia be increasingly able to come nearer to a direct perception of the Etheric Christ. This will become clearer to us if we compare what has been said in the present chapter with the content of the lecture of 14 April 1914 (*Inner Nature of Man and the Life Between Death and a New Birth*, APC 1959). In this lecture Rudolf Steiner describes at some length how in our time it is only through the working of the Christ-impulse in the earthly aura that man is enabled to preserve his ego-consciousness until 'the midnight hour of existence', that is, until that moment when, from worlds which lie still higher than that sphere whither the soul can rise in the present cycle of evolution between two incarnations, the Holy Spirit descends upon it, awakening it to new life and *fructifying* it with the wisdom of the spiritual

cosmos in order that it might find the way back into earthly incarnation *in the right way*. However, if in his last earthly life a man has been able to acquire a conscious and purely spiritual relationship to the Christ-impulse, as is now possible thanks to anthroposophically orientated spiritual science, he will after death experience the imagination of the Son of Man with considerably greater intensity. For a power will flow forth from this imagination into his soul which will not only enable him to preserve his ego-consciousness until the 'midnight hour', but will subsequently further strengthen the fructifying and awakening activity of the spirit at the highest point of the life after death. As a result of this, the Spirit-impulse which has been strengthened by the Christ-impulse (the companion of the soul on its way down to the Earth) will immediately, before a person's descent into physical existence, be able to call forth the cosmic imagination of the Sophia before his inner eye with such power that this can work as a spiritual force in his etheric body also after earthly birth. Through this means the foundation will be laid for the gradual transformation of the etheric heart into a new Sun organ of cognition which will enable him consciously to perceive the Etheric Christ on the Earth. Thus in the full cycle of human existence there unfolds before us first the path from Christ to Sophia and then the path from Sophia back to Christ in His new etheric form. (In its more microcosmic form, this path finds its expression in the cycle of the year, as has been expounded at some length in the author's book, *The Cycle of the Year as a Path of Initiation*, Part XI.)

Novalis, too, refers to this path, albeit in a completely different form. In his words, one must in order to approach the mysteries of Isis Sophia (to lift her veil) first reach the sphere of 'immortality' (see his words quoted on p.166), a sphere to which Christ can lead us in our time. This is the path from Christ to Sophia. Once he had achieved this and lifted the veil from the holy image, man had an experience of himself in his higher, spiritualised being (see Novalis' words quoted on p.166). This is an experience of true Anthropos, corresponding to the second half of the path—from Sophia back to Christ. At the same time, this is also a living testimony of Novalis' prophetic insight into the mystery of the future incarnation of Anthropos–Sophia amongst mankind, the foundation for which was laid in the twentieth century through the establishing of *Anthroposophy* on the Earth.

557. Regarding the mysteries of death and birth as the two fundamental aspects of the mysteries of the pre-Christian period of evolution, see *Rudolf Steiner and the Founding of the New Mysteries*, op. cit., ch. 4. The so-called Spring and Autumn Mysteries—described by Rudolf Steiner in the lectures of 19 and 20 April 1924 (*The Easter Festival in the Evolution of the Mysteries*, op. cit.)—may be regarded as their later and thoroughly enfeebled continuation.

558. That the entering of birth and death into earthly evolution was called forth

by the division of humanity into two sexes, together with the capacity to procreate that is associated with this division, is attested by Rudolf Steiner in the lecture of 4 June 1907 (*Theosophy of the Rosicrucian*, RSP 1966) and in his book, *Cosmic Memory*, op. cit.).

559. Like the metamorphosis of the human larynx (see note 552), the metamorphosis of the heart will also pass through three stages: at first, the changes affect only the 'astral' heart, then the 'etheric' and only later the supersensible parts of the physical heart.

560. In the lecture of 29 April 1909 (GA 57, Typescript Z 26), Rudolf Steiner refers to the threefold representation of Isis in the art of ancient Egypt. In the first, Isis feeds Horus in an earthly way. In the second, she hands him the 'crux ansata', the spiritual power of Osiris, while she is portrayed with a bull's horns on her head. These bull's horns refer to the process of the spiritual fructifying of Isis (the Virgin) by the forces of the cosmic Spirit (the Bull). (See further in *The Twelve Holy Nights and the Spiritual Hierarchies*, op. cit., ch. 1.) Finally, Isis is depicted, in the most esoteric representations, with a lion's head, whereby reference is made to an even more distant future when the heart organ, which has a direct connection with the spiritual forces that are sent down by the Sun from the constellation of the Lion, will be transmuted into a new organ of spiritual reproduction.

561. Lecture of 17 December 1907 (GA 98).

562. Lecture of 5 November 1907 (GA 98). In connection with these words of Rudolf Steiner it should be observed that the heightened interest displayed in our time towards the sphere of physical relationships between the sexes is the strongest manifestation of the forces that are *opposed* to the future mysteries of the Divine Sophia. Interests of such a kind are consciously supported and disseminated by those occult circles in the West which have set themselves the task of preventing the sixth cultural epoch from happening at all.

563. Lecture of 17 December 1907. The quotation that follows is from the lecture of 5 November 1907.

564. Thus there arises on Earth a kind of reflection of that higher macrocosmic process of the fructification by the spirit referred to in note 556.

565. Regarding the spiritual continuity between the Grail Mysteries and Rosicrucianism, see *Occult Science—An Outline*, op. cit., the chapter entitled 'Present and Future Evolution of the World and of Mankind', and also the lecture of 24 June 1909 (*The Gospel of St John in Relation to the Other Three Gospels*, op. cit.).

566. Lecture of 26 June 1908 (*The Apocalypse of St John*, op. cit.). In the course of earthly evolution the separation of the Sun from the Earth took place during the so-called second root-race (the Hyperborean). According to the law of reflection, its repetition—albeit on a higher plane—is the sixth root-race, whose time will come after the 'War of All Against All' and which in its turn will consist of seven smaller periods similar to our present

cultural epochs. During this sixth root-race, towards its end (in approximately its sixth sub-race), the re-union of the Earth with the Sun will take place.

567. Lecture of 13 May 1921 (*Materialism and the Task of Anthroposophy*, RSP/AP 1987). According to the law of reflection, the Moon, which left the Earth during the Lemurian epoch (the third root-race), must again unite with it by the end of our post-Atlantean period of evolution (the fifth root-race), a period which will conclude with the 'War of All Against All'.

568. That the division into two sexes was connected with the departure of the Moon from the Earth is confirmed by Rudolf Steiner in the lecture of 4 June 1907 (*The Theosophy of Rosicrucian*, op. cit.) and in his book, *Cosmic Memory*, op. cit.), he also refers to this from a somewhat different point of view in the lecture of 13 May 1921 (see previous note).

569. In the lecture of 28 October 1917 (GA 177, Typescript R 35), Rudolf Steiner, from a somewhat different point of view, refers to the seventh millennium of the Christian era as the time when women will become barren. Moreover, if evolution takes its course wholly in the spirit of *rightly* evolved Angelic Beings, human beings will be able to reproduce physically only until the sixth millennium (ibid.). Or in other words: 'Only in the sixth post-Atlantean cultural period will physical reproduction still be possible on the Earth; it is in accordance with the wisdom of [the Spirits of] Light that the reproductive impulse appropriate for this post-Atlantean age, in its seven cultural epochs, will not continue beyond this point' (ibid.). Against the will of the Angels or Spirits of Light who guide earthly evolution, however, physical reproduction will continue on longer than this, not only to the seventh but also to the eighth millennium. This will be brought about by the influence which the retarded Angels or 'Spirits of Darkness' will exert upon mankind. Their impulses in the seventh cultural epoch will work with particular power from the American continent. In this connection, the peoples inhabiting Eastern Europe will have a task of the greatest significance in the sixth epoch. Rudolf Steiner speaks of this as follows: 'The European East will develop strong inclinations not to allow physical reproduction to go beyond the sixth cultural epoch but to lead the Earth over into a more spiritual, more psychical existence' (ibid.). And this will become possible pre-eminently because it will be amongst the Slavic peoples that the impulses of the Holy Grail will be working at that time with particular power (regarding the connection of Eastern Europe with the impulses of the Holy Grail, see the lecture of 3 November 1918, *From Symptom to Reality in Modern History*, RSP 1976). Novalis probably had something of a premonition of this future condition when he wrote in one of his fragments: 'Blossoms are allegories of consciousness, or of the head. The purpose of this higher blossom is a higher form of reproduction—a higher means of preservation. Where human beings are concerned it is the organ of immortality—of a progressive reproduction of the personality.'

570. Rudolf Steiner speaks in the lecture of 11 April 1909 (*The Festivals and their Meaning* op. cit.) about the possibility of an inner contradiction between a person's *own* astral body and his etheric body that bears within itself an 'imprint' of the etheric body of a higher Being. In the same context he also refers to St Augustine as an especially obvious example of such a contradiction.

571. For further details about this see *Occult Science—An Outline*, op. cit., the chapter entitled 'Knowledge of the Higher Worlds'.

572. An archetype of such a mystic union of rose and lily or 'rose-soul' and 'lily-soul' can be found in the medieval legend of Flor and Blancheflor. (This legend was subsequently retold in literary form by the Provençal poet Konrad Fleck in the thirteenth century and as such has come down to us today). Rudolf Steiner referred to this legend, behind which are hidden quite definite historical events associated with the preparation for and evolution of the Rosicrucian stream, in the lecture of 6 May 1909 (GA 57, Typescript AQ 9:1). There he speaks in the following words of how the symbols of the rose and the lily have been understood, from the beginning, in the circles of esoteric Christendom: 'The rose—Flor or Flos—was seen as a symbol for the human soul which has received the impulse of the ego, of personality, which allows the spiritual to work out of its individuality and has brought the ego-impulse down into the red blood. While the lily was the symbol of the soul which can only remain spiritual when the ego remains outside it and only approaches it from without. Thus there is a contrast between the rose and the lily. The principle of self-consciousness has entered wholly into the rose, whereas it remains outside the lily.' With a certain modification in accordance with the present epoch in human evolution, these words of Rudolf Steiner can, with certain reservations, also be applied to the relationship of Novalis and Sophie von Kühn. And, in a quite different historical soul-mood, they also bear a relationship to the event which was described in note 534.

573. Lecture of 22 December 1908 (*The Christmas Mystery: Novalis as Seer*, op. cit.).

574. It would be a complete misunderstanding of the occult and karmic foundations of Novalis' biography to suppose that these words refer only to the soul of the dead Sophie von Kühn. For as Rudolf Steiner has frequently pointed out, the *Hymns to the Night* represent the poetic expression of the all-encompassing cosmic revelations experienced by Novalis, which in their character and content extended far beyond the realm of personal, earthly things (see further regarding this in the lecture of 26 October 1908—GA 108—and 22 December 1908, *The Christmas Mystery: Novalis as Seer*, op. cit.). The passage of the Hymn here quoted refers to the revelation which the poet-seer has received from the sphere of the cosmic Sophia ('the world Queen, the high herald of sacred worlds') through the spiritual mediation of her personified representative, the Luke Mary, whose spirit-being the 'released new-born spirit' of Novalis

encounters in the higher worlds or the world of 'night'. She it is to whom he later refers through the image of the 'lovely Sun of the night' that shines upon him from the realm of the Sophia.

575. This can be seen especially by comparing these lines from the third 'Hymn to the Night':

> 'I grasped her hands . . .'
> 'Upon her neck I wept . . .'

with the following lines from the fifth Hymn, which are about Mary:

> If you, their blessed salvation,
> Will clasp them to your breast.

(See also *Spiritual Songs* XIII, lines 5–6.)

A further reason for thinking that where in the *Hymns to the Night* the word *Geliebte* ('beloved') is used it always refers to the Luke Mary (see the first and third Hymns) is that Christ is given the parallel designation of *Geliebter* [the masculine form of the same word] (see the fourth and sixth Hymns).

576. See note 575.

577. Thus we see that in Novalis' work the two principal pillars of the future spiritual temple of the sixth cultural epoch, which were spoken of in note 544, are present from the very beginning. This dual leitmotif is then reiterated in the poetic cycle, the *Spiritual Songs*, of which the part that is dedicated to Christ was, in the older editions called specifically 'Spiritual Songs', and the other part 'Songs of Mary'.

578. Richard Samuel, *Die poetische Staats—und Geschichts auffassung Friedrich von Hardenbergs (Novalis). Studien zur romantishen Geschichtsphilosophie*, Frankfurt 1925, quoted by Gerhard Schulz, *Novalis Werke*, Munich 1981.

579. The poems in question are the twelfth and thirteenth 'Spiritual Songs', and in particular the verses quoted in the present work on p. 116. (See also in connection with these two verses what was said in notes 293 and 325 about similar spiritual experiences in Raphael's life.)

580. See the lecture of 6 September 1910 (*The Gospel of St Matthew*, op. cit.).

581. The Mary of the Luke Gospel died in the year 12 at the age of 25 (see note 530), and as she ascended into the spiritual world took with her the etheric body of the Solomon Jesus, who died at approximately the same time (see the lecture of 21 September 1909, *The Gospel of St Luke*, op. cit., thus giving rise to a quite special relationship of this etheric body with the cosmic sphere of the Sophia. Herein also lies the deeper reason of the connection which arose between the Master Jesus and the Sophia-impulse, inasmuch as in all his subsequent incarnations on the Earth he 'made use of' this

etheric body. However, a fuller exposition of these relationships would lie beyond the scope of the present work.

582. Lecture of 11 January 1910 (unpublished)—see note 430 and the quotation from the lecture referred to that appears on p. 187.

583. See the 'Ergänzende Bemerkungen' to the lecture of 28 September 1924 (*The Last Address*, op. cit.) published in the German edition of 1981. [The relevant portion of these 'supplementary remarks' is included, at least in part, in the English edition of 1967 op. cit.—Translator's note.]

584. See the lecture of 12 September 1908 (*Egyptian Myths and Mysteries*, AP 1971).

585. Lecture of 23 September 1912 (*The Gospel of St Mark*, op. cit.). These words of Rudolf Steiner are a spiritual–scientific commentary on verses 51–2 of the fourteenth chapter of St Mark's Gospel. That the figure of the 'youth who ran away' refers to the Cosmic Christ is borne out by the following words of Rudolf Steiner: 'And it was to them [the women at the grave] that the youth, that is, the Cosmic Christ, first appeared' (lecture of 24 September 1912, see above).

586. In the lecture of 3 October 1913 (*The Fifth Gospel*, op. cit.) Rudolf Steiner characterises the relationship of the Cosmic Christ to the human Jesus principle immediately after the Baptism in the Jordan in the following way: 'At the beginning of Christ's life on Earth, directly after the Baptism in the Jordan, the connection with the body of Jesus of Nazareth was still only very slight. The Christ Being was still quite outside the body of Jesus of Nazareth. This was because what was living in the Christ Being as He went about the Earth was still something wholly super-earthly.'

587. This union of the two Johns has often been the subject of works of art that have been based on a more or less dim awareness of this mystery. Here, apart from Raphael's *Transfiguration* (see note 482), mention should be made of Altdorfer's picture, *The Two Johns* (Regensburg); that of Machiavelli, *John the Baptist and John the Evangelist* (National Gallery, London); and in particular the representation of the two Johns in the central part of the Isenheim altar-piece (*Crucifixion*) by Matthias Grünewald.

588. The Gospels at this point speak in an amazingly concrete way about the presence of the entelechy of Elijah–John in the supersensible surroundings of the Hill of Golgotha. Thus in two of them, Matthew and Mark, there is a description of how at that moment when the last words of the Son of Man sounded from the Cross 'some of the bystanders', as though under the influence of a higher power, became for a moment partly clairvoyant and were able, to a certain extent, to behold the mystery of the presence of Elijah in the events that were taking place: 'Some of the bystanders hearing it said, "He is calling Elijah"' . . . Others said, "Wait, let us see whether Elijah will come to save Him"' (Matthew 27:47 and 49; see also Mark 15:35–36). And Elijah really does come!—though not in a physically visible way but in the form of an *inspiration* which at this moment reveals,

to those who are inwardly capable of receiving its influence from the surroundings of the Hill of Golgotha, the very essence of that higher revelation which he, as John the Baptist, had once proclaimed to mankind. Then, as we read on in the Gospel of St Mark: 'And when the centurion [St Matthew's Gospel adds: 'and those who were with him guarding Jesus', 27:54], who stood facing Him, saw that He thus breathed His last, he said: "*Truly, this man was the Son of God*"' (15:39). That is exactly the same testimony which John the Baptist—as the first of all mankind—pronounces immediately after the Baptism of Jesus in the Jordan out of the forces of conscience, the new organ of knowledge: 'And I have seen and have borne witness that this is the Son of God' (John 1:3). And it is this capacity of recognising Christ on the Earth through the forces of conscience that Elijah proclaims in this scene to those who are standing at the foot of the Cross. Thus in the reference by the Evangelists to Elijah immediately after the words of the Son of Man, and in the 'Johannine testimony' of the centurion and Roman soldiers that follows it, we have an indication not only of the actual presence of Elijah–John in the supersensible surroundings of the Hill of Golgotha but also of his spiritual participation in all these events even as far as the physical plane.

In the so-called 'Gospel of Nicodemus', which tells of the descent of Christ Jesus into the underworld after His death on Golgotha, there is also a mention of John the Baptist and Elijah. John the Baptist is depicted as going before Christ and proclaiming to the souls in torment in the underworld about His coming and their imminent release; while the figure of Elijah meets the liberated souls in a higher spiritual sphere.

589. Lecture of 30 January 1913 (GA 62, Typescript Z 27).
590. As Emil Bock has already observed, the majority of the pictures of the Madonna with the Jesus child in the world of art should be regarded as being of the Luke Mary. On the other hand, the Solomon Mary of St Matthew's Gospel is, as a general rule, portrayed in the burial scene (Pieta). See note 530. An exception is to a certain extent the famous 'Pieta' by Michelangelo in St Peter's Cathedral in Rome, which depicts the Solomon Mary permeated to such a degree by the forces of the Luke Mary that she, for all her actual age at the moment of the Mystery of Golgotha, is portrayed as being quite young (see the lecture of 29 April 1909, *Isis and Madonna*, Mercury Press, Spring Valley, 1987).
591. Lecture of 6 October 1923 (*The Four Seasons and the Archangels*, op. cit.).
592. A particular secret of the *Sistine Madonna* lies also in the fact that it is, so to speak, a connecting link between the past and the future. Thus on the one hand, it points towards the Egyptian Mysteries of Isis, these being a memory of the ancient Lemurian age when human beings were still in direct communion with this Goddess, and on the other hand, to the future mysteries of the Divine Sophia, shining towards us from the future in the image of the Virgin clothed with the Sun (regarding the relationship of the *Sistine Madonna* to the ancient Egyptian images of Isis with the child Horus,

see the lectures of 4 and 5 August 1908, *Universe, Earth and Man*, op. cit.). In this sense, Rudolf Steiner was able with full justice to say of this picture: 'The whole story of human evolution is contained in a wonderful way in this picture of the Madonna' (lecture of 22 December 1908, *The Christmas Mystery, Novalis as Seer*, op. cit.).

593. Lecture of 29 April 1909 (GA 57, Typescript Z 26). Later in the same lecture Rudolf Steiner formulates this thought as follows: 'The human soul as it is fructified out of the World-Spirit is made manifest in the Madonna . . . Then we see with what devotion our soul, as the eternal feminine in us, longs and searches for the divine Father Spirit who is born out of the universe and to whom we give birth as a Sun in our own soul . . . And on the other hand, the Madonna contains that which can be born out of the human soul: the true, higher man that slumbers in every human being, all that is best in man, what as spirit weaves and flows through the world.

594. The traditional Russian Orthodox iconostasis consists, as a rule, of five rows of icons one above the other with the following themes. The first row (reckoning from above) is that of the 'Father'. In these icons are portrayed various figures of the Old Testament, the Patriarchs and so on. At the centre—in the majority of cases—is *God the Father*, sometimes depicted with the Son God and Spirit God borne by Him in His bosom from eternity. The second row is that of the 'Prophets'. In these icons are represented the Old Testament Prophets who proclaimed the coming of the Messiah to the Earth. At the centre of this row there is sometimes Mary with the Jesus child in her lap. This tradition of depicting the prophets and Initiates of the pre-Christian era as beholding the future birth on Earth of the Divinity from a pure virgin is the last memory of the ancient initiatory experiences of mankind which still existed in the Egyptian Mysteries of Isis and Horus and later in the Eleusinian Mysteries, the spiritual focus of which was the contemplation of the image of the Virgin with the holy child Jacchos in her arms (see the lecture of 14 December 1923, *Mystery Knowledge and Mystery Centres*, op. cit.). The third row is the most important row in the iconostasis—the 'Deesis'. In the icons of this row, certain particular representatives of humanity and spiritual Beings appear before *Christ* as the 'new Spirit of the Earth'. The fourth row is the 'festive row'. It is devoted to the principal Christian Festivals, connected as they are with the most important events of the Gospel narrative. Their celebration in the course of the year, according to those who fashioned the iconostasis, is an expression of the working of the *Holy Spirit*, amongst mankind. And the last row is the so-called 'local', where there are icons which in one way or another are associated with the particular church and its patrons or with its locality. While the order of the five rows of the iconostasis can be varied to some extent in accordance with different kinds of outward circumstances and for other reasons, and sometimes even the number of rows reduced, the 'Deesis', its spiritual

362

focus, can never be omitted or altered in any way that would affect the arrangement of the principal figures within it.

The three principle figures of the 'Deesis': Christ in the radiance of the cosmic aura surrounded by the Luke Mary and John the Baptist, are also met with in certain works of Western European art—in, for example, Raphael's *Disputa*.

Thus we have two kinds of images. The one, as in the 'Deesis', alludes to the spiritual scene in the *supersensible* surroundings of the Hill of Golgotha; the other to events on the *earthly* plane. In the case of the latter, the crucified Son of Man is portrayed at the centre, and around Him beneath the Cross the Solomon Mary and John the Evangelist (see, for example, Grünewald's *Crucifixion* in the picture gallery at Karlsruhe).

595. This same motif can also be seen on the second apocalyptic seal (see GA 2284/285, also in John Fletcher, *Art Inspired by Rudolf Steiner*, op. cit., and note 354).

596. The presence of *Gabriel* is a sign that in the 'Deesis' the Luke Mary is depicted (although in many icons she does, it is true, also bear features of the 'other Mary'). This is further confirmed by the fact that in the Gospel of St Matthew the annunciating Angel is not referred to by name and appears not to Mary but to Joseph (see note 439).

597. See the lecture of 27 September 1911 (*Esoteric Christianity and the Mission of Christian Rosenkreutz*, op. cit.). The theme of the 'Virgin Sophia' as the mediator between the uncreated and created worlds can also be found in early Rosicrucian works. See, for example, *Mystery figures of the Rosicrucians from the sixteenth and seventeenth centuries*, Plate 1 in the second volume, Altona 1788. In the eighteenth century the Rosicrucian movement in Russia was intensified considerably through the elucidatory endeavours of Novikov (1744–1818) and his friend Gamaleya, who at that time were translating into Russian *Mystery-figures of the Rosicrucians*, many works of Jacob Boehme and some of Saint-Martin.

598. In certain icons of this type the throne on which the Sophia is sitting was depicted with seven pillars supporting it, in accordance with the words of the Proverbs of Solomon: 'Wisdom has built her house and hewn out her seven pillars' (9:1). These seven columns in the temple of the Divine Sophia are none other than an allusion to the sphere of activity of the Sophia forces in the macrocosm, which—in the language of the starry script—stretches from the constellation of the Virgin to the constellation of the Fishes (see note 538).

599. Lecture of 15 January 1910 (unpublished). See note 430.

600. Genesis 6:1–6.

601. See *Erinnerungen von Marie Steiner* ('Memoirs of Marie Steiner'), volume II, the section entitled 'Am Vorabend des Michael-Tages' ('On the Eve of Michaelmas Day'), Dornach 1952.

602. Albert Steffen, *Wiedergeburt der Schönen Wissenschaften*, Dornach 1946. 'Die

Botschaft von Novalils' is also available in a separate edition, published in Dornach in 1972.

603. See the Foreword by Ita Wegman to *Aus Michaels Wirken* by Nora Stein von Baditz (Stuttgart 1983).
604. Lecture of 15 June 1915 (*Preparing for the Sixth Epoch*, op. cit.).
605. Lecture of 11 June 1922 (GA 211, Typescript Z 234).
606. Lecture of 20 September 1912 (*The Gospel of St Mark*, op. cit.).

Notes to Appendices

1. Lecture of 25 June 1909 (*The Gospel of St John in Relation to the Other Three Gospels*, AP 1982).
2. *Mysterium magnum oder Erklärung über das erste Buch Mosis*, ch. 18 (published in 1623).
3. Jacob Boehme, *Aurora*, ch. 18, 2.
4. Ibid, 1.
5. *Die Sagen der Juden*, Frankfurt 1862.
6. See G. Schulz, *Novalis Werke*, Studienausgabe, Munich 1981: commentary section.
7. Genesis 2:7.
8. See the lecture of 21 December 1909 (*Festivals of the Seasons*, AP 1928).
9. Revelation 10:8–11.
10. Friedrich Hiebel, 'Novalis in frühester Verkündigung der Anthroposophie. Sein Denkbelebungsimpuls im Idealismus der Goethe-Zeit'. Published in *Die Drei*, issue of February 1987.
11. The 'Barr Manuscript', part 1 (*Correspondence and Documents, 1901–25*, RSP/AP 1988).
12. Ibid.
13. See note 10.
14. See, respectively: *Goethean Science*, Mercury Press, NY, 1988 (formerly *Goethe the Scientist*); *The Theory of Knowledge Implicit in Goethe's World Conception* (AP 1978); *Goethe's World View* (*Goethe's Conception of the World*) Mercury Press, NY, 1985.
15. See, for example, the lectures included in GA 188, some of which may be found under the title of 'Goetheanism as an Impulse for Man's Transformation and Reflection on Resurrection' (Typescript R 60).
16. See, for example, Novalis' fragments quoted on p. 135.
17. *W.J. Stein/Rudolf Steiner—Dokumentation eines wegweisenden Zusammenwirkens* (Dornach, 1985). Rudolf Steiner is, of course, characterising here only *one particular aspect* of Anthroposophy.
18. See *Goethe's World View*, op. cit.
19. In the article entitled 'Michael's Suffering over Human Evolution before the Time of his Earthly Activity' (*Anthroposophical Leading Thoughts*, RSP 1973) Rudolf Steiner speaks of how Goethe, who aspired throughout his life to an experience of 'man', was able to attain to this only to a very limited degree and, moreover, only by turning *to the past* as it has been preserved in the culture of ancient Greece. As to finding it *in the present* (that is, in the consciousness soul) through a direct experience of the

working within it of the Christ-impulse, this he could not do. (See what was said about Goethe in note 412 and in chapter 12.)

20. Lecture of 17 June 1923 (*The Anthroposophic Movement*, H. Collison, 1933).

21. Lectures of 28 and 29 November 1919 (*The Mission of the Archangel Michael*, AP 1961).

22. Rudolf Steiner speaks as follows about the participation of the will in the process of sense-perception: 'Everything is streaming, all-prevailing will inasmuch as we go towards the sense world . . . He [man] approaches what is real through being connected through his will with all that pertains to the sense world' (lecture of 28 December 1911, *The World of the Senses and the World of the Spirit*, Steiner Book Centre, N. Vancouver 1979).

23. See note 26 (below).

24. See in this connection the lecture of 28 November 1919 (see above).

25. The article entitled 'Michael's Mission in the Cosmic Age of Human Freedom' (*Anthroposophical Leading Thoughts*, op. cit.).

26. Lecture of 14 October 1911 (*From Jesus to Christ*, RSP 1991).

27. Lecture of 28 November 1919 (*The Mission of the Archangel Michael*, op. cit.).

28. Lecture of 13 February 1923 (*Awakening to Community*, AP 1974).

29. Lecture of 28 November 1919 (see above).

30. Lecture of 6 January 1918 (*Ancient Myths. Their Meaning and Connection with Evolution*, Steiner Book Centre, N. Vancouver, 1981).

31. The full context of these words is: 'Some results of observing the human soul as natural science observes nature.'

32. That when he uses these words Novalis has in mind not simple groundless fantasising but a higher faculty of cognition is borne out by his understanding of the relationship of art to philosophy and to science. The following words of his bear witness to this: 'The poet is simply the highest degree of the thinker . . .', which is to say that for Novalis, by analogy with these words, 'the power of imagination is the highest degree of the power of thinking'. Or two further observations of his: 'The division between poet and thinker is only apparent . . .' and 'physics is nothing other than the study of *imagination*' (and 'physics' means here 'science as a whole'). Thus we can also say that in the 'power of imagination', as something which is directly associated with the working of the human ego, we have Novalis' first premonition of what Rudolf Steiner was later to call 'moral imagination'.

33. *The Philosophy of Freedom*, ch. 5, RSP 1988, AP 1986.

34. Ibid. chapters 5 and 7. Thus in the Fragments quoted above and also below, Novalis cites the following categories, which correspond to the fundamental contrasts that appear in the first part of *The Philosophy of Freedom* as the contrast between 'percept' and 'concept' or 'thinking':

our world	intelligence
object	mental picture
experiments	contemplation
materiality	intellect
beholding	mental picture
willing	mental picturing
object	concept
beholding	concept
fact	concept
senses	spirit-world

In *The Philosophy of Freedom* Rudolf Steiner also mentions the following antitheses: 'I and world' (inner and outer); 'spirit and matter'; 'subject and object'; 'thinking and appearance' (ch. 2).

35. Ibid. ch. 9. The two quotations that follow are from the same source.
36. This has a direct relationship to *The Philosophy of Freedom*, op. cit. In the lecture of 19 December 1920 (*The Bridge between Universal Spirituality and the Physical Constitution*, AP 1958) Rudolf Steiner says: 'And freedom and love belong together, as I have already pointed out in my *Philosophy of Freedom*.' This refers to the following places in his book: 'Only when I follow my love for my objective is it I myself who acts.' 'Man is free in so far as he is able, at every moment of his life, to be his own guide.' This means that only deeds accomplished *out of love for the objective* can be free. Moreover, 'acting out of freedom includes rather than excludes moral laws, but proves to be *on a higher* level than actions which are merely dictated by such laws.' (Quotations are from ch. 9.) That is to say, one is speaking here of a *higher* morality than is possible when one follows moral laws or precepts that are given from without.
37. In the lecture of 12 June 1919 (*Some Characteristics of Today*, Collison 1932) Rudolf Steiner says: 'I called one of the chapters in my *Philosophy of Freedom* of 1894 "Moral Imagination". From a spiritual–scientific point of view one could also say: the imaginative moral impulse.' While in the twelfth chapter of *The Philosophy of Freedom* Rudolf Steiner writes: 'Thus what the free spirit needs in order to realise his ideas, in order to be effective, is *moral imagination*. This is the source of the free spirit's actions. *Therefore it is only men with moral imagination who are, strictly speaking, morally productive.*'
38. This is a further instance where Novalis' inner experience approaches remarkably close to the principal results of *The Philosophy of Freedom*. Thus in the ninth chapter Rudolf Steiner writes: 'When we are contemplating *thinking* itself, two things coincide which otherwise must always appear apart, namely, concept and percept.' Novalis expresses the same thought in his particular formulation, although instead of the word 'thinking' he uses the word 'I'. This is because Novalis is, through his experience, well familiar with what Rudolf Steiner speaks about later in the same chapter: 'The true "I" does indeed lie within the essential nature of thinking . . .

This can be observed once thinking is observed without prejudice. The "I" is to be found within thinking.'

39. In reading this Fragment of Novalis one is involuntarily reminded of Rudolf Steiner's cycle of three lectures entitled *Balance in the World and Man*, Steiner Book Centre, N. Vancouver, 1977 (formerly *The World as a Product of the Working of Balance*), and of his individual lectures containing a description of the sculptural Group in Dornach. The following words of Rudolf Steiner may also be cited here: 'In world-existence we have to do with the forces of Lucifer, which represent one pan of the scales, with those of Ahriman, representing the other, and with the state of balance, which is represented by the Christ-impulse' (ibid.).

40. *The Riddles of Philosophy*, op. cit., the chapter entitled 'The Age of Kant and Goethe'.

41. When Rudolf Steiner speaks here of the 'spiritual world', he has in mind a wholly real relationship of the soul to the higher realms of existence, a relationship which he was to describe in his later writings. According to his own testimony in the lecture of 12 August 1924 (*Karmic Relationships*, vol. VIII, op. cit.) it was in the period between the years of 28 and 35 (that is, during his work on *The Philosophy of Freedom*) that he had particularly significant experiences in the spiritual world, and he perceived all the events that took place there in full consciousness. In the 'Hague conversation', albeit from a somewhat different viewpoint, he again refers to this same theme: 'Although *The Philosophy of Freedom* merely offers a description of this [man as a spiritual being], it is nevertheless true that anyone who struggles through to an experience of freedom will find the Hierarchies around the spiritual man that he will then perceive. For they are all within man, and in spirit-vision whatever is within man appears as a spiritual environment. Hence although they are not actually mentioned, they are nevertheless included in *The Philosophy of Freedom*.'

42. Both the quotations that follow are taken from the lecture of 30 May 1908 (*The Gospel of St John*, AP 1962); and in the lecture of 10 January 1915 (GA 161, Typescript Z 273), Rudolf Steiner speaks the following words: 'Then you will see how in the free, emancipated thought-life of today philosophy does indeed present something that reaches right into the consciousness soul, but how within this life in the consciousness soul it must, at first in a philosophical way, take hold of what comes from the Spirit-Self, for otherwise philosophy would necessarily fall into decadence and disintegrate.' This 'taking hold, at first in a philosophical way, of what comes from the Spirit-Self within the life of the consciousness soul' was what Rudolf Steiner accomplished in his *Philosophy of Freedom*.

43. In Russia the 'great Festivals' are: Christmas, Epiphany, Easter, Ascension, Whitsun, St John's (the birth of John the Baptist) and the Festival of the 'Beheading of John'.

44. It is for this reason that the chief figures in the majority of Russian fairytales are Ivan the peasant's son and Ivan Tsarevich. Of Old Testament

figures, the prophet Elijah was most especially revered in Russia (see note 72 to the main part of the book). This is why the chief hero of Russian bylini (epics) was called Ilya Muromets.

45. See the lecture of 17 April 1917 (*Building Stones for an Understanding of the Mystery of Golgotha*, RSP 1972).

46. See the lectures of 18 and 22 August 1911 (*Wonders of the World, Ordeals of the Soul, Revelations of the Spirit*, RSP 1963).

47. See note 45.

48. Ibid. In other lectures, for example in that of 23 March 1924 (*Karmic Relationships*, vol. I, RSP 1972) Rudolf Steiner indicates that this town will lie in Russia. It should be added that the ending of the Palladium legend did not only have a spiritual outcome, of which more will be said in this appendix, but also an Ahrimanic counterpart, which found its outward expression in the so-called 'Testament of Peter the Great' and in all the occult-political power struggles connected with him.

49. See the lecture of 22 August 1911 (see above) and note 50, and also what is said about Pallas Athene in Ernst Uehli's book, *Mythos and Kunst der Griechen* (Dornach 1979).

50. Lecture of 24 December 1917 (GA, 180, Typescript NSL 117).

51. Lecture of 26 August 1911 (as note 46). Moreover, in the lecture of 6 April 1909 (*The Principle of Spiritual Economy*, AP 1986) Rudolf Steiner speaks of how many pictures of the Madonna and Christ Jesus, until the beginning of the Middle Ages, originated in clairvoyant experiences which were evoked by the working of imprints of the etheric body of Jesus of Nazareth (the Nathan Soul) in human souls.

52. Lecture of 2 December 1906 (GA 97, Typescript Z 60).

53. Lecture of 3 February 1907 (GA 97).

54. In various connections Rudolf Steiner often refers to the fundamental 'pedagogical law', that in true pedagogical practice there is always an awakening and transforming influence of the higher member of the teacher's being on the corresponding lower member of the pupil. For example, the teacher's ego works upon the pupil's astral body, while only the teacher's Spirit-Self can rightly work upon his ego, and so on. See in this regard the lecture of 26 June 1924 (*Curative Education*, RSP 1972). This enables us to understand why in the scene of the Annunciation, as it is described in St Luke's Gospel, it is not an Angel but an Archangel who appears to Mary as the messenger from the spiritual worlds. For the latter has a fully developed Life-Spirit and, hence, is able directly to influence the development of the Spirit-Self, which stands one stage lower in evolution. (See also note 82.)

55. The lecture is contained in *The Gospel of St John*, op. cit.).

56. Lecture of 18 February 1916 (GA 168, Typescript NSL 217).

57. Rudolf Steiner speaks about the 'moral quality' of the sixth cultural epoch in the lecture of 15 June 1915 (*Preparing for the Sixth Epoch*, AP 1957).

58. See note 56.

59. This aspect of the future working of the Spirit-Self is already being prepared amongst mankind in our time through the gradual awakening of the new faculty of clairvoyant vision in imaginatvely beholding the karmic consequences of one's own actions. The development of this new capacity will be brought about by the appearance of Christ in an etheric body and also through His becoming the 'Lord of Karma'. For this reason Rudolf Steiner also refers to the connection of this central spiritual event of the twentieth century with the beginning of the working of the Spirit-Self amongst mankind, a process which is like the first glimmer of the dawn of the approaching sixth cultural epoch. (See the lecture of 14 October 1911, *From Jesus to Christ*, RSP 1991, and note 196 to the main part of the book.)

60. Lecture of 15 June 1915 (*Preparing for the Sixth Epoch*, op. cit.).

61. Rudolf Steiner speaks about the connection of the Buddhi principle with the impulse of love in, for example, the following words: 'Christ is not merely wisdom, He is love incarnate: a high divine kama that is at the same time Buddhi; a pure streaming kama that wants nothing for itself . . . an inverse kama. Buddhi is the inverse of kama' (lecture of 4 November 1904, in *A Christian Rosenkreutz Anthology*, ed. P.M. Allen, Rudolf Steiner Publications, Blauvelt NY 1968).

62. Lecture of 30 May 1908 (*The Gospel of St John*, op. cit., morning lecture); the quotation that follows is taken from the evening lecture.

63. Ibid.

64. In the lecture of 3 February 1913, which was given on the occasion of the first general assembly of the newly founded Anthroposophical Society, Rudolf Steiner made a clear indication of the connection of Anthroposophy with the impulse of the Spirit-Self. Thus he first characterised the modern fifth post-Atlantean epoch: 'We know that we are in an age in which the Spirit-Self is being prepared, that we do indeed still stand firmly within the evolution of the consciousness soul but that the evolution of the Spirit-Self is being prepared.' And then, on this basis, he described from a particular viewpoint the evolution of the forces of the Sophia amongst mankind: her gradual descent from the exalted Goddess of wisdom (such as, for example, Pallas Athene was for the Greeks) to the ever more abstract philo-Sophia (philosophy) in order—after passing through a complete union with the image of man—from our time onwards to appear before him as an objective spiritual being as Anthropos-Sophia (Anthroposophy). Rudolf Steiner concluded the lecture with the indication that the three stages in the evolution of the Sophia forces that he had described correspond to three members of man's being: 'And I shall now leave it to all those who wish to examine ever more closely how from the destiny of *Sophia, philosophy and Anthroposophy* they may again demonstrate, in some detail, how mankind evolves further through those soul-members which we refer to as *intellectual soul or mind soul, consciousness soul and Spirit-Self.*'

65. See further about this aspect of the seventh cultural epoch in ch. 12.

66. Lecture of 3 February 1907 (GA 97).
67. Lecture of 30 May 1908 (morning) (*The Gospel of St John*, op. cit.). See also ch. 12.
68. Lecture of 15 February 1909 (*Christianity in Human Evolution*, AP 1979).
69. Lecture of 6 July 1909 (*The Gospel of St John in Relation to the Other Three Gospels*, AP 1982).
70. In our fifth post-Atlantean epoch this is possible only for Initiates or for those who have entered upon a path of spirit-pupilship.
71. Lecture of 30 May 1908 (morning) (*The Gospel of St John*, op. cit.).
72. In addition to all that has been said regarding the connection of the Palladium with the Festival of the 'Intercession of the Virgin' ('the Protecting Veil of Mary'), there is the further fact that from the very beginning it has everywhere served as a protective power.
73. See, for example, the lecture of 3 April 1917 (*Building Stones for an Understanding of the Mystery of Golgotha*, op. cit).
74. In esoteric Christianity there is—apart from the imagination of the palla of the Sophia, which points towards the future descent of Manas in the sixth epoch—a further imagination, which speaks of the mystery of the descent of Buddhi in the seventh cultural epoch. This is the imagination of the 'seamless tunic of the Lord', which is mentioned only in the Gospel of St John (19:23–24). It refers to the working of the forces of Christ's Life-Spirit, after the Mystery of Golgotha, in the airy environment of the Earth, a member which will become a full reality amongst mankind only in the seventh epoch. In the evening lecture of 30 May 1908 (*The Gospel of St John*), op. cit., where he characterises the physical Earth as the outer garment of Christ, Rudolf Steiner also speaks of His tunic as surrounding its atmosphere: 'The air has not been divided; it remains the common possession of all. It is the external, material symbol for the *love* which is hovering about the earthly globe, a love which will later find its fulfilment.' Hence in the central icon of the Deesis (see Plate 8), Christ is portrayed surrounded by a rectangular aura, which is the last echo of the knowledge of the mystery of the seamless tunic as the substance of love or Buddhi which spreads out freely to all four quarters of the world in the airy environment of the Earth (see note 61). This difference between the aura of the highest wisdom (Manas) and the aura of the highest love (Buddhi), is shown with remarkable precision in the icon of the 'Intercession' (see Plate 10). The first aura is associated more with man's head, and the second with his heart. Thus Mary's palla covers her head, while Christ's tunic, which is thrown over His left shoulder and left arm, extends to His heart.
75. Of particular significance in this connection is another icon of the 'Intercession' which was painted at the beginning of the sixteenth century and can be found in the 'Russian Museum' in Petersburg.
76. See the lecture of 19 September 1910 (*The Gospel of St Matthew*, RSP/AP 1965).

77. Lecture of 15 June 1915; the next two quotations are taken from the same source.
78. In Russia, the inspirations of one or another spiritually advanced ascetic or saint usually stood behind the icon-painters. For example, the inspirations of St Sergei of Radonezh found their artistic expression in the work of Andrei Rublyov.
79. The original is in Petersburg, in the 'Russian Museum'.
80. See the lecture of 21 September 1909 (*The Gospel of St Luke*, op cit.).
81. See the lecture of 25 June 1908 (*The Apocalypse of St John*, op. cit.). The nineteenth century Russian poet–philosopher Evgeny Baratynsky expressed this quality of the human ego in the following lines:

> Two regions: of darkness and of light
> We would investigate with equal might.

82. Rudolf Steiner speaks about the gates of the Sun and the Moon, which open the way to the mysteries of the future and the past, in the lecture of 25 January 1924 (*Karmic Relationships*, vol vi, RSP 1989). Moreover, the way that these two Archangels are portrayed in the icon has a further meaning. According to Rudolf Steiner, the Angels are, within the sphere of the Third Hierarchy, the representatives of the impulse of the Holy Spirit (they have a fully developed Spirit-Self); while the Archangels are the representatives of the Son or Christ, in that they have a fully developed Life-Spirit (see the lecture of 20 February 1917, *Cosmic and Human Metamorphoses*, Spiritual Research Editions, Blauvelt, NY 1989). Thus in the icon the Angels, above on the right, are *below* the 'palla of the Sophia', while the Archangels are above it, in that they are Beings who inspire the Spirit-Self from the higher sphere of Buddhi or the Christ-sphere.
83. See note 23 to the main part of the book.
84. See note 72 to the main part of the book.
85. See note 305 to the main part of the book.
86. See the lecture of 4 November 1904 (in *A Christian Rosenkreutz Anthology*, op. cit.).
87. From 1837 until 1857.
88. See note 325 to the main part of the book.
89. Lecture of 15 February 1909 (*Christianity in Human Evolution*, op. cit.).
90. Even the very fact that, in the darkest time of the Kali Yuga when materialism in Europe had become most widely diffused, a Russian artist living in the West (in Italy) worked for *twenty years* on a theme which is of such central importance for earthly evolution as a whole, is a matter of considerable significance.
91. In this connection it is also of interest that Alexander Ivanov received a certain stimulus towards *his* interpretation of the outward form of John the Baptist from an acquaintance with the original of Raphael's fresco, *The Mass of Bolsena*, in Rome. The figures in its left corner, together with

the gestures of their hands as they reach up towards the altar, are distantly reminiscent of the gestures of John the Baptist's hands in Ivanov's picture.

92. See Chapter 3.

93. Out of a definite artistic intuition Ivanov places John son of Zebedee directly beside John the Baptist. Although he was, of course, guided only by the exoteric traditions of the Church, the artist through this compositional decision is nevertheless himself unconsciously indicating that there is a special connection between the two Johns (see note 587 to the main part of the book).

94. See the lecture of 2 May 1910 (*The Christ Impulse and the Development of Ego Consciousness*, AP 1976). Herein lies one of the reasons why most of the closest disciples of Christ Jesus incarnated at the Turning-Point of Time as—in a social sense—'simple people' (for example, fishermen and so on), although in the past they had had incarnations of importance.

95. It is evident from numerous preparatory studies for the painting that at first Alexander Ivanov wanted to portray Jesus after the Baptism in the Jordan. However, after several unsuccessful attempts, he turned his attention to the more human aspect of this scene and portrayed Jesus approaching the place of the Baptism, that is, immediately *before* it. In this connection, one of the sketches for the head of Jesus that has been preserved, which was painted in oil about 1840, is of particular interest. There we find beside the head of Jesus the heads—familiar from antiquity—of Apollo of Belvedere, Venus and Zeus, from the union of whose individual features the artist sought the foundation for the features of Jesus: the upper part of the face from Apollo, the middle part from Venus, and the lower part from Zeus. (Michelangelo once also did something similar when he used as the model for Christ's head in the *Last Judgement* that very same statue of Apollo of Belvedere.) Turning in this way to images of the gods of antiquity and particularly to that of the Sun god Apollo in his quest for a model for the head of Jesus would not by any means be incorrect if the artist had set himself the task of portraying Jesus *before* his Baptism in the Jordan. In such a case, the reason for the resemblance of Jesus to representations of Apollo, Venus and Zeus, the god of the Sun, the goddess of love and the leader of all the Greek gods, could be understood in that, according to Rudolf Steiner, the images of the Greek gods and that of Apollo in particular are memory-projections into the fourth cultural epoch of the third pre-earthly stage of the Mystery of Golgotha, which the entelechy of Jesus of Nazareth accomplished in the spiritual world at the end of the Atlantean age (see regarding this the lecture of 30 December 1913, *Christ and the Spiritual World, and The Search for the Holy Grail*, RSP 1963). What appeared in Jesus' countenance *after* the Baptism in the Jordan as impulses of wonder, love (compassion) and conscience (see note 495) had its correspondence *before* the Baptism in the Jordan in the memory that lived in Jesus of the cosmic impulses of which

the images of the Greek gods Apollo, Venus and Zeus were the projections that the ancient Greek formed in his consciousness.

96. This ancient wisdom of earthly evolution can, according to ancient Hebrew teaching, be termed the 'wisdom of the snake'. John the Baptist refers to this when he addresses the Pharisees and Sadducees with the words, 'You brood of vipers' (Matthew 3:7).

97. In this respect, many of the closest disciples of Christ Jesus in their incarnations at the Turning-Point of Time were in a certain sense related to the leading representatives of the later inhabitants of Europe, which were to receive Christianity in the coming centuries (cf. note 94).

98. See the lecture of 1 October 1911 (*The Etherisation of the Blood: The Entry of the Etheric Christ into the Evolution of the Earth*, RSP 1971) and also the lecture of 28 November 1919 (*The Mission of the Archangel Michael*, op. cit.) where Rudolf Steiner speaks in detail about the entry of the Christ-impulse after the Mystery of Golgotha into the rhythmical system of the human organism. In St Luke's Gospel, there is also a reference to the working of the Christ-impulse after His Resurrection from the dead in the human heart. After it had been revealed to the two disciples on their way to Emmaus that the unknown companion who had accompanied them throughout their journey was the Risen One, 'they said to one another: "*Did not our hearts burn within us while He talked to us on the road* and revealed to us the meaning of the Scriptures?"' (24:32).

99. See *The Education of the Child* (RSP 1975).

100. Is not the memory of *this* 'representational function' reflected in the title of Novalis' essay, *Christendom or Europe* (1799)? See also note 94.

101. See the lecture of 8 May 1910 (*The Christ-Impulse and the Development of Ego Consciousness*, op. cit.).

102. Rudolf Steiner speaks with particular clarity about the Russian people as the 'Christ people' in the lecture of 2 November 1918 (*From Symptom to Reality in Modern History*, RSP 1976).

103. Lecture of 5 May 1910 (*Metamorphoses of the Soul*, vol. 2, RSP 1983).

104. Lecture of 2 May 1913 ('Christ at the Time of the Mystery of Golgotha and Christ in the Twentieth Century'; contained in *Occult Science and Occult Development*, RSP 1983. [The English edition includes only a small part of the passage quoted by the author.] See also the lecture of 20 May 1913 (*The Festivals and Their Meaning*, op. cit.).

105. This is confirmed not only by the Christian impulse which worked very strongly in Eastern Europe (as it also has in recent times) but still more by the outward circumstances that, for example, in Russia even at the end of the nineteenth century more than 90 per cent of the population were unable to read or write and hence could not take any part in the evolution of materialistic civilisation.

106. Of course, the directions of West and East have an altogether different significance in the spiritual world than they do in the physical. Nevertheless, the projection of certain *spiritual streams* appears in the

earthly world in forms such as to enable one to speak of these directions. Rudolf Steiner himself gives numerous examples of such a reflection of spiritual processes within the earthly sphere in association with the various directions of the world. The most significant example is to be found in the Foundation Stone Meditation, which was spoken for the first time on 25 December 1923 (other examples are contained in the lecture of 21 January 1917, *The Karma of Untruthfulness*, Part 2, RSP 1992, and in that of 25 November 1923, *Mystery Knowledge and Mystery Centres*, RSP 1973).

107. In the lecture of 28 March 1913 (*The Effects of Occult Development upon the Sheaths of Man*, APC 1945; *The Effects of Spiritual Development*, RSP 1978), Rudolf Steiner speaks of how the historical Mystery of Golgotha introduced forces into earthly evolution which were able to protect mankind in future from the unwarranted influences of Ahriman; and the second supersensible Mystery of Golgotha—together with the subsequent appearance of Christ in an etheric body—from the unwarranted influences of Lucifer. This corresponds to the direction in which the Christ-impulse moves: in the first case from East *to West* (that is, towards those regions of the Earth where the forces of Ahriman are predominant), and, in the second, from West *to East* (that is, towards these regions of the Earth where the forces of Lucifer are predominant).

108. Of course, this does not mean that this faculty of a metamorphosed conscience will in the coming centuries appear *only* in the East of Europe. Here it should merely be pointed out that the Slavic peoples have a stronger 'natural' predisposition for *such* a transformation of conscience, a predisposition which stems in particular from the spiritual connection that exists between the future descent of the Spirit-Self principle into earthly evolution and the entry of the Etheric Christ into humanity (see in this regard note 196 to the main part of the book).

List of GAs referred to in Notes

GA 53   Ursprung und Ziel des Menschen. Lecture of 16 March 1905 in *Esoteric Development*, AP 1982.

GA 57   Wo und wie findet man den Geist? Lecture of 29 April 1909 in Z 26 *Isis and Madonna*; 6 May 1909 in AQ 9:1 *The European Mysteries and their Initiates*.

GA 62   Ergebnisse der Geistesforschung. Lecture of 30 January 1913 in Z 27 *The Mission of Raphael*.

GA 94   Kosmogonie. Populärer Okkultismus. Das Johannes Evangelium.

GA 96   Ursprungsimpulse der Geisteswissenschaft.

GA 97   Das Christliche Mysterium. Some lectures appear in typescript, viz. NSL 160 *Dante's Divine Comedy*; Z 60 *The Mystery of Golgotha*; Z 208 *The Three Paths of Initiation*; Z 216 *Notes from the Lecture on Stones*; Z 259 *The Social Question as a Problem of Soul Life*; Z 307 *Parsifal*; Z 412 *The Christian Mystery*.

GA 98   Natur- und Geistwesen—ihr Wirken in unserer sichtbaren Welt. Lecture of 5 November 1907 not translated; 1 December 1907 in NSL 251 *Man's relationship with the surrounding World*; 4 December 1907 in Z 366 *The Elemental Kingdoms*; 17 December 1907, no translation; 25 December 1907, *The Mysteries*, lecture on the poem by Goethe, Mercury Press, Spring Valley 1987; 2 February 1908 in Z 396 *The Group Soul of Animals, Plants and Minerals*; 29 April 1908, NSL 161 *The Relationship between Worlds and Beings*; 7 June 1907 *Ascension and Pentecost*; *The Festivals and their Meaning*, RSP 1981; 9 June 1908 Z 405 *Whitsuntide*; 14 June 1908 NSL 107 *Shadow Beings, Phantoms, Demons created by Man Himself*.

GA 100   Menschheitsentwickelung und Christus-Erkenntnis. Lecture of 29 June 1907 in NSL 263–76 *Theosophy and Rosicrucianism*; 16–20 November 1907 in EN 50 *Notes of 8 Lectures on St John's Gospel*.

GA 108   Die Beantwortung von Welt und Lebensfragen durch Anthroposophie. Lecture of 22 December 1908 in *The Christmas Mystery: Novalis as Seer*, Mercury Press, Spring Valley, 1985; 26 October and 14 December 1908, no translation.

GA 109   Das Prinzip der Spirituellen Ökonomie. Lecture of 28 March 1909 not translated; some lectures appear in *The Principle of Spiritual Economy*, AP 1986; Lecture of 7 March 1909 in AQ 11:4 *Intimate Aspects of Reincarnation*.

GA 118   Das Ereignis der Christus-Erscheinung in der ätherischen Welt.

GA 125   Wege und Ziele des geistigen Menschen. Lecture of 23 January 1910 in EN 46 *Extract from a lecture given at the "Novalis" Lodge*; lecture of 27 December 1910 in AQ 19:4 *Yuletide and the Christmas Mystery*.

GA 127 Die Mission der neuen Geistesoffenbarung. Lecture of 26 December 1911 in *The Festivals and their Meaning*, RSP 1981; 14 June 1911 in NSL 359 *Faith, Love and Hope* (notes); 11 February 1911 in AQ 22:2 *The Representative of Life*; 25 February 1911 in AQ 21:4 *The Work of the Ego in Childhood*.

GA 143 Erfahrungen des Übersinnlichen. Die Wege der Seele zu Christus. Lecture of 9 May 1912 in AQ 18:1 *Ancient Wisdom and the Heralding of the Christ Impulse*; 16 May 1912 AQ 8:1 *Calendar of the Soul*; 29 December 1912 not translated.

GA 150 Die Welt des Geistes und ihr Hereinragen in das physische Dasein. Lecture of 13 April 1913 not translated.

GA 152 Vorstufen zum Mysterium von Golgotha. Lecture of 5 March 1914 in Z 411 *The Three Super-earthly Events preceding the Mystery of Golgotha*; 27 May 1914 in Z 422 *Progress in the Knowledge of Christ*; 18 and 20 May in *The Festivals and their Meaning: Michaelmas*, RSP 1981.

GA 158 *Der Zusammenhang des Menschen mit der elementarischen Welt*. Lectures of 9, 14 and 15 November 1914 in Z 144 *The Connection of Man with the Elemental World*.

GA 161 Wege der geistigen Erkenntis und der Erneuerung künstlerischer Weltanschauung. Lecture of 10 January 1915 in Z 273 *Perception of the Nature of Thought, Sun Activity in Earthly Evolution*.

GA 168 Die Verbindung zwischen Lebenden und Toten. Lecture of 16 February 1916 in NSL 153 *Relationships between Living and the Dead*; 18 February 1916 in NSL 217 *Concerning the Life between Death and a New Birth*; 22 February 1916 in NSL 234 *The Ego-Consciousness of the So-called Dead*.

GA 177 Die spirituellen Hintergründe der äusseren Welt. Der Sturz der Geister der Finsternis. Lecture of 28 October 1917 in R 35 *The Fall of the Spirits of Darkness*.

GA 180 Mysterienwahrheiten und Weihnachtsimpulse. Alte Mythen und ihre Bedeutung. Lecture of 24 December 1917 in NSL 117 (untitled).

GA 188 Der Goetheanismus, ein Umwandlungsimpuls und Auferstehungsgedanke. Lectures 3, 4, 5, 10, 11, 12 January 1919 in R 60 *Goetheanism as an Impulse for Man's Transformation*.

GA 194 Die Sendung Michael. Lecture of 6 and 7 December 1919 in Z 415 *The Michael Revelation*.

GA 209 Nordische und mitteleuropäsche Geistimpulse. Lecture of 25 December 1921 in Z 22 *Two Christmas Lectures*.

GA 238 Esoterische Betrachtungen Karmischer Zusammenhänge: Vierter Band—Zehn Vorträge und eine Ansprache (letzte Ansprache).

GA 245 Anweisungen für eine esoterische Schulung.

GA 264 Zur Geschichte und aus den Inhalten der ersten Abteilung der Esoterische Schule 1904 bis 1914.

GA 284/5 Bilder okkulter Siegel und Saülen. Lecture of 5 May 1909 in Z 147
Raphael's 'School of Athens' and 'Disputa'. Some texts and reproductions included in John Fletcher: *Art Inspired by Rudolf Steiner*, Mercury Arts Publications, 1987.

GA 292 Kunstgeschichte als Abbild innerer geistiger Impulse. Lecture of 5 October 1917 not translated.

PLATES

1. The Prophet Elijah in the desert

2. The Prophet Elijah's fiery ascension to heaven

3. John the Baptist

4. Raphael (self-portrait)

5. Novalis (Friedrich von Hardenburg)

6. John the Baptist, by Alexander Ivanov

The Archangel Michael   Mary   Christ in His Spiritual Might

8. Central part of the Deesis, from the Iconostasis by Theophanes the Greek

7. Christ's Appearance before the People by Alexander Ivanov

John the Baptist   The Archangel Gabriel

9. Sophia, the Wisdom of God

10. Intercession of the Virgin

Illustrations

Frontispiece: Bust of Novalis by Friedrich Schaper (from Novalis' grave in Weißenfels)

Plates:

1. The Prophet Elijah in the desert. Icon from the thirteenth century (detail). Tretjakow Gallery, Moscow.

2. The Prophet Elijah's fiery ascension to heaven. Icon from the sixteenth century (detail). Tretjakow Gallery, Moscow.

3. John the Baptist. Icon from the fourteenth century. Hermitage, Petersburg.

4. Raphael (self-portrait) 1506. Uffizi, Florence.

5. Novalis (Friedrich von Hardenburg). Oil painting by Franz Gareis. Weißenfels museum.

6. John the Baptist, by Alexander Ivanov. From the period 1840–1850. Tretjakow Gallery, Moscow.

7. Christ's Appearance before the People. Oil painting by Alexander Ivanov. From the period 1837–1857. Tretjakow Gallery, Moscow. Original size: 540 cm × 750 cm.

8. Christ in His Spiritual Might, Mary, John the Baptist, the Archangels Michael and Gabriel. Central part of the Deesis, from the Iconostasis by Theophanes the Greek. From the end of the fourteenth century. Cathedral of the Annunciation, Kremlin, Moscow.

9. Sophia, the Wisdom of God. Icon from the seventeenth century (detail). Private collection. Reproduced by kind permission of Beuroner Kunstverlages, Beuron.

10. Intercession of the Virgin. Icon from the first half of the fifteenth century. Tretjakow Gallery, Moscow.